GREAT RIVER

The Rio Grande
in North American History

VOLUME ONE

Indians and Spain

GREAT

The *Rio*

VOLUME ONE

Indians and Spain

R I V E R

G r a n d e

in

North American

History

by PAUL HORGAN

RINEHART & COMPANY, INC. *New York*
1954 *Toronto*

*Published simultaneously in Canada by
Clarke, Irwin & Company, Ltd., Toronto*

*Copyright, 1954, by Paul Horgan
Printed in the United States of America
By The Haddon Craftsmen, Scranton, Pa.*
Library of Congress Catalog Card Number: 54-9867

works by Paul Horgan

Novels

The Fault of Angels
No Quarter Given
Main Line West
A Lamp on the Plains
Far From Cibola
The Habit of Empire
The Common Heart

Shorter Fiction

The Return of the Weed
Figures in a Landscape
The Devil in the Desert
One Red Rose for Christmas

History and Belles-Lettres

Men of Arms (*juvenile*)
From the Royal City
New Mexico's Own Chronicle (*with Maurice Garland Fulton*)
Biographical Introductions to Volumes 1 and 2 of Diary and Letters of
      Josiah Gregg (*edited by Maurice Garland Fulton*)
Great River: The Rio Grande in North American History
      VOLUME ONE: Indians and Spain
      VOLUME TWO: Mexico and the United States

to Charles Arthur Henderson

a letter of dedication to serve as a preface

Dear C.,

let me give you this book, which has been in the making so long
a time—ever since, really, I was brought to the Rio Grande at Albuquerque as a small boy in 1915. You were an earlier immigrant to New
Mexico—where, as in our continent, everybody, far enough back, was an
immigrant—and from you I have learned much about my subject,
particularly about the spirit behind the image of man so small and so
great, so various and so tenacious, against the river empire where for
centuries there was no such thing as a short journey.

Neither in these volumes is my passage through the river's story
a short one. How could it be? The river is nearly two thousand miles
long, its historical course takes us through something over ten centuries
of time and through the chronicles of three cultures. To do it anything
like justice, I have wanted to produce a sense of historical experience,
rather than a bare record. This required me wherever possible to see
events, societies, movements, through human characters in action. Without, I hope, departing from the inflexible limits of respectful scholar-
ship, I took every opportunity to stage a scene. What this may have
cost in brevity was perhaps made up for by a presentation of experience
with which the reader might be able to identify himself. If here and
there I halted the narrative of events to describe various ways and
customs of the peoples, then I had precedent for it; for Herodotus did
this, to our enrichment. Only when events are rooted in the soil of the
culture might they seem to have true reality.

Perhaps it would interest you to see a few comments on the
writing of history which have seemed to clarify for me my own view

of the task. Here is one which I found in an essay on *The Literary His-torian* in the *London Times Literary Supplement* for January 16, 1953:

> Macaulay wrote to stimulate the reader, not to contribute an original piece of research. He wrote, in fact, much as he talked. . . .

Here is another, out of Aldous Huxley's essay *Vulgarity in Literature:*

> What is the smallest amount of simplification compatible with com-prehensibility, compatible with the expression of a humanly significant meaning? It is the business of the non-classical naturalistic writer to dis-cover. His ambition is to render, in literary terms, the quality of immediate experience. . . .

And in his *Journal* for July 21, 1850, Eugène Delacroix gave me comfort for those passages in which I may have translated the experi-ence of the past with an accent other than that of conventional historiography:

> The historian's task appears to me to be the most difficult of all because he needs to give unceasing attention to a hundred and one things at the same time, and must preserve through quotations, precise recitals of events, and facts that are only relatively important, the en-thusiasm that gives life to his story and makes it something more than an extract from the newspapers. . . . We need to be very bold. Without daring, without extreme daring, even, there is no beauty. . . . (Trans-lated by Lucy Norton. London, Phaidon Press, 1951.)

For I agree with Professor Nevins that the writing of history, in addition to being a technical craft, is also an art. Its proper aim is to produce, in literary form, to whatever degree the author may command, a work of art.

To realize this purpose may require the historian to invoke certain flexibilities of method. Here's one that I've invoked in order to give the reader an immediate sense of locality in the vastly scattered backgrounds of the river empire. To accomplish this I have in many cases used recent or modern place names in speaking of persons and events belonging to earlier times. For example, "Mexico" properly speaking was not the name of a nation, or a whole national region, until 1821; but I use it for events in its area before that date rather than the officially correct designation "New Spain" because by doing so I hope to give the modern reader a more ready sense of where he is on the map. Similarly, pressing ahead with narratives of events occurring near the sites of modern river towns, I use their modern names—e.g., "near Eagle Pass"—as a quick means of orientation, trusting to the reader to understand my freedom with historical time.

Perhaps you will notice that in the flow of the narrative I have not used footnotes or running references with superior numbers to identify sources. I followed this course not because I did not have precise references for my facts, or because I did not want to share these with the reader; but because it seemed to me more to the reader's advantage to give him the story without diverting his interest to the anatomy of my framework. But of course I must identify my sources, under two obligations: one is to acknowledge my debt to those authors whose works I have consulted; the other is to provide anyone interested in the source material—its range and authenticity—with general evidence for my statements. Accordingly, such information appears in brief form at the end of each volume, with the sources listed by chapters, from which the reader may refer to the complete bibliography at the end of volume two, in Appendix C.

I am, of course, deeply indebted to a great number of men and women who have helped me in every phase of my long task. Contributing much to whatever successes my work may show, they are in no wise responsible for its failures. Let me list such benefactors, many of whom you will know.

For help in locating source materials and for other good acts of guidance I thank United States Senator Clinton P. Anderson, and Mrs. Luna Diamond of his office staff; Ernst Bacon, who helped me to travel the river's source country; the Most Reverend Dr. Edwin V. Byrne, Archbishop of Santa Fe, and his predecessor, the Most Reverend Rudolf A. Gerken, who gave me access to various records of the Church in New Mexico; Kenneth Chapman and Stanley Stubbs of the Laboratory of Anthropology at Santa Fe; J. Frank Dobie, of Austin, who gave me both books and advice; Edward Corrigan, of Laredo, who directed me to information about the Republic of the Rio Grande, an elusive subject; Colonel Martin L. Crimmins, of San Antonio, who shared with me his information on the forts of the Rio Grande; Major General and Mrs. Hunter Harris, Jr.; Dr. Rex Z. Howard, of Fort Worth, who supplied me with useful photographs of Saint Bernard's Mission at Guerrero, Coahuila; Peter Hurd, who gave me valuable materials, whether published or remembered out of his own experience; William A. Keleher, of Albuquerque, who gave me the freedom of his library and of his judgment in literary and historical matters; Victor J. Smith, of Alpine, Texas; James L. Threlkeld, of Albuquerque, who lent me his support as a bookman; Mrs. J. P. White, of Roswell, who let me study her folio copy of the Percier designs after Isabey for the *Sacre* of Napoleon; and Mrs. John Boylan, who typed many of my source notes.

You can imagine how much I owe to libraries and librarians. I must pay my grateful respects to William Dix and members of his staff at the Princeton University Library; Mrs. Dollis Stevens, librarian of the New Mexico Military Institute, and her predecessor, Mrs. Charlotte Gaylord; Mrs. Albert Ely, formerly librarian of the Museum of New Mexico, and Augustus Gaylord, a later incumbent of the position; Arthur McAnnally, former librarian of the University of New Mexico, and Miss Ruth Russell and Miss Williams of his staff; Miss Haydée Noya of the Henry E. Huntington Memorial Library at San Marino; Miss Fannie Ratchford, Miss Winnie Allen, and other officers of the University of Texas Library; Miss Erin Humphrey of the Reference Department of the El Paso Public Library; and Miss Katherine Brand of the Manuscripts Division of the Library of Congress. I must give my thanks to these officers and library staff members of the United States Department of Agriculture at Albuquerque: Miss Marian W. Dorroh, Al Jarrett, Mrs. Clemmie Shirley, Harper Sims; and to Hubert Ball, chief engineer of the Middle Rio Grande Conservancy District.

You'll find a detailed record of my great indebtedness to authors of printed works in the General Bibliography (Appendix C). Here I must mention with particular admiration and gratitude certain works appearing in the bibliography which were of recurrent value to me: Charles Wilson Hackett's edition of Mr. and Mrs. Adolph Bandelier's *Historical Documents Relating to New Mexico, Nueva Viscaya and Approaches Thereto, to 1773,* of which, by the way, you gave me your copies; Eugene C. Barker's edition of *The Austin Papers;* the publications issued through the University of New Mexico Press by the Coronado Cuarto Centennial Commission, and those of the Quivira Society; the works of Herbert C. Bolton; Carlos E. Castañeda's *Our Catholic Heritage in Texas, 1519-1936;* the works of J. Frank Dobie; the *Report* of Commissioner William H. Emory; the works of Cleve Hallenbeck; the works of Edgar L. Hewett and Bertha Dutton; the southwestern books of Erna Fergusson; General Tom Green's *Journal of the Texian Expedition Against Mier;* Joseph C. McCoy's *Historic Sketches of the Cattle Trade;* Salvador de Madariaga's volumes on the Spanish American empire; Tocqueville's *Democracy in America;* Twitchell's catalogue of the *Spanish Archives of New Mexico,* and his *Leading Facts of New Mexican History;* the two volumes of the *Diary and Letters of Josiah*

Gregg, discovered and edited by Maurice Garland Fulton; Cleofas M. Jaramillo's *Shadows of the Past (Sombras del pasado);* William A. Keleher's *Turmoil in New Mexico, 1846-1868;* Constance Rourke's *American Humor* and *The Roots of American Culture;* Bancroft's *History of the North Mexican States and Texas;* Rives's *The United States and Mexico, 1821-1848;* Yoakum's *History of Texas;* and *Coahuila y Texas en la época colonial,* by Vito Alessio Robles.

In addition to people whose printed works gave me so much that was useful there were many others whose conversation contributed to my work. Among these were Judge Harbert Davenport, of Brownsville; Dr. Bertha Dutton, of Santa Fe; the late Mrs. Clara M. Fergusson, of Albuquerque; Brigadier General William J. Glasgow, of El Paso; J. Brinckerhoff Jackson, of Santa Fe; Mrs. D. S. McKellar and Sheriff Lehman, of Eagle Pass; Virgil Lott, of Roma, Texas; Stuart Rose, of Philadelphia; John Sinclair, of Tiguex, at Bernalillo; and Seb. S. Wilcox, of Laredo.

As you know, I turned to historical motion picture film to find impressions of living character in the animated images of certain figures who appear near the end of my story. I thank the Film Division of the National Broadcasting Company for help in locating, through Lloyds Film Storage Company of New York, and in making available for study, historic film footage showing Villa, Pershing, Carranza, Wilson, Funston, Obregón, and an episode of desert fighting during the Punitive Expedition of 1916. I wonder if my bibliography is the first to list factual motion pictures as serious historical reference material. I should like to think so. But even if it is not, I shall rest content to be among the earliest of historians to show the way to scholarly use of such a vivid medium of enlivening the past.

I am glad to record that I profited from critical readings given variously to portions, or to all, of my typescript by the Rev. Fray Angélico Chavez, O.F.M., Carl Carmer, and Allan Nevins. During my labors I was often given a chance to read aloud to friends from the work in progress, so to weigh my effects and discover lacks. For such help I thank Henriette, Peter, and Peter Wyeth Hurd; Robert and Barbara Anderson; Constance and Vernon Knapp; Dwight Starr; and Remi and Thomas Messer. Henriette Wyeth Hurd, Margaret Duffield, Mary C. Nicholas, Stuart Rose, Virginia Rice, and Daniel Longwell read the whole work in typescript, and their comments were of much value to me. I am grateful to Edward Nicholas for hospitality he gave me while I was at work on the last phase of the book.

To three superintendents of the New Mexico Military Institute I give full thanks for their consideration of me. During the last years of my service as an officer of the school, Colonel D. C. Pearson and General Hugh M. Milton II both granted me extended leaves of absence from my duties to permit me to give all my time to this book, and General Milton further helped me with gifts of source material. Colonel Charles Francis Ward, in a gesture of true generosity, permitted me to use his edited manuscript, yet unpublished, of his great-grandfather's Mexican War diary.

Part of my study was done under the auspices of the John Simon Guggenheim Memorial Foundation. I warmly thank Dr. Henry Allen Moe, Secretary-General of the Foundation, for his sensitive and generous administration of my Guggenheim Fellowship.

Finally, to my agent, Virginia Rice, who sustained me with more than merely professional confidence throughout my years of work on this book, I offer all gratitude.

Here, then, in whatever part I have managed to divine its meaning and stay its likeness, is your country and mine.

P. H.

Roswell, New Mexico,
16 March 1954.

Contents

Maps

Riverscape

I.

Creation

Space.

Abstract movement.

The elements at large.

Over warm seas the air is heavy with moisture. Endlessly the vast delicate act of evaporation occurs. The seas yield their essence to the air. Sometimes it is invisible, ascending into the upper atmosphere. Sometimes it makes a shimmer in the calm light that proceeds universally from the sun. The upper heavens carry dust—sea dust of salt evaporated from ocean spray, and other dust lingering from volcanic eruption, and the lost dust of shooting stars that wear themselves out against the atmosphere through which they fly, and dust blown up from earth by wind. Invisibly the volume of sea moisture and dust is taken toward land by prevailing winds; and as it passes over the coast, a new condition arises—the wind-borne mass reflects earth temperatures, that change with the earth-forms inland from the sea. Moving rapidly, huge currents of air carrying their sea burdens repeat tremendously in their unseen movement the profile of the land forms over which they pass. When land sweeps up into a mountain, the laden air mass rolling upon it must rise and correspond in shape.

And suddenly that shape is made visible; for colder air above the mountain causes moisture to condense upon the motes of dust in the warm air wafted from over the sea; and directly in response to the presence and inert power of the mountain, clouds appear. The two volumes—invisible warm air, immovable cold mountain—continue to meet and repeat their joint creation of cloud. Looking from afar calm and eternal, clouds enclose forces of heat and cold, wind and inert

3

matter that conflict immensely. In such continuing turbulence, cloud motes collide, cling together, and in the act condense a new particle of moisture. Heavier, it falls from cold air through warmer. Colliding with other drops, it grows. As the drops, colder than the earth, warmer than the cloud they left, fall free of cloud bottom into clear air, it is raining.

Rain and snow fall to the earth, where much runs away on the surface; but roots below ground and the dense nerve system of grasses and the preservative cover of forest floors detain the runoff, so that much sky moisture goes underground to storage, even through rock; for rock is not solid, and through its pores and cracks and sockets precipitation is saved. The storage fills; and nearing capacity, some of its water reappears at ground level as springs which find upward release through the pores of the earth just as originally it found entry. A flowing spring makes its own channel in which to run away. So does the melt from snow clinging to the highest mountain peaks. So does the sudden, brief sheet of storm water. Seeking always to go lower, the running water of the land struggles to fulfill its blind purpose—to find a way over, around or through earth's fantastic obstacles back to the element which gave it origin, the sea.

In this cycle a huge and exquisite balance is preserved. Whatever the amount of its element the sea gives up to the atmosphere by evaporation, the sea regains exactly the same amount from the water which falls upon the earth and flows back to its source.

This is the work, and the law, of rivers.

2.

Gazetteer

Out of such vast interaction between ocean, sky and land, the Rio Grande rises on the concave eastern face of the Continental Divide in southern Colorado. There are three main sources, about two and a half miles high, amidst the Cordilleran ice fields. Flowing from the west, the river proper is joined by two confluents—Spring Creek from the north, and the South Fork. The river in its journey winds eastward across southern Colorado, turns southward to continue across the whole length of New Mexico which it cuts down the center, turns southeastward on reaching Mexico and with one immense aberration from this course—the Big Bend—runs on as the boundary between Texas and Mexico, ending at the Gulf of Mexico.

In all its career the Rio Grande knows several typical kinds of landscape, some of which are repeated along its great length. It springs from tremendous mountains, and intermittently mountains accompany it for three fourths of its course. It often lies hidden and inaccessible in canyons, whether they cleave through mountains or wide level plains. From such forbidding obscurities it emerges again and again into pastoral valleys of bounty and grace. These are narrow, at the most only a few miles wide; and at the least, a bare few hundred yards. In such fertile passages all is green, and the shade of cottonwoods and willows is blue and cool, and there is reward for life in water and field. But always visible on either side are reaches of desert, and beyond stand mountains that limit the river's world. Again, the desert closes against the river, and the gritty wastelands crumble into its very banks, and nothing lives but creatures of the dry and hot; and nothing grows but desert plants of thirsty pod, or wooden stem, or spiny defense. But at last the river comes to the coastal plain where an ancient sea floor reaching deep inland is overlaid by ancient river deposits. After turbulence in mountains, bafflement in canyons, and exhaustion in deserts, the river finds peaceful delivery into the sea, winding its last miles slowly through marshy bends, having come nearly one thousand nine hundred miles from mountains nearly three miles high. After the Mississippi-Missouri system, it is the longest river in the United States.

Along its way the Rio Grande receives few tributaries for so long a river. Some are sporadic in flow. Reading downstream, the major tributaries below those of the source are Rock Creek, Alamosa Creek, Trinchera Creek and the Conejos River in Colorado; in New Mexico, the Red River, the Chama River, and four great draws that are generally dry except in storm when they pour wild volumes of silt into the main channel—Galisteo Creek, the Jemez River, Rio Puerco and Rio Salado; and in Texas and Mexico, the Rio Conchos (which renews the river as it is about to die in the desert), the Pecos River, the Devil's River, (another) Rio Salado and Rio San Juan. The river commonly does not carry a great volume of water, and in some places, year after year, it barely flows, and in one or two it is sometimes dry. Local storms will make it rush for a few hours; but soon it is down to its poor level again. Even at its high sources the precipitation averages only five inches year-round. At its mouth, the rainfall averages in the summer between twenty and thirty inches, but there the river is old and done, and needs no new water. In January, at the source the surface temperature is fourteen degrees on the average, and in July fifty degrees. At the mouth in the same months the averages read fifty and sixty-eight. In the mountainous north the river is clear and sparkling, in the colors of obsidian, with rippling folds of current like the markings on a trout. Once among the pastoral valleys and the desert bench terraces that yield silt, the river is ever after the color of the earth that it drags so heavily in its shallow flow.

Falling from so high to the sea, and going so far to do it, the river with each of its successive zones encounters a new climate. Winter crowns the source mountains almost the whole year round, in the longest season of cold in the United States. The headwaters are free of frost for only three months out of the year, from mid-June to mid-September. Where the river carves its way through the mesas of northern New Mexico, the seasons are temperate. Entering the Texas desert, the river finds perennial warmth that rises in summer to blasting heat. At its end, the channel wanders under the heavy moist air of the tropics, mild in winter, violently hot in summer.

3.

Cycle

Landscape is often seen as static; but it never is static. From its first rock in the sky to its last embrace by the estuary at the sea, the river has been surrounded by forces and elements constantly moving and dynamic, interacting to produce its life and character. It has taken ocean and sky; the bearing of winds and the vagary of temperature; altitude and tilt of the earth's crust; underground waters and the spill of valleys and the impermeable texture of deserts; the cover of plants and the uses of animals; the power of gravity and the perishability of rock; the thirst of things that grow; and the need of the sea to create the Rio Grande.

The main physical circumstances of the Rio Grande are timeless. They assume meaning only in terms of people who came to the river.

BOOK ONE

The Indian Rio Grande

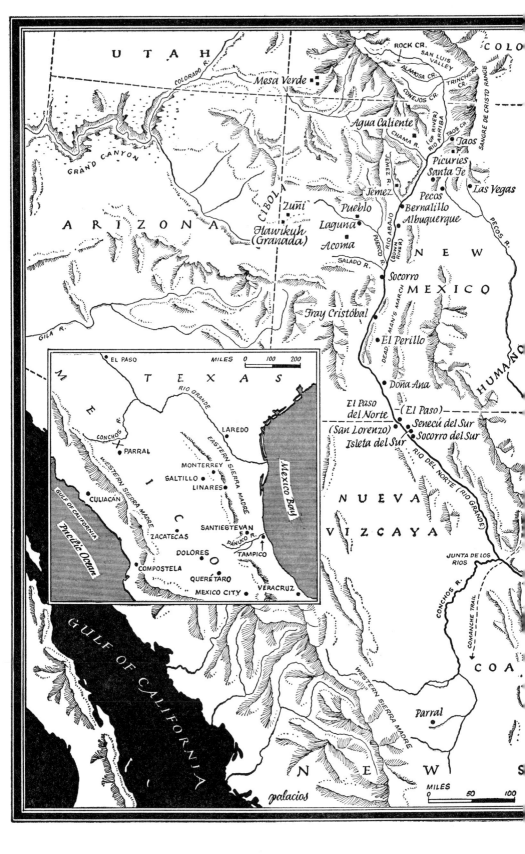

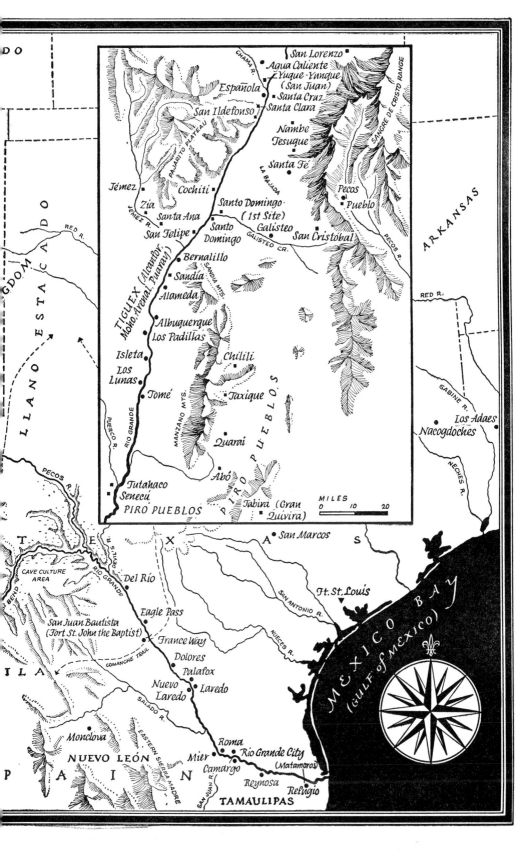

I.

The Ancients

THERE WAS NO RECORD BUT MEMORY and it became tradition and then legend and then religion. So long ago that they did not know themselves how long, their ancestors, the ancient people, moved. They went with the weather. Seasons, generations, centuries went by as each brought discovery of places farther toward the morning, across vacant Asia. They were guided that way by the lie of mountains, whose vast trough lay northeastward and southwestward. There was toil enough for people in taking their generations through valleys, without crossing the spines of mountains. But valleys end at the sea, and finally the people saw it too. The Asian continent ended, except for an isthmus of land or ice that remained above the waters. They crossed it, not in a day, or a year perhaps; perhaps it took lifetimes to find and keep what the bridge led to. But lost memory has no time, only action; and they came to North America, bringing their animals, their blind history, their implements and the human future of two continents. Once again they encountered mountains which became their immovable guides. The entire vast new land lay on an axis of north and south, and its greatest mountains did also. Having entered at the north, the people must move southward, between the sea and the mountains.

Movement, however laborious, slow and lost in dangers it may have been, was the very nature of their lives. Through age after age it took them down the continent, across another isthmus, and into the great continent to the south, until the antipodean ice fields were joined by the disorderly but urgent line of mankind. Movement was what kept them alive, for they lived by hunting animals that followed the seasons.

They knew how to twist vegetable fibres until they had string.

13

They could bend a branch until it made a bow by which a string could be tautly stretched. With bow, then, and arrow, they brought down game. There was another weapon, a throwing stick, with which to kill. Fish in the streams were taken with the harpoon. Its points, and those of arrows, were chipped from stone; often from glittering, sharp volcanic glass. Birds and fish were snared with nets. These measures travelled easily. They were light, efficient, and imaginative.

There were others called alive in their consequence. To make fire, the ancient people set a wooden drill into a socket in a small wooden hearth, and rotated the drill with their palms. Smoke came. They blew upon it. Coals glowed and under breath burst into flame. It was possible to cook. They heated stones and in vessels of wood or bark, even of animal hide dried and toughened, cooked the booty of the hunt. When it was time again to move, valuable leftovers could be carried in baskets invented and woven as baggage. With them travelled, or crouched to eat, a clever, fond and valiant friend whose ancestors too had made the timeless migration. He was the dog.

Throughout ages of lost memory the people possessed the new continents and found great regions within which to rove, above and below the equator, as loosely scattered groups. Vast localisms determined their ways—whether they pursued animals on plains, or hunted for berries in mountains, or clung to the unvarying climate of warm zones in one luxuriant wilderness after another. It took a mystery of the vegetable world to unfold for them in slow discovery a new way of life. There was a seed which could be eaten. It could be planted. It could be watered and made to grow at the hunter's will. It could multiply. It could be carried far and planted elsewhere. Wherever it took root it afforded food. It made a place where the people could stay season after season. It kept the hunters home, and their women and children and dogs, relieved of their wandering in search of life itself. Up from the warm zones of the earth it travelled from tribe to tribe, until most of the people who lived in the huge valleys and basins of the cordilleras knew how to use it, and using it, gradually discovered the arts of living together. Their histories were changed by it. The laws of its growth created their dwellings, their sense of property and brought them their gods, and its crushed seed became their most habitual and sacred offering in prayer. It was maize, or Indian corn.

In becoming farmers the ancient people looked for the most suitable places in which to remain. Corn needed water. Water flowed down the mountains making streams. In the grand valleys were many isolated mountain fragments standing separate whose heights were secure against animal and human dangers. When people could stay where they chose to stay there was time, there was imagination, to improve their conditions of life. A surplus of corn required some place in which to store it, safe against waste and thieving little animals. Dry caves in rocky cliffs seemed made by nature for the purpose. But food was wealth and people protected it in the caves by hauling stones, making enclosures which they sealed with clay which dried solid. The wall of a bin protecting food could be extended to make walls which gave shelter. Boldly beautiful rooms were made in the cliffs, some of masonry, some carved with obsidian knives out of rich soft yellow tufa itself. Arising independently, some at the same time, some at other times, and almost all on the western slopes of the continental divide in the American Southwest, many such cliff cities of the high plateaus were settled and developed by hunters who learned how to become farmers. After thousands of years of migration across continents in search of the always moving forms of live food, it took only a few hundred years of settled agriculture for the ancient people to discover how to satisfy their prime hunger, and find time and ways in which to recognize other hungers and give form to their satisfaction, socially, morally and spiritually. And though in their slowly developed mastery of how to grow corn they needed not only the seed but also water, they established their plateau cities not by the banks of the three or four great rivers that rose in the mountain system that had pointed the path for their ancestors, but on mesas and in valleys touched by little streams, some of them not even perennial in their flow.

Nor did all of the ancient people find the secret of maize. Some who found eastern gateways in the mountains spread themselves out on the great plains where for long succeeding centuries they continued to rove as hunters, governed by solstice and the growing seasons of animal feed. In time the wanderers heard of the plateau cities and their riches stored against hunger and the hardships of travel. Raids resulted, and battle, devastations and triumphant thefts, leaving upon the withdrawal of the nomads new tasks of rebuilding and revival according to the customs of the farmers who long ago had given up the bare rewards of the chase for hard but dependable and peaceful cultivation of the land.

If there was little regular communication between the scattered cliff cities of southwestern Colorado, northeastern Arizona, and northern New Mexico, and if there were local differences between their ways, still they solved common mysteries in much the same fashion and in their several responses to the waiting secrets of earth, sky and mind, they made much the same fabric of life for people together.

2.

The Cliffs

The fields were either on the mesa top above the cliff cities or on the canyon floor below. At sunup the men went to cultivate their crops. Corn was planted a foot deep, and earth was kept piled up about the stalks, to give them extra growing strength and moisture. Every means was used to capture water. Planting was done where flood waters of the usually dry stream beds came seasonally. But there were long summers without rain. The winter snows filtered into porous sandstone until they met hard rock and found outlets in trickles down canyon walls. The people scooped basins out of the rock to collect such precious flow, from which they carried water by hand to the growing stalks. The mesa tops were gashed at the edges by sloping draws which fell away to the valley floor, like the spaces between spread fingers. Between the great stone fingers the people built small stone dams to catch storm waters running off the plateau. Occasionally springs came to the surface in the veined rock of the cliffs and were held sacred.

Seeds were planted and crops cultivated with a stick about a yard long which could poke holes in the earth or turn it over. The prevailing crop was red corn, and others were pumpkin, beans and cotton. Wild sunflowers yielded their seeds which were eaten. When the crop was harvested it became the charge of the women, who were ready to receive it and store it in baskets which they wove to hold about two bushels. Flat stone lids were fashioned to seal the baskets, which went into granaries built by the men. Part of the seed was ground between suitably shaped stones, and part was kept for planting. If meal was the staff of life, it was varied by meat from wild game including the deer, the fox, the bear, the mountain sheep and the rabbit.

As they lived through the centuries learning how to work and build together, the ancient people made steady and continuous progress in all ways. If their first permanent houses had only one room with a connecting underground ceremonial chamber and storeroom, they increasingly reflected the drawing together of individuals into community life in a constantly elaborated form of the dwelling. The rooms came together, reinforcing one another with the use of common walls, and so did families. The rooms rose one upon another until terraced houses three and four stories high were built. The masonry was expert and beautiful, laid in a variety of styles. The builders were inventive. They thought of pillars, balconies, and interior shafts for ventilation. They made round towers and square towers. And they placed their great house-cities with an awesome sense of location, whether on the crown of a mesa or in the wind-made architectural shell of a long arching cave in the cliffside. The work was prodigious. In one typical community house fifty million pieces of stone were quarried, carried and laid in its walls. Forests were far away; yet thousands of wooden beams, poles and joins were cut from timber and hauled to their use in the house. From the immediate earth untold tons of mortar were mixed and applied—and all this by the small population of a single group dwelling.

The rooms averaged eight by ten feet in size, with ceilings reaching from four feet to eight. There were no windows. Doors were narrow and low, with high sills. The roof was made of long heavy poles laid over the walls, and thatched with small sticks or twigs, finally covered with mud plaster in a thick layer. The floor was of hard clay washed with animal blood and made smooth, in a shiny black. Walls were polished with burnt gypsum. Along their base was a painted band of yellow ochre, taken as raw mineral from the softly decaying faces of the cliffs where great stripes of the dusty gold color were revealed by the wearing of wind and water. Round chambers of great size and majesty were built underground for religious and ceremonial use. Many cities had a dozen or more such rooms, each dedicated to the use of a separate religious cult or fraternity. One had a vault with a covering of timber which resounded like a great drum when priests danced upon it.

In the ceremonial kivas men kept their ritual accessories and the tools of their crafts. They made tools out of bones—deer, rabbit, bird, and of deerhorn and mountain sheep horn. Their knives and hunting points and grinding tools and scraping tools for dressing skins and gravers for carving and incising and axes and chisels for cutting and shaping wood and mauls for breaking rock were made out of stone.

Baskets were woven for light, mobile use at first, when the people kept moving, and as they found ways to settle in their cities they continued to use baskets for cooking, storage and hauling. But more durable and more widely useful vessels could be made out of clay; and so the women developed in connection with domestic arts the craft of pottery. Their early attempts imitated the construction of basketry, with long clay ropes coiled into enclosing form which was not smoothed over on the surface. But for greater comeliness and better protection against leakage and breakage the surfaces of pots were eventually made smooth and fired with glazes. Natural mineral pigments gave each locality its characteristic pottery style—now red clay, again ochre, white gypsum, iron-black.

In warm weather the people lived naked; in cold they wore fur-cloth and feather-cloth robes and leggings, and dressed skins. Thread was made from yucca fibre. Both men and women wore ornaments created out of beads—stone, shell, bone. Feather tassels, bright with color, hung from garments. Small pieces of chipped or cut turquoise were put together in mosaic for pendants and bracelets. Fashion had its power, modifying out of sheer taste rather than utility various details of dress. The sandal fringe of one period was missing from the next.

For hundreds of years this busy life with all its ingenuities, its practices whose origins lacking written record were lost among the dead ancestors, its growing body of worship of all creation, its personal and collective sorrows, its private and communal joys, rose and flourished with the affirmative power of living prophecy. Were they being readied to imagine a greatness beyond themselves in the future? Already they had found for the material face of life a grace and beauty whose evidence would endure like the mountain stuff out of which they had made it. The people grew their nourishment on plateaus that reached toward the sun. They put about themselves like garments the enfolding substances of cliffs. They looked out in daylight upon breathtaking views of intercourse between sky and ground, where light and shadow and color and distance in their acts of change made in every moment new aspects of the familiar natural world. Amidst the impassive elegance of mountains, valleys and deserts they fulfilled their needs with intimacy and modesty in their use of natural things. With no communication through time but the living voice, for they had no records but their own refuse, the power of their hooded thoughts brought them a long

way from the straggle out of Asia tens of centuries before to the flowering
civilization of the cliffs, the plateaus and the canyons.

And at just the long moment in their story when all material
evidence seemed to promise life more significant than that which they
had so laboriously made so beautiful, mysteriously, in city after city
among the plateaus, they left it never to return.

3.

To the River

Their departures were orderly. Not all occurred at the very same
instant, but all took place late in the thirteenth century and early in
the fourteenth, and all gave evidence of having been agreed upon. Their
houses were left standing. Their rooms were neat and emptied of
possessions needed for travel and new life elsewhere. But for occasional
bits of corn and stalk and tassel the food bins were bare. The dead
were left in peaceful burial according to regular custom. Few personal
objects—clothing, jewelry, ceremonial effects—were left behind. Fires died
in their proper places. There was no sign of the applied torch. Sudden
natural calamity—earthquake, flood, lightning-set holocaust—played no
part. The cities, one by one, at the point of their highest development,
were left to time and the amber preservative of dry sunlit air.

Again the people left no record, and carried none with them,
written, or even pictorial, to explain these abandonments. Perhaps for
a few generations memory told the story, until gradually it was lost in
the recesses of time. The only records which can be consulted are those
of the natural world. They have been much invoked and disputed by
experts.

The trees have testified. By counting the rings of annual growth
in the cross section of a trunk, a system of dating has been devised. By
comparing the thickness and thinness of the successive rings, periods of

relative wetness or dryness have been tabulated. According to such information the century of the migrations from the plateaus coincided with a period of increasing dryness, until crops could no longer be watered, and the people were faced with living on the seed corn and finally starvation. A search for new watered lands was the only recourse.

Erosion has been blamed. Too much timber was cut for building use. Bared forest lands permitted too rapid runoff of storm-water. Gullies were lengthened until their waters became ungovernable for flood-farming. Old fields had to be abandoned and new ones begun farther from the houses and from water sources.

But erosion presupposes flow of water, and the drought theory contradicts the erosion theory. And though some scientists say that the entire region during its whole period of occupation by people has been slowly growing drier, they say further that the rate of desiccation would not in itself account for these migrations. And one of the greatest of the communities—in Chaco Canyon—was abandoned a century before the tree-ring evidence of the great drought. On top of this, lately, the whole responsibility of the tree-ring theory has been shaken by comparison of ancient rings formed when there were no written records with more recent rings which when checked against modern meteorological records show no consistent correlation with thickness and thinness of the rings in wet and dry periods as scientifically recorded. The drought theory holds no firm answer.

In the canyon of the Rito de los Frijoles the river is an ever-flowing stream. Yet the cliff dwellings there and the houses of the canyon floor were abandoned just like communities near streams which were intermittent and for the most part dry. Lack of water was not a motive for the silencing of the Rito.

The mystery has been attacked in other ways.

Did the soft rock of the cliff dwellings disintegrate too fast and force the people to move? But the rooms are still intact today.

Were there epidemics of other disease? Burials reveal no evidence of unusual numbers of deaths in any one period.

Was the prevailing diet of corn meal—hard and coarse, and especially when old as hard as gravel—the cause of disease? Recovered skulls show teeth ground down to the bone as a result of chewing the tough meal. Tooth decay led to abscesses, lodged poisons, rheumatism, arthritis and diet deficiencies. Did the people go to look in new places for other foods? But wherever they resettled, corn remained their staple food, and does today.

Did nomadic enemies cut off water supplies and drive the people from their towns? There would have been battles, and if defeated, the city dwellers would have left their homes in disarrayed flight. There was no evidence to indicate siege and defeat.

Did the pattern of community life become so complex as the towns grew that political quarrels between clans and religious fraternities broke apart the order of existence and made communal life impossible and migration imperative? If so, then why did not one or more clans survive dissension and continue in possession of the houses? But no one was left behind. And when the people found their new homesites, they recreated the same social pattern they had expressed in the cliff cities, in some instances building even larger cities with greater populations and more group divisions.

All efforts to explain the mystery on the basis of physical or material motives come to nothing. What is left? Where might the explanation lie? The people left beautiful cities and looked for new places to live. Consulting the favor of the natural world, many of them came at last through the barrier mountains to the river, the big river, P'osoge, or the big water, Ha^{n}n^{y}ap'akwa, or just the river, Tšina, where they found scattered settlements of people raising corn and living in primitive pit-houses. Life was already blessed there. The new settlers joined the old. The Pueblos of the Rio Grande were founded. What drove the people from the silent cities they had left behind them might well have been something they carried within themselves; something with more power over their acts than heat or cold, rain or dust, sickness or war or dissension. If they had reason to believe that their gods had abandoned them where they lived, the people would have had to go and find them again, in order to live at peace with the world of nature. As everything had its abiding spirit, not only things that grew, but inanimate things, and places, so with the loss of that spirit would be lost blessing, protection, safety. In fear and trembling the people would have had to abandon a place, no matter how splendid, from which the ruling deity had withdrawn. Any event, natural or imaginary, which would withdraw the gods of a place would make it accursed, and dangerous to life; and no matter how great hitherto it may have become, it would be abandoned.

They told stories through the centuries of such a motive for migration from various places. What was believed true of one place could be so of another.

In cliff towns of the Pajarito Plateau west of the river the people said that A-wan-yu lived among them, their deity. He was the plumed snake, creature of both air and land. A time came when they lost favor with him. He abandoned them, retired to the sky, and became the major galaxy of stars which reached across the central heavens as the Milky Way. Without him the people were at a loss. They gathered their life and its objects and, leaving their rooms in modest order, went away to build new cities on the river.

At the greatest of cliff cities (Mesa Verde) the people began to build a temple to the sun. It sat upon a crown of the mesa between valley and sky. Using the skin-colored stone of the place, they quarried and shaped their blocks and raised their walls in expert masonry. The temple contained many rooms. The largest was a round one in the center. Little junipers whose shape echoed the pull of the wind grew all about the temple. Close to its doors the mesa's cliffs swept away to the valley floor far below. It was a noble site facing the rising sun. To reach it with stone and timber took prodigious work. The work went slowly. The walls rose carefully to the same successive heights day by day or year by year. But they were never finished. Before they could be, all human life departed from the mesa, with its fields on top, its farms below in the valley, and its magnificent community houses high up in the faces of the cliffs. What if before the sun temple could be completed there was no god to receive in it? The people could only leave what they had partially done, with all of its walls unfinished at the same height, and go away.

Long later, in another ancient town, east of the river, the people kept a great black snake in the kiva, who had power over their life. They fed him the fruits of the hunt—deer, antelope, rabbit, bison, birds. From him they received all they needed to eat and to wear—corn, squash, berries, fruit of the yucca and cactus; shoes, leggings, shirts of soft deerskin. One night at midnight he left them. In the morning they found that he was gone. He left his track and they followed it. It took them down a dry river of white stones and clay (Galisteo Creek) which at last entered into the big river (Rio Grande), where the track was lost in the ever-flowing water. They returned to their town and discussed their trouble. "The snake has gone. What are we going to have of those things which he gave us? He has gone away. Now we also must be going away," they said. They worked together at the sorrowful job of taking up their things, and went down the dry river to the big river, where they found another town already living. There they took up their lives again amidst the gods of that place.

Fear of their gods may well have sent the cliff people from the mesas to the river. Bringing their high culture from the plateaus, the people wedded it to the primitive human ways they found along the Rio Grande, and once again with the approval of the gods made for themselves a settled life, sure of land, water, and corn, and of what explained fear and what creation.

4.

The Stuff of Life

i. creation and prayer

Most intimately they could watch creation as a child was born. So from the womb of the earth itself they said all life came forth long ago. The underworld was dark and mysterious. People and animals lived there and knew their mother, who was kind and loving, even though she remained far from the daily lives of her children. So they accounted for the impersonality of nature. As all life came from the underworld, so it returned there in death. To come in life and go in death, people and animals had to pass through a lake between the underworld and the world. The first people climbed up a great fir tree through the waters of the lake and entered this world. The place where they emerged was in the north and was called Shipapu.* Emergence into the world was a tremendous act, full of awe for what was left behind, and of fear and respect for what was found above, on the earth and in the sky. A thing ever afterward could be made sacred simply by saying "It came up with us."

With them came spirit, and could dwell in everything upon the

---

* With many variants, like all proper names in the myths.

earth. All spirit was like that of people. Rock, trees, plants; animals, birds, fish; places, directions, the bodies and acts of the sky; the live and the dead; things found or things made—all had the same spirit and behaved in the same ways as men and women. Some spirit was good and some bad, and accordingly had to be propitiated or guarded against. And sometimes spirit would leave its visible form and be gone. If it was bad spirit, people could rejoice; if good, they must mourn at having lost favor with the powers of their lives.

Everything in the world was part of the same living force, whether thought, action, object or creature. Of all this the earth was the center, and all things existed in order to help people to live upon it. And the center of the earth—earth's navel—was in the center of each group of people and their own city. All things reached out in widening circles of awareness from the very point of the self, individual, and the group, collective. From the center, then, of person and place, reached the six directions, each with its animal deity: north, with the mountain lion; west, with the bear; south, with the badger; east, with the wolf; the zenith, with the eagle; and the nadir, with the shrew. North and west produced the snow; south and east the rain. So the reach of Pueblo belief went across the earth, and into the depths underground and into the heights of the sky, and all tied to the place of emergence which was imitated with a stone-lined pit in the center of each ceremonial chamber, and sometimes out in the open in the very center of the town placita itself. All forces interacted to make life; and of these, none was greater in effect, sacredness and poetry than the sky, with its heroes, goddesses, and ancestors.

"Our Father Sun," they said. Some said that even the sun had ancestors—two mothers, who before the people came from the underworld saw that people must have light in order to see. The mothers fashioned the sun out of a white shell, a pink abalone shell, a turquoise and a red stone. They carried him to the east and in the morning climbed a high mountain. They dropped the sun behind the mountain; and presently he began to rise, taking his way over trails that ran above the waters of the sky, toward the evening. He set toward the lake which lay between the world and the underworld. He went down through the lake and when it was night on the earth he shone dimly below in the underworld. In the morning again he arose and again the people saw him with joy. What they saw was not the sun himself but a large mask that covered his whole body. By his light everyone saw that the world was large and beautiful. The sun saw and knew, like any other person.

And others said that he walked through the sky dressed in white deer-skin which flashed with countless beads. His face, hidden by a mask, was beautiful. They said he was the father of the twin boys, Masewi and Oyoyewi, the young gods of war, who protected the people by killing their enemies. The concept of evil, menace, hugeness of danger was defeated by the dream of small, immature mortals—the very cast of hope in people who first imagined their survival and triumph, then willed it, and then achieved it through the spirit which towered to victory over threatening forces. Power and strength came from the sun, as they could plainly see in the daily life all about them. "Our Father Sun" governed the overworld.

But when he went down through the sacred lake at evening the world was dark. He needed a companion god in the sky at night. So they said that the two mothers who made the sun also made the moon, taking a dark stone, different kinds of yellow stone, turquoise and a red stone, and placed it in the sky, where it followed by night the same trails which the sun followed by day. The moon was a mystery, and some said it was a man, others a woman.

Because the moon travelled slowly, not always giving light, the stars were needed, and were made out of crystal which sparkled and shone. At morning a great star shone into the dawn, and at evening another flashed slowly in the west even before the daylight was all gone at the place where the sun went below. They were clear in the heavens, along with many others, hanging near in power and beauty when the night was clear and dark, making at least some things certain and pure in a world where evil spirit could bring about change among people and things, and cause fear.

When clouds came, they brought rain, which blessed the earth and made things grow. Who loved the people and blessed them? The dead ancestors, who once were people, and who came back as clouds to do good for those whose life they already knew, with its constant hope, need and prayer for rain. Clouds were prayed to. The prayers took many forms. Feathers were used to imitate clouds and were put on top of headdresses and sacred masks. Visible prayers were put together out of little sticks decorated with feathers. These could be set about and left as invocations from earth to sky. The dead who departed to life in the clouds were in some places prepared with white paint on the forehead, and feathers and cotton placed in the hair, so that cloud would go to cloud and come back bringing rain.

Lightning, they said, was born of mischief by Masewi and Oyoyewi.

The twin war godlings once came to an empty kiva in a village of another world. While all the people were elsewhere the boys stole bows and arrows from the kiva wall and tried to escape unnoticed; but they were seen, their theft discovered, and they were chased by outraged people. Just where they had come from their own world to the other one, and as they were about to be taken, the adventurers were picked up by a whirlwind and thrust back into their own world, where they went home. On the way, Masewi sent an arrow high up to the sky. It made a grand noise. The womenfolk saw it and fainted. The boys shot many more arrows. These were the first bolts of lightning known by the people. Some days later here came rainclouds, bringing the arrows back and delivering rain with many flashes and noises. Arrows fell. The twins were glad their arrows came back to them. Sky arrows were holy to hunters, who prayed to lightning when they got ready to hunt. Thunder was made by an old goddess. They said medicine men could send for thunder and receive it at any time. The wind had a divinity, too, sometimes man, sometimes woman. There was an aged god of the rainbow. When the war twins wanted to visit their father the sun, they walked on the rainbow which quickly took them to him in mid-sky.

The Pueblos said, then, recognizing the exchange of influences and acts between earth and sky, that the Old Man of the Sky was the husband of the Old Woman of the Earth. All things came from their union, just as the child came from the union of man and woman. Mankind and the animals, the earth and the sky with all their elements, all had the same kind of life; and a person must be in harmony with the life in all things. The way to find it was in religion. Prayer and observances were part of all daily life. Bound upon the earth with other living things, the Pueblos said that the same life belonged in everything, and that life was either male or female. Everything they believed came within the frame of those two ideas.

Prayer took many forms.

Sometimes it was only the person who prayed; and sometimes the whole family, or fraternity, or town. Prayers were always visible, a stuff was used, in an act, to make plain the desire locked in the heart. Of all prayer substances, the most common was meal, ground once, from white corn. It had life in it, it came from something that once grew, it fed life in people, its seed made more life in the ground. The Pueblo person took it in his hand and breathed upon it as he prayed. "Eat" he said to it, and then he sprinkled it into the air, or over the ground, or upon the person, place, thing, or animal he wanted to bless. At sunrise he would go out and sprinkle meal and say a prayer. When holy men, or hunters, or warriors went by his house before or after doing their work, he would come to his wall, breathe upon meal, and sprinkle it before their steps. His fingers were bunched at his lips holding the pinch of meal. In breathing upon it he gave his living essence to it. His inward prayer made an arc of spirit from him to all godliness; and his arm when he swept it widely to sprinkle the meal had a noble reach in it; for a gesture can always be bigger than the little member which makes it.

Sometimes pollen from flowers was used and spread in prayer in just the same way.

Another form of prayer, one which lasted longer, and could be left to bear testimony and intercede by itself, was the prayer stick. It was used in every group ceremonial in some pueblos, and often a whole ritual was built around it. It was also used privately. Much care, ingenuity and taste went into its making. The prayer stick was as long as from the wrist to the end of the middle finger. It was cut from oak, willow, spruce or cottonwood. Its stem was richly painted with colors taken from the earth. There was turquoise color, made out of malachite or copper ore mixed with white bean meal. Yellow ochre came from canyon or gully faces, exposed in stripes by long weather. Shale made black. Pale clay made white, iron-stained sandstone made red, and from cactus flowers or purple cornhusk came violet. The colors were mixed with water from sacred springs, and with flowers from the bee-plant. Honey was sprayed on the paint after it was applied. The sky was called by feathers bound onto the prayer stick. Turkey, duck, hawk and eagle; flicker, jay, bluebird, oriole, towhee, yellow warbler feathers were used. To speak to cloud spirits, downy or breast feathers were bound in with the feather bundles. Beads were added sometimes.

When the prayer stick was made, it was prayed over and exposed to smoke. It was breathed upon and given its intention. Then it was taken to do its work. Perhaps it was set up in the house where it would stay for life, expressing its prayer forever. It might be taken to the fields and buried; or set in the riverbank; or taken to a holy spring and established at its lip; or carried high into the mountains to make a remote shrine; or put away with stored food; or sealed up in the wall of a new house; or carried in the hand during ceremonials; or put to earth with the dead. If a prayer stick was left in an exposed place, they could tell by whether it stood or fell how the spirit of its maker was. If it fell, he must have had bad thought while making it, and his offering was in consequence rejected.

Sometimes prayer and its acts were delegated. Certain persons became priests and acted for everyone else. It was agreed that nature did what the priests told it to do. The priests spoke to the world in grander ways than anyone else. When they meant "four years" they would say "four days," for example. But everyone knew what they meant when they sounded special. It was part of their having power. People watched to see that the priests used their power when it was needed, such as those times every year when the sun had to be turned back. All summer long the sun moved farther to the south, toward the badger. The weather was colder. Every year, in the same month, there came a point beyond which the sun must not be permitted to go. They would know by watching the sun come to a natural landmark when the limit of his southern journey was reached. At that point, on that day, it was the duty of the priests to halt the sun; and with prayer, ceremony and power, make the sun start northward in the sky once again, in its proper way. Half a year later, when the sun touched the point to the north, with the mountain lion, beyond which it must never be allowed to go, the priests brought it back toward the south again. So the natural cycles were preserved. What nature had already ordered was ordered once again by the people in their prayers. To rise above, govern and hold the natural world they imagined their own control of it and solemnly sanctioned the inevitable.

Other ways to pray and gain favor were found in imitating what nature looked like and did. And here the great group prayer was made, when the people came together in ceremony to tell nature what it must do for their lives.

They gave great splendor to the group prayer, and prepared for it with rigor, always in the same ways which had come down to them out of memory. A certain society of men learned invocations and chants which lasted for hours, and had to be word-perfect. They learned choruses and strict drumbeats to accompany them. Sacred costumes were made, and the materials for them came from expeditions, often to the mountains and even farther—boughs of the pine tree, skins of the fox and the rabbit, the deer, the buffalo, the bobcat; feathers from eagles, the bright parrots of the south; and from nearer home, gourds to dry and fill with pebbles from the arroyos, cornhusks to weave into head-dresses, paint to put on the body. Groups of men and groups of women worked at practicing over and over the steps of the dance to be used in the ceremony. They must stand—the men separate from the women—just so, and to the beat of the drum, they must lift and put down their feet so, all exactly together; they must turn, and pause, and advance, facing newly, and the women's bare feet must be lifted only a little and put down again mildly, while the men must smartly raise their feet in their soft deerskin shoes and bring them down to pound on the ground with power. The singers and the dancers and the drummers learned perfect accord. Implements were made in the ceremonial chambers to be used on the day of the group prayer which was held in the plaza of the town. All persons, young and old, worked toward the day. Men and women could not lie together for a certain period before it. Only certain foods might be eaten. For several days before, those who were going to take part made sure to vomit many times a day. The dancing ground was swept clean. If there was any refuse about the houses it was taken away. Thoughts were put in order too. Some of the figures in the dance were going to be the clowns, the spirits who mocked and scolded humanity, whose very thoughts they could see. And above all, there would be certain masked figures who came there from the other world. All the women knew that these were gods themselves—the spirits of rain and growth—who wore wooden coverings on their heads, trimmed with downy feathers, painted to represent the deities of the sky. These were the most mysterious and powerful of all the dancers. They had naked arms and breasts and legs like any other men, and wore foxtails on their rumps. and had pine boughs banded upon their arms, and wore the woven belts and the rabbit-fur baldrics and deerskin shoes, and used the gourds like the real men, but the women said they were not real men, they were actual gods, called the kachinas, and upon them depended the rainfall, the crops and the yield of the hunt. All year, said the women, their masks were kept in the ceremonial chamber, and when time came for the group prayer, they came like gods and put them on, and appeared in the ceremony. The men knew something else. They knew that long ago, before anybody could remember, or think of it, the kachinas really came and danced with the people. But for a long time they had not really come. It was actually certain men who put on the masks and appeared as the kachinas. But they never told the women of the substitution. Children did not know of it, either; and only boys, when they reached a certain age, learned of it, and kept the secret among their sex. If the gods were properly imitated, then they would do as their imitators did, and make the motions which would produce rain, growth and game.

When the day came the whole pueblo was ready. Those who did not dance sat in silence upon the rooftops or against the walls upon the ground. All was still in the early sunlight. The houses, made of earth, looked like mesas, and cast strong shadows. People waited as nature waited for whatever might come. The ground before the houses was empty and clean, dazzling in the light. What would break the silence, and release the bodies full of prayer?

It was a thunderclap which came suddenly and rocked from wall to wall, in the voice of the drums. The drums told the thunder what to do; and thunder, born of storm, would bring rain.

At once the first dancers came like creatures of the air out of the door in the flat roof of the ceremonial chamber; and at the same instant song began and the drums sounded with it. The chorus appeared from between two houses and came to the plaza.

Then the dancers came, great ranks of them, the men in front, the women behind them, led by a man holding a long pole into the air, decorated with eagle feathers that spoke to the sky, as from one cloud to another. They all advanced as slowly as a shadow from a high cloud on a still day; but they never ceased their movement. The men pounded the stamped ground. The women padded softly upon it. The men commanded nature. The women waited to receive it. Slowly the long columns reached out and out into the dancing-ground until they were all seen. They crossed it. They faced and returned. The chorus and the drummers sang and beat without falter. Everyone was exactly together in rhythm and action. The evolutions of the dancing and singing groups were made so gradually and in such slowly changed relation to one another that they seemed like the slow wheeling of the stars overhead at night.

In their right hands the men held the rattles of dried gourds containing seed pods or pebbles. With these at intervals they clattered upon the ground the sound of seeds falling; and again they showered together upon the earth the sound of falling rain.

In their left hands the men and women carried bunches of eagle feathers which like those on the banner that towered above them and went with them in their grave evolutions invoked the clouds of the sky.

In their left hands the women carried pine boughs; and pine boughs were bound upon the arms of the men. These were a prayer for everlasting life, for the pine tree was always green.

The men proclaimed by their presence the seed, and invoked it, and wet it, pounding their power into the earth, and ordered that it live and grow.

The women impassively like the earth itself showed by their presence how the seed was received and nurtured.

With their pine boughs spaced throughout the ranks, they looked like a little forest. Advancing powerfully against the light they were like a movement of the earth in an analogy of slow time. The voices of the singers barked together and made order out of the sounds of the animal kingdom. The arms moved, the legs rose and fell, the bodies travelled in such unanimity and decorum that they all seemed like a great woven construction, something man-made, some vast act of basketry, the parts tied and yet flexible in supple buckskin; again, moving against the sidelines, they seemed like a cliff advancing; or if the watchers shut their eyes and only listened for a moment, they heard the singing voices clapping flatly back from the facing houses, and the clatter of seeds, the swipe of rain, the breeze of pine trees, the rattle of little shells tied to costumes, and in all of it the spacious and secret sound of the sky into which all other sounds disappeared and were taken to the gods.

All day long the insistent pounding of the prayer went on.

The clowns—koshare—played about the undisturbed edges of the formal dancing groups. They were painted white, with here and there a black stripe. They were naked, and used their nakedness in comic outrage and in joking punishment of generative power. They leaped and ran. They now went soberly by the dancers and jogged like them and then broke away to enact a burlesque at a corner of the dancing-ground. A little boy or two, painted like them, capered along with them learning the mocking idiom of the people's self-critics. Against so much work and preparation and proper devoutness in the great dance, it was necessary to send a different kind of prayer through the antics of the koshare—all the things the people knew about themselves but would not say separately. Fun included hurting. About that there was nothing odd. Much of life hurt.

The masked gods moved with the men.

The singers and drummers, massed closely together, turned and changed formation, now into a solid square, now a circle, but so slowly that the watchers hardly saw the change take place, but only realized it the next time they looked. The drums smote the air every time the dancing feet charged the ground with the day's stern message, in beat, beat, beat. Every now and then, as dictated by the words of the chant, and the phases of prayer, the whole united government of bodies and voices and shaken air would suddenly break, missing a beat, and break again, missing another, making a clap of silence, a falter like a loss of light, a chasm in design, until, still in absolute union, legs, arms, voices, drums would resume the steady pounding by which the power of that town was driven, beat, beat, beat, into the earthen and airy body of nature.

And the whole day long it pounded.

According to the season, the dance took its theme from different gods. With them all, it practiced imitation of nature to influence nature. The rainbow dance with its arches of willows carried by women suggested rain as the rainbow could never appear in a dry sky. The turtle dance reminded the powers of water, for water came with turtles. The corn dance showered the sound of seeds and rain on the ground. The parrot dance with its blaze of feathers woven on costumes made nature think of the warm south where the parrots lived, and the hot sun, also, which made crops grow. The eagle dance, in which men soared along the ground with eagle wings tied to their arms, reminded of how strong an eagle was, and how such strength could cure anything. Before huntsmen set out, the dance would imagine and predict success for them— sometimes in the deer dance, with men garbed in deerskin and hunted down by other dancers as heroes; or the antelope, the elk, the buffalo, all costumed accordingly, and full of respect for the habits of the beloved adversary and victim who would be brought to death in order that the people might live. In the animal dances, little boys sometimes went costumed as bobcats and coyotes, jogging under the dancing bodies of men who impersonated deer or buffalo. Sometimes a boy dancer was a turkey, bridling and flaring with a suit of feathers.

To imitate was to induce, in gesture, sound and article.

To impersonate was to become.

To endure ordeal was to know not exhaustion but refreshment.

For when evening came the dancers, the singers and drummers were not tired. They were stronger than ever. They were lifted up. In giving they had received. The great ranks ended their slow stately evolutions, and the men retired to the kiva. The women sought their houses. The chorus broke formation and entered the kiva. The clowns went trotting lazily over the town. They capered benignly now. Dwellers came forward from their rooms and breathing upon corn meal dusted it into the air before the clowns who took the tribute with a kindly bend of painted nakedness. The spectators drifted to their rooms.

Such a pueblo typically sat on an eminence above the river, and near to it. The river was a power which like the light of the sky was never wholly lost. It came from the north beyond knowing, and it went to the south nobody knew where. It was always new and yet always the same. It let water be taken in ditches to the lowest fields. Trees grew along its banks—willows, cottonwoods, young and old, always renewing themselves. The water was brown, as brown as a body, and both lived on earth as brown. The river was part of the day's prayer.

Evening came down over the west, like thin gray smoke pulled over color, and the evening star stood like a great trembling drop of water on the soft darkness of the sky.

Before daylight was all gone, the pueblo was silent but for the little sounds of ordinary life—voices lost in narrow walls, a dog, someone breaking branches for firewood, children. The twilight was piercingly sweet and clear. The river went silent and silken between its low banks where grasses grew and saplings and little meadows sprung up out of mudbanks. Sky and town and valley were united in deep peace after the hard wonders of the dancing day. And at that hour the men of the dance came through the sapling groves to the river. The deepening yellow dusk put color on the water. The men came in their ceremonial dress. They took it off and went naked to the river's edge. There they breathed upon the pine boughs which they had worn, and the baldrics of rabbit fur, and sometimes the gourd rattles, and cast them upon the sliding surface of the water. They sent their prayers with the cast-off branches and the skins which, wherever they were borne by the river wherever it went, would go as part of that day's pleading will. Then entering the river the men bathed. The brown water played about them and over them and they thanked it and blessed it. Silken as beavers they came out and dried. Now their voices rang and they laughed and joked and gossiped about the long hard day, for its ceremony was over, and its make-believe, and could be talked about quite ordinarily. They felt strong and refreshed. It was good to have such a river, and such a town, and to have done such a work as that of today. Everything about it told nature what to do; everything was done in exactly the right way; all the ways were right, because, said the men, "they came up with us."

So the idea of creation, and so the ways of propitiating the creators.

ii. forms

There in that long stretch of New Mexico valley (which even so was but one seventh of the whole length of the river) the Pueblo Indians ordered the propriety of their life to the landscape that surrounded them.

This act was implicit in all their sacred beliefs. It recognized the power, nearness and blaze of the sky; the clarity of the air; the colors of the earth; the sweep of mountain, rock, plain; and the eternity of the river. Environment directly called forth the spirit and the creations of the people. The weather had direct effects upon vegetable growth, and the life of waterways, and the change in land forms. It had equally direct effect upon the human personality and its various states and views of life. The presence of mountains; the altitude of the very valley itself; the outlying deserts beyond; the effects created by the interchange of influence and response between that particular land and that particular sky—all had effect and expression in the Pueblo world.

The natural forms rising from a landscape created by surface water action, and wind, and volcanic fury—that is to say, river, desert and mountain—bore intimate fruits in their imitation by the forms of Pueblo life. The cave became a room. The room became part of a butte. The butte, joined with others like it, resembled a mesa, terraced and stepped back. The Pueblo town looked like a land form directly created by the forces that made hills and arroyos and deserts. Daylight upon the face of a pueblo looked the same as daylight upon the face of a cliff. Who knew how much this was accidental, and how much devised by the Indian in his sense of propriety in the natural world, his reverence for all its aspects, and his general application in imitative symbols of all the living and enduring forms he knew about him? Even where his town stood above the river, the river dictated his farming methods; for the irrigation ditch leading from the river to the fields below the town was in itself but a tiny river in form, with the same general laws of flow, and reach, and structure as the big river. People not too long the owners of such a concept would not find it a naive one, to be taken for granted. It would instead be a grave and reassuring fact, to be thankful for along with all of the other energetic expressions of the landscape, among which the Pueblo Indian prayed passionately to be included as a proper part— not a dominant part, not a being whose houses and inventions and commerce would subject the physical world until he rose above it as its master; but as a living spirit with material needs whose modest satisfaction could be found and harmonized with those of all other elements, breathing or still, in the dazzling openness all about him, with its ageless open secrets of solitude, sunlight and impassive land.

So every act and relationship of Pueblo life included the intention to find and fulfill such harmony. The whole environment found its way by spiritual means into all of Pueblo life. Works of art captured the animal and vegetable and spiritual world—always in objects meant for use, never display for its own sake. The work of art, in the sense that all elements were brought together—colors, emotions, ideas, attitudes—in harmonious proportion and mixed with fluent skill, the work of art was the act of living, itself. No one part of it had significance alone, just as each feature of the landscape by itself meant less than what all meant and looked like together.

Worship entered into every relation between the people and their surroundings. The mountains were holy places; temples standing forever which held up the sky. Gods lived in them, and other supernaturals. The priests of the people went to the mountains to call upon the deities of the four points of the compass. The various pueblo groups identified their sacred mountains differently. For one of them, the northern one was Truchas Peak; the eastern one was the Lake Peak of the Santa Fe range; the southern one was the Sandia range, which they called Okupi^{n}n, turtle mountain; the western one was Santa Clara Peak of the Jemez range, which they called the mountain covered with obsidian. All of them rose far back and above the Rio Grande, into whose valley they all eventually shed water.

The action of the river upon land forms was recognized at times by the Indians. Near the pueblo of San Ildefonso is a great black mesa on the west of the river, faced across the river on the east by high ground. This place they called P'o-woge, "where the water cut through." In the midst of supernatural explanations of natural conditions this was suddenly a cool and observant conclusion; not, however, to the disadvantage of another idea, which was that in the great cave on the north side of the black mesa there once lived (they said) a cannibal giant. His cave was connected with the interior of the vast, houselike mesa by tunnels which took him to his rooms. His influence upon the surrounding country was heavy. Persons did the proper things to avoid being caught and eaten by him.

Lakes and springs were sacred too, and natural pools. They were doorways to the world below. If everything originally "came up" with the people through the sacred lake Shi-pap, the same action could be imagined for other such bodies of water. Many of these were springs which fed the river. Gods and heroes were born out of springs, and ever afterward came and went between the above and below worlds through their pools. Every pueblo had sacred springs somewhere near-by. There was every reason to sanctify them—physical, as life depended upon water; spiritual, as they had natural mystery which suggested supernatural qualities; for how could it be that when water fell as rain, or as snow, and ran away, or dried up, there should be other water which came and came, secretly and sweetly, out of the ground and never failed?

Some of the rivers that went into the Rio Grande dried up for months at a time. In the Pueblo world, the most important tributaries were Taos, Santa Cruz, Pojuaque, Santa Fe and Galisteo Creeks on the east, and on the west, Jemez Creek, the Chama River. Of these only the last one had perennial flow. Its waters were red in melting season and colored the Rio Grande for many miles below their confluence. But the courses of them all bore the valley cottonwood. It was the dominant and most useful tree in all the Pueblo country. Its wood was soft and manageable, and it supplied material for many objects. Its silver bark, its big, varnished leaves sparkling in the light of summer and making caverns of shade along the banks, its winter-hold of leaves the color of beaten thin gold lasting in gorgeous bounty until the new catkins of spring—all added grace to the pueblo world. The columnar trunks were used to make tall drums, hollowed out and resonated with skins stretched over the open ends. The wood was hot fuel, fast-burning, leaving a pale, rich ash of many uses. Even the catkins had personal use—eaten raw, they were a bitter delicacy in some towns. And in that arid land, any tree, much less a scattered few, or a bounteous grove, meant good things— water somewhere near, and shade, and shelter from the beating sun, and talk from trifling leaves.

The feeling, the sense, of a place was real and important to the people. Almost invariably for their towns they chose sites of great natural beauty. The special charm of a place was often commemorated in what they named it. On the river's west bank stood a pueblo called Yunge, which meant "Western mockingbird place." The name was a clue to the sense of the place, for above its graces of flowing water, rippling groves and the high clear valley with its open skies would rise the memory of the May nights when the prodigal songs of the mockingbirds year after year sounded all night long in the moonlight. The birds sang so loudly as to awaken people from sleep. Night after night a particular voice seemed to come from the very same tree with the same song. It was like a blessing so joyful that it made an awakened sleeper laugh with delight, listening to that seasonal creature of the river's life. In the daytime little boys on rooftops caught moths which also appeared in May and whistling to the mockingbirds released the moths which the birds in an accurate swoop caught in midair with their bills.

Everything in the landscape was sacred, whether the forms of nature, or those made by people—altars, shrines, and the very towns which were like earth arisen into wall, terrace, light and shadow, enclosing and expressing organized human life.

iii. community

It was an organized life whose ruling ideas were order, moderation, unanimity. All ways were prescribed, all limits set, and all people by weight of an irresistible power took part in the town life. Examples of such controls elsewhere suggested that they must come from a ruler, a presiding head of state whose decrees could only be obeyed, on pain of despotic gesture. But the Pueblo people had no ruler; no despot. The irresistible power which ordered their communal life was the combined and voluntary power of the people—all the people, in each town, giving continuity to inherited ways by common agreement.

Everybody, together, in a pueblo, owned all the land, all the religious edifices and ritual objects. Assignment of use was made by a council of elders. Heads of families were granted the use of portions of land, which could be reallotted every year, according to change in families through marriage or death. Religious properties were assigned to proper organizations.

Crops grown by families upon their assigned plots belonged to them alone. Families owned objects which they made for their own use. Families were given permanent possession of rooms in the pueblo for as long as the family existed and could build additional space as needed. When a family died out its apartments were abandoned and went into ruins.

Since property was entirely for use, and not for sale or trade within the pueblo, everybody lived upon the same scale. Their rooms were alike. Their holdings in food, clothing, furniture, were about the same. Living closely together, they interfered very little with their immediate neighbors, though within the family there was no privacy and no desire for any. Outbursts of feeling, emotion, violence, were bad form, and so was indulgence in authority for its own sake, instead of for the propriety it was meant to preserve. Nobody was supposed to stand out from everyone else in any connection but that which had to do with official duties. Everyone understood that certain work—official or religious—had to be done by someone who was given, by common consent, the authority to do it. But nobody was supposed to propose himself for the job, or go out after it. If he was chosen for it, a man with real reluctance but equally real obedience to the wishes of his associates accepted it and did his serious best while in office. If anybody in such a position showed the wrong attitude, or indeed, if anyone at all transgressed against the accepted way of things, he was shown his error in the ridicule he received from other people. He did not like to be laughed at in the town, or made sport of by the clowns in the dances, and he would mend his ways if he had gone too far out of line. There was no excuse for him to feel differently from anybody else, and to behave accordingly. As there was a proper way to perform all acts, everyone not only understood ritual but performed it. United in gesture, the pueblo had a strong sense of its own identity. Everyone agreed how things were and had to be and should be. Understanding so, there could be few disappointments in life, and few complete bafflements.

Certain towns had thin, narrow, long stones which rang with a clear song when struck. They were hung by deerskin thongs to the end, outdoors, of a roof beam. The singing stones could be heard in the town and the near-by fields. To summon men for meetings, the stones were struck. Meetings were held often, for the town had many organizations, each with particular work to do.

In some towns, all people were divided into two cults—the Summer, or Squash, People; and the Winter, or Turquoise, People. Other towns knew four seasons of the year, and organized accordingly. All towns had secret societies with particular social duties, all religious in form. At the head of the pueblo, as guardian of all spiritual lives, was the cacique. He served for life. He had many duties, for no important act was ever done without ritual, and it was he who blessed and approved all ceremonies. In his own life he invoked holiness with fasting and prayer. That he might be free entirely for his sacred offices he was relieved of all other work. His house was built for him. Other people planted for him and cultivated his crops and made his harvests. In his shrines he kept fetishes which had to be fed with rabbit meat. Men went on special hunts to bring him rabbits, and the sacred food was prepared by his appointed helper, who cooked the rabbits, and also kept his house for him, making fires, sweeping the packed earthen floor, and ministering to his needs.

The cacique made important appointments to the priesthood. Two of these were the war priests, named for the twin boy-gods Masewi and Oyoyowi. They held office for a year. Part of their duty was to observe the cacique in the performance of his duties, and to admonish him if he was negligent. Each year he appointed ten assistants to the war priests. His influence was great, his position among the people that of the fountainhead of all spiritual belief and practice. He was both father and mother to them, a living analogue of the source of their lives. Upon his death his successor was chosen by the war priests from his own secret society.

The cult was a medium through which the people could formally take part in the religious life of the pueblo. Everyone belonged to one or another of the cults in the town. Membership was hereditary, except that a girl who married entered the cult of her husband. If she was widowed she could choose between remaining in the cult of her husband or returning to that of her father. The cult had a head who was in charge of all its activities. The most sacred of objects were the masks used in the kachina dances—those great group prayers in which the gods of rain were believed by women and children to be actually present in the dance. These masks, and the costumes that went with them, and the miniature carved figures representing the godly kachinas, were kept by the cult leader as his own personal duty. He alone could mix the turquoise green paint used in decorating the masks. Not everyone could have masks. Only married men of mature experience could have them. With the mask came powers—the wearer turned into someone else. His real person was hidden not only from the spectator but delivered from himself. Behind the mask he was the godlike being which the people saw. He escaped into a new and sacred dignity, leaving behind him the weak man of every day to whom he must return when he doffed his mask again but surely with some lingering joy and a new strength.

The cult had its ceremonial home in the large chamber of the kiva, sacred to its own members. It was usually circular, sometimes underground, generally above ground. Here was the very house of power and ritual. It was entered through a hatch in the roof, by a tall ladder which leaned down to the floor. A small altar stood in the room, sometimes against the wall, sometimes free. Before it was a small round hole. This was called by the same name as the original place where the people came up into the world—Shipapu. A shaft built into the wall brought air to the altar, and with it could come and go the spirits addressed in prayer. Smoke from fires built before the altar was carried out through the entrance hatch in the roof by the spirits of the kachinas. On another plane of experience and discovery, the air descending through the shaft made the fire draw, and set up circulation which drew smoke to the roof and out into the air through the hatchway. At about the height of a kneeling man, a deep shelf or seat ran around the wall of the interior. The wall was sometimes painted with sacred images and symbols of weather, animals, birds, plants, and human actions, all with ritual purposes.

The whole kiva itself was a powerful symbol. It was like a small butte with a flat top, a land form often seen. In its interior it gave passageway to the two worlds—the earth-world above, through the hatch to natural life of land, creatures and sky; and the netherworld below, through the portal of the world's womb from which all had come so long ago. Both worlds were made to join in the kiva. Here the holy pigments were prepared, and the costumes for the dances. Inherited rituals were studied and learned here. Sacred objects remained in the kiva when not in use out of doors. Fetishes were fed there. Boys were initiated there into knowledge and power of which they had known only animal intimations. There dancers painted and dressed for their outdoor ceremonials, and when readied came in a crowding line up the ladder through the hatch, over the roof and down to the ground. To perpetuate the kiva in filling vacant kiva offices, there the members met in conclave. There in the significant number of four times—invocation of the whole world through its four quarters—ceremonies were prepared during four days of vomiting and other purifications.

Each kiva group was dedicated to the ceremonial work of one of the seasons. Since ritual and its texts were elaborate, and long, and transmitted only by memory with no written records, and since every phase of community life was accompanied by its ceremonial observance, no one cult could learn and execute the liturgy for all occasions. Yet certain events, like the great corn dance, called upon two or more cults to perform in the plaza, alternately throughout the day-long invocation of the spirits of fertility and growth, when one group would dance while the other waited to take its place, with all joining at the end.

So the religious life of the people was formalized in groups that separately represented neither the whole town nor a single clan but drew symmetrically upon the population until all were included, empowered in the same terms, and actors of the same myths. Religion was not a thing apart from daily life. It *was* daily life, a formalization, an imitation of nature, an imagined control of the elements, and of what was obscure in the spirit of men and women.

In addition to the major divisions of the kiva groups, which cut boldly through the whole company of the town for organized religious acts, there were smaller groups with specialized missions whose members were not chosen along the lines of kiva organization. These were the secret societies. Each had its unique purpose. There was one in charge of war. Another appointed all holders of major nonreligious offices. Another comprised the koshare, the clowns of the dances who served also as the disciplinarians, through censure or ridicule, of individuals who offended against the unspoken but powerful sense of restraint and decorum that governed behavior. Several others were curing societies, and together constituted the medicine cult. And another embraced the hunters of the town. All selected and initiated their own members throughout the generations.

Of the secret societies those which did battle on behalf of the people against illnesses of body and spirit had the largest number of members. Their work was highly specialized and in much demand. Almost everywhere there was reason to call upon them, for even a suspicion of illness was enough to invoke the powers of the curing societies. It all related to what the people said was behind illness—any illness but the little commonplace ones that came and went in a day. No, there were other kinds that came from nowhere, lasted a long time, and had strange effects. They were not accounted for in ordinary ways. Something was at work, something wicked, something unseen, and clever, and dangerous because it might be right here, anywhere, abiding for the while in a bird, or an animal, or a person, or a rock, none of whom knew it. Possibly an ant, or a toad, or a buzzing insect contained the responsible thing. One day well, the next day sick—the invalid, they said, must have received the sickness in his sleep when nobody was watching, and the awful thing had its chance to happen. Once again they had struck, those powers of evil and illness, of whom everybody knew, and sooner or later encountered. They were witches, male and female, who were invisible, who put themselves into innocent creatures and objects, and who did their worst work in all success because people could not recognize them and prevent them from creating harm and havoc. All witches worked upon the same purpose—to make people sicken and die. Sometimes they put spells also upon useful animals to make them die. The danger was so real and so prevalent that everyone kept a sharp watch for suspicious behavior on the part of persons, animals and things. And yet much else had to be done, daily, and so the people gave to the curing societies the special responsibility of keeping vigil against witches, and of taking proper action when the blow fell.

It was they said most fortunate that the doctors of the medicine societies were able to receive extraordinary powers from the real medicine men of the spirit world—the ones who were animal-gods and heroes, whose benign influence reached to all the quarters of the world, and to the zenith and the nadir too: the mountain lion, the bear, the badger, the eagle, the wolf, and the shrew. Thanks to these powers, the doctors were able to recognize witches where no other person could possibly do so. Once identified, the witches could be unmasked and worked against. It was hard work, calling for exactly learned methods, and sadly enough there was always the possibility of failure. Still, everything possible had to be done, and if in the end the doctors lost their patient, the people did not hold it against them, but realized that in this case the opposing powers were the stronger, and could not but prevail. Witches were powerful, that was just the point of being so careful about them, and working so energetically against them. Witches especially tried to destroy the young men. It was particularly evil of them thus to strike against the strength of the present and the seed of the future.

When a person was bewitched into sickness, great forces went to work to save him. His people sent for the doctor of a medicine society who came to the house. Family and friends were there. The prevalence of witches was of much concern to everyone. The doctor followed a procedure known to all, for it was established long ago. He removed his clothes, returning to his animal estate naked. He went to the patient whom he examined with thorough care, feeling him all over his naked body to determine the location of the malevolence which had invaded him. He prayed. If there was a fracture he made splints and set the bone. If there was lameness he massaged. If there was an eruption he lanced it with a flint knife. If no visible ailment showed he administered medicines brewed of herbs and water. He anointed the sick body with his curative saliva. He was disembodied from his daily self. The patient and the people knew him as a power in tune with greater powers, and as he worked, they felt in themselves the energy he brought and the conviction of recovery he carried. Hope arrived with him. Witches might be strong, but here was strength too, in every curative gesture, word and thought. At the end of the treatment, the doctor resumed his clothes and left, with instructions to summon him again if the patient did not improve rapidly.

If he was needed again, he then assembled all the other members of his own medicine society and unless the patient was critically ill, the doctor worked with them for four days in ritualistic preparation for the major cure which they were to undertake. If the patient seemed to be dying, they went to him in the first evening. Otherwise on the evening of the fourth day (the people said great virtue resided in the number four) they went to the house of sickness. The doctors undressed. To frighten the witches they painted their faces black. Over their heads from ear to ear they each fastened a band of white eagle-down, and around their necks hung necklaces of bear claws. Each doctor held two eagle wing feathers and a gourd rattle. The medicine society was ready to go to work.

The doctors in turn came to the patient and felt over his body to determine the seat of illness. When they found it they would know into what member the witches had shot their evil, and what was its nature. The whole cure led to the extraction of the evil object from the patient's body.

Meantime there were prayers and chants. Paintings of colored meal were laid upon the swept floor by a medicine priest. He sprinkled grains of color through his fingers, drawing lines with delicacy. He aimed the dropping meal with his thumb that sifted it, to compose in flax yellow, turquoise blue, berry red, skin brown, black, and white, a design full of magic power against sickness and witches. Before he changed from one color to another, he cleaned his fingers by twiddling them in a little pile of clean sand, like the sand that was spread down as the general background of the painting. It was almost hypnotic, to see the curative design come to being out of the little pouring streams of colored motes. Where nothing was, now power dwelt. How fortunate to know that it came manifest on the side of good, against evil! And then medicines were mixed and administered. The doctors partook of them along with the patient.

The proceedings were dangerous, they said, because such a gathering of virtue and opposition would in itself attract witches who would do their utmost to defeat the forces of good. Therefore, the war priests attended also, Masewi and Oyoyewi, to defend the doctors at their hopeful work. They stationed their assistants outside the house of illness with bows and arrows with which to shoot the witches if they came close. Nobody was in any doubt—the witches were there, and the last act of the curing drama was soon to come, after everything proper had been done in the sickroom. It was sober and urgent in feeling—so many personalities, so much gesture, such powerful singing, all the medicines—and the patient alone and bare in the midst of it felt these forces pulling at him and empowering him to recover. The doctors labored mightily.

Feeling the flesh of the patient, one of them found what they had all searched for—the place of illness, and the physical cause of it: turning to the assembled powers, he indicated the place, and then he bent to it and sucked upon the skin, or he operated with his hands, until he was able to come away from the sufferer and show everyone the cause of the trouble which had been stricken into the sick man by the witches. It was sometimes a thorn; again, a little snake, or a lizard, or piece of rag, or a pebble; any small foreign substance might turn out to be the seat of trouble. Only a trained doctor, they agreed, could ever find it, and bring it forth for everyone to see.

And now it was time to do battle directly with the witches who lurked outside. Already they had been partially defeated with the discovery of their projectile in the flesh of their victim. The doctors would finish the cure by physically punishing the witches so they would hardly dare to repeat their wickedness soon again.

Taking up each a sleeve made of the skin of a bear's leg (the power of the deity of the West) the doctors covered their left arms and took flint knives in their right hands. Linking arms they went out into the dark of the night in the open air before the house, and there as they knew they would they came upon the witches, who were invisible to all but them. A fearful struggle followed, as the people could hear in the sickroom. The patient could hear how mightily he was being avenged and—all hoped—freed of his trouble. There were shrieks and thunders, blows and wounds and imprecations without, as the doctors fought in the dark. The whole town was aware of the battle. The witches were strong and terrible. They might lead the doctors away. The sounds of the fight came and went. Now and then there was a human scream as a witch killed a doctor, who fell down dead, in proof that the enemy was formidable and the cure hazardous. Gradually all sounds whimpered down to nothing, and the guardian war priests went to look at the evidence of the struggle. On the ground they found the dead doctors. The other doctors who survived on their feet helped to carry the dead ones back to the curing chamber. There, with measures known to the doctors as part of their powers, the dead men were revived.

But the witches were repulsed. Sometimes a witch was killed by a shot through his heart with a flint-tipped arrow. Witches were known to have escaped the very grasp of a doctor, leaving only their clothes in the doctor's hands—but that was proof, anyway, of how close the battle was. There was much to talk about when the whole thing was over. The medicine meal had to be swept up, the pictures destroyed, the ceremonial equipment taken away. The Masewi always stood up, at the end of the curing labor, and told all how the patient had been cured. How strenuous the efforts; how huge and powerful the witches; how deep-seated the disease, and how wise the doctors to find it; how satisfactory the way in which all had participated; how fortunate the patient.

Then with the luxurious thoughts of the aftermath, the people went home. Now and then for the next several days one or another of the doctors would call informally upon the patient until he was well entirely, or dead. If it was death instead of cure, everyone however saddened knew where it came from and sighed over the awful power and strength of the witches, whose thundering blows and calls and general tumult they had heard through the darkness several nights before in the town. No wonder the doctors had not prevailed. If it was cure, that was not surprising, they said, for who did not recall the fury of the encounter with the witches, the valor of the doctors, the expertness of their ritual? No wonder witches could not endure such powerful attacks.

Thus comfort through organized observances.

The whole year had its cycle of them.

All winter the river ran shallow and lazy from the faraway north, and deep against the sky of the whole valley the snow was locked on the peaks by cold air. The fields by the pueblo were dry and the irrigation ditches which ran to them from the river were overgrown with the dry golden stalks, the pink brush, of the past year's weeds. In March* it was time to clean the ditches and then with prayer, dancing and prayer sticks, open the ditches to bring the river water in upon the spring plantings. The masked gods came from the otherworld to attend. They were seen right there in their masks among the dancers.

In April with four days of preparations the assembled kiva groups of the pueblo held a dance for the blessing of corn, which would come to summer harvest. Water, rain, were the greatest of blessings, and all was asked in their name, and in their image, gesture, and sound. The curing societies during this month went into retreat for purification and for prayer, again invoking rain, upon whose coming the lives of plant and person and animal alike depended. They retreated to their houses which they called, during the retreat, Shipapu, the same as the place of origin, through which everyone had come up. The retreat over, dances

---

* For convenience I have used modern calendric names, which of course were not accessible to the Pueblo Indians of the Rio Grande in the period before recorded history.

followed, again with the gods in their masks, who also had spent the same time in retreat at the real Shipapu. Well into the summer, retreats and emergence ceremonies continued.

In early summer the ceremony was held by the curing societies to pull the sun to the south, where his hot light would make long days and help things to grow.

In full summer they danced again for corn. Sometimes they started out in clear day, with all the kiva groups in fullest magnificence under a spotless blue sky which gave back heat like stone near fire. Rain could never come from such a sky. But all day they pounded the prayer into the ground and showered the sound of falling drops of rain from the air to the earth while the heat grew and grew and the shadows of the houses stood like triangles painted on pottery in black paint; and presently they might see without giving any sign what loomed in the north and the west against the ringing blue—dazzling white thunderheads marching slowly and powerfully over the sky toward this town, these fields and seeds. The blessings were vast and visible; and late in the day as the prayer still beat its way into the ground, the light might change, and the clouds meet over all, and brown color of the bodies and the town and the earth all alike would turn dark like the river as rain came and fell upon them and answered them and the sparkling green shoots of the corn in the fields. Sometimes it rained so hard and long that the earth ran and the gullies deepened, and new cracks appeared leading to them, and rocks rolled scouring new ways to the river, and the river rose and flowed fast carrying unaccustomed things sideways in the queer sailing current of flood.

In September as the border of summer and winter was reached the Summer People and the Winter People both held dances. Autumn brought hunting dances too, and some of them were given later in wintertime. In November came the feast of the dead, when all the ancestors came back to the pueblo to visit for a day and a night. It was a blessed occasion and a happy one. And before long it was time to urge the four curing societies to watch the sun, and call it back to the north before it went too far southward.

In midwinter the kiva groups chose their officers for the next year, and held dances to honor them, to bless them and to make them know the right ways. The curing societies now frequently in the winter held general cures for everyone. People could come to the curing cere-monies with their ailments and have them included with the other ills against which the doctors gave battle. They purged everyone, the whole town, of evil spirits. Again they cried out and struck blows against the witches, while all heard the encounters, and were reassured.

In February the koshare danced, the clowns, the critics, who hazed the people, sometimes to laughter, sometimes to shame, the spirit of irony and perversity thus accounted for and made useful.

And it was by then observed that the sun was safely on his way north again, and there was a ceremony to confirm this and give thanks.

Then the winter's weeds stood thick again in the ditches, and the path of life from the river to the fields had to be readied. Once again it was time to burn the weeds away, clean the ditches, let the river in, and set the plantings of another year.

It was an organized life based upon the desire for peace. The Pueblos rarely went to war unless they had to resist attack. The war society with its chief captains Masewi and Oyoyewi maintained the magic necessary to use in times of crisis from without the town. The war society was also a medium for the forgiveness of killing. Its members—all men —were those who had brought upon themselves the danger of having killed someone. This danger was the same whether the killing was accidental, murderous, or in sanctioned conflict. If there was blood upon a man he had to join the war society to wipe it out. He then became a defender of his people. He was confirmed with ceremony. After his initiation he went—like all boys and men after initiations and dances— to the river to bathe his body and his thoughts.

As for thoughts, when grave matters were in the air, requiring the judgment of the cacique and his council, these leaders fasted. They did penance the better to make wise decisions. Their fasting was known about. At home they abstained. In the kiva they abstained. They spoke to no one of what lay heavily upon their thoughts, but their concern was plain to all. Soon there was wonder, and gossip, worry; something was brewing; what would it be; was there anywhere to turn but once again to blind Nature?

But at last the council would speak to them. At evening, the town crier went to his rooftop. Perhaps the sky was yellow behind him and the house fires sent their smokes upward in unwavering lines of pale blue above the earth's band of twilight. The murmur of talk was like the sound of the river beyond its groves. Facing four ways in succession, the crier told four times what the council had decided and what it wanted of the people. On their roofs, or by their walls, or in their fields, the people heard him, and gave no kind of response; but they all heard and in proper order and time did what was asked of them.

iv. dwelling

When the Pueblo builders came to the river they found dwellers in little shelters built of upright poles stuck in the ground with brush woven among them and covered with dried mud. The walls of the cliff cities which had been left behind were of chipped flat stone anchored with earth. Now by the river there was no stone to be had, and the outlines, the terraces, the pyramids of the cliff towns were reproduced in the river material—clay, adobe, mixed with brush or straw from dried grasses native to the valley. At first even the upright poles of the scattered *jacales* along the river were used, in modified design. The poles were set close together in double rows. Between the rows wet earth was poured. The faces of the walls, outdoors and in, were built up with adobe scooped together a handful at a time and patted, puddled, into place. Layers were allowed to dry, and new layers for strength and thickness were added. When a wall was thick enough it could support beams; cross branches could be laid on the beams and plastered over, to make a ceiling, and a roof. Once a smooth level was managed on the roof, it could serve as a floor for a second storey, which in turn could support a third, and a fourth, until the great hive with all its cells had a porous strength shared by all its supporting uprights and laterals. There was no entrance at ground level. Ladders took the dweller from ground to all levels above.

The cities were much alike in form, varying most in color. The Rio Grande long ago cut down through different layers of buried color, revealing each at widely separated places along its course. The local soil made the walls, and gave them their color. The prevailing hue was pale, the Indian tan of dried river mud, wherever the pueblos sat on or near the river course in its most pastoral character. Where lava still showed in the soil in spite of centuries of weathering after forgotten upheavals, the earth, and the town, had a gray look, as at San Ildefonso. Up the Chama river, the ancient pueblo of Abiquiu had a dusty vermilion adobe, taken from the red hills and cliffs. A faint pink clay went into the pueblos of the Piros farther down the Rio Grande near Socorro.

The form of the pueblos was not found only on the Rio Grande. Those cities, and the typical life they showed, were common to great areas and long gaps of time. Just as certain tribes of Pueblo Indians came to the river to resettle, so others went westward and grew their cities in northwestern New Mexico and northeastern Arizona. Even deep in Mexico, and long before them in time, the Rio Grande Pueblos had their counterparts among the Aztecs, whose houses, temples, rituals and organization suggested theirs. Much came northward with the seed of corn and of ways to cultivate, invoke and protect it.

In the community house each family had a room. It was private, for its only entrance was through a hatch in the roof, entered by a long ladder. It was small—about twelve by fourteen by seven or eight feet. The walls were painted with gypsum and water whitewash. Much gypsum was available in the river country. The beams overhead were brought from forests far away. The length of the timbers determined the size of the room. Smoke from fires built on the floor went up through the hatch in the ceiling. Little openings in the walls let a draft in and gave a view outward, and in times of trouble served as a hole through which to fly arrows. Blankets of cotton and yucca fibre mats made beds and places to sit upon. There were also drum-shaped stools carved out of cottonwood trunks, and hollowed out on top.

If the family grew, a room next door was built, connected by a low opening to the first room. Each family prepared its own food. Food and water were kept in pottery vessels, and cooked in them. Pottery bowls were used to eat from. The pots were more than just receptacles. They were works of art, and more, they were made as acts of devotion, just as the poetry and song and drama and design of the dances were. All imaginative creation and skilled craftsmanship went to fulfill a direct purpose which was partly religious, partly esthetic and always utilitarian. A pot was made in a certain size and shape for a certain purpose; beyond that it was decorated with designs which spoke of the potter's desire for blessings from the natural world and its gods. By representing the forms of life associated with fertility, rain and growth, the Indian painter called them into being on his own behalf. Handling pots decorated with such symbols, the family had daily communion with the powers. The designs were without meaning for their own sake. Their value was not inherent in their lines, masses and colors, but dwelt in their spiritual message. They were outpourings of wish, not of artistic pleasure. As all forms of art and craft went to express the unanimous belief and observance of the people, so every person was in some degree an artist or a craftsman. The arts like all other phases of Pueblo life were communal in their purpose and realization.

The people of the Rio Grande had no metal crafts. Their products

were all made with stone or bone tools, and with fingers. Raw material
and finished object remained close to each other. What was inherent in
the one determined the form of the other.

Pueblo symbols for bird, or cloud, lightning or rain, animal, or
man, or mountain, were used by all makers. There was a common
graphic language in each tribe. Its designs were not meant to be realistic,
nor were they purposely grotesque. They were stylized images hallowed
by long usage and accepted as descriptive. The typical Pueblo pot carried
bands of design around its circumference combining specific symbols
with abstract lines and spaces. Even these last had a suggestive power.
Though they represented nothing, they seemed to recreate the spaces
and the angles, the sweep and line of the Southwest, the shafting of light
in the sky, the bold mesa, the parallels of rain and the dark spots of
juniper on hills otherwise bare. There was a genius common to all
Indian artisans—a tepee recalled a pine tree, a pueblo was a mesa, a
clay cist was a seed pod. Whatever its conscious motive, however symbolic its style, the impulse to record life was an ancient one; and in
any degree of its fulfillment always respectable as art.   ·

The needs of daily use called forth in the Rio Grande town
Indians a profuse and vigorous creation of pottery. They took the same
material of which they made their houses and with it made their vessels,
and somewhat by the same method, building up surfaces of moist earth,
letting them dry, adding more, and exposing the final form, in the one
case, to the baking sun, and in the other, to the fire of the kiln. The
decorations of the pottery were rich, often using two or three colors,
some of which had a glazed finish. Black, white, red and natural clay
color were the most common. A syrup of the yucca fruit was used with
paint and water. The designs were painted with a brush made of yucca
leaves. The line was flowed firmly, the sense of balance and proportion
was exquisite, and the use of color was both strong and delicate. In
such artistry there seemed to be an impersonal obedience to laws of
harmony and grace which dwelled deep in the common spirit of the
people. They said that life existed in everything; and that when they
made a pot, they gave personal life to it, just as all creatures, places
and things had personal life. Believing so, they knew a responsibility not
to art and its abstract aims, but to life and its hope of perfection. They
dared not make even a pot with less than their utmost skill if it was
to live a good life. Allowance was invariably made for its spirit to breathe
and come and go in the painted design on its surface. Somewhere in
the decoration there was always left an opening in the design, a gap,

a space not closed, so that life might enter there or flow from it. Wherever decorative design appeared—on textiles, walls, or on the half-sections of gourds fashioned into ladles—the ceremonial gap was represented.

v. garments

The pueblo people wove cloth and wore it hundreds of years before they came to the river. They made thread from the native cotton, and used a true loom, and whether they invented it or acquired it from Mexico no one can say. Cloth came from yucca fibres, too. On their clothing they painted or embroidered designs, much like those which they used in making baskets and pottery. Their costumes were rich and complete, according to the season. In summertime, the children went naked, and the men and women wore as little as necessary. In cold weather they had plenty to cover themselves with, some of it magnificent. They domesticated the wild turkey for the use of his feathers. Turkey tail feathers were part of the dance paraphernalia, and the soft little feathers of breast and body were tied with yucca fibres to make rich, warm blankets that could be worn as cloaks or slept in. Turkeys evidently had no other use, for the Pueblos did not eat them; but a glaring and straining bunch of live turkeys tied together by the legs made a ceremonial gift to visitors who came to the pueblo.

The people's clothes took their prevailing color from the natural hues of cotton and yucca fibre. Designs were added in colors taken from the earth and plants. There was a rich red, from clay. Mustard yellow came from rabbit brush, and a soft golden yellow came from ochreous earth. Larkspur and blue beans yielded a delicate blue stain, and copper sulphate gave again the brilliant blue-green dye which prevailed in the kachina masks.

A man dressed himself in a breechclout of cloth when he wore no other clothing. Otherwise, he wore a broad kilt wrapped about his waist. It was held in place by a richly decorated sash whose ends hung down. His shirt was a square of cloth with a hole cut for the head. Around his head he wore a cloth bandeau. His legs were sometimes covered by the superb buckskin leggings which he imitated from those of the hunting Plains Indians. The leggings were not joined, but hung separately from the sash or breechclout by leather thongs, from the crotch to the ankle. They were often gathered at the knee with ties of rawhide. On his feet he wore soft skin mocassins. Over all he wore a robe or cloak, now of turkey feathers, again of rabbit fur cut in strips and laced together with yucca thread. Tied to interesting points of his costume he wore, if he was fortunate, a number of the little copper bells and beads made far away in Mexico, and very rare in his river country. But some of the bells came northward in trade, and possibly some were made by wandering metalworkers from far to the south who came to the river and used local metals; but without leaving their skill behind them, for the pueblo people had no metal crafts in that time. Such an ornamental bell was about an inch, open at the bottom, and had a pebble strung on a thread for its clapper. The beads were an inch long and shaped in tight little cylinders. The bells seemed to be cast by some lost method and the beads were hammered. The man wore jewels, too, as many as he could contrive, out of strings of turquoise, bone inlaid with bright stones, black, red, or blue; and bits of shined rock in any beautiful color. He wore strings of precious color about his neck, and hung them from his ears, and wrapped them about his arms. Finally, on many occasions, he used paint on his skin as decoration, whether in the dance, in ceremonies for the sick, in rites of the hunt, or in war.

A woman wore a mantle four or five feet long, and about three feet wide, which she wrapped about herself under the left arm and over the right shoulder and held together with a long decorated belt that went several times around her waist. She wore nothing on her head and, except in bad weather when she used mocassins, nothing on her feet. Like her husband she wore as much jewelry as she could get, and in her uses of the dance and other ceremonies, she wore paint, but only on her face.

As among people anywhere, the children wore miniature imitations of adult costumes, except in hot weather, when they wore nothing at all.

The skins of the people were the color of moist river-earth. Their eyes were black and so was the thick hair of their heads. In general they were not tall. The men, from the exercises of their rituals, the ordeals of work, were lean and muscular. The women early lost the figures of maidenhood and grew heavy, moving modestly and calmly about their duties, fixed in their pivotal positions as the bearers of life, the holders of all that brought stability to the family.

vi. man, woman and child

For in the analogy of woman as the repository of continuing life, it was the wife and mother who was custodian of the family dwelling, and all communal property. Growing up among her relatives, she was courted by her suitor, who sometimes played to her upon the flageolet in the evening on the hills at a little distance from the town, when the fading light was still clear, and the day's sounds were dying away. If she heard him with favor, and took him as her husband, he joined her in the circle of her blood relations, who helped her with materials to build new rooms for her own life. She herself made the walls out of earth long ago laid down by the passage of the river. She received her husband in the shelter of her own life, with her person, her house and her years. It was hers to make all the enfolding and conserving gestures of life, whether as maker of shelter, of children, or of pottery. She took her husband for life and he understood that he was to have no other woman. A daughter born meant that the mother's family was increased, for the child would in her time bring a suitor to the same family premises; while a son born meant that one day he would leave and find his mate in another settled family bound together by its matron. From mother to daughter the home was passed on; not from father to son.

The father and mother rarely separated from one another; but if it came to pass that the marriage must end, it was the man who was removed, leaving the dominion of the family secure with the mother and her relations. He would one day find his few personal possessions set out upon the doorstep of his home by his wife, whereupon he would weep, take up his things, and return to the house of his mother. For it was there that he went at important times; and if his mother was dead, he would find his sister there, to whom he gave his ancestral allegiance.

A woman in her house produced the clothes worn by her husband and children. She prepared the food and cooked it. The staple of the diet was corn, and she ground the meal, often before sunrise. While her husband sang to her a song which celebrated the act of grinding corn, or beat upon a drum, she worked the kernels in time with his rhythm. She put the corn upon a large flat stone and ground it with a smaller bar of stone, and in time the first was hollowed out like a dish and the second was rounded off at the edges by the work. Her hands grew hard and big and her fingernails wore down as she labored. For each batch of meal she used several different stones, going from coarse to smooth, always refining the flour and roasting it after each grinding. Sometimes several women ground corn together at night. If a woman wanted to make a gift to a man, she would give corn bread or any cooked food.

She kept her house immaculate and the roof above it and the space before it. Her broom was made of slender branches of Apache plume (or poñil) bound to a willow stick. When she swept her floor she first sprinkled it with water or blew a spray of water from her mouth. Her soap was made from yucca roots. To make cord or rope she boiled the succulent leaves of the yucca and when they cooled she chewed them until they were soft, and then drew out the stringy fibers which she worked together.

Her day was busy and her duties were serious. Much depended upon her, not only what needed to be done, but also how. From her mother she had learned the proper ways of life, and it was her own obligation to transmit these to her own daughters. Even hopes and desires had their proper gestures, to be made in the image of what she wanted. If she wanted a son and had none, she went to find a stone that had the shape of a man's generative member. From this she scraped a little stone dust and put it into water and drank. She prayed. She deeply knew her animal womanhood and enacted its appointed nature in harmony with what she saw of life all about her.

A man's purposes and duties were all plain, too.

If he owned no house, anyhow he governed the town. He explained life through religion and ordered, preserved and executed the ceremonies which he said kept the year and its seasons in their proper passage. He provided raw food by farming and hunting. Like the seed for children, the seed corn belong to him. All the powers latent in the fields were his, and so was the rubble after harvest. Harvested food and stored corn was, he said, "my wife's." If he wanted to make a gift to a woman, he gave the products of his work—game, firewood, embroidered or woven cloth, which it was his to produce. He ruled the river and brought its water to the fields for irrigation. And in times of danger from other peoples, he made war.

The Pueblo people were peaceful. They said they never carried war to others, but gave battle only in defense of their own lands, towns and families. One Pueblo tribe sang a song of war which told of no glory, no brag, no zest for a fight.

> So we have bad luck
> For we are men.
> You have good luck
> For you are women.
> To Navaho camps we go
> Ready for war. Good-bye.

Bad luck—but ready, they sang, with realism and a larger bravery.

The Pueblo warriors painted themselves, for there was power in paint, and to go out to save their community life was in itself a ceremony. The surface of their bodies, perceptive of touch, caress and wound, was beautified with designs that came alive with movement—the lift and fall of breathing, the haul and suck of the belly in exertion, the climb and pound of limbs. Flesh became a living temple of esthetic and spiritual feeling. It was an act of both art and religion, and the warrior's mortal humanity, his bodily stuff dear because it was not immortal, was the very material of his craft. Using the colors of the earth itself, the great source and repository both, the act of devotion combined in tragic wholeness the Pueblo man's concepts of himself and his gods. Upon his own nakedness he used his earth in the symbols of what he believed in.

First he put on his skin a layer of tallow. Over this went the colors—gypsum white that clothed but did not conceal his legs; red, from clay or crushed amaranth blossoms, on arms and chest; lines of soot black edging designs; yellow from the dust of sunflower petals. He ceremonially washed his hair in yucca suds. Wearing only invocations as armor, he went to the enemy carrying his loins wrapped in buckskin. A buckskin baldric hung over the left shoulder, and above the left shoulder peered the bow case and the quiver, from which arrows could be slipped with the right hand, the left holding the bow. From a tight belt were slung a stone knife and a club, a pouch of sacred objects to bring power, and a little bag of ground meal to be used with water as food on the campaign. Bad luck—but ready for war. The Pueblo men were devoted to their soil. Their towns rose from the river earth like shapes of nature. Their fields were cunningly cultivated. The seed corn secured them life. Their wives gave houses to live in to generation upon generation. There was every reason to stay at home and live well. But their most powerful enemies came from the plains where nothing grew but food for the wandering herds of buffalo, whose flesh made meals for the marauders, whose droppings gave them fire, whose vast seasonal whims took them drifting like cloud shadows over the exposed prairies. The invaders had little to lose and much to gain. But the pueblo people had everything to lose and they fought for it and kept it. Their ways came up with them from a long time ago, and gave them strength.

They lost few of their reluctant prehistoric wars, though perhaps a town here, a scatter of houses there, might suffer and be abandoned. They could come home and make sacrifices of thanksgiving with ceremonies, smoking clay pipes filled with red willow bark, and telling of battle. They had earned their ease. When they wanted to relax and gossip, and be purified, the men took sweat baths together, putting heated stones in a closed room, and pouring water upon them, and finally going to the river to bathe. The river always purified. It seemed to bring some thoughts from far above, who knew from where, and carry others far downstream, who knew whither. Using the river, a person could dream awake, like a child.

The people treated their children tenderly, from the time of birth to the entrance into adult societies. Ceremony and symbol accompanied the child into the world, and at every stage of life thereafter attended him.

The mother unbraided her hair and wore her clothing unknotted that her unborn child might learn to come easily without stricture into the world. A midwife delivered him. In slow or dangerous deliveries, medicine priests might be sent for. They had measures. With invocations, they would hold the laboring woman up by her hips. Again, they would burn pine-nut shells on live coals in a medicine bowl, placing it under her blankets to sweat her. They would massage her belly and call forth the child.

When the baby was born, the midwife cut its cord and wiped its eyes. If a boy, she put his legs and feet into a black pottery bowl so that he might have a heavy voice, and then handed him to his maternal grandfather. If a girl, the midwife put her in the grinding bin for a moment to make her a proper woman, and handed her to her maternal grandmother. The midwife took the afterbirth to the river and threw it into the water which took it away in purification. For her help she received a gift of fine meal.

The paternal grandmother or aunt took up corn meal and with it sprinkled on each wall of the room four little parallel lines, saying to the infant, "Now I have made you a house, and you shall stay here." In his blankets the baby was laid between two unblemished ears of corn that would guard him until he was given his name. His mother chose a woman to name him, which would be done after four sunrises. Before dawn on the fifth day the sponsor came to the baby's house. Taking him up, and accompanied by the mother, she went outdoors just before sunrise and as the sun rose she presented him to the light, and spoke his name. The sun was his spiritual father. All then returned to the house and feasted. The sponsor was given a gift of meal. The child was given an ear of corn so that he might always know plenty. Then he was put upon his cradleboard and was so carried on her back by his mother for the first year of his life. Thereafter he was taken from it and taught to walk. Young girls and old men helped to take care of him in his infancy. Through him, the one could learn motherhood, the other could contemplate the cycle of life.

A girl grew up learning the ways of the household from her mother.

Between five and nine years of age, a boy was taken by the men for schooling in the man's duties of government and ceremony. He was initiated into a kiva. He was too small to learn anything of the ritual or to understand the revelations that awaited him later, and that in their stunning force would bring him almost at one stroke from the sweet useless thoughts and illusions of boyhood to the purposeful impostures used by men. As a little boy in the kiva, he was brought into direct relation with the spirit powers, and given strength. He learned through fear and pain, for the masked kachinas came to his initiation bearing yucca whips with which they whipped him until he cried. Their lashes drove out the badness in him and made him ready for a good future. His elders nodded and approved as he cried under the punishment of his innocence. Now he had his allegiance, and though understanding nothing of what he did, perhaps he might impersonate an animal in one of the dances, and trot cleverly among the legs of the dancing men.

At adolescence, ready with new powers and desires, the boy was again the victim of a kiva rite. Again the masked gods came and whipped him, harder than before. He venerated them. He felt that the greatest power in the world was chastising him directly. He knew the gods, for they danced in their masks at all the great ceremonials. He knew they came from the sacred lake far underground to the north, where all life had come up. He knew the gods had come down to be about him on this day. It was terrible to be so near to the gods and to receive punishment from their own hands. But he bent himself under the painful honor and valiantly endured what he must.

And then more horrifying than any of the blows he had taken, more shocking than any other discovery of growth, an incredible thing happened to him. The masked gods who were savagely whipping him suddenly stopped, faced him, and lifted from their heads and shoulders their bright copper-green wooden masks with feathers and designs, and showed themselves to be men—neighbors, or uncles, people whom the boy had always known and taken for granted.

The boy was stupefied with terror and amazement.

Then the dances? Who were the gods there?

They were the same men who here, at the kiva ceremony, now removed all their masks. All were men. None was a god. But only men knew this. Women and children still believed that it was the real gods who came masked to the pueblo. Here: let the boy learn how mortal the masked figures were: take this whip. The boy was made to whip the unmasked gods who had whipped him. They put a mask on him and he knew how it felt to be the impersonator of a god from the sacred lake. When he learned enough he would be able to act out what all the other people believed of the gods. He now owned a tremendous secret which he must never, never betray. They spoke of one boy who had told, and what had happened to him. It appeared that they had cut off his head and then, using it like a ball in a game, had kicked it to the sacred underworld.

There would be much learning and several years to go through before they were men; but boys passing the stage of discovering the gods were no longer children. There were other stages. They could not smoke until they had qualified in the hunt, killing deer, buffalo, rabbit and coyote. If before this anyone found them smoking, they were thrown into the river, in punishment.

Though punishment played less part in the lives of children than fear. Unless children behaved well, they would be in danger from giants and bogeymen who knew all. Once a year the bogeymen, wearing fearful masks, came to the pueblo and knew exactly which children to visit and scold. They knew all the bad things that parents had been harping on. They appalled the children, who had heard of one giant, for example, who went every day to a pueblo near the black mesa in which he lived, and stole children, took them home, and ate them. The bogeymen made threats. The children shivered. And then their parents in anguish begged them not to take the children or hurt them, they were sure the children would be better boys and girls from now on, wouldn't they, children? With sobs and shudders the children promised. The bogeymen rattled their masks. No, who could be sure. Threats and horrors were renewed.

The parents pleaded. Promises were repeated. At last the dreadful visitors consented to go, for this time. But remember and beware!

Happier children were favored with the protection of the masked gods, the kachinas, who rewarded their goodness.

In the morning, waking up, one of the children in the family was sent out to make a prayer, sprinkling sacred meal or pollen to the sun. Then came duties, and then play. The boys tried all the games played by the men. They practiced the kick-race, which the men ran on a course sometimes as long as forty miles, circling out by landmarks and back to the pueblo. Two teams played, each kicking a lump about five inches in size made of hair stuck with pinyon gum. The men could kick the ball twenty yards. The boys tried. They also played a game using a curved stick with which they knocked a deerskin ball filled with seeds. The winner was the one who broke the ball. They liked to run relay races, wearing tufts of down to make them light as birds. All running games were valuable, they said, because they kept the sun running in its course. The boys pitched little stones at a larger target stone. They threw darts and practiced with bow and arrow. Boylike, they discovered things to do with things, and took the fruit of the ground-tomato which had a puffy envelope over it and, by smacking it against their foreheads, made a fine loud pop.

Children were desired and cherished and given all that their families could give, of things and powers and certainties. The blessings of life came from the parents, the ancestors, to whom gratitude and veneration were due. On the hot afternoons of the summer, when the sky blue had golden shimmers over it from heat, and the cottonwoods were breathless and the river ran depleted in and out of their shade, there rose on the hot silver distance the big afternoon rain clouds, with their white billows and black airy shadows. They had promise and blessing in them—rain and life. The people pointed to them and said to the children with love and thanks, "Your grandfathers are coming."

vii. farmer and hunter

The people did not consider that the cloud that made the rain that fell on the mountain thus made the river. Long ago, when they lived on the mesas and plateaus, far from the valleys, they needed water direct from the clouds to make their crops grow. In dry times they took water out to the plants in jars and spilled it carefully on the roots. Sometimes when heavy rain brought fast floods, they channelled the runoff to their fields. Running waters took usually the same channel, deepening it, widening it, turning its soil over. The people began to use such places in which to plant, so that their crops would receive the water that fell and ran.

When they came to the river and through generations settled their life along its farming plain, they saw that if water could run into the river from all the uplands, then on the immediate floor of the valley it was in many places possible to run water out of the river to the fields. Nearly a thousand years ago Pueblo people were irrigating their fields through well-laid canals and ditches. The river had in some places sharp steep deep walls of rock which ran for many miles. But most of these hard-buried canyons opened out as the river went downstream into wide flat valleys whose floor on each side of the riverbed was lush with growing grasses, plants and trees. In such places the people placed many of their towns. The river was accessible. They used it and it sustained them.

There were thirty thousand people, living in at least thirty, perhaps up to seventy, towns on the Rio Grande of central and northern New Mexico. They cultivated in all about twenty-five thousand acres, through irrigation from the river and its tributaries, and by the use of controlled floodwater. They grew corn, beans, pumpkins, gourds and cotton. They said it was the leaves that made the plants grow, because when the leaves dropped off, the plants stopped growing. The leaves could be watched. Roots were below ground and could not be watched. But even things that could be watched might mean nothing. Pollen from corn was sacred and used in many a prayer; it was part of the great plant which gave life; but nobody noticed what pollen did to make more corn.

Seed corn was kept into the second season before it was planted. Each town used its own, and refused to plant that of other towns, for, they said, the corn was the same as the people. Sowing was assisted by much prayer. Under the waxing moon of April the corn was planted, so it would grow as the moon grew, for under a waning moon the corn paused in its growth. Each farmer made his own prayer, and conducted his own ritual. One said this:

Mother, Father, you who belong to the great Beings, you who belong to the storm clouds, you will help me. I am ready to put down yellow corn and also blue corn, and red corn and all kinds of corn. I am going to plant today. Therefore, you will help me and you will make my work light. You will not make it heavy and also you will make the field not hard. You will make it soft.

The river water was let into the ditches to run to the fields. As the sluices were opened, the farmers prayed and threw feathers upon the first seeking ruffles of the muddy water in the dry ditches whose winter reeds had been burned down. As plants grew the farmers cultivated them with sharpened sticks. Each plant had its own little crater of shaped earth to conserve water. The fields were laid in long narrow strips touching at their ends to the river course so that each would have access to water. The farming lands were owned by the town, and each family man's share was assigned to his use by the cacique's council.

The growing plants had enemies that had to be watched out for. So, in a place commanding a good view of the fields and the country beyond them, the old men who could no longer do the work of irrigating and cultivating served as guardians of the fields. For this duty a lookout was built, eight or ten feet square and two stories high. Four posts held up the deck of the second floor and a brush roof over the top. There were no side walls, for the view had to be clear. But brush was some-times set along one side as a windbreak. Under the platform, in the ground, there was a first floor made of a shallow pit with a fireplace and food storage. The guard sat up on top. Women came and prepared his food in the pit below him, while he kept up his watch against enemies. Sometimes they were Navahos, Apaches, Comanches who grew no food for themselves but knew where to find it all done for them. Sometimes it was birds who came to flock through the tender new plants and strip them clean. Small riverside animals sometimes found a crop to their taste and had to be scared away. The watchman often had a dog with him who could give chase, or bark an alarm, or simply doze and scratch companionably and affirm by his devoted presence how suitably things were arranged, with one to lead and one to follow, and behind both, the need, the power and the responsibility of the earthen town whose life came from the river.

As crops matured, the people danced for rain in late spring, full summer, and early fall. Then came the harvest. First the melons were taken in and stored, and then the corn. In many towns the ground was swept clean before the corn was brought through the streets from the fields. Everyone, men, women and children, took part in the harvest, which lasted for several days. It was a happy time, full of social exchange and pleasure. Neighbors helped one another. The storage bins were ready. The year's hard work was over for a spell. Peace and plenty repaid virtue. The winter was coming when nothing would grow. The days would be bright, the nights cold, sometimes there would be ice on the river. The cottonwoods would turn golden and keep their dried leaves. The stalks and grasses by the water would be rods of rusty brown and black and pink and pale gold. In the fields, the corn husks would dry and crackle in the wind. The ditches would be clogged with withered weeds. Vegetation did not rot. It dried up. A seed planted then would be lost. But it did not matter, for now in harvesttime there was enough food to last through the coming months, and people could live.

If the summer was the man's season, then winter was the woman's. For the harvest was hers, and she knew what to do with it to make all its produce into good dishes to eat. There were two meals a day to prepare, the first in midmorning, when everyone had already been at work for several hours; the second in late afternoon, when smoke from cooking fires stood plain against the setting sunlight. The mother and her girls prepared the food. They had to have enough on hand in case anyone appeared at mealtime. This often happened. Brothers and sisters, aunts and uncles, grandparents, felt free to go visiting and to take a meal in the family at any time. Friends sometimes came, too, with the unspoken question, What do you suppose she is going to serve this evening? They would find out, and whatever it was, they would know it represented the best the family could offer, for the news would travel fast if the guest found any evidence of poverty, carelessness or clumsiness in the meal. The company sat in a circle on the floor. The tone was one of gaiety and good humor, for it was not good manners to be gloomy or disagreeable while dining. The room was small, the air smoky, the floor hard, but with much to say, and plenty to taste, they all enjoyed themselves.

The staff of life was maize. It was prepared in many ways. It was boiled in the whole ear, or the ear was toasted over charcoal fire, and the corn was eaten off the cob. It was ground into meal and cooked as a mush and eaten hot. For anniversaries and dances and weddings, corn bread was made in fancy shapes called flowers, with fluted designs, or shell-coils, or petals, or little hunks pinched out into spikes. Thin large wafers of corn dough mixed with fine cottonwood ashes were baked into tortillas. Corn meal, ground fine, and toasted three times, was carried by travelers, who needed only to add water to it to have a nourishing dish called pinole.

Roots of wild onion and mariposa lily were cooked for green vegetables. Milkweed was eaten raw or boiled. Seed pods were boiled, and seeds often made into dumplings with corn dough. The berries of the ground-tomato and nuts from the oak and pine were eaten raw. Pumpkins were given as presents, and served uncooked, and also could be preserved. The housewife cut off the rind, opened one end of the pumpkin and scraped out seeds and pithy fibres, and put the pumpkin to dry overnight. The next day she tore it carefully into long, spiral strips, and hung each strip to dry on a cottonwood sapling which she had trimmed as a drying rack. When the pumpkin meat was dry, it could be bundled together and stored, until it was wanted for stewing and making into pies.

The people had meat on special occasions. They liked mountain sheep, deer, squirrel, prairie dog, mountain lion, badger, fox and the fat field mouse. Meat was cut into little strips and, unsalted, hung out in the sun to dry, after which it could be stored without spoiling. Fresh meat was cooked on sticks held over a fire of coals, or included in a stew with vegetables. Fat and marrow were the tastiest parts. When the ducks came down the river in the fall, or went back up in the spring, they snared them and cooked them between hot stones. They did not eat fish, for this reason: they said that two pueblos faced each other across the Rio Grande near the confluence of the Chama and the main river. The towns belonged to two groups of the same ancestry. Desiring intercourse, they said they would see that a bridge was built over the river between them. Their medicine men built it, reaching out from one bank with parrot feathers, and magpie feathers from the other. When the feather spans met, people used the bridge until evil witches one day overturned it, causing people to fall into the river, where they became fishes. The people said they must not eat their own bewitched relations.

They made tea from the leaves of coyote plant, coreopsis, mistletoe, and thelesperma, and if they wanted the bitter brew sweetened, they used corn syrup. Young girls whose mouths were pure were chosen to make the sweet syrup. For days before they worked, they kept spurge root in their mouths to clear their breaths. Then they chewed fine corn meal until it became a paste. This was added to a mixture of water and corn meal, and the cornstarch and the saliva of the maidens combined to make sugar. There was no alcoholic drink.

The people took much of their food from wild nature. After the corn harvests they went to the mountains to gather the little sweet nuts from the piñon tree, and crops of acorns and wild plum. Men and women, young and old, went on the expeditions, and for the young, these were occasions of love-making and courtship. To the children who stayed home in the pueblo the elders would bring back sticky juniper boughs loaded with frost-purple berries.

The pueblos never domesticated animals for food. One tribe did not even have a word meaning animal. Each kind of animal had a specific name, and each creature had its own identity, like a living person. The dogs they lived with, perhaps the domestic mouse, the turkeys they kept for feathers, could no more be eaten than a person (for it was a long time since human sacrifice had taken place among them, even though to the south in Mexico it still was performed daily in untold numbers). But the wild animal was fair game, and the hunt was one of a man's glories. It made him not only a provider, proud to bring home that which kept life going. It gave him a challenge, and it told him of his own animalhood which he must use with all his craft and power if he was to succeed over other creatures. The mountain lion was his hunting god, a symbol of the killer who saw with a piercing yellow stare, who moved as softly as cloud, and who killed with claws like lightning. On a mountaintop above one abandoned plateau city, hunters had long ago carved two stones into the likenesses of the mountain lion, and later hunters carried little images of him in clay or stone when they went out.

Some useful animals were found near home—the prairie dog, whose bark the men could imitate to perfection, the beaver along the river, whose meat was good to eat, whose fur was needed in dance costumes. All the animals they hunted had many uses—food, hides and fur for clothes, bone for instruments, sinew for stitching and for bowstrings, leather for drumheads, pouches, bags. They said in one of the towns to the north that the animals of the hunt lived together far off to the west in a great kiva, and when the people needed them, they were sent out to be hunted. They were clever, and every skill had to be shown by the people, and by their dogs. Before a good hunting dog went out with his master, he was given food containing powdered bumblebees which would buzz and sting inside him and give him power.

Some hunts took place far away and lasted several days, some just for a day, near-by.

The deer hunt was often sacred if the meat was to be used in a ceremony. The deer was hunted by many men, who scattered until they could surround him. They closed toward him. They forced him to a trap, made of a great snare of yucca fibres, sometimes over two hundred feet long. They took him alive, and smothered him to death, so that his blood would not be spilled and his meat contaminated and made useless in the rites for which they took him. If the deer was captured for food and other use, he was killed with a knife. So with other animal victims too. When they came back dead with the hunting parties, they were received in the pueblo with great respect. Many more animals would be needed for food, and if they heard from the spirits of those already taken and killed how gentle the people were, how respectful of the loved creatures whom they had killed out of need, then when the hunters went out again, the wild quarry would be kind and come to be captured and killed and given honor. So they laid the bodies of the deer, and the other animals, on fur rugs, and covered them with blankets, and hung precious ornaments on them of turquoise and shell. The animal dead lay for a little while in pathetic splendor before being put to many uses.

Deer hunts were held in fall and spring, rabbit hunts many times a year, and for several different purposes. The ceremonial treasures of the kiva had to be fed—the kachina masks, the scalps collected in warfare, the sacred fetishes made by the medicine priests. Rabbit meat went for that, and the hunts were held in spring and fall. Other rabbit hunts were held in honor of the cacique and the war captain, to supply them with food and fur. The men alone hunted for these. In the fall, when harvesttime brought high spirits and symbolized sharp change in the year's life, rabbit hunts were held for the girls, in which they were permitted to join. The koshare were in charge of the hunt, and, holding authority from all the people and the gods, performed without resistance from the people whom they mocked, chastised and humiliated. They seemed to act on witless impulse, and they also gave freedom to the spirit of the perverse and the sardonic which lived somewhere in everyone, and never otherwise escaped into comic mockery of life and its origin. The power of the koshare was absolute when they took charge. They called the girls and men and boys to the hunt, telling them the time and place to assemble. Woe to them if they were late. What happened to them was the worst kind of punishment—they were made objects of derision. The koshare watched for those who came late, had them lined up in the presence of all the other hunting men and girls, and ordered them to show their sexual parts to everyone. The victims were half-ashamed, half-satisfied at making a sensation, and all went on the hunt in high spirits.

The men were armed with throwing sticks with which to kill rabbits. The girls did not kill. They all walked to the hunting place. Girls brought food along for lunch. When a man killed a rabbit, all the girls broke loose in a run and each tried to be first to pick up the dead game. Whoever touched it first could keep it, and take it home. At lunchtime she was the one who had to feed the man who killed the rabbit. The koshare watched to see that all was properly conducted. After lunch the hunt was resumed. The party spread out and drove the rabbits within an always contracting circle. Now and then someone, a man, a girl, would be far out on the circle, and might disappear together behind a protecting bush or rock. If they were certain they had not been noticed, they had forgotten the koshare, who came to see what they were doing. If they were coupled together carnally, the koshare broke them apart, and took them back to the party in captivity for the rest of the day. News of the arrest, and what for, would spread, and everyone with amusement would wait for what came next, for all knew what must follow. At the day's end, when the hunt was over, and the whole party gathered together to return to the pueblo, the koshare produced their prisoners and had them resume and complete before everyone the act which had been interrupted. After this, all went home. The girls took their trophy rabbits with them, and cooked them for their families to eat.

On the hunts they encountered members of the reptile creation, but did not fear them. The rattlesnake was the only poisonous snake in that part of the river world, and though the people knew of its dangerous nature, they did not regard it with horror. Some of them used the murderous snake in ceremonies as messenger to the cardinal points of the world. The swift, a little gilded lizard, was the supernatural of the sixth, or downward, point of direction. Turtles sometimes lay in their path. They saw many of the harmless horned lizard, or horned toad, and blue and green racer snakes, brown bull snakes, little water snakes with black and gold stripes running the length of their bodies. Deep and dim was the memory of past life which came stepping down the generations in talk; the people knew of a curious mixture in nature between snake and bird, each of whom was born in an egg. They made prayers to their image of the feathered serpent, and believed prodigies of a bird that could crawl and a snake that could fly. Land and sky with all their separate mysteries were brought together in that god, and in thread and paint the people made his picture again and again.

To find certain game the hunters had to go far away from home. For the big bear they went deep into the mountains to the north, and for the bison whose robe was so rich, whose meat was so good, and whose head and horns were such mighty ornaments for the dance, the men of the pueblos went to the eastern plains. Out of their own valley of the Rio Grande, they followed a pass eastward to the valley of another river, the Pecos, which began its life between high mountain walls. But the eastern wall ended more or less due east from the central Rio Grande world, and the hunters came up a grand escarpment to the plains not long after crossing the Pecos. They had to go carefully in some years, for the plains people sometimes came that far west, and not always for peaceful purposes. But with care and good fortune, the Pueblo men could advance to the immensity of flat land and hunt the buffalo. They could see, it seemed, forever, if time and distance there became one. The horizon was clear and flat and the light was stunning. Stiff grass grew everywhere, and in dry years was brittle and yellow. From time to time they would see far away what looked like a grove of trees. But there were no trees on that plain. Those tree trunks, rising to dark blurs of joined treetops were actually the legs of buffalo against the white lower sky, and the heavy tree crowns were their bodies—all optically enlarged in the shining air. The buffalo at first were not afraid. Sometimes they moved off in answer to scents on the wind. Sometimes they watched the hunters approach. When the attack came they would heave and run away together. The hunters had their plans. They set great snares and then as in the rabbit and deer hunts they separated and began to drive the buffalo inward to the trap. They set fires around the circle they made and the big herds ran against them in confusion and were turned back as the burning circle narrowed. In high weather, the sky was blinding blue and the sunlight white. Strenuous buffalo-colored smoke blew upward in rolling clouds. Fire in daylight at the edge of the hunt showed yellow and red and brighter than the air. There were yells and commotion. Silvery waves of heat arose. The buffalo stormed from side to side. Their eyes glared sidewise in terror as they fled to their doom. Behind them came the naked hunters shining with sweat and triumph, making calls and motions of menace. Blue, black, straw, curly smoke and pelt, running flame and figure—the picture ended with the capture and the kill.

It was a different picture when they hunted buffalo in the winter. They found the great herds black against the snow and searched until they found deep drifts piled up on unseen obstacles by the hard north wind that made storm on those plains. Spreading out on the white flat land, in a thin line of dark dots, the hunters began to drive the herd toward the drifts of snow. In the end, the buffalo got in deeper and deeper, until at last they could flounder no more and were caught for red slaughter on the white drift.

There were years when plains people, the Comanches, came west bringing buffalo furs and horns to the river people to exchange for corn, corn meal and other precious things. Products and stories, habits and words, beliefs and wonders—there was much to trade.

viii. travel and trade

The Rio Grande pueblo world had corridors to other worlds. Mountain passes to the east gave upon the great prairies. Deserts and mountain parallels to the west finally led to the sea. The river's own valley led south to Mexico through a pass which opened on a vast plain just as the river turned southeastward on the course which finally took it to the sea. With these roads open, the people yet did not travel them very far, and only the hunt took them away from their pueblo world. The river towns knew one another, and exchanged visits, and took part in one another's dances, and showed, and sometimes traded, curious rare objects that had come from nobody knew just where, or by what crawling pace, through what perilous distance. A stranger now and then appeared, walking, moving into the sight at first like a fleck of dust that bobbed on the glaring distance and seemed to come hardly nearer. He would be noticed. Someone saw him and told. Without seeming to, many people watched, as they went on with their work. Where was he from. What would he want. What did he bring. Was he alone. Perhaps he finally arrived half a mile away and sat down and stared at the pueblo for a while and rested. And then moving gradually so as not to be noticed, he came closer, and was at last where people could hear him, and see his ingratiating nods, as he unpacked his pouch and revealed bits of color.

Perhaps he came from northern Mexico, where he obtained from another man who got it from another farther south who in turn had it from a hunting party in the jungle a bundle of macaw feathers—sunflower yellow, scarlet, sky blue, copper green. For their rarity, beauty and sacred meaning, they were wanted for ceremonial use on masks, headdresses, robes. Sometimes the trader brought with him a live macaw with its feathers still in place. That was a treasure. The bird changed hands and after an honored lifetime of yielding its blazing feathers to the needs of ritual, was buried in the pueblo with ceremony, prayers and fetishes.

Perhaps he came from the deserts to the west, bringing a rare red paint, chips of agate, and fine baskets which had come to him through many hands.

If he came from the plains, the trader might have with him not only the useful products of the buffalo, but also worked buckskin, moccasins, odd foods.

The pueblos were a thousand miles from the sea, with every danger of weather, distance, time, human and animal conflict, desert and mountain between. Yet the trader, walking, for there was no other way to travel, might have with him a pouch of little sea shells that came either from the ocean to the west or the gulf to the southeast. The trader may never have seen the sea; but others had, and what they found came slowly and through many relays to the upper river whose origin and whose end, in relation to its populated part, none of the people knew. The shells were acquired and made into necklaces, pendants, fringe. From the western sea came over sixty species of shells, and from the gulf, nearly a dozen. Red coral beads came through tribe after tribe, from the seacoast inland.

The trader may have brought stone tools to offer, or a few pots to exchange for the kind made by the women here in the town.

And beyond all that, there was much to tell about and to hear.

The walking trader might come alone, but often he had company. Even so, in such a wilderness, reaching so far and open without forest and with little water, it took an intermittent multitude toiling on foot in tiny, scattered bands across rocky space immeasurable time to make their mark. But they made it. Trails were established, first in relayed knowledge of landmarks, and then in barely worn but visible pathways that were like the first tributaries of communication struggling to feed a stream of knowledge.

The incoming traders looked for things to take back with them when they left. News of what was to be had always took people to country strange to them. In the river towns, traders saw the accumulated produce of the pueblo farms. There was corn meal to be had, either coarse, or ground fine in pinole. Dried pumpkin seeds, squash were bartered. Irrigation ditches ran to cotton fields, and picked cotton was made into cloth, and cloth could be carried away in bulk, or in the form of shirts, kilts, sashes, or shawls. Mineral and vegetable dyes were used to decorate such garments. The traders might trade for the knowledge of how to use such colors.

There was one color and substance they wanted most, for the river pueblos had much of it, and prized it dearly. It was turquoise, and the people knew of a place, the only place in the river world, where it could be found in the earth. South of the site of Santa Fe, they mined turquoise for centuries in undisputed ownership. They made necklaces and ear pendants of the rich green-blue stone, usually carving little discs which they pierced and strung on yucca fibre. It was their principal jewel, and as such it was given to the gods in costumes, vessels, masks, fetishes with sacred meaning—and sometimes with magnificence: in one ancient town there was a superb basket, made in the shape of a cylinder, paved with 1,214 turquoises. If the people had treasure to bury, it was turquoise, and bits of red coral, which they put into large jars and hid in the earth.

Not only trade from far away made trails. The river people themselves went travelling to fulfill their needs, one of which was salt. They knew where to find it, in great deposits across the mountains to the east of the Rio Grande, and about in a line with the southernmost of the river pueblos. There, across that mountain range from the river valley, lived other town people who spoke a different language. They occupied ten or more communities, and their life faced out across the great plains to the east. Mountains behind them divided them from the river world. Precariously they survived the wandering fighters of the plains who came periodically to make war. Their bleak riches were the salt deposits which lay in a series of shallow, white lakes surrounded by low curving hills whose skyline seemed like the idling path of a circling and banking vulture. In some years the lakes were dry and the salt glistened dry at the sun. In others, a milky water filmed over the beds and rippled like cotton cloth when the wind came. Little vegetation grew about the lakes. They were like part of the underworld exposed. Nobody stayed by the brackish water for very long, but gathered up salt, and made whatever trade was necessary, and returned on the trail through the mountains to the river.

They saw much along the way. There were long-abandoned towns here and there, and from the ruins the travellers could learn something about the vanished inhabitants. Wanderers sometimes came to the pueblo world from down south on the river where, they said, there once flourished life in river caves that was long since gone. The river went more or less straight south, as you left the pueblo cities, and for the most part, the best—though not very good—trails were along the west side, for on the east, mountains came very close to the river and made travel difficult if not impossible. But finally after its usual succession of canyons and flat, fertile valleys, and after finding a pass between the ends of two mountain ranges, the river turned southeastward across a hard desert. Travellers had little reason to go there. They said that as far away as many days of walking, the river entered mountains which no man could enter, and disappeared between high rock walls into deep shadow. There were few people there.

But news of the other people who had once lived in river caves far away drifted with the wanderers. (These were the caves of the Big Bend and below.) The Pueblo dwellers listened, though the facts were scattered and few. Still, they could recognize by their own ways what other people must have been like.

The caves were in a great rocky wall of a river far to the southeast. (Was it the same river? It might be. And yet it was very far away. Rivers came from many places. Who could be sure?) The rocks were marked with lines like the flow of water. Water once made the caves and filled them and then left them as the river deepened. People came to live in them for part of the year, passing the rest of the seasons on the flat plain above the river cliffs. On the cave walls and on near-by rocks they made pictures by scratching with hard stone. They drew animals and the four directions and made marks to show time passing, and more often than anything else they drew hands in outline on the rock. There: hand, meaning a person was here; the thumb spread, the fingers straight. On a wall, hand. On a flat stone up on the plain, hand. I, long ago, hand now, and forever, said the rocks, without saying who, exactly.

From the river they took smooth large pebbles the size of the palm of your hand and painted upon them various yellow, blue and gray lines and made certain spaces which sometimes looked like a man, sometimes like nothing to see but like something to think. They carried these, or made offerings of them in ceremonies, or buried them. They took their colors from rock and berry. With a hollowed bone from a deer's leg filled with color that could ooze from a little hole in the end, they drew their shapes and spaces.

They had no corn, but near their places up on the plain above the cliff they gathered berries and yucca and ate of them. In time bushes and stalks grew nearer to the cave entrances, as seeds were dropped near the shelter. Paths and toe holds—the only way to the caves—led from the plain above. The men fished in the river where they could get to it. They used hooks made from bent thorns of devil's-head cactus, and yucca fibre nets weighted with round stones, and stone fish-knives. With a throwing stick from which they discharged spear and arrow they hunted running animals. With bone daggers they struck a wounded animal to death.

There were not many caves—less than a dozen, and only one family lived in each, at a time. They built fires under the overhang of rock, using long slender wooden drills which they palmed to spinning against a wooden hearth to make smoke, spark and flame. From the dry hard brush of the plain they gathered little bundles of kindling.

Like many people they wore few clothes in warm seasons, when the men went bare, and the women wore skirts made of yucca fibre that was corded and woven into matting. In cold times, they all wore blankets of lechuguilla fibre twisted with strips of rabbit fur. Traders rarely came their way, and so they had no turquoise, no red coral for necklaces. Instead, they strung together something that made beads, that was fairly hard to get, even dangerous, and was therefore valuable and not entirely commonplace. It was the vertebrae of the rattlesnake.

What they used more than anything else were baskets and other articles woven from fibre or straw or tender twigs. They made no pottery. But baskets served to cook in and eat from. The children had toy baskets to play with. Even bracelets were made of basketwork. They came to know, as anyone might, how to make baskets from watching birds. The parent birds brought little twigs and bits of grass to make a nest, twining them in and out until a little cup-shaped wall was made. There the nestlings were safe as they grew. A woman of the river caves in time would have her nestling and must carry him with her and keep him. If she wove a nest for him out of fibres, she might make other things in the same way.

As children grew within each family, they met new times of life during ceremonies which told them fearful things and made them able. The gods lived in the sun, in fire and in the snakes of the canyon and the plain. People of the river, and those far away to the south beyond the river in Mexico, prayed to the same powers. Shaped stones and modelled clay represented other powers to help men make and keep life through the day's hard work of providing shelter and food—coyotes, bears, lions, frogs, wolves.

All about them on both sides of the river, ranged other people who hunted everywhere, never staying to live and worship and grow in one place; but always prowling to kill. They were Comanches, Apaches, Lipans. Lipantitlan was the rippling name of the domain where they roved. They came to the caves, perhaps many times, and in the end, they finished forever what was trying to fix its life there above the river in the rocky walls. It was like much life in many other places of the desert and mountain land. It did not last very long, but it made signs, even in death.

A body was buried in rock shelters or under piled rocks in the open. Its limbs were gathered against itself and bound. A few of its meagre possessions were placed with it—things to work with and to pray. Woven fibre matting was wrapped around all, and where at last it lay, a blanket of cactus leaves, thick and bristling with sharp needles, was put to protect and cover all. On a flat rock face near-by was a picture that said "Hand," and meant "Forever."

Below, in its rocky trough, the river went on and presently—not very far off—was joined by another big river from the north—the Pecos of today. The two streams came along the flat sides of a great rock wedge that ended sharply, like a stone hatchet. They went on as one river when they met below the hatchet edge.

All along the river there were wandering people, even at the coast where the brown water went into the green sea. People travelling inland followed rivers, and those by the sea followed the shore. Out of Mexico went travellers up along the coast, coming to the mouth of the river, crossing it, and going on beyond to see what they could find. The travellers met trouble at times, for the people who roved the great vaporous sea-plain were hostile. They were naked hunters, always moving, and they attacked not only animals but people, and when they made any kill, they ate of it. Otherwise on the sandy plain where the sky all day long changed from thick to thin and back again, there was little to be had except roots in the sand and food from the sea. They snatched the white crabs of the beach and fished in the surf and in the end-waters of the river that passed through empty wilderness to meet the tide.

In news that came to the river pueblos from travellers who had seen, or heard, all of it, there was little of any other cities that lived anywhere else along the river. Towns at the river's mouth were made of sand grasses that blew away in hurricane or fell down dry if the rovers left them for long. A few dug-out pits roofed with yucca stalks clung to the river in the middle desert (southeast of the site of El Paso) whose people grew corn and went to the buffalo plains to hunt. But it was much harder country than the pueblo valleys up north—rockier, hotter, barer, dryer. Sometimes the desert part of the river failed to run. Its mountains were too far away to renew it. It was, there below, a river to cross, not to live along. The pueblo people were the only ones, with their many towns up and down the green, gold, blue, black and pink valley of their world, to whom the river through a thousand years gave continuing life, and connection with one another.

People from the farthest north pueblo, Taos, which was on a plateau too high for the growing of cotton, came south to the central towns below the volcanic canyons of the river, where the land forms stepped down immensely and the farms lay two thousand feet lower in altitude, and traded for cotton cloth.

During November men from the red rocks and plains of the west came on travels to see dances and to make trades, and went home again to their own towns, that were made of shale and mud plaster.

Other travellers, the Navahos, wandered with the seasons, and sometimes reached the western edge of the river world. If fixed with the spirit of war, they struck, thieved, and fled. If at peace, they threw up their mud cells, like wasps' hives, and dwelled in them awhile. If someone died in a Navaho hut, it was fearfully abandoned and a new one built by the survivors. The house meant nothing in itself. Thus, neither did a town, or a place. The Navaho moved, always just ahead of his hunger and his fear.

Stable, relatively secure amidst all such movements and motives, the river people received the trails as they were made, and maintained themselves at home by their work, their search for harmony with the visible world, and their endless propitiation of forces of whose existence they dreamed but whose nature they did not know.

ix. personality and death

Imprisoned in their struggle with nature, the people sought for an explanation of the personality they knew in themselves and felt all about them, and came to believe in a sorcery so infinitely distributed among all objects and creatures that no act or circumstance of life was beyond suspicion as evil or destructive. Neighbors might be trusted; but they had also to be watched in secret, for who knew who among them might finally turn out to be a witch? If every object, every animal, every man and woman quivered with the same unseen personal spirit, to whom prayers might be said, and of whom in anxiety blessings could be asked, then they could also and with terrible swiftness turn out to be agents for evil. Long ago, they said, the young war gods Masewi and Oyoyewi, the powerful twins, lived amongst the people, and protected them by killing witches and giants. Nature was vast and people were little and danger was everywhere. But (in the universal canon of faith which brings to every Goliath his David) there was the very cast of hope in the people who imagined their survival and triumph in the midst of menace, then willed it, and even by implausible means achieved it.

But at great cost.

Anyone suspected of sorcery was put to death, often in secret, often by individuals acting without formal sanction. What would identify a witch? A vagrant idea in someone's head; a dream (for dreams were always seen as truth, as actual life encountered by the spirit freed from the sleeping body); a portent in nature; perhaps a conspicuous act, aspect or statement, anything too unusual, too imaginative in unfamiliar terms; persistent misfortune or sickness among the people which must be blamed upon someone—the notion could come from anywhere. If only one or two people knew of the witch, he might be secretly killed. If everyone suspected him and knew about him, he would be accused and pressed to confess. In their search for a victim the people sometimes fixed upon an ancient person who had outlived his family and, obtaining a confession through torture, exiled him to another pueblo or simply killed him. Sometimes people in one town would discover a witch in another town who was causing them grief, and would murder him virtuously. Retaliation, inspired by the highest motives, would follow.

The killing of witches at times reached such numbers that whole towns were nearly wiped out by it.

Otherwise believers in peace, and calm, measured life, the people sanctioned their only outbreak of violence in connection with punishment of witches, whose machinations, they said, threatened the communal safety of life. Was that very communality itself an expression not so much of the dignity of men and women as their fear—a fear which put them always on guard, created a propriety of the commonplace, and held as its core a poisonous distrust of one another? The old people told the children that no one could know the hearts of men: there were bad people—witches—everywhere. Evil resided in them, and never came from the gods. The gods were exempted from doubt or blame. All believed so and, believing, all followed the same superstitions in the same strength of mind. Such strong beliefs, laced through with such compelling fears, created a personality common to the people as a whole.

Men went out during the night to encounter the spirits at sacred sites. They went in fear and returned trembling, whatever their experience, for they went to garner omens for themselves. Going home from the shrine they must not look behind them, no matter what might seem to be following them. They would consider gravely before they would tell what they had encountered, for what had been gained could be lost if not kept secret. It would not be a sin to tell—there was no guilt in the people since they were not responsible for what nature did to them—but in telling a secret, new power against menace might be lost. Ordeals were spiritual rather than physical. Endurance of torture was demanded only of witches.

The personality had many private faces, each with a new name. A man had his name given at birth as a child of the sun. When he joined a kiva, he received another, and another when he entered any organization, and he was nicknamed after his various duties and kinds of work. The personality was renewed and purified by ritual acts, such as vomiting. Before all ceremonial dances, all taking part were required to vomit in the early morning for four days (four was a powerful number in all ways). They said that those who vomited breathed differently from those who had not. "After you vomit four days you're *changed.*" A man thus purged left the daily world and entered the supernatural.

The personality was clever. A man prowling in hostile country wore sandals made of wooden hoops wound with thongs of rabbitskin. His footprints were round; from them, he was sure, nobody would tell which way he was coming or going.

The personality could be shared: images of men or animals were made in gestures of menace, to frighten trespassers away from property.

And the personality was vain, for the people of this town looked down upon the people of that town, saying that those others did not hunt so well, or farm, or fight, or sing, or dance, or race, so well as we do, the poor crazy things, with their silly ways, and their bad imitations of what we do which they stole by watching us secretly. But this was a pitying superiority, without anger or quarrel.

The most immediate medium of personality was talk. The people of the river world did not all speak the same language, but were divided into two general groups, Keres and Tewa, each of which had its localized variations. But all derived from the same mother tongue long ago far in Mexico, and ventured northward with the farming people and their maize. In spite of differences in language the river pueblos with minor local variations lived under much the same beliefs, customs and ways of work. Their language was expressive and exact. The men spoke it with voices that seemed to try to escape from smothering. They formed some words deep in the throat. Others were framed lightly on the lips. Some ideas were given through little pauses in a series of sounds, and a tiny round-mouthed silence became eloquent. Their words were never written even though in Mexico the mother tongue of the Aztec people was used in written form. The pueblo people taught all their knowledge by word of mouth. The greatest body of it had to do with ceremony and ritual. "One who knows how"—that was a man of power who remembered all that had been told to him. For the dances those "who knew how" had to memorize tremendous amounts of ritual, word-perfectly. Such men showed great powers of mind which their life in other directions hardly equalled. The great movements of time and the seasons, the acts of life and work, the inherited stories of the gods, the forms of prayers, all had to be stored in mind, along with their many variations and combinations, until a vast body of knowledge rested trembling and precarious on the spoken thread of the generations that was spun from elder to youth. Thus even the act of literature was not individual but co-operative, since it took one to tell, and another or more to listen, and remember. Much of what was so recorded in memory was to be kept secret among those "who knew how." If a man betrayed them, he was punished. The war captains put him naked within a circle drawn upon the ground. He must not lie down, but stand or sit. If he moved to step across the circle he was shot with arrows by the captains.

People within a language group visited one another's towns.

Before he went, a man had his hair washed by the women of his family
before sunrise, and his body bathed in yucca suds. They gave him a
new name for his venture. At the end of his journey, if he found a friend
awaiting him, he took his hand and breathed upon it, and clasping it
with both hands lifted it toward the sky without words, for joy muted
his speech.

"May I live so long," prayed the people, "that I may fall asleep
of old age." The personality ended with death and had to be exorcised
from living memory, and become one with all ancestry, impersonal,
benign and beyond fear. When a man lay dying among his relatives
they sent for the doctors of the curing society that combatted witches.
Then doctors came and undressed the dying man to examine him carefully. If he was already dead, they put a cotton blanket over him. His
people brought all his clothes to the doctors who tore little holes in
each garment to let its life, too, escape and leave the dead cloth. They
folded the arms of the dead across his breast, tying his wrists together.
His legs they closed up against his body. They wrapped him in this
huddled position with cotton blankets. His clothes were included. A
feather robe was folded about him next, and lastly, a yucca matting was
bundled over all, and tied with a woman's sash. Crouched in silence
within its wrappings the body was a restatement of the attitude of birth,
when the unborn infant was folded within the womb; and bound by a
mother's cincture to the womb of all it was now returned. The doctors
rinsed their mouths and washed their hands, saying to each other,

"Now he is gone."

"Yes, he is gone back to Shipapu."

"The place from where all emerged."

"He is gone back to Shipapu."

The family took the body out of doors to burial in the open ground,
or in a rocky crevice, or in a midden. With it were placed water and
food. The food was cooked, so the dead could feed on its aroma. The
dead man's turquoises, his weapons, his tools were buried with him,
for he was now about to set out on his journey to the underworld from
which all life had come, and his spirit would need the spirits of all such
articles to use in the life that awaited him. He was on his way to be
one with the gods themselves. At the end of his journey he would take
up again what he did in the world, whether as hunter, farmer, priest,
or dancer.

Four days after his burial, his personality was finally expunged
with ceremony. The doctors returned to his house and arranged an altar

on which they laid sacred ears of corn, bear paws, a medicine bowl and kachinas. They sang songs and ceremonially cooked food for the ghost to smell. They made a painting on the floor with colored corn meal. He was gone, and to confirm this and help him where he now would be forever, they made a bundle of offerings containing moccasins in which he might journey, a dancer's kilt and turtleshell rattle and parrot feathers and necklace which he might use to start rain from the ghostly world. They buried this out of doors. Underground, he would find it. Doctors then dipped eagle feathers into the medicine bowl on the altar and sprinkled the meal painting, the sacred implements and the people. They swept the walls of the dead man's room with the eagle feathers to brush away his spirit, and they went to other houses where he had last been seen and did the same. Returning to the house of the ghost, they sang again, and all settled down to a feast provided by the family. A few morsels were thrown aside by the doctors for the spirits. At the end of the repast, the doctors arose and were given finely ground grain for their services. They destroyed the painting and took up its colored meal in a cloth which they gave to a woman, who carried it to the river. There she threw it into the water which for all his life had flowed by the dead man, had sustained him, purified him, and which now took away his last sign forever, through the shade of cottonwoods and into the sweet blue light of distant mountains beyond the pale desert.

5.

On the Edge of Change

So the Pueblo people agreed without exception in their worship, their work, their designs for making things in the largest to the smallest forms, their views of property, the education of their children, the healing of their sick, and their view of death.

A clear and simple and within its limits a satisfactory plan of living together was understood by everybody, and complied with. But tragically it lacked the seed of fullest humanity. Mankind's unique and unpredictable gift was not encouraged to burgeon in Pueblo society. Individuality, the release of the separate personality, the growth of the single soul in sudden, inexplicable flowering of talent or leadership or genius, were absent. In harmony with all nature but individual human nature, the people retained together a powerful and enduring form of life at the expense of a higher consciousness—that of the individual free to unlock in himself all the imprisoned secrets of his own history and that of his whole kind, and by individual acts of discovery, growth and ability, to open opportunities that would follow upon his knowledge for all who might partake of them. It was costly, that loss of the individual to the group. The essential genius of humanity, with all its risks, and yet too with its dazzling fulfillments, was buried deep in the sleeping souls of the Indians by the Rio Grande.

They solved with restraint and beauty the problem of modest physical union with their mighty surroundings.

But only to their gods did they allow the adventure, the brilliance, the gift of astonishment that came with individuality. Those mythic heroes, those animal personifications ranged sky and earth and underworld performing prodigies, releasing dreams for the dreamers, perhaps beckoning inscrutably toward some future in which the people too might find freedom before death to be individuals in nature instead of units among units in a perfected animal society whose loftiest expression of the human properties of mind and soul was an invisible tyranny of fear that bent them in endless propitiation before inanimate matter.

The deep alien sadness of such a life was born with dignity. They lived like figures in a dream, waiting to be awakened. Possibly if left to their own time and development, they would have awakened by themselves to discover another and greater environment than the physical one to which they were already accommodated with economy and tenacity. The inner environment of the conscience, the responsible and endlessly replenished human soul, the recognition of God within mankind above a multitude of gods without—these might have come as their own discoveries to those people who already had climbed far from forgotten antiquity.

But men of another order were making ready to come to the river as ministers of enlightenment and shock and the strongest necessity of their epoch.

BOOK TWO

The Spanish Rio Grande

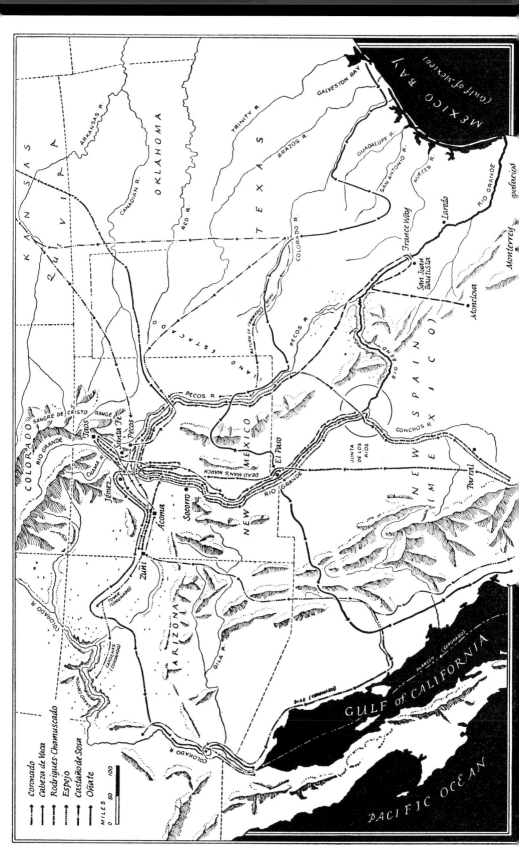

I.

The River of Palms

As it came to the sea at the gulf of mexico the river turned from side to side in looping bends and dragging effort like a great ancient dying snake. The land was white with sea shells and crusty with salty sand. On the low dunes hard tall ranks of grass stood up in thin blades that cut if touched. The sky was low, even in sunlight. Air over the sea thickened and thinned as wind and moisture played. Someone watching the sea where the river flowed its brown water into salty gray waves that broke shoreward forever, someone looking and idly turning his head, saw the low lines of the whole world—pale horizon, vapory sky, wide-shadowed green sea, the mist-white shore with its reed huts scattered close to the river, and the drying nets, and the powdery browns of the people moving at what they did. Warm in the fall, the days expected nothing new. The search for clams, crabs, oysters went on, and the dwellers watched for signs that the edible root of the sand dunes was coming into season. Now and then a memory of outrage by other people inland, or from up and down the coast, returned and brought caution. Enemies always came on foot. Sometimes all their dogs and children and women came too, and waited in the land haze for the outcome of battle. On some days the distance was blue with misty heat and the aisles of palm trees along the river could be taken for smoke far away.

Looking to the land for food and protection, and to the sky for weathers that told the immediate future, the beach people kept no guard seaward, where the water birds dived with sounds like splintering rock, and the clouds now met and hung over everything and again separated and travelled like misty pearls and trailed shadows like mother of pearl over the waters that were never still, and yet always the same, forever long as anyone remembered, forever and forever.

Yet the sea, the light, the clouds, had the power of making image and marvel out of nothing, phantoms to loom and fade. Perhaps it was so with the vision of change that became visible on the sea one day.

One, then another, and another, and another, sharp cloud came clear of the horizon. They moved close on the surface of the water. They rested on dark bulks. They came toward shore, all four of them. They were not clouds, then, but houses on the water, with trees standing out of them holding up great mats in the air. All four moving slowly could turn in accord like birds. Each time they turned they crossed a line nearer to the beach. Before long they were moving in the water that was made brown by the run of the river into the sea. The mats were shaken and changed, the bulks drifted, and all four came into the arms of the river, and in the moving houses were men amazingly decorated. Voices stranger than any before echoed across the water.

Twenty-seven years after Columbus's first discoveries, it was a day in the autumn of 1519 Anno Domini when four ships of Jamaica stood in through the veils of sea air to the mouth of the Rio Grande, and the point of view was about to be changed for the next three hundred years from that of the river Indian to that of the European soldiers, sailors, civil servants and friars—for surely chaplains came too—on board the little fleet.

With their coming, the golden haze of the Indian story along the river began to lift. Hitherto, the river people had been without individuality. Time was unrecorded and experience was halted within each generation. There was no way of setting down the past and of letting it recede. The ancient people were trapped in an eternity of the present tense.

Now against the moving backdrop of the civilized world, the little fleet dropped anchor in the brown river water, and someone on board recorded the act. Leo X was Pope, the earthly source of all legitimate authori'y. The Emperor Charles V, King of Spain, was planning to go to Germany to preside at hearings of Martin Luther. In England Henry VIII was King, and the righteous author of an essay condemning Luther for defection from the Faith. In France, as guest and employee of Francis I, Leonardo da Vinci died. Ferdinand Magellan was nearing Tierra del Fuego in his first voyage around the globe. There were no European colonies anywhere in North America. Deep in Mexico, to the south, the passion to conquer smoldered like hidden coals under the courtesy with which the Captain-General Hernando Cortés approached the Emperor Montezuma high in his capital.

The four ships of the little fleet were under the command of Captain Alonso Alvarez de Pineda. With him were two hundred and seventy Spanish men-at-arms. They had been afloat since the previous spring. Their orders, issued by Francisco Garay, governor of Jamaica, directed them to coast along the shores of Florida as far as they might in order to find a water passage to the Orient. For a while the term Florida signified the whole immense crescent of the Gulf of Mexico. Pineda logged rivers and bays, but he had not found the strait for Cathay when in August he came upon other Spaniards already ashore at Veracruz.

There was an incident at Veracruz. Pineda anchored his fleet in the harbor. The ships were reported to the Spanish commander ashore —Cortés, who at once went with fifty soldiers to investigate. No newcomers were welcome on that shore. Cortés had already sunk his own ships. His men were ready with his own spirit to take Mexico, for by now they had seen with him the gifts brought with soft messages by ambassadors from Montezuma; and they lusted for such a country. The feathered ambassadors had laid before Cortés an image of the sun, beautifully chased, of pure gold, the size of a carriage wheel, alone worth more than twenty thousand crowns; a larger disc, of silver, which was the moon; a helmet full of raw gold to the value of three thousand crowns; thirty excellently modelled gold figures of ducks, dogs, lions, deer, monkeys and tigers; ornaments—rods, collars, plumes of feathers, fans, all done in gold or silver; headdresses of precious green parrot feathers. The Emperor's messages in presenting the gifts said that he would not welcome the Spaniards in his capital. In return, Cortés gave the ambassadors three shirts of Holland cloth and a Venetian glass cup to take to their lord, with the answer that having come so far, he could not fail his own monarch the Emperor Charles V by not pressing forward to visit the ruler of Mexico in his palace. Mexico was rich. The soldiers knew it now for a fact in their own terms. Was every unknown land in the new world a treasure house? An ancient theme sounded again fatefully. Cortés wanted none to help, and none to share, in the ravishment of Mexico. Coming to the Veracruz beach with his soldiers to see who anchored offshore and what was wanted, he did not see Pineda, but met a notary and two soldiers from the anchored fleet, who in ceremony took possession of these lands for Governor Garay of Jamaica.

Cortés at once had them arrested and denuded. Putting three of his own men in the clothes of the captives, he sent them in the landing-party's own boat to hail the ships to send ashore. A small boat with twelve men in it put in to the beach, and four came from it through the surf carrying crossbows and guns. Cortés's men sprang out of hiding and surrounded them. The small boat pushed off in alarm, and as it reached the nearest anchored ship, the fleet was already making sail. It departed.

So Cortés knew from his captives that the coasting expedition was also charged with laying claim to lands; and Pineda knew that a ruthless and powerful campaign was afoot in Mexico. Plunging heavily northward, the four ships travelled along the barren coast which at that season was also mild. There were no signs of other Spaniards, there were nothing but naked brown staring creatures as Pineda brought the squadron to the mouth of the river that reached inland and showed its course by its aisle of palm trees. The tallest masts of the vessels reached as high as the highest palms. At rest, the ships looked heavy and swollen, with their high bows and bulging sides and tall, suddenly narrowed housing at the stern where rows of windows framed in gilt carving flashed slowly when the hulls veered. Either under sail, or with sail furled as now, the ships looked to be nodding forward, across their own bowsprits.

Seen close to, their mystery vanished. Their clinker-built planking was crusted with barnacles. When an unloading port in the side was opened, and men leaned out gazing, a wave of foul air was let go. What looked like a cloud on the horizon was dirty coarse sailcloth with faded heraldic painting on it. The hulls were perhaps a third as long as the masts were high. A small boat was launched over the side to bring Pineda ashore. It was then proper style to step into the surf when the boat grounded and, drawing a sword, slash the blade into the waves, stating at the same time that these waters, and this land, and all in their provinces, now came under the possession of His Most Catholic Majesty.

Company from the ships followed the captain ashore. They were in general slender and muscular people, not very tall, but finely proportioned. Their heads were narrow, their faces oval, their hands and fingers long, their shoulders sloping. Moving with grace, and a certain suggestion of repose, they yet could in an instant flare into violence, sparring with blade or pike swift and deadly. Their skin was tough and swarthy, taking the light with a faint tarnish of gold, and turning in shadow with warm darks that suggested embers buried but alive and ardent. They kept their dark hair cropped like caps hugging their tall skulls. Many of them, even youths, wore mustaches that curved out about the mouth to meet sharply pointed beards under the lower lip. The lips were exposed, ruddy and sharply scrolled. These swarthy faces flashed alive with startling whites—the whites of eyes set off by the piercing black of their pupils, and the whites of teeth showing through lips parted for the breath of interest. Their eyes were set deep and often showed black shadows under the carved shell of their brows. In the faces of old men, the eyes were like black gems that reflected suffering, resignation and irony from the world all about them. The eyelids roofed over from a little curved fold deep in the socket. In the faces of young men, the eyes, suggesting a taste for life to be both given and taken, shone with calm animal charm. Above metal gorget or velvet collar a white ruffle of starched linen, sometimes edged with lace, gleamed along the dark jaws, bony or bearded, of those lean, perfervid faces.

Those men were not all dressed alike. Some—the leaders, the elders—wore shining pieces of armor at the neck, the breast, the arms, the thighs. Others wore chain-mail shirts, hauberks, under their ordinary shirts of Holland linen. Some had jackets of many layers of quilted cotton, that could turn or break the blow of an arrow. Some wore metal helmets shaped like deep slices of melon, that were morions, and others had hats of leather and felt shaped like little round boxes with tufted brims and jeweled brooches and expensive feathers from eastern Africa. There were suits of brocade or velvet, stained and worn from travel, padded and puffed at the shoulders and elbows. The hips and loins were covered with trunks made of leather or heavy cloth, slashed and puffed to show other stuff and color beneath. Their legs looked long and slender and ceremonial, encased in tight thick hose that reached to the groin. Soft leather boots were worn either rippled up tight on the thighs or loosely pulled down about the calves in many folds. Shoes were flat-soled-and-heeled, and had puffed and slashed toes revealing contrasting color. Everyone had cloaks, some with embroidery of gold and silver bullion, some plain, but all voluminous and expressive in gesture, whether thrown about the face for warmth or secrecy, or lifted by a sword at the rear like the rooster's tail, and all hanging as richly from the shoulders of a hungry private soldier as from those of a hereditary gentleman.

At the waist, aslant the codpiece, nestled the dagger with hilt turned to receive the left hand instantly. At the left side, from a baldric of leather studded variously with precious stones, or gold, silver or brass rivets, hung the sword with basket guard, silver wire-wrapped hilt, and a cross guard below the grip that signified when necessary the crucifix. The private soldiers carried a variety of tall weapons—pikes, halberds, spears, lances—and some had maces, including the morning star from Germany with its long-spiked ball dangling from a length of chain. A platoon handled the heavy crossbows that with their carved and colored ornaments, graceful curved bows and stout thongs at a glance suggested some sort of plectral instrument for music. A few elite soldiers handled the heavily chased flintlock muskets bound to walnut or blackthorn stocks with thick bands of copper, brass and silver. A hardly bearded youngster in white hose and quilted body mail, with indifference masking pride, might carry the royal standard on a tall pole tipped with silk streamers and a sharp iron point.

They gave in the light every color as they came out of the foul ships and crossed to the shore. They found the Indians friendly in their leathery nakedness. A sizable squatters' town reached along the river at the mouth. Supplies must be at hand. The beach was wide and sloped gently, so gently that the tidal marks of certain seasons showed far back in the sharp-grassed marshes. The air was balmy. As far inland as could be seen the ground was flat and easy to explore. Pineda's ships were ready for overhaul. Here he ordered them careened.

The Spanish company spent forty days about the mouth of the Rio Grande, which they called the Rio de las Palmas. While some of the men worked on the ships—scraping barnacles, recaulking, repairing—others went into the country. They traded with the Indians, though for what and with what nobody said. Travelling eighteen miles upriver from the mouth, they found forty Indian towns—wattled reed and mud houses to come to for sea food seasons, and to leave when the roots and berries inland were ready to be eaten. There was no report of seeds planted and crops raised for food. Pineda told in sweeping general terms of the whole land he had seen, from Florida to Veracruz, and found it good, at peace, productive, healthful. He saw Indians with gold ornaments but did not say where. But of all the places he had seen he chose the River of Palms to recommend for colonization when at the end of forty days, the ships were floated, and the expeditioners embarked for their return to Jamaica, four and a third centuries ago, laden with the most desirable cargo of their time—knowledge of new lands. They were the first Europeans to see any part of the Rio Grande.

2.

Rivals

A year later in the summer Spaniards came back, again by sea, to the mouth of the Rio de las Palmas. News of this swiftly crossed the wilderness to the south, where the chief of the Pánuco River was a native ally of Cortés. It was not long until in Mexico City Cortés received an inquiry to know whether the cacique Pánuco should be friend or foe to the white men at the Rio de las Palmas. Pending an answer from Cortés, he would send the strangers at the north some women and food. If the answer ever came, it was not preserved.

There were a hundred and fifty foot soldiers, seven cavalrymen, some brass cannon, and building brick and lime, with several masons, in three ships under Diego de Camargo on the lower river in that summer of 1520. Again the visitors came from Governor Garay of Jamaica, who declared in his official reports to the crown that the men of the previous year had been eager to return to their river; that they had promised the natives to do so; that it was important to keep their word to the Indians; that the Indians longed for Christianizing; and that three ships were idle and available at Jamaica for the venture. Behind the florid virtue of colonial prose lay harder fact. Cortés had made plain in his encounter with Pineda's men that other claimants to Mexico would be briskly handled. A colony, an organic evidence of true claim, would have to underlie any argument that might arise over frontiers. The Rio de las Palmas lay conveniently north of Cortés, and yet near enough to the river Pánuco where a position could be taken, and an attitude struck, to bound Cortés on the north, and extend Garay to the south. And what professional colonizer in a time of colonial genius forgot the rewards that came to the successfully bold? Literally lord of frontiers, of marches, such a one could hope to be created marquis, and know glory, before wearing a carved coronet on his tomb.

Camargo sailed up the Rio de las Palmas for about twenty miles,

winding on the long and repeated curves of the river, above whose low
banks that seemed like the sea floor his fat heavy little ships bulged like
sea monsters cast out of their element, and could be seen from miles
away on the flat coastal wilderness. The masts moved slowly among the
palms, and came to rest between Indian towns on the banks.

The stone masons, the bricks and lime, in the ships were intended
for the building of a fort as the first unit of civilization on the river for
defense against Indians and, possibly against other Spaniards from the
south, should the boundary challenge ever be given.

Perhaps motives were never really concealed.

The Indians were friendly as Camargo and his people landed.
Pineda had come and gone in peace, while the Indians watched what
he did, and gave him their frail products in return for his cheap colors
and shines and pretties, and let him march, if he would, seeing and seeing
as if he hungered with his eyes.

Now Camargo settled heavily among the river Indians. He would
have food from their stores, for his men. Superior strength in armament
at times felt like personal virtue, justifying all, as in a police psychology.
Other Indian possessions may have seemed suitable to take—dwellings,
women, lordship, honor, liberty. The record of provocations on the one
hand, and of treacheries on the other, was meagre. But one day a group
of Indians turned against the Spaniards, and open hostility flared on
both sides. Camargo made a show of arms, but the river people fought
back, and a battle driving them to the ships in the river cost the
Spaniards eighteen men and all seven horses of the cavalry. Abandoning
one of their ships, the Spaniards weighed anchor in the other two and
headed downriver. Indians pursued them in a great fleet of canoes. The
clumsy towering ships like great bullheaded fish, imprisoned by the
meanders of the river, were exposed to the stinging missles and cries of
the Indians in the canoes, and others on the low banks. The distance they
had to travel to reach the sea was twice as long by water as by land. But
at last they came to the roiled water of the mouth, crossed the shallow
bar, and headed south following the coast.

The ships were in bad repair. Unlike Pineda, these expeditioners
had not careened their vessels, which—"idle and available" at Jamaica—
may have been no good to start with. On board were few stores, because
of the unexpected flight from the river country. The stoutest men on
board ship were permitted to land on the coast, to make their way overland to Veracruz, foraging for their keep, and heading for the promises
of Mexico. The ships went on for Veracruz by sea. The same ambitions

filled their companies. Nearing Veracruz, and other Spaniards, one of the ships had to be abandoned. It sank, after the men on board had safely moved to the other ship, which reached Veracruz only to settle and sink in the harbor after ten days.

A little while later, reinforcements came from Jamaica to join Camargo's colony on the river. It was nowhere to be seen. But the passion of Cortés, shaking the Mexican kingdoms for their gold and glory, called to the men of Garay's second expeditionary force who, when they had to leave the Rio de las Palmas, turned southward, irresistibly drawn into hardship, catastrophe—and unity with the power of their time.

Three years later, on July 25, in 1523, Governor Francisco Garay himself finally arrived at the Rio de las Palmas from Jamaica with an army of seven hundred and fifty officers and men in sixteen ships, armed with two hundred guns, three hundred crossbows, and artillery. A town was to be founded here and called Garay. The civil administration had already been established, and the alcaldes and councilmen appointed, before the Governor's expedition had left Jamaica. He had never heard from his other two forces of 1520; but he believed that their attempts to found a colony were successful. His purpose was not only to make his capital on the River of Palms, but also to make good his claims—based on Pineda's voyage in 1519—to all the region reaching south to the Pánuco River, despite the fiery shadow of Cortés which had already fallen across the territory. Cortés, Cortés—the name, the legend reached into the mind and affairs of every man who turned himself and his fortunes toward the New World.

Garay sent a subordinate up the river to fix upon a proper site for his city. The Governor waited at the arms of the river for a report. It came in four days, when his scouting officer returned to say that what he had seen made him conclude that the river country was unsuitable for the founding of the city of Garay.

Many men were dismayed when the Governor, almost as though seizing upon a pretext for his action, abandoned the plan to settle the Rio de las Palmas. Some urged him to remain. But he turned his face toward the south where on the Pánuco River, as he already knew, Cortés had established the town of Santiestevan. Was this to be endured by that officer of the crown who swore he had a claim to the Pánuco prior to the claim of Cortés? Garay was heard to declare that he would fight for his claim, and ordered the bulk of his army ashore, to join him in an overland march from the Rio de las Palmas to the Pánuco. The fleet he directed to follow the coast. Through hardship and loss, both land and sea forces made their way south to give battle. But what genius of success attended Cortés? On his very way to oppose Garay by force of arms rather than by legal sanction, he received in the jungle a new royal grant giving him jurisdiction over the Pánuco, superseding the one earlier made to Garay, who came only to be swept magnetically into the power of Cortés—Cortés, to whom Garay's soldiers and sailors were eager to desert, Cortés, who never forgot anything, Cortés, to whom the Rio de las Palmas at the north was an outpost, possibly strategic, to be kept sharply in a corner of his mind, and be done about when the time came.

Garay bowed to the royal cédula and in due course was kindly, even sumptuously, received by Cortés in Mexico. There in the court of New Spain, he met another of the conqueror's defeated rivals—Pánfilo de Narváez, who had undertaken to represent the Governor of Cuba in a matter of landing in Mexico and arresting Cortés—a venture which had cost Narváez his small army, his reputation, his freedom, and one of his eyes. The two prisoners, given every privilege, exchanged old hopes and severed dreams. To proud men, the very kindness of Cortés could be terrible; for only to rivals rendered harmless could he show so much. Governor Garay died before the new year, of a broken heart it was said, after leaving Cortés as executor of his will, and Narváez as the inheritor of his hope to colonize the River of Palms.

It was the destiny of this river from the first to be a frontier of rivalries, a boundary of kingdoms, a dividing line between opposing ambitions and qualities of life. During the next three years, three Spanish leaders considered themselves the rightful masters of the Rio de las Palmas.

Cortés planned to settle a colony there in 1523, to help in carrying out the Emperor's command to find the Strait of Anian, which all believed to open from the coast between Florida and the Rio de las Palmas and to lead by water to Cathay. But affairs in central Mexico took all his attention.

Intrigue in the colonies and at Court worked away to crumble Cortés from below. As a result of representations made to him, the Emperor in 1525 removed the Pánuco from the jurisdiction of Cortés and created a new province of Pánuco-Victoria Garayana, reaching all the way to Florida and including the Rio de las Palmas. Nuño de Guzmán, appointed governor, sailed for his new province which he reached over a year later.

And meantime, with the return of Narváez to Spain petitioning for command of the lands once granted to Garay, the Emperor made still another grant, establishing the province of Florida, reaching from the Atlantic coast to the Rio de las Palmas. Narváez was made adelantado.

Messages, even royal commands, with their replies, took a year for the round trip, for the fleet sailed from Spain in April and returned from Veracruz in the fall. To such delay, again subject to the vagaries of the ocean, and the soundness of little ships and of men, there was added the formal obstructionism of government with its dedicated waste of time. It was no wonder that for years Cortés knew nothing of the royal patents made to Guzmán and Narváez.

Once in residence at the Pánuco, Guzmán established slave trade among the Indians of his region, and word traveled swiftly through the Indian jungles and deserts and river valleys of the cargoes of stolen Indians shipped out at fat prices for the enrichment of the Governor and his followers. He knew of the forty and more reed towns on the Rio de las Palmas; what was more, Pineda had seen Indians wearing golden ornaments somewhere along the Gulf Coast. Guzmán sent his cousin Sancho de Caniedo north to the River of Palms with orders to found a town on its course, reconnoitre the country, and claim it for Guzmán in the name of the King. It was an act of typical ruthlessness, for Guzmán knew then that Narváez by royal authority had been given command of the land taking in this river. He held to his prior claim. There was no news of Narváez. Slaves and gold to the north—let his brave cousin march. Caniedo went overland and spent five months exploring the territory. But where were they, the forty towns on the river? And where the people, with or without golden jewels? He found no towns and no tribes, only a few roving Intlians who said yes, there were people, but they had scattered themselves away from the river, far away from what they knew about. To the south, Indian men and women of tribes persecuted in the slave trade had vowed to have no children rather than let them grow up to be captives for sale. Such news travelled. Caniedo returned from the empty lowlands of River of Palms to Guzmán at the Pánuco with neither slaves, gold, nor establishment of a city. Guzmán was later transferred to a command in the western coastal region of Mexico, where after a successful campaign he became the cruel governor of Nueva Galicia.

On September 3, 1526, from the city of Tenochtitlan, where he had come after months of arduous pacification of Yucatan and Guatemala, Cortés wrote to the King, ". . . I have a goodly number of people ready to go to settle at the Rio de las Palmas . . . because I have been informed

that it is good land and that there is a port. I do not think God and
Your Majesty will be served less there than in all the other regions
because I have much good news concerning that land. . . . " That
announcement had the air of forestalling in the King's mind any rival's
similar plans for the River of Palms. On the great map of New Spain
Cortés laid a paw here, a dagger point there, a knee elsewhere, a scowl
yonder; while he pursued whatever local battle required his presence.
Now deep in the tropics, away from communication for two years, he
finally heard from a loyal friend in Mexico the capital that his government had proved treacherous; that his death and his army's had been
proclaimed and all their possessions confiscated; and that Narváez, his
miserable, once-disposed-of rival, had been granted the River of Palms.
For a whole day the great commander kept to himself. His soldiers outside
his tent could hear that "he was suffering under the greatest agitation."
After Mass the following morning he told them the terrible news, and in
the midst of their dejection made plans for a secret return to Mexico, to
confound his traitors, regain his empire, and once more beguile the
Emperor with triumphs. But in his large affairs, as in his small, a spell
seemed to have been broken. The genius for success had abandoned
him. Soon he was in Spain arguing for more power; the Emperor de-
liberated, complimented him, relieved him of his major command, and
created him Marquis of the Valley of Oaxaca. He returned to Mexico,
a lion still hungry but with claws drawn. He never saw the Rio de las
Palmas; for, a decade later when he asked for another part of the same
long river, far to the north, he was denied in favor of a young officer, a
late-comer to Mexico, of whom nobody among the veterans of the
Conquest had ever heard.

Meanwhile, Pánfilo de Narváez with his royal charter, four hundred men, eighty-two horses, four ships and a brigantine rode out of the
harbor of Xagua in Cuba. His course was charted for the mouth of the
Rio de las Palmas. His pilot had been there before, with Garay, and
was believed to know the whole crescent of the great Gulf, from Pánuco
to Florida. But it was a year of storms, and in early April of 1528
Narváez and his company were driven from their course by a wild south
wind that blew them into the west coast of Florida, where they landed
on the fifteenth. They were far—how far they could not know—from the
River of Palms; but amidst hostile demonstrations by Indians, who yet
wore a few golden trinkets, and discoveries of the wrecked ship and the
deerskin-wrapped corpses of earlier Spaniards, Narváez concocted high
plans. The fleet was to proceed along the Gulf Coast to the Rio de las

Palmas, while he and the cavalry and the bulk of the footmen marched to the same future capital by land. There they would meet, and the city would rise, and it would not be Cortés who built it, or poor Garay, but the Adelantado Pánfilo de Narváez, with his failures in Mexico wiped out, his one eye flashing enough for the other one which Cortés had cost him, his marvelous deep commanding voice proper to a wise governor of fabulous lands united to Spain and ennobled by his own courage and zeal. The fleet caught the wind to sea, and in due course, Narváez moved overland into the wilderness, according to plan. He never reached the river that was the western boundary of his vast province. The ships of his original fleet looked for the River of Palms, there to meet him, but either did not sail far enough or passed the lazy waters of its bar-hidden estuary at night, for they never found it. They returned to their starting point on the Florida coast, but there was no sign of their captain-general. They sailed back and forth for nearly a year searching for him and the three hundred men who had disembarked with him; but to no avail; and in the end they gave up and sailed for Veracruz, in New Spain.

For seven years nothing was known of the fate that befell the remainder of the Narváez command. But when the news finally came, those who heard it were lost in marvelling at how it arrived.

3·

Upland River

A thousand miles upland from the mouth of the Rio de las Palmas, dug-out villages roofed with straw, twig and mud sat by the banks of the river. It was the same river, though nobody then knew this. The river-banks were low, here and there shaded by willows and cottonwoods. A little distance back on either side, the ground was hard with gravel. Narrow deserts reached to mountains that lay parallel to the river. The leaves were turning yellow, for the first frost had come, and the hunting parties from the villages had already left for the buffalo plains to the northeast, leaving only a few people at home to care for old persons and to guard the stored harvest of beans, squashes and corn. In mid-November, if the wind was from the north, hard dust was blown up to sting the face, and the sky was wan with long white streaks. If the breeze was southerly, midday was warm and blazed with empowering light out of the blue, and sharp, dry scents came off the scaly desert and somehow told of well-being.

To the most northerly of these river villages, near the site of modern El Paso, now came walking in mid-November, 1535, two Indian women, one of whom was the returning daughter of a man who lived there. With them were two extraordinary persons, a man whose skin was light, though burned by sun and wind, and a man whose skin was black. These men showed signs of having suffered from near-starvation over a long period. They were sparsely clothed in animal skins. The women said that three days away were two other white men, escorted by a large throng of Indians of the prairies who dared not approach closer because of long-standing enmities with the village people. There was much to tell the villagers about the strangers, who were great doctors able to cure the sick and raise the dead. If the two already there in the town by the river were made welcome, the other two who waited three days away would come also. Yes, let them come, said the town people. With that, accompanied by many of the river people, the strangers set out to join their companions. Toward the end of the three days' journey, the white man, with five or six of the villagers, went ahead to prepare the meeting, and a few miles later met the other two white men who waited in the desert with their crowd of roving prairie people. The white strangers greeted one another with joy, sharing the news of settled towns where food was to be had. They then proceeded to meet the gift-laden procession that was approaching, and with which walked the black man.

The meeting in the desert was ceremonious. The river dwellers brought gifts of beans, squashes, gourds, robes of buffalo fur, and other things. These were bestowed upon the strange doctors in friendship. Now the plains people and the river people confronted one another. They did not speak one another's tongues, and were enemies. The doctors gathered up the gifts they had just received and gave them to the roaming people who had come there as escorts, and asked them to go back to their own people and away from their enemies, which they did.

With the others, the doctors then marched to the river dwellings, and as night came with the November chill they reached the houses. Great celebrations were held for the visitors, who gave thanks in prayer for having found those people, with whom they stayed all night and a day. On the second morning they began to travel again, accompanied by the people, going up the river which ran brown and shallow between earthen banks below two mountains that made a pass. Messengers went ahead. On the streambanks beyond the mountains the doctors found other towns where they were received with different signs of friendship. When the strangers came into houses they found the people seated facing the wall, with lowered heads, and their hair hiding their faces. In tribute to the visitors the householders had heaped all their possessions in the middle of the room from which, when greetings had been exchanged, they gave presents of robes and animal skin. The people were strong and energetic, with beautiful bodies and lively intelligence. The young and able men went wholly naked, the women and old feeble men clothed in deerskin. They freely and aptly answered questions put to them by the strangers.

Why did they not plant corn?

Because all they had left was seed corn on which they were living. How was this?

Because there had been no rain for two years. Seed put into the fields was stolen by the moles, who could find nothing else to eat, since nothing grew in the dry years. The summer sun destroyed what the winter cold had not killed. The people begged the doctors to invoke rain for them from the sky, and the doctors acquiesced.

Where did the corn come from?

From that place where the sun went down.

Ah. And how did a man reach that place?

The shortest way to it was in that very direction, to the west, but the proper way was to go up the river toward the north. Even so, anyone would have to walk for seventeen days before finding anything to eat except chacan (juniper berries) which even when ground between stones was too dry and bitter to enjoy, though birds ate it, and brown bears in the mountains. Here, they said, try it, producing some. The strangers tried, but could not eat it.

And the river trail, then, how was it?

Passable, until the river turned west at the point of a mountain which could not be followed, for it came sharply down to the river and there was no path. All the way there were many people who spoke the same language as here, but who were enemies. They likewise, in towns, had little food in the dry years, but they would be friendly to the doctors, and present them with gifts of their riches, such as hides and cotton cloth. But it would be wise not to go that way, but take another journey toward the buffalo plains where the village hunters were.

Hunger was everywhere in the immense land, through which the river crawled brown by day, white in the twilight, shadowed by the vast moving clouds, walled now near, now far, by mountains of bare rock against which the pale dust stirred upward off the deserts whose constant change in motion could be seen only from great distance. Which way to turn? The strangers debated, remaining two days with their informers, who gave them beans and squash to live on, and who showed them how to cook. They took a large dried gourd which they half-filled with water from the river, and making fire with a hard wooden drill which they rapidly palmed to make its point turn in a small pit let into a flat piece of wood from which embers would presently come, they heated small stones readily picked up from the crusty gravel of the desert. When the stones were hot they were taken up with sticks and dropped into the water in the gourd. When the water boiled, the cooks dropped their raw food into it, and replaced stones that cooled with others just heated.

There was much to consider if the strangers were to take their way safely toward the goal they blindly sought. At the end of two days they made up their minds not to go directly to the west, or to cross the deserts northeastward toward the hunting plains, but in spite of the advice they had received, to go up the river as far as possible, and then turn west for the corn country; for it was in going always toward the sunset that they believed their salvation lay. Leaving the people, who would not go with them, they walked on the trail up the river's east bank. Every night they came to other people who received them with gifts of buffalo robes, and offered them chacan, which they did not eat, but lived instead on little stores of deer suet that they had hoarded against starvation. For fifteen, sixteen, or seventeen days the three white men and the black man made their way along the depleted river from village to village. And then, below the shoulder of the mountain that made them change their course (the southern tip of the Caballo range) they crossed over to the other bank, and diminishing as they toiled away from the river until they were mere specks in that speckled land, they finally vanished into the west.

Behind them were seven years of impossible endurance and determination to survive—impossible, except that they endured and survived; for these four were all that remained free and alive in 1536 out of the whole armored and bannered company that had landed in April of 1528 on the west shore of Florida with Pánfilo de Narváez, by royal charter hereditary Grand Constable, Governor, Captain-General and Adelantado of that kingdom in fantasy. The mission of Narváez—to know the country from Florida to the Rio de las Palmas—was at last carried out by members of his company, however unexpectedly.

One of the four starving travellers was the royally appointed Treasurer of the Rio de las Palmas. His name was Alvar Núñez Cabeza de Vaca, and he came from Jerez de la Frontera in Spain. He did not know his own river when he found it. The others were Captain Alonso del Castillo Maldonado, of Salamanca, and Andres Dorantes de Carrança, of Béjar, who owned the last man of the four, the Moorish Negro slave Estebanico.*

The river saw them no more. But with them they carried its image and its legend. Weeks later they came among people who told them more of life to the north. There was a great river—and again it was the same river—where lived many people in big towns with immense houses. They were people of wealth, and had many fine and desirable things, like these blue stones, and these green arrowheads, five of them—here, take them—which, the Spaniards thought, shone like emeralds. Emeralds treated like common flint for arrowheads! For such treasures, Indians went on a long trail crossing the deserts and mountains to the great house-cities of the north on the river, and traded yellow, scarlet, blue and orange macaw feathers, and the tiny green breast feathers of little parrots for them. At the right times of the year the trail was well-travelled.

The four travellers followed it to the south, and took with them in experience and memory all they had seen and all they had been told, that would soon reveal a whole new world to those whom they at last met—Spanish soldiers bearded and helmeted, mounted on horses, armed with swords and lances, at the outposts of the slave trade in the province of New Galicia whose governor was the former governor of the River of Palms, Nuño de Guzmán.

They were delivered from their prison of space. The wilderness of their tremendous passage ceased to be an abstraction as soon as they found succor amongst those who could hear what they had to tell, Spaniard to Spaniard.

---

* One more survivor of the Narváez entry was still alive, a prisoner of Indians in Florida. He was Juan Ortiz, who suffered abominable captivity before his rescue a few years later by De Soto, and died before seeing his Spanish homeland again.

4.

The Travellers' Tales

They were given clothes to wear, and after seven years of nakedness they could scarcely endure the feeling of cloth. They were given beds
to sleep in, but for many nights could not sleep anywhere but on the
ground. Their rescuers wept and prayed with them giving thanks for
their delivery out of the barbarian lands. But there were bitter discoveries to make again of rapacity and greed among their own kind as
represented by Governor Guzmán's men at Culiacan. Still, every sense of
the value inherent in their extraordinary—and exclusive—news of vast
new kingdoms helped to urge Núñez Cabeza de Vaca and his companions
on to the city of Mexico, where they arrived on Sunday, July 25, 1536.
Here there were two men who, more than anyone else, wanted to see
them, to question them, and to glean their treasure of information.

One was the Viceroy, Don Antonio Mendoza, maintaining in his
palace a state proper to the direct representative of the Emperor
Charles V, with sixty Indian servants, three dozen gentlemen in his
bodyguard, and trumpets and kettledrums.

The other—how could it have been otherwise so long as he
breathed?—the other was the Marquis of the Valley of Oaxaca, Cortés,
starving for a renewal of conquest, and gnawing on his pride like a dog
on a bare bone. Still restless, he still saw the new continent as exclusively
the vessel of his aging energies.

The sabbatical refugees were splendidly received, now by the
Viceroy, now by Cortés, and given fine clothes and other gifts. On the
feast day of St. James the Apostle, a bull fight was arranged with a fiesta
to honor the heroes. Núñez Cabeza de Vaca was put up at the viceregal
palace. Interesting interviews followed.

What was the extent of the seven-year journey?

The travellers drew a map for the Viceroy and on it traced their
immense passage that spanned the continent from ocean to ocean.

And what had befallen them in that seven-year passion of survival? The travellers had much to tell:

How seven years before with the whole company they had set out with the Grand Constable in Florida to find the rich inland country of Apalachen where they were promised gold and food, and how when they got there all they saw was a starving tribe of belligerent Indians; how days of roaming brought them nothing better; how the Governor fell ill and irresolute; how they tried to find the sea again and, having found it, how they wondered whether they could build boats in which to go by water to the River of Palms; how they had no tools or crafts with which to build boats; and yet how one day a soldier volunteered to make pipes out of tree branches and bellows out of deerskins; how they turned their stirrups, spurs, crossbows into nails, axes, saws and other tools, and set to work; how in twenty days with only one real carpenter among their number they constructed five boats about thirty feet long, caulked with palm fibre, and rigged with ropes made from horsehair, and sails made from Spanish shirts, and oars carved out of willow; how two hundred and two men embarked for the River of Palms in the five boats on the twenty-second of September in 1528, and how when all were loaded, the sea reached to within the spread of a thumb and little finger of the gunwales, and how men could hardly move for fear of swamping; how nobody in the party knew navigation; how they drifted west in hunger, and thirsted when the water containers made from the whole skins of horses' legs rotted and would not serve further; how it was when men died from drinking sea water; how when they landed now and then to forage they were attacked by Indians; how winds and currents drove the boats apart from one another; how the Captain-General dissolved his command, saying it was each man for himself, and how he himself in his boat vanished out to sea one night in high weather and was never again seen; how two of the boats were blown ashore and broken on a barren island near the coast; how those who escaped, now only eighty in number, came to land naked and skeletal; how they passed the winter there amidst Indians, digging in the shallows for roots until January; how with spring all went to hunt blackberries; how they agreed to demands by Indians to effect cures of the sick, praying the Pater Noster and the Ave Maria, which healed the infirm; how certain Indians on meeting one another sat and wept for half an hour, then how he who was visited rose and gave the visitor all he owned who went away often without a word; how they were enslaved as root diggers by the Indians; how Núñez Cabeza de Vaca became a trader between coastal and inland people, taking from the shore such things as sea snail, conch shell for use as knives, sea beads, and berries, and bringing from inland in return skins, reeds or canes to make arrows of, hide thongs, ochre for face-painting, and tassels of deer hair; how one of their companions refused to leave the island to try for freedom overland, and how Núñez Cabeza de Vaca tried each year for several years to persuade him, and, having succeeded, only saw him give up and return to the island where he died; how others of the company died until eighty became fifteen, and those became four, threatened and terrorized by Indians through the years of captivity and constant movement from sea to plains, from plains to rivers, according to the seasons of food; how the company sliced and dried the flesh of their companions who died, and ate it to live; how the Indian people ate ant eggs, and spiders, worms, lizards, poisonous snakes (even those that bore at the tips of their tails little horny pods that shook with the sound of castanets), the droppings of animals, powdered fishbones, and other things to be remembered but not told; how the mosquitoes caused such torment that the people at times set fire to forests and grasses to drive them off; how they saw buffalo, some tawny, some black, with small horns; how the ground fire-hot from the sun in summer burned their bare feet as they wandered naked; how the four friends were separated many times when their Indian masters of different tribes met and parted; how one day after years they heard of the remains of one of the five poor boats and were shown by Indians the weapons and clothes of the occupants who had been too weak to resist as they were killed by the people of the coast; how the friends escaped and came to friendlier tribes inland among whom they became, all four of them, powerful doctors of medicine, making cures by the grace of God, and even as Núñez de Cabeza de Vaca did, restoring to life an Indian admitted to be dead; how after six months with those people, in famine, they found the prickly pears ripening and regaled themselves though the fruit was green and so milky it burned their mouths; how when the Indians set them to scraping skins to cure they scraped diligently and ate the scraps which would sustain them for two or three days; how going naked under the sun they shed their skins twice a year like snakes, and carried open sores on their shoulders and breasts, and were torn by thorns in the heavy brush of the inland country; how they came to be with other Indians who were astonished by their appearance and who overcoming their first fear put their hands on the faces and bodies of the strangers and then on their own faces and bodies almost as though to banish the mystery of human separateness in a gesture of common identity; how the Indians saw and heard better and had sharper senses than any other people they had ever seen; how one day they were given two gourd rattles by Indian doctors who said these had come floating by a river from the north; how another day they saw a hawk's-bell of copper, carved with a face, which they were told came from a country where there was much copper; how in a new tribe they came among, the men hunted rabbits driving the animal ever closer to each other and finally striking it with a club most accurately thrown; how these people were hospitable and hunted deer, quail and other game for them, and at night made them shelters of mats; how as they moved, the people, three or four thousand strong, went with them and asked of them cures, blessings, and breathings of sanctification upon their very food, until their duties became a great burden; how these people never spoke to one another, and silenced a crying child by scratching it from shoulder to calves with the sharp teeth of a rat in punishment; how through the summers and winters of seven years these and countless other memories came with them in their powerful will to keep walking to the west, to the west; how they avoided the courses of rivers that flowed south and east which would return them to the miseries of the seacoast and its barbarians; and how they looked for rivers that flowed south and west, which might lead them out of the unknown land toward the mapped places of New Spain. . . .

And by the grace of God, they had indeed found their countrymen. Now—continued the voice of government—after all the abuses and hardships so admirably survived, was there then information as to the material resources seen along the journey?

Nothing but the utmost in degrading poverty for the first six years, until the travellers moved westward through mountains, and encountered the river where the corn-raisers lived. Given rain, it must be good country. They saw it.

Was that all?

Not all, for though they did not actually see, they heard of great cities on the river to the north, with many storied houses, where there were great riches, according to the people who told them so, and in fact, there was some evidence, for the people gave them some turquoises, and five arrowheads carved out of emerald.

Emerald? Where were these? Could they be examined?

Unfortunately, they had been lost in a frontier fracas with Governor Guzmán's men, but were perfectly real, a bright, polished, though not transparent, green.

And these fabulous arrowheads came from the cities to the north, on the river?

Yes, and had been obtained by trade with southerly Indians, who bartered parrot feathers for them. There were other things of interest, and possibly of value—beautifully made shawls better than those made in Mexico, bangles and ornaments of beads, including coral that was traded inland from the South Sea, that great ocean lying to the west.

Yes, yes, shawls and beads—was there by any chance any sign of gold and silver and other metals?

Not directly, save for a copper hawk's-bell come upon in the prairies far inland. The trading Indians were asked, as of course all people were asked every time they met anyone, whether gold and silver were in use in the great river houses. The reply was no, they did not seem to place much value on such substances. However, in the mountains through which they had come, reported Núñez Cabeza de Vaca, he and his friends had themselves seen many signs of "gold, antimony, iron, copper, and other metals."

In other words, though the natives did not employ them, there were deposits of natural wealth?

So the trading Indians had said.

This was curious, in the face of earlier reports that came officially to the viceregal government, through an Indian belonging to Governor Guzmán, who said that as a child he had gone with his father—a trader—to those northern river cities, and he well remembered them, there were seven of them, where there were whole streets made up of the shops of gold- and silversmiths. Still. They might well be the same cities. —What was the way like? A road? Landmarks? A trail?

A trail, principally, once past the northern outposts of Governor Guzmán. It was employed for the travel of traders. There were many such guiding paths to be seen, made by the people who went from place to place for food and barter.

Could the way be followed by strangers to the land?

Probably—certainly, if anyone went along who had once travelled it.

Good. The refugees would please prepare a written report of all they had seen, as fully as possible, to be forwarded to the home government.

It was like the imperceptible rising of a pall of smoke from unknown land which became slowly visible.

All the evidence was translated into visions of wealth. But after all, experience made it seem plausible that the northern country should be another Mexico, another Peru, where in their own terms of gold and silver the conquerors had found wealth so real and heavy that the treasure ships returning to Spain with only the King's fifth of all colonial income were worth whole fleets of raiders to the French and British. From the very first evidence at the tropical coast, with Montezuma's gifts to Cortés of golden suns the size of carriage wheels and the rest, there was promise in every report of an unknown land.

Cortés believed that he held moral and legal right to all new conquests in the continent he had been the first to overcome. He spoke privately and urgently with Núñez Cabeza de Vaca, and was not amazed at what he heard. In 1528, had he not already petitioned the Emperor for a patent to the northern lands, where this river was that they spoke of? Now it must certainly be his to exploit. Everything would appear to justify his selection as commander of an expedition to the great house-towns of the north—experience, ability, seniority, not to mention what might be due to him in gratitude for his past discoveries, pacifications and enrichments.

But the Viceroy had been given a firm understanding of the crown policy toward Cortés. All honor, consideration, respect—but no power. Power in the hands of the Marquis of the Valley tended to become too personal; too possibly enlarged until the crown itself might in its colonial relationship come to appear somewhat diminished, which would be unsuitable. As interest grew in the conquest of the north, there was talk that the Spanish Governor of New Galicia, Francisco Vásquez de Coronado, would be named by the Viceroy to organize and command the new colonization. He had come to Mexico in the suite of the Viceroy a year or so before, and had shown himself to be an able man of government. The Viceroy conversed with him—secretly, for fear of Cortés—and arrived at a plan for further investigation of the north before the full expedition should be sent. The Bishop of Mexico had a remarkable guest, a certain Franciscan friar, called Marcus of Nice, who was known to be bold, saintly and selfless. Let him go north to find, if he could, the seven cities of Cíbola, of which such firm evidence had already been noted, and let him pacify the Indians as he went, and return with news. To guide him, the Moor Estebanico, who had already walked on much of the traders' trail in the northern wilderness, would be sent along. Núñez Cabeza de Vaca had earlier declined an invitation to return to the north, and had sailed for Spain. The other two survivors were settled in Mexico. The Moor was the best one to go.

The plan was agreed upon in the summer of 1538, and from New Galicia Francisco Vásquez de Coronado dispatched the friar and the Moor, with Indians who knew the immediate north, in the mid-spring of 1539. Fray Marcus was robed in a gray zaragoza cloth habit. Estebanico, fleetly accompanied by two greyhounds, went clad in bright clothes with jingle bells at his wrists and ankles, carrying as a badge of importance one of the gourd rattles long ago acquired in the inland plains whither it had floated by river. The party travelled on foot. The Viceroy's orders to the friar said, in part, "You shall be very careful to observe the number of people that there are, whether they are few or many, and whether they are scattered or living together. Note also the nature, fertility, and climate of the land; the trees, plants, and domestic and wild animals there may be; the character of the country, whether it is broken or flat; the rivers, whether they are large or small; the stones and metals which are there; and of all things that can be sent or brought, send or bring samples of them in order that His Majesty may be informed of everything. . . . Send back reports with the utmost secrecy so that appropriate steps may be taken, without disturbing anything. . . ."

Would Cortés be listening?

The faithful friar was back in Mexico by early summer, making his reports first to Governor Vásquez de Coronado at Compostela, and later to the Viceroy in the capital. He told a temperate story, as full of fear as of conjecture, and earnestly hopeful of truth, in spite of its hearsay with occasional exaggerations and inaccuracies. It was a story with its regrets, too. He had gone faithfully northward, observing the land, passing from people to people, by whom he was cordially received, with food, triumphal arches, and requests for blessings. Estebanico he sent ahead with Indian guides, who were to return on the trail to tell the friar what his black man had seen: a small cross if he had seen a moderate-sized settlement, two crosses if a larger one, a great large cross if a big city. Day by day the messengers came back with ever larger crosses, until they bore one as high as a man. The great cities so long imagined must surely be coming into view. . . .

Meantime, Indians from the west coast brought shells of the kind known to contain pearls. There were deserts to cross, but the land became gentle again, and the journey was feasible. Finally one day came weeping messengers with bloody wounds who told of how Estebanico had halted at a great city at the base of a high mound. There he sent to the chief his ceremonial gourd rattle with its copper jingle bells. On seeing this, the chief hurled it to the ground, crying that it belonged to people who were his enemies and ordering its bearers to retire from the land. But Estebanico had refused, an attack had followed, the Moor had been killed by arrows, along with many of his Indian party. Those who returned to report declared that this took place before the first of the cities of Cíbola, which they said had many stories with flat roofs, doorways paved with turquoise, and other signs of wealth.

Friar Marcus then believed all was lost. His Indian companions were angered against him, for he had led them into a land of danger where many of their relatives had been killed along with Estebanico. He opened his sacks containing articles of trade, gifts received farther back on the trail, and made them presents, and declared that faithfully he would go forward and see but not enter the city of Cíbola. Two of the Indians finally agreed to go with him, and at last he saw the city with his own eyes, from a safe distance. It looked as he had expected—terraced, made of stone, and larger than the city of Mexico, which itself had over a thousand souls. Even so, the Indians told him it was the smallest of the seven cities. Giving thanks to God, he named it the new kingdom of Saint Francis, built a cairn of rocks surmounted by a cross, and solemnly possessing the whole of Cíbola for the Emperor and the Viceroy, retreated to his waiting party.

One more matter needed observation—a valley many days' journey to the east, where he was told that in well-populated towns there was much gold which the people used for vessels, for ornaments of their persons, and for little blades with which they scraped away the sweat of their bodies. He believed that he saw only the mouth of that valley which lay at the end of the mountains of the north. There he planted two crosses and took formal possession, and hurried back to Compostela and Governor Vásquez de Coronado.

What he told was fitted ardently into the statements of Núñez Cabeza de Vaca, and into the long-sustained expectation of a true discovery of the lost cities of Atlantis—a dream kept alive in a time of marvels and credulities by Europeans whose exploits had already been marvellous enough to render any rumor plausible.

Excitement was high and gossip general. The Viceroy sent to Cortés, as a common courtesy, a brief of the friar's report. From his hacienda at Cuernavaca, the Marquis replied with thanks and a formidable offer to co-operate in any expedition of settlement sent to Cíbola. Presently he was in the capital, scornfully letting it be known that in fact he had himself supplied Friar Marcus with most of the information which other people accepted as having been gathered at great personal risk by the Franciscan in his northern journey. The feeling of movement was in the air.

People felt which way the wind was blowing. Cortés called upon Francisco Vásquez de Coronado, whom he knew to be in the confidence of the Viceroy, and proposed himself for the expedition to conquer, settle and exploit Cíbola. Vásquez de Coronado faithfully reported the hungry offer to the Viceroy, who rejected it sharply, and gave his young provincial governor a wigging into the bargain. It was as well to have the position made clear: he had already recommended Vásquez de Coronado to the Emperor for appointment to the command of the expedition to the north; and with no further word to the great, the difficult, the restless Marquis, the Viceroy by royal authority on January 6, 1540, issued the commission to Vásquez de Coronado, with the order "that no impediment or hindrance whatsoever be placed in your way in the discharge and exercise of the office of captain-general in the said lands, that everyone accept your judgment, and render and have others render you, without any excuse or delay, all the assistance that you may demand from them and that you may need in the performance of the duties of your office. . . ."

It was time to move rapidly.

Cortés was only waiting for the spring sailings from Veracruz to hurry back to Spain, where he meant to press his claims personally upon Charles V.

Already a fleet and an army had left Spain once again for Florida. Núñez Cabeza de Vaca had hoped to return to the new kingdom of his long suffering as commander of the present Florida fleet, but he was too late with his petition to the King. A veteran of the Peruvian campaign, Don Hernando de Soto, had already received the commission. De Soto sailed with much of Núñez Cabeza de Vaca's information in his head, imagining that he understood the country of his grant, all the way from Florida to the Rio de las Palmas.

Núñez Cabeza de Vaca was a fateful man; for in Compostela, and Culiacán, and the city of Mexico, another expedition in consequence of what he had seen, heard, and suffered, now made ready for the north, where waiting to be found in the distance of time and rumor, beyond the cities of Cíbola, was the valley of the long river, with its people who grew corn and wore mantles of cotton.

5.

Destiny and the Future

In midsummer of 1540 the Pueblo World of the river had the news of what was happening at the rocky towns to the west, in the deserts, where Zuñi people lived. New men had come, in shining garments, with tremendous animals on whose backs they rode. It seemed that these animals, with their great teeth in their long bony heads, ate people. There was a battle at the town of Hawikuh, where before the town the Indians made a line of sacred meal on the ground which they told the newcomers not to cross. One of the strangers advanced and made a long statement with a one-handed gesture to his brow, his breast, and each shoulder. More came up behind him. The Zuñis sounded their war horn, and were ready, with leather shields and bows, arrows, lances and maces. The women and the little ones and the old ones were sent many hours before to the hills beyond the town. The war captain gave the signal and arrows flew. Then came the men with the high animals, and gave war, making loud sudden noises with flashes of fire and smoke, and thrusting with hard knives as long as a leg. The Zuñis broke and ran to their town, the invaders followed, and a hot fight brought the surrender of the town in a little while. The new men broke into the food stores and ate like starving dogs. They made peace, and treated everyone kindly, though they had killed twenty Zuñis in the battle. Their chief was a grand lord who had been hurt in the fight, wearing a helmet of gold. He now recovered, and remained with his men at Hawikuh. Various chiefs from other pueblos went to see him, bringing him gifts of turkeys, animal skins and food. To them he gave marvellous little things never before seen, some to be worn, either as ornaments, like the flashing beads, or on the head, like the red caps, others to be played with, like the little bells. He made much of a sign to be given with fingers, crossed one over another, squarely, or fixed in wooden pieces.

It was the mark by which they did everything. They could always be recognized by it.

Nobody knew who the newcomers were, with their light coloring, their immense animals, and their frightful noises. They brought with them a great amount of things they needed, and they sat down and put their legs one over the other as though to stay.

Long ago this world had heard of a white lord who would come to rule them. He would come from the south, as these men had come. Was this he?

There were people always moving on the long trails that went from the western deserts to the eastern plains. The news came along steadily.

One day in August of that summer the old chief of the pueblo of Pecos,* that stood at the gateway to the plains to the east of the river, came to the river pueblos on a journey. With him he brought a few of his people, including a young chief who wore long mustaches. He had heard of what had happened to the Zuñis, and he was going to see for himself. Word had travelled that the new man at Hawikuh would be glad to see chiefs from the country. The newcomers at Hawikuh were strange people, and bold men, and should be met and examined. Travelling by the pueblos on the river, the chief from Pecos and his party crossed over to the west and made their way in the August heat over the desert to the town where the amazing thing had happened.

When he arrived with his party at Hawikuh, he was without delay taken to see the commander of the invasion, whose name was given as General Don Francisco Vásquez de Coronado. The travellers identified themselves. The old chief of the pueblo of Pecos, because of his position, was at once called Cacique, and the young chief, because of his long mustaches, was called Bigotes. Friendly greetings were exchanged and gifts—on the one hand little glass dishes, and pearl beads, and little bells; on the other, dressed animal skins, and leather shields, and head-dresses.

Bigotes spoke for the callers. He was a tall, handsomely made young man, a person of authority. He said they had come in response to the General's invitation to the people of this land to meet him as friends. He put his hands on himself and then toward the General. If the other soldiers and the General wished to come to his own land—he pointed to the east—then they would be welcomed, and in the air he made designs to enlarge his meaning.

* Pecos was then called Ciqúique.

The General was touched, and showed his gratitude. He was him-self a tall and handsome young man, with dark gold hair, mustaches and beard, and blue eyes. He gave himself a fine bearing and was beautifully dressed, with leather, velvet, brocade and linen. He indicated that he would know more of the lands from which Bigotes and his friends came.

There to the east, told Bigotes with word and hand, lay the plains, so wide, so flat, so far, where the cattle were, with great bodies, little hooves, heads lowered, short curled horns, and beards, thus, from the chin.

The General knew of those before, from the reports of Núñez Cabeza de Vaca. One by one the pieces of the map fell into place. He wondered if the hides that had come as gifts might be from such cattle? But the hair on them was so matted and snarled that it was impossible to picture from them the appearance of those plains cows.

Bigotes could show them. He took one of his men and turned him so that all could see his nakedness. There on his body was a painted picture of one of the cows. On his breathing skin they could see how the cattle were.

The General and his men were delighted. The interview con-tinued, with descriptions of the trails to the east, towns to see, one on a vast high rock, a river with more towns, and then mountains, with the plains beyond. The General for his part explained who he was, for whom he came here, his purpose in the land, the power of the Emperor, and the will of God, whose Son to save the world died on the Cross: thus: cross.

Now it was clear that there was much to see and the General wanted to ask one of his first captains to go to see it. He presented Captain Hernando de Alvarado, commander of the artillery. Captain de Alvarado, with twenty soldiers, and the chaplain Fray Juan Padilla, was to accompany the Indian visitors on their return to their homelands, and take up to eighty days if necessary to make a proper reconnaissance of the territory to the east.

Bigotes and Cacique found that this could be arranged, and at once proposed to accompany Alvarado as his guides and to sponsor him in friendship among the people they would meet and whose towns they must pass as they went, toward the land of the cattle.

So it was settled. The General had already sent other expeditions to the west and the northwest, who would report back to Hawikuh which he now called Granada, both because it somewhat resembled the town in Spain, and also to honor the Viceroy, who came from the old Granada. Captain de Alvarado now with his little force of sixteen cavalry, four dismounted crossbowmen and a chaplain, along with the Indian party would be able to furnish much information. The General would remain at Granada until he received all reports from his scouting forces in the field. Then, in a position to move wisely, he would decide where to take the bulk of the army, which awaited his word in the Sonora Valley to the south, and establish its winter quarters.

The General saw Alvarado and his company off to the east on Sunday, August 29, 1540, which was the feast day of the beheaded St. John. The unknown lay vastly all about him to the west, the north and the east. His health was restored to him after the wounds he had suffered in the battle for Hawikuh, when because of his gilded armor and his place of command in the vanguard of his troops he had been the chief target of the Indian defenders. Storming the walls among his men, he had suffered piercing arrows and a rain of heavy stones thrown down from the parapets. Alvarado and another captain, García de Cárdenas, had saved his life and borne him away unconscious, and for the duration of the battle they had thought he must die.

But now the town was at peace, the Indians made paintings for him on hides, showing the animals of the region, that he could send to the Viceroy, and he worked on his reports, and awaited news from his field forces.

Not too many years before an odd thing had happened in Salamanca, his home in Spain. It was the kind of thing to which thought now and then returned. It seemed that in his young days he had a friend who was an adept in mathematics and other sciences. One day they had a conversation in which destiny and the future came up. The mathematician looked at him and told him that he was destined in the future to find himself in faraway lands.

Faraway?

Yes, and furthermore, that he would become a man of high position and much power.

Position? Power?

Yes, but alas, he was to suffer a fall from which he would never recover.

A fall?

The mathematician told him no more; but already at Granada in the Indian wastes of the most remote northerly marches of the Indies of the Ocean Sea, the General of the Army Francisco Vásquez de

Coronado was undertaking new kingdoms for the Crown. Was the prophecy two-thirds fulfilled?

6.

Faith and Bad Faith

On the evening of September 7, 1540, Alvarado and his company on the way to the plains came to a river which Indians called P'osoge, or Big River. Upstream, they said, were many towns, and downstream a few others. Here the banks were gentle, with cottonwoods and willows and wild fields of grass. On the west side were gravelly terraces and on the east, a band of desert rising far away into a long range of blue mountains parallel to the river. The evening light there arched yellow and vast overhead and the full river ran brown and silky to the south. The Spaniards were near the site of the modern Indian town of Isleta.

The river they named the River of Our Lady, because they had discovered it on the eve of her feast day—the Rio de Nuestra Señora.

Alvarado ordered his tent pitched, and at once sent Indian guides bearing a cross to the river towns of the north, to announce his coming.

The march from Vásquez de Coronado's headquarters at Granada had taken a week, during which they had passed other towns, notably Ácoma, the citadel on the rock. Alvarado declared that it was one of the strongest ever seen. The town, of three- and four-storied houses, sat on a great mesa of red rocks four hundred feet high, or, as Spaniards measured, about as many feet as a shot from a harquebus would travel. The ascent was so difficult that, he said, they were sorry they tried it. It was a well-provisioned town, with corn, beans and turkeys. They passed on eastward and came to a big lake with abundant trees that reminded them of those of Castile. And then they reached the river.

On the next day came Indians from twelve pueblos with friendly greetings. They formed a little procession and came to Alvarado's tent, the group from each pueblo following in turn. An Indian played on a flute as they marched. After circling the tent, they entered and presented the Captain with food, skins and blankets, and an old man spoke for all of them. In return Alvarado gave them little gifts, and they withdrew.

Alvarado pursued such a good beginning. His party moved northward along the river. They saw its groves of cottonwoods and its wide fields, and the twelve towns of the province where they were, which was called Tiguex, and the two-storied houses built of mud. In the fields by the towns they saw cotton plants, and they took notice of the rich produce of melons, beans, corn, turkeys and other foods that the people raised, and they saw that the people, following the ways of the farmer, were more peaceable than warlike. Here the people did not go naked, but wore mantles of cotton and robes of dressed hides, and cloaks of turkey feathers. Their hair was worn short. Among them, the governing power lay with the elders of the town, who made certain odd statements, such as that they could rise to the sky at their pleasure. Alvarado believed that they must be sorcerers.

Lying all about the river country were other provinces with eighty scattered towns. From these the leaders came to greet Alvarado in peace. With Bigotes guiding him, he continued his progress up the river from town to town until he came to a black canyon cutting through a high plain. He ascended the plain for there was no passage in the canyon. On the plain he came to a town remarkable for its size and the number of its stories, and for the fact that it lay in two parts, with a creek running between. He understood it to be called Braba, and was invited to lodge there. But he declined with thanks, and camped without. It was the pueblo of Taos. He thought it had fifteen thousand people. The weather was cold. It appeared that the people worshipped the sun and the water.

Wherever they went, Alvarado's company planted crosses and taught the people to venerate them. In the bare ground before the towns, the large crosses stood, and to them the Indians prayed in their fashion. They freed sprinkles of corn meal and puffs of pollen before the crosses. They brought their prayer sticks of feathers and flowers. To reach the arms of the cross, an Indian would climb on the shoulders of another, and others brought ladders which they held while another climbed, and then with fibres of yucca they were able to tie their offerings to the cross, bunches of sacred feathers and wild roses. . . .

All this Captain de Alvarado and Fray Juan de Padilla wrote to the General at Granada, telling him of good pasture land for the horses and domestic animals, and sending him a buffalo head and several loads of Indian clothing and animal skins, and a map of the country they had seen, and advising him to bring the army to the River of Our Lady for the winter, as it was much the best country they had yet seen. The report was dispatched by courier.

With this first duty done, Alvarado with his own men and the Indian guides departed from the river to go east to see the cattle plains.

His report to the General brought early and positive results. Don García López de Cárdenas, captain of cavalry, with thirteen or fourteen cavalrymen and a party of Indian allies from Mexico and Hawikuh, came to the river with orders to prepare winter quarters for the whole army. The main body of the army was moving up from northern Mexico to join the General at Granada, and would come to the river in good order and season when preparations were completed. The campaign was proceeding in all propriety.

Cárdenas came to the twelve towns of Tiguex, and near the most southerly, on the west bank, he began to prepare campsites in the open, opposite the site of modern Bernalillo. It was October, and the bosky cottonwoods were turning to pale bronze above the brown run of the river. The days were golden and warm, but the nights were beginning to turn cold. The soldiers shivered in their open camp.

Now and then, when the light was gone, and all was quiet, and the smokes of evening no longer dawdled in the still air above the pueblo near-by, an Indian here, and another there, would quietly appear among the soldiers in their camp. They looked to see where the sentries were, and if they were on guard. In their expressionless way the Indians would seek out soldiers and communicate a suggestion to them. Did they want to wrestle? And a soldier or two, off duty, would get up, and with every appearance of good will, take up the challenge. The wrestling pairs went at their game. Something about the way of the Indian wrestlers made the Spaniards think. It was almost as though the Indians with a buried idea were trying out the strength of the soldiers. The nights were cold. The soldiers shivered.

A hard winter was coming. One October night the snow fell on the soldiers in the open fields. What would the whole army do when it arrived to camp on the river?

Cárdenas presented himself to the chief of the near-by pueblo on the west bank, which was called Alcanfor, and asked him to move his people into other pueblos of the province, to leave the Spaniards a town to themselves. where not only the small advance guard but the main body of the army, when it arrived, could be given shelter. The Indian governor gazed upon him and finally agreed to do as he asked. Taking nothing but their clothes the Indians left their houses, and the soldiers moved in, settling themselves and making arrangements for the arrival of the General. The garrison—only fourteen cavalry soldiers and a handful of Indian infantry from the west and south—hoped for the early arrival of the General and the whole army. Amidst the pueblos they felt alien and uneasy.

One day an Indian from Arenal, a town a few miles up the river, came to Alcanfor accompanied by the elders of his pueblo. He asked to see Captain López de Cárdenas. He was received, and at once launched into a vigorous complaint, making eloquent signs and enactments with his hands, his arms, his body. The elders with him seemed to sustain his case. Cárdenas strained to understand, and gradually the story of the visitors began to come clear.

They said that a soldier came on a horse to Arenal and presently rode up to the walls and saw a woman on the terrace with her husband. The soldier dismounted and called up to the man if he would come down and hold his horse for him. The man went down the ladder to the ground to hold the horse, and watched as the soldier climbed up to the roof. Since all rooms were entered from the roof, the man was not surprised when the soldier like all visitors went there and vanished into a room from the top. The man patiently waited holding the horse. He heard a commotion somewhere in the pueblo, but thought nothing of it at the time. In a while, the soldier reappeared, came down the ladder, mounted his horse and rode away. The man then went to his part of the pueblo and found to his horror that his wife had been carnally assaulted by the soldier. When she resisted, there followed the commotion heard below and outside. The soldier seized at her garments as if to tear them from her. He had presented himself violently upon her, and if he had not actually ravished her, he had tried to. It was an outrage. The man who told the story, here with the elders, was the woman's husband. He demanded punishment and redress. The elders supported him.

It was grave news for Cárdenas to hear. He agreed that if true, the outrage must be redressed. Did the husband believe he would know the soldier?

Yes, yes.

Cárdenas sent for the whole garrison of Spaniards, and when the fourteen were all present, he asked the Indian from Arenal to point to the guilty man.

The Indian searched the faces and examined the clothes of the soldiers, but could not recognize his man. He angrily told how impossible it would be to find him if the soldier had meantime changed his costume. But having held the horse, the Indian would never forget how it looked, and he now demanded to see all the horses of the garrison.

Cárdenas obliged him. The party moved to the horse stalls on the ground below, and the Indian went down the line until he came to a dappled gray covered with a blanket. That was the horse, he was certain of it.

It belonged to Juan de Villegas, who owned three horses, one coat of mail, one buckskin coat, and pieces of armor. What did Villegas have to say to the charge?

He denied it. He reminded the Captain that the Indian had not been able to recognize the man whom he accused, and asked if it was any more reasonable to think the Indian was any more certain about the horse?

The argument had weight. Captain López de Cárdenas was obliged in the face of no better evidence to drop the matter. The Indians went away with their story dishonored.

There was, somehow, a feeling of more trouble in the air. It was something of a relief when Captain de Alvarado returned to the river from the eastern cattle plains. He came dragging four people in iron collars and chains, and he had an animated story of his adventures to tell Cárdenas and the others at Alcanfor:

Eastward, through a mountain pass, beyond which were many other pueblos in ruins, and a turquoise mine, and another spine of mountains, there was the largest town yet to be seen by any of the explorers. It was Pecos, where Bigotes and Cacique had come from. There the chiefs and their Spanish friends were received with drums and flageolets, and gifts of clothing and turquoises. There the soldiers rested for a few days, feasting, and listening to stories of the kingdoms of the plains that lay beyond.

The stories were told by two captive Indian slaves who came from the plains and belonged to Bigotes and Cacique. One, a young man, was called Isopete. The other, because he looked like one, was named the Turk by Alvarado. These two must be the guides for a march to the cattle country. Bigotes decided to stay behind when the rest of them set out.

They went south by a river (the Pecos) with red rock and water and then left it to follow a smaller river, eastward. The Turk learned to speak a little Spanish. With that, and by gestures, he began to talk about a land of Quivira far to the east. Gold, silver, silks. Rich harvests. Great towns. Alvarado listened as they travelled. Soon they were in sight of endless herds of buffalo, and they hunted among them, bringing the big running bulls down with lances. Several horses were killed by the charging buffalo and others were wounded. If the cattle stood and stared with their bulging eyes sidewise, the soldiers killed them with harquebuses.

Gold, continued the Turk, and for proof, there was a gold bracelet that he himself had brought from Quivira when captured by Bigotes.

Where was the bracelet then?

Bigotes had it, at home, in Pecos.

Was he sure?

Very sure, and he added other details of precious wealth in the far plains kingdom.

Alvarado's commission of eighty days was then over half spent, and he decided to turn back to Pecos to take from Bigotes the Turk's golden bracelet as proof of what lay waiting for the General in Quivira. He ordered his party back to Pecos. The Turk cautioned him. He must on no account mention the bracelet to Bigotes. But on arrival, after receiving new gifts of provisions, Alvarado demanded the bracelet.

Bigotes and Cacique were bewildered. What bracelet?

The bracelet of gold they had taken from the arm of the Turk, here.

They declared that the Turk was lying. There was no such bracelet.

With that, Alvarado retired to his tent, and sent for Bigotes and Cacique. When they appeared, he had them clapped into chains for denying him what he asked for, and ordered the Turk to be kept in arrest as a witness. Trouble followed. The people of Pecos hearing what had happened to their chiefs came to Alvarado's camp crying bad faith, and discharging arrows. Presently the Turk escaped. A parley followed. Alvarado agreed to release the captive Cacique if he and his men would bring back the Turk. When they did so, Alvarado put them back in chains again, and again there was an outcry from the Indians. And then the land of Pecos was threatened by enemy Indians from another province. Alvarado and his men helped the Indian war party to go and defeat the enemy. The captive chiefs were released for the campaign, but in the course of it, the Turk once again escaped, taking Isopete with him. Once again Bigotes and Cacique were sent to recapture the slaves, and returning without them, were still again put in chains.

"I will keep you so until the Turk is delivered to me," declared Alvarado, whereupon the fugitives were brought back by other Indians. The battle campaign was abandoned as suddenly as it had been started, and Alvarado, bringing his four prisoners in iron collars and chains marched westward to report to the General at Granada. But coming to the River of Our Lady he found Cárdenas and the others already at Alcanfor, and heard that the General himself with a large advance guard was on his way to the river. Alvarado halted there to wait for him with the enlivening news of the golden bracelet and all that it must mean.

7.

Facing Battle

At Granada, to the west, by late November, the main body of the army had arrived from the south under command of Captain Tristan de Arellano. The General received them warmly, and gave orders that they should rest for twenty days and then follow him east to the river, for he was leaving with thirty men to establish his winter headquarters at Alcanfor. He took a different trail from that of Alvarado and Cárdenas, striking to the southeast, meeting cold weather and for three days finding no water. Just before coming to the river he passed through a province of eight pueblos called Tutahaco, where the people were peaceable. Hearing of further towns down the river, the General sent Captain Francisco de Ovando, perhaps his most popular officer, to explore them and rejoin him at Alcanfor in the Tiguex province. Then turning upstream the General made his way in the winter valley, with all its dry golden, earthen pink and river-brown colors, to the town commandeered by his advance guard, where he arrived in the afternoon of an early December day, pleased to see the garrison established under Cárdenas, and especially pleased to find Alvarado already returned from the cattle plains. The very first evening, the General sent for Alvarado to tell his

story. Alvarado, who brought the Turk with him, made his report. The
General then turned to the Turk. What, then, was this country like to
the east of the cattle?

Oh, there was a vast river, two leagues across, where the fish were
as big as the Spanish horses. On it floated great numbers of long canoes,
carrying sails, with more than twenty oarsmen on each side. At their
prows were large golden eagles. Under canopies at the stern the lords
of the country took their ease. The ruler of that kingdom slept in the
afternoons under a large tree in whose branches were hung countless
little golden bells which beguiled him as they rang in the breeze.

The Turk spoke earnestly and openly. It was impossible not to
believe him.

Was he sure of what he meant by gold?

Acochis, he replied. That was gold.

The General showed him some ornaments made of tin. Was this
gold?

The Turk leaned over and smelled of the tin, and said that of
course it was not gold, he knew gold and silver very well, and in fact,
did not, as it happened, himself, care for any other metals.

Then there was silver, too?

Yes, all the ordinary table service was of silver, and larger pieces,
like pitchers, bowls and platters, were of gold.

(Hardly thirty years before, the Emperor Montezuma had sent
Cortés, at the seacoast, an image of the sun as large as a carriage wheel,
and all of solid gold. . . .)

The General was enthralled.

What of the golden bracelet, then?

The Turk repeated that it had been wrested from him by Bigotes,
and hidden at Pecos.

How could it be obtained?

Why, if they would let him go there alone, without Bigotes, the
Turk would find it and bring it straight back to prove all he had
been saying.

The General excused him, and he was led away. Alvarado advised
strongly against releasing the Turk. He had long tried to escape from
his enslavement; now could he be trusted to do as he promised? Bigotes,
with the other captives, was at Alcanfor and could be questioned. With
the advice of Fray Juan de Padilla, the General ordered him and
Alvarado together to question Bigotes further. Much depended upon
what they could learn from the young chief.

That night the Captain and the friar took the prisoner to the fields near the pueblo and interrogated him. Bigotes denied everything all over again. They concluded that he was lying. Alvarado knew what was commonly done in cases of that sort. He ordered some of the army's dogs turned loose upon Bigotes. But even though bitten on an arm and both legs, the prisoner refused to confirm the Turk's story. Later, the lacerated Bigotes, with Isopete and the Turk, was delivered in shackles to Cárdenas for safekeeping. Cacique, the fourth prisoner, an old man, though not chained was also retained in custody. The news of their treatment filtered through the pueblo settlements, behind whose impassive walls it made bitterness among the river people.

But now for the moment the General had more immediate problems to solve. The garrison was growing, and in less than three weeks his main force would arrive. Most of them were used to warmer southern climates. Already some of the Mexican Indians and Negroes with the army had died of the freezing weather. It was a sharp December in the river valley. He would need additional clothing for his troops. The Indian people seemed to have ample supplies of cloth of their own manufacture—cotton, and yucca fibre in which strips of rabbit fur were twisted. A requisition would have to be levied.

The General sent for an Indian who was called Juan Alemán, after a man in Mexico of the same name whom he resembled. Juan was a chief of Moho, a pueblo fifteen miles up the river. He had shown himself to be friendly. The General now asked him to collect from all twelve towns of Tiguex a requisition of three hundred articles of clothing or cloth with which to dress the soldiers.

Juan Alemán replied that he was unable to speak for more than one pueblo, as each was independently governed and would have to be approached separately.

With this, the General designated officers to visit the pueblos one by one and collect the levy. The order was promptly carried out. Some of the Spaniards did their duty considerately, others roughly. But in all cases the Indians had no chance to prepare for the demand, and time and again submitted by taking the clothes off their backs to hand to the soldiers, some of whom while foraging also took the opportunity to come away with corn, turkeys and other edibles. The river people lived from season to season, for the most part. Privation for them must follow the stern removal of their modest possessions, even though, in obedience to the strict command of the Viceroy, nothing was taken from the native people without reimbursement. But beads and little bells would not keep the people of Tiguex warm as winter fell, or feed their mouths as their harvest, gleaned with dances of thanksgiving, was so fast depleted by the strangers in their midst.

Thought moved behind the earthen brows within the earthen walls.

The soldiers were but men like others, as the playful wrestling had shown on those autumn evenings in the Spanish camp. Any man could die like another; but not so readily if he rode a huge beast that could trample over obstacles and people with furious power, and bear away its rider to safety faster than a man could run.

One day there came running from the Spanish pastures near Alcanfor a Mexican Indian wounded and bleeding who was one of the guards with the garrison's herd of horses. He cried that another guard had been killed by arrows, and that the horses were being driven across the river and north toward the pueblo of Arenal by men of Tiguex.

In a very real sense the horses could mean life itself to the Spanish. Cárdenas, taking some men with him, galloped out in pursuit. Footprints led him across the river and as he went he came upon many horses already killed with arrows. Others were alive and scattering in the river groves. He rounded up all he could and started back to the corrals, passing the pueblo of Arenal, which was barricaded behind new palisades. Within there was a wild concert of yells, exhortations, sportive chorus. He heard captured horses braying and dashing wildly about. The Indians were driving them as in a bull ring, and shooting arrows at them. He made a demonstration outside the palisades, and got their attention. He offered them forgiveness and peace. They reviled him and mocked him with obscene motions. He returned to his own pueblo with the rescued portion of the herd and reported to the General.

Vásquez de Coronado called his staff together for a council of war. His captains and his two Franciscan chaplains sat with him. All factors were weighed. The main army was not yet at the river, though surely it must by then be on the march. With the river towns in revolt, it would be impossible to conduct any explorations of the cattle plains and beyond, where the real objective of the whole expedition seemed now to lie. The uprising must be put down or between the prizes of Quivira and the long road home to Mexico there would be unpredictable dangers. The advance garrison was not large; there was risk in giving battle at this point; yet there seemed greater risk in not doing so. The General asked for votes. Each captain in turn, and the friars, voted to make one more offer of peace and, if it were rejected, to fight.

Captains Diego López and Maldonado were ordered to go respectively to the pueblos of Arenal and Moho. There they made announcements in official style offering peace and asking for specific complaints as to any individual misbehavior on the part of the army. If evidence supported charges, the guilty soldiery would be punished in the presence of the Indians.

In answer, the Indians, from their terraces where they seethed in tumultuous crowds, with their ladders drawn up, cried their defiance to the sky and brandished like flags the tails of the Spanish horses they had killed. After the officers were nearly killed at both pueblos through trickery, they returned to the General and war orders went out.

Captain Don García López de Cárdenas would command a force to subdue and capture the pueblo of Arenal, without delay. Attention would be turned later to Moho and other rebellious towns.

Sixty cavalry, and an infantry detachment, including Mexican Indians, were ordered in readiness. Veterans of Mexico and Cortés among them knew all over again the feelings facing battle. All night long before great battles the soldiers one by one moved slowly forward in line to confess their sins to the chaplains with the army. Loosely buckled great rowelled spurs chased in gold and silver on metal openwork clanged and tinkled as the horsemen moved up in line to the field confessionals. When had Indians first learned that Spaniards could be killed like other men? Perish it, whenever! After battles in the war of Mexico the soldiers used to dress their own wounds with the fat of Indians. Who remembered the hot jungle night when it rained just before a battle in Mexico—against Narváez and his invaders who sought to overthrow Cortés—and how just at that instant in the heavy air above the ground, a multitude of fireflies appeared in the wet darkness, and to the soldiers of Narváez looked like the lighted matches of Cortés's musketry, and seemed like a vast force?

In the cold valley of the Tiguex river hovered absolution and memory on the one hand, and on the other, a passion to protect an ancient breathing life within the hard-walled hives of the pueblos.

8.

Battle Piece

In daylight, the east mountains of bare rock looked near. Below them lay the band of desert; below that, the sandy terraces to the river, edged with groves brittle in winter. The pueblo rose in cubes of earth, casting sharp triangles of ink-blue shadow. The roof terraces were peopled. The ladders were up. Silence held the strain of looking. Presently from the south there was movement through the dry trees and out to the opening about the celled house. The light stung itself on metal and broke in rays as the column turned and halted. One man went forward and motioned a few others to follow him. They advanced quite clear of the troops and halted facing the plain walls along whose tops clung the minutely striving creatures dimly glistening like bees in great swarm. To them the man spoke out. At a distance his voice sounded thin but earnest. He motioned with his arms, offering. The swarm buzzed in rage from the roofs and replied with threatening motions. The man cried out again. Again the clustered bodies of the hive showed defiance. For two hours the exchange of offer and refusal continued. The man on the ground then returned to the mounted column and all rested motionless for a few moments. Then a movement began to detach one horseman after another from the column, as they set out and formed a circle all around the pueblo. When the movement was completed, there followed another pause and then came a long valiant cry that weakened as it went through the air until it might have been a wail, crying "Santiago . . ." and the men outside the pueblo began to advance on horseback and on foot against it. From the roofs downward: arrows and stones, wild dancing convulsions loathing and loathly, handfuls of powdered mud from puddled walls, screamed incantations. From the ground upward: slicing flights of arrows from crossbows, and volleys of lead bullets lumbered in gentle arcs by the harquebuses, and charges forward on horseback to cover efforts on the ground against the very walls. The walls were not excessively high, for the bodies of a few men leaning upon them, and the feet and hands of others climbing upon these, and holding, and the scramble of a few more upon those, let the top of the first rise of wall be reached. There swords flew, flashing, and wooden maces beat against them and upon helmets. The clinging strife against the wall fell down and rose again and fell and rose, and through the hours prevailed with its armored bodies flowing at last over the roof edge to stay, like a stain that once spilled would spread and flow until it stained all. Colors changed. Fluid crimson altered the rooftop as it altered naked earthen brown. Sounds wound on the air, the break of wood and steel, bone and life. With failing light and yellow evening the men from the ground were everywhere on the rooftops, and the people of the hive, but for their dead, were vanished below within the cells, into which the long delicate prongs of their ladders were drawn after them. Silence came with night, and hardly a movement, save that of the calm river going in its shallow valley. With morning, on the roofs, the leader of the armored men made another scene of exhortation, casting his voice awide and turning himself to be heard down below in the pits of darkness where remained silence and defiance. After an interval, then, separate small storms followed when the attackers tried to capture each cell by itself with its occupants. But the structure was thick, the entrances small, the cells many and interconnected, and advance was slow. There was a pause for a new undertaking, directed from the captured terraces, and then, below, on the ground, came men bearing a heavy burden against the walls. It was a huge log. With its end they began to thunder upon the ground wall of the big house slowly, in regular rhythm, shaking the earth house as if with deep drumbeat. Behind the battering ram there was a gathering of dry winter brush and bough. Fires sprang alive in the daylight and carried smoke into the blue. The giant drumming went on and wall-earth began to crumble. Cakes of earth fell aside, then whole clods, sliding like talus, then white dust shaken from the interior walls, and the hive was opened at its lowest level. Now the fires were taken brand by brand to the breach, and thrown in, and wood brought, and added, and the air shuddered in and out as drafts fought, but finally the whole cellular house acted as a chimney, and the smoke was drawn whistling from the banked fire on the ground outside through the rooms and out onto the roof terraces. With it were drawn the people inside, stumbling and crying, who clawed at themselves to see, and hugged themselves to breathe. They swarmed to the edges of the roof, where many were thrust by swords. Some hung down from the roof and dropped and ran and were ridden down by mounted men. Others were stopped as they ran on the ground, and were laid low by swords or bullets. Still others, taken as they fled from the walls, were made to keep running but tightly held until they reached the roaring fires into which they were thrown and in which they were kept at the points of long lances that spitted them if they strove to reach the cool air. Near-by there were stakes driven into the ground with faggots piled about them. To these many captives were dragged and tied, and the fires lighted about them. All appeared to happen with speed, wild understanding and inevitability. A tent for the mounted commander stood safely apart. Into it a large throng of escaped or surrendered people were put. The burning bodies at the stakes were in their view. Seeing those they tried to break from the tent to escape again but from outside men with blades thrust at them through the walls of the tent and those who survived to throw themselves forth were seized and piled onto the fires that grew and grew making flame and smoke high in the air by the mild river below the sandy sweeps that reached to the bare rock mountain on the east. Presently the mountain grew dim and the smoke from the fires seemed heavy in its rise. Winds swept over the reeking ground. The air turned colder. A thick snow began to fall upon the flames, the dying who still moved, the open dead at quiet, the excited animals and the armored men at their last tasks. The snowfall was gentle and sober. It softened broken edges and darkened the day and fell so fast that it muffled the hooves of the mounts as the column of troopers assembled from their various works about the little plain of the terraced city and with movements now modest and slow rode away southward through the thickened air. By evening all was quiet and no fires burned, and late in the night a handful of last inhabitants in the hive found their way safely out and ran away in the shadows of their house which was destroyed by the events of those two days.

Returning at the head of his troops through the snowfall from the ruins of Arenal, Don García López de Cárdenas was met outside the headquarters at Alcanfor by the General himself, who embraced him heartily and approved his whole action in the victorious battle.

9.

The Garrison

The snow was still falling on the next day when the main body of the army under Captain de Arellano arrived from the west to join the General at Alcanfor. It was a dry snow that fell thickly but lay lightly and soldiers in the open field slept warmer all night for the cover silently made upon them.

The General's forces were now all with him but for a small rear guard left in the northern march of Mexico in the Sonora Valley. The army could look up the river and see the thickened air above Arenal still smoking from yesterday's battle. They were eager for news, and heard all, especially the Turk's promises of the great wealth that awaited them in the eastern kingdom of Quivira. When would they leave? When the river of Tiguex, as they now called it, was pacified. They would be on the river for a while. A self-supporting army in the field moved slowly at best.

There were three hundred and forty men-at-arms enrolled in the now-assembled force, including two hundred and thirty cavalry, and sixty-two infantrymen. These were all of European blood, mostly Spanish, but with an occasional foreigner, like the five men from Portugal, and the Scotsman, and the German bugler from Worms, and the Sicilian, the Genoan, and the Frenchman. Like a bridge between the Old World and the New, a native of the island of Hispaniola was on the muster roll. These were young soldiers. The youngest was seventeen, most of them were barely over twenty, hardly any over thirty. The General himself at thirty was an elder of the army. Many of them were nobles and gentlemen, come to seek their fortunes in the New World. Their blood pounded with longing and promise. By their young beards they looked older than they were, and by their cap-cropped hair younger. In their great appetite for the unknown they went to take more than to give; and like all youth what they desired most if they did not say it was experience, without which there was shame before other men, and inequality of opinion. Many of them were fellows of high spirits and wild behavior, and there was talk in Mexico that as they were unmarried and dissolute, without work or property, and with nothing to do but eat and loaf, and make trouble for more settled people, it was a good thing that they went with the army and left the city in peace. It was legally noted that they left of their own will and happily.

They were armed variously with double-edged swords, crossbows, daggers, lances, harquebuses and maces; and protected, some with pieces of plate armor, gorget, cuirass, corselet; others with coats of mail, breeches of mail, one with only sleeves of mail; and helmets of casque, morion and sallet design, the last with beaver to protect the jaw and chin; and steel gauntlets and shields. Such equipment ranged in value from the splendor of the General's gilt armor with its plumed sallet to the buckskin coat worn by most. They brought with them a few bronze mortars that discharged stones.

Three of the private soldiers brought their wives. One of these men was a tailor. His wife served as nurse and seamstress, and rode seven thousand miles with the expedition on a horse. The military company were served by close to a thousand Mexican Indians, many of whom were accompanied by their wives and children. With the main body of the army came the flocks of sheep—over five thousand rams, ewes and lambs. The pace and distance of the daily marches of the army were determined by how steadily and at what speed those grazing little animals could move. The army brought five hundred head of cattle. Six hundred pack mules carried supplies and equipment. Five hundred and fifty-two horses belonged to the soldiers.

Alcanfor received the army shortly before the new year of 1541. The pueblo was crowded but as a fortress it was also safe. The herds and the flocks were guarded in corrals and pastures outside the walls. The snow continued to fall. Spanish soldiers whiled away their off-duty time. They would talk with the chaplains—Fray Juan de Padilla and Fray Luis de Escalona. Fray Juan had been a soldier himself in his youth. He knew how to talk with them. There were two Indian lay assistants with him, the oblates Sebastián and Luis. The soldiers went to confession, heard Mass, attended vespers, and cooked, and some wrote letters that two years later would be received in Spain, if ever. Playing cards could be made out of the heads of drums. They gambled at cards, playing "first" and "triumph," which were not prohibited by the command, and "doubles" and "lamb-skin-it," which were. Throwing dice was also forbidden and popular.

Captain de Ovando was back from the explorations downstream, to report that he had found four towns, built like the ones at Tiguex, occupied by friendly Indians. He saw no wild people, but as he had stayed with the river, this was not surprising, for the wandering Indians seemed to keep to the plains.

Heavy snowfall kept the garrison confined at Alcanfor, though the General had determined to demand the submission of the rest of the Tiguex nation and to obtain it if necessary with further battle. About a week after the arrival of the army it was possible to send Captain de Cárdenas and a party of forty horsemen and some infantry up the river with the ultimatum. They crossed to the eastern bank and presently came among the upriver towns which they found abandoned. At one of these they discovered a number of dead horses. In retaliation, Cárdenas burned the town and returned to headquarters. Word presently came that the Indians driven from their refuge in the bare and frigid hills were collecting at the pueblo of Moho, on the west bank about ten miles north of Alcanfor. In common defense, the river people, though accustomed to live under local rule in each town, now gathered under the general rule of Juan Alemán. Again and again the General sent his message of clemency and power, calling for all to submit to His Holy Catholic Caesarian Majesty. Captain de Maldonado took it to Moho first, only to return with reports of treachery and defiance. Cárdenas went forth once more with his cavalry and infantry, and found the Indians clustered on their roof edges at Moho waiting for him with Juan Alemán to speak for them.

Arriving within earshot, Cárdenas made his proclamation with large gestures.

Alemán responded. It was good to have the Captain there. Much could be settled without war. Let the Captain dismount and come forward alone, and he would meet him likewise on the ground before the pueblo.

Cárdenas gave his sword, lance and horse to an orderly to hold for him and went forward, but not without a few guardsmen following him. Alemán advanced from the pueblo unarmed, but also followed by his bodyguard. As the two leaders met, Alemán held out his arms with a smile and embraced Cárdenas about the body—and tightly held him immovable. The Indian bodyguard sprang forward and rang blows with wooden maces on the Captain's helmet. They took him away from their chief and carried him rapidly toward a narrow opening in the palisade. People on the roof crying execrations sent arrows and stones down on the visitors. At the entrance, Cárdenas freed himself enough to brace against its sides as the Indians worked to drag him through into captivity and death. Three of his horsemen rallied and charged to the palisade to rescue him. They brought him free of danger. He was wounded in the leg by an arrow.

But in spite of his wound and the weather he went upstream to the next pueblo, after leaving a detachment on guard at Moho. Once again he met abuse, arrows and defiance. He returned to Moho, gathered up his rear guard, and followed the trail in the snow back to Alcanfor. The General then determined to give battle with his whole army.

I0.

Siege

They came in full array a few days later to Moho, and made camp about the spring outside the pueblo. The German bugler from Worms sounded his trumpet. The call to surrender and the offer of amnesty were given in the proper form, with the notary officiating. The frieze of defenders on the terraces became animated with obscene mockery. The General gave an order. The troops moved out to surround the town which stood on a level plain of barren gravel from which the wide slow curves of the river could be seen to the north and south. Stout tree trunks were planted deep in the earth to form a palisade before the walls. The defenses were better than at Arenal, for the walls themselves were built of upright timbers solidly side by side and woven with willow branches from the riverbanks, and thickly plastered over with river silt. Here the town had not one continuous terrace of roof at each level, but several platforms separated by wide gaps. There were towers with portholes near their tops. It was a large town with deep granaries well-filled.

On the second morning, and on almost every day thereafter until the issue was decided, the General repeated the overtures for peace, but without submission by the Indians. With the battle cry invoking Saint James of Compostela, the patron of Spain, the army attacked from all sides.

Recalling the stratagem of Arenal that brought victory, they breached the palisade and brought battering rams to the walls. But the stout construction of the first storey defeated the attempt to open a hole and set fires. The Indian force was larger than at Arenal, with people from many towns gathered within. Moho was more than a single hive, it was several, as the plan of the clustered rooms with spaces between clusters revealed. Small battles took place in separate places at the same time against the fortress.

Stones flew down on the attackers who tried to climb the walls. Many soldiers fell, hurt and stunned. On one wall, soldiers raised ladders and fifty reached a roof terrace. They fought across gaps firing at Indians on the same level. From higher terraces stones fell and arrows whistled. To help them in their preparations for war the Indians called upon deathly nature. They shut rattlesnakes into willow cages and thrust arrows among the snakes who striking at the arrowheads flooded their venom on the flint or obsidian points, where it dried in tiny crystals but did not lose its power. Now from the portholes in the towers they sent the poisoned arrows and where these struck they left festering wounds that killed or disfigured.

A soldier ascended to one of the portholes bringing wet mud with which he tried to plaster it shut. He was killed outright by an arrow that quivered deep into his eye.

Another was struck in an eyebrow by a poisoned arrow, but lived, saying that he was saved by his devotion to the rosary.

Nearly a hundred soldiers were wounded by arrows in this first day.

When the cold night fell the soldiers retired to their camp where the physician went to work on the living casualties, who numbered nearly a third of the army. It was costly; too costly. The General resolved on a siege of the pueblo. He controlled the water supply. How long could the Indians live on whatever water they had stored?

The army lived in the field, and its tents and settled ways and traffic of supply between the camp and Alcanfor suggested the existence of a new town. The besiegers were as troubled as the besieged. The weather continued cold. It was wearing to be vigilant yet inactive. Twice it appeared that the water within Moho must be all gone, and that peace would follow at once; and twice, the Indians were saved by what gave the soldiers such discomfort: it snowed. The Indians melted the snow and stored the water in their clay vessels.

Life for the army became a routine.

Every day the invocation to surrender and come forth peacefully was made.

Daily the Indians refused. Their argument was that the Spaniards had broken their trust, they still kept Bigotes, Cacique, the Turk, and Isopete as prisoners, they would not keep their promises.

Keeping siege, the General yet had time for other duties. One of these was to listen to the Turk, who still a prisoner continued to show great eagerness to interest his jailers. What he said filtered through the camp. The siege of Moho seemed to be an irritating obstacle in the way of the proper business of the army, which lay to the east, in the land called Quivira, where——

Why, yes, there was gold, the Turk said, there was so much of it that they could load not only horses with it, but wagons.

What else?

In Quivira, on a lake, the royal canoes had golden oarlocks. The ruler lived in a great palace, hung with cotton cloth.

Quivira?

Yes, Quivira where there was much gold and silver, but not as much as could be seen even farther east, in other kingdoms, called Harahey and Guaes.

Even more? It sounded like the richest country of all the Indies so far, including Mexico and Peru.

Yes, even more, and in that land lived the king—the Turk even knew his name, which was Tatarrax—who said his prayers from a book, and addressed them to a woman who was queen of heaven.

Then it was, surely it was, a Christian country?

During the siege of Moho the General made a friendly trip to Pecos. When the war on the river should be ended, he would start for Quivira. Pecos lay on the way. It would be well to resume friendly relations with so powerful a city on his line of march. He took with him the aged Cacique whom he restored to his people amid their acclamations. But where, they wondered, was Bigotes, and where the Turk and Isopete, the slaves?

He could answer that. They were still at the great river, but had actually presented him with a plan to lay before their countrymen, which was this: if the people of Pecos helped in the conquest of Tiguex, the General would reward them with the gift of one of the conquered pueblos. At the victorious end of the war, Bigotes and the others would be released.

The people thought, and replied that it was not convenient to do as he proposed. It was early spring. The planting had begun with prayer and observance. But if he commanded them, they would obey.

The General did not insist since they hesitated to volunteer. He returned to the river where he found his people suffering from the cold, and inaction, and impatience. In the third week of February, 1541, he ordered another attack upon Moho. It was inconclusive, like the first, and it lost the army five killed, including its well-loved young Captain Francisco de Ovando, who while crawling on his hands and knees toward an opening in the defenses was seized by the enemy and taken within the walls where he was put to death, despite the efforts of his soldiers to save him.

This event was sad, and it became mysterious, and all things seemed related in odd powerful ways when something was discovered about the Turk in connection with it.

Cervantes, a soldier who was the guard at the Turk's prison, looked in at him one day, whereupon the Turk asked how many Spaniards had been killed in a recent fight.

Cervantes stonily replied that no soldiers had been killed.

No, said the Turk, Cervantes was lying, for the Indians had killed five Christians, including a captain.

Yes, admitted the guard, now that he was forced to say so, the Turk was correct. But how could it be? The Turk was under lock and key, he saw no one, talked to no one, heard nothing.

All the Turk would say was that he knew it already, and needed no one else to tell him.

Cervantes was not satisfied, and when opportunity came, he spied upon the Turk and was dumfounded at what he saw, and saw at once that it explained everything. He swore under oath that he saw the Turk talking to the Devil who was enclosed in a jug filled with water. It must have been the Devil who told him what he knew. What a mystery. What if everything else the Turk knew—gold, silver, little bells in trees, wagons full of treasure—were just as true as the death of Captain de Ovando, whom all knew as a distinguished young fellow, very honorable, gracious and well-beloved?

The siege dragged on. Soldiers experimented with building some cannons out of heavy timber, thickly bound with ropes. But these were a failure.

The General sent to the pueblo of Zia, to the west of the river, asking for clothing for his shivering army. The people were generous, and sent back some cloaks, hides and blankets.

In the middle of March the Indians at last asked for a truce in which to discuss a proposal. It was granted. The Indians declared that their water supply was falling rapidly. They believed the Spanish did not harm women and children. Would the General consent to accept theirs, and let the siege be resumed? He agreed. Soldiers rode forward and escorted Indian women and youngsters out of the walls. Young Captain Lope de Urrea, from Aragón, went back and forth on his horse, without his helmet, receiving Indian babies in his arms, and delivering them to safety. His men warned him to wear his helmet, but he refused. When all who were coming out had come (some women with their children refused to leave the besieged town), the Captain rode back to the walls and asked on behalf of his General for surrender and peace, promising all fair treatment. The Indians became angered and warned him to withdraw. He persisted. The Indians threatened. Soldiers called to Urrea to put on his helmet, he was in danger, and he called back that the Indians would not harm him, and took up his persuasions again. An Indian sprang an arrow toward the feet of Urrea's horse with a last warning that next time he would aim to kill. The Captain shrugged. He gently turned his horse and rode at a walk away from the walls, putting on his helmet indifferently. As he passed beyond the range of arrows, the Indians began to howl and fire vollies. The siege was resumed.

But spring was advancing. The snowfalls ended. The water supply in the crippled town was finally vanishing. Moreover, the season of planting and propitiation, the birth of the future, were passing by, and if unattended, would end in physical hardship and spiritual sorrow for the Indians. One night at the end of March they began to steal away out of their walls toward the river. Forty mounted soldiers were on guard. The alarm was given. An Indian arrow pierced a soldier's heart and he died at once. Another soldier was seized and taken and was never seen again. The soldiers attacked, the camp was aroused, and a battle followed in the darkness. Many Indians were killed, and soldiers were wounded, as the Indian retreat continued toward the river. The water was high and cold, the current fast. Hurrying for freedom, the Indians came to the bank and were pursued by the cavalry, and few escaped wounds or death. The river took away the bodies and blood of those killed while trying to cross. Some reached the east bank in the dark. It was an icy night, filled with the sounds of arms and voices. The investment of Moho was over. It had lasted fifty days.

In the morning, soldiers went over the river and found wounded and half-frozen Indians lying there, whom they brought back to be restored and treated as servants. Other soldiers entered the pueblo to see what they could find, for all provisions were to be gathered for the commissary. Soldiers looked out for jewels and other treasures, and discovered instead the ashes of mantles, feathers and turquoise strings burned to save them from the Spaniards. They found stores of maize, and recognized again that Indians of the river did not own anything except their food and their cotton clothes and their robes made of turkey feathers and rabbit fur.

The soldiers found something that, had it succeeded, might have prolonged the war indefinitely. It was a well, dug within the protection of the walls of Moho, but the well had caved in, and thirty Indians had died in it.

They explored further. In one section of the surrendered town there was a small group of people who still resisted. They would be taken in a matter of days.

And somewhere in the fallen town, the soldiers came upon a sight that awed them. They found the body of Captain Francisco de Ovando, dead forty days, naked, whole but for the wound of his death, white as snow, and incorrupt, "with no bad odor."

The General commanded a portion of the pueblo of Moho burned as a warning to the people of Tiguex. He sent for Bigotes, the Turk and Isopete so they too might see. His policy was prevailing everywhere, for farther up the river during the last days of the siege, another pueblo had been taken by a mounted detachment who forced the Indians to abandon it. After a few days, in early April, the General heard that the people were returning to some of the upriver towns to fortify them. He sent Captain de Maldonado to do what needed to be done. A day or so later, the General saw smoke in the north over the valley, and asked what it meant. He was informed that Captain de Maldonado had burned a town. With that image—distant smoke rising from the mud-plastered timbers of a Rio Grande pueblo in the springtime groves of willows and cottonwoods far below the air-blue mountains—the Tiguex war was won.

I I.

The Eastern Plains

The weather warmed, and then froze again, and solid ice reached across the river. If they were all going east it would be well to start while they could cross on the ice, the whole army of fifteen hundred people, and a thousand horses, and five hundred cattle, and five thousand sheep. On April 23, 1541, the train passed from Alcanfor over the frozen river and began the long march to the eastern plains in search of Quivira and its treasures. Bigotes and Isopete, freed of their collars and chains, were on their way to be restored to their pueblo of Pecos. The Turk was the principal guide, still raving of wonders to come. The slow procession went north along the east bank, passing the burned town of Arenal, empty like all the other pueblos of Tiguex. Rounding the northern end of the Sandia mountains, the army drew away eastward and out of sight of the river.

Seventy-seven days later, all but the General, his chaplain, and thirty mounted men and six footmen returned to the river to settle once again at Alcanfor. The town was still empty of Indians, like all the others, and so long as these Spaniards were in the nation of Tiguex, no Indians ever came back to live there.

The army returned in low spirits and unwillingly. On their march to the plains with the General they had met one disappointment after another, though they saw strange sights of passing interest. Farther and farther east the visions of the Turk had taken them to the very limit of caution. They left Bigotes at Pecos, and moved out to the plains where they saw Indians who lived in tents and used dogs as beasts of burden, and noticed that if his load was badly balanced the dog barked for someone to come and set it right. They heard of a big river to the east and many canoes. It was all familiar—the Turk had mentioned such. They came to flat highlands in whose irregular faces were deep-slashed canyons of red rock and scrub oak. In such places, the plains cattle stampeded, the army lost horses, Captain de Cárdenas broke his arm. Now and then they encountered groups of Indians who lived in straw huts on the prairies and hunted the buffalo for materials of food, shelter and arms. Among such a people they found an old blind man who told them something amazing. Six years ago, as they figured it, he and his people had been farther to the south, and there they were visited by four great doctors, one of them black, the other three white, who gave blessings, healed the sick and wanted to go toward the sunset. The army knew who these were—Núñez Cabeza de Vaca and his companions. They were awed that in so great a wilderness they should come upon the trace of the man long gone who more than any other seemed responsible for their whole hard journey now.

What was wrong? Where was the gold? The Turk took them now in one direction, now in another, keeping up a flow of promises and explanations for his change of plans.

Isopete, the Indian slave brought from Pecos, declared that the Turk was lying. There was such a country as the Turk said, but there was nothing in it that the General sought.

But still they marched, seeing in one place a white woman with painted chin, and in another a wild hailstorm. The stones, as big as oranges, dented armor and killed animals. Trembling, the people wept and prayed and made vows. Each day they heard how far they had gone according to the soldier whose duty it was to count steps by which the leagues could be computed. In all that wilderness, they were appalled at how little mark so great a throng of men and women and beasts made upon the grasses of the plain. They left no trail, for the grass in the wind waved over their path like the sea over a galleon's wake.

One day the General called a halt for a council of his captains. The leaders agreed upon a decision. The army was to turn back to the Tiguex River, there to settle at Alcanfor once again, and scour the valley for supplies against the next winter. The General and thirty picked horsemen and a handful of infantry, together with Fray Juan de Padilla, and Isopete, and the Turk, once again in chains for his ineffectual performance of his duties as guide, would go farther to the east to see what they could see. The General's smaller force could proceed more swiftly than the long lumbering straggle of the burdened army, and could live off the animals of the plains more readily. The army begged to be taken along, saying they would rather die with the General than return to the river without him who might never return. He was firm, though he promised to send swift couriers to fetch them after him again if he came upon the treasure of Quivira. They saw him go, and waited a fortnight for word from him, while they hunted the buffalo, and killed five hundred bulls whose meat they dried for winter storage. The hunters often lost their way back to camp, for the land was so flat and so barren of marks that in midday with the sun overhead there was no way to know where to turn. At the end of every day the army in camp built fires, blew horns, beat drums, fired their muskets to guide the huntsmen home. Only at sundown could they get their bearings.

But no word came from the General, and at last the army turned to the west. Plains Indians served as guides. Each sunrise a guide watched where the sun rose, and then facing westward sprang an arrow whose course they followed. Before they overtook it, they let go another, and so each day they drew the line of their course through the air until they came once again to the river, on the ninth of July.

Captain de Arellano was in command of the army. He lost little time in sending out detachments to forage for the winter supplies, one to the north, one to the south, both to follow the river.

Captain Francisco de Barrionuevo led his men to the province of Jemez, containing seven pueblos, where the people were generous and gave supplies. This lay on a stream that entered the Tiguex River from the west. On the main stream, at a powerful tributary with red water which they called the Chama, the soldiers came to two cities called Yuque-Yunque whose people fled to the mountains at the approach of the mounted strangers. These towns were on opposite banks of the river and in Indian tales were once connected by a bridge of parrot feathers, that had been upset by witches so that many people fell into the river and were drowned and became fish. Here the soldiers made an abundant haul of food and pottery with a high glaze over many curious designs. Some of the pots held a shiny metal—they thought it might be silver, and their hearts leaped—used for the glaze. Following the main river again, Barrionuevo came to Taos, where Alvarado had been before him a year ago.

To the south another officer led a party to the towns previously seen by Ovando. Going farther than his lost fellow officer, he followed the river until, as he reported later, it disappeared in the ground. He stated that it made him think of the Guadiana River in Estremadura, in Spain, and that it made him quite homesick. The people down the river told him that much farther down, it reappeared with much water. It was the country of drought where Núñez Cabeza de Vaca had seen the low or dry river, like travellers in certain years long later. Where the river reappeared, it was brought back to life by the never-failing, full and clear green water of the Rio Conchos out of Mexico.

The garrison at Alcanfor gathered their stores and explored the silent towns of Tiguex, and saw the kivas underground, some round, some square, with their walls painted in sorcerers' markings, and some large enough in which to have a game of ball. They saw how the floors were paved with smooth stones, which reminded them of the sunken baths of Europe. They foraged in the fields where the Indians sowed their seed corn without plowing, but only waiting for the snows that would cover the earth in winter, and fatten the seed out of which would break the sprouts in summer. The snow clouds came off the mountains by the river and nourished the valley floors. Great flocks of cranes, wild geese, crows and thrushes came to eat the seed, and even so, the crop of one year was enough to last for seven, with a litter of ungathered corn left in the fields. Corn was the staff of life for the river people. They did not eat human flesh, or sacrifice it, like the Mexicans of twenty years before, who took youths to the tops of their temples and under the open sun tore their living hearts out with obsidian knives, in such quantity that at a certain temple the conquerors had seen one hundred thousand corpses near the walls. As well as they could tell, the army at Tiguex accounted for the existence of sixty-six towns in the new land, with Tiguex in the center of them all. They believed the Indian population to number twenty thousand.

The pueblo people and their ways were so different from all others so far met with in the Indies of the Ocean Sea, remarked the soldiers, that surely they must have come from the coast of Greater India, that lay to the west of this land. The soldiers declared that the river rose in the mountains to the northeast, and that the towns were settled all along it until it disappeared underground. There was speculation. Might it not have been better to go north, rather than follow the Turk eastward? To be sure, the land between Norway and China, they realized, was very far up. But as something was known of Greater India, its treasure should perhaps have been attempted instead of that lying across the barren cattle plains. . . .

In Tiguex. as they stated, there was not even anything to steal, though the jars and pots made by the women of the pueblos were fanciful and curious, but otherwise the rooms in the towns were bare and clean. They could only hope that when the General returned to the river he would bring the news all had sought so hard.

Toward the end of summer Captain de Arellano decided to go to look for the General. Picking forty men, and giving the command of the army on the river to Captain de Barrionuevo, he started east. At Pecos he found the people unfriendly. There was a skirmish near the town and two Indians were shot. The misfortunes of Bigotes and Cacique were not forgotten. Pecos stood near the pass through which the General's return must come. Why did he not come? It was late in August, and the rains were falling everywhere, the rivers would rise, the homeward travellers would have trouble crossing them if they waited much longer. But at last word came by Indian traveller that the General was actually on his way. Arellano decided to wait for him at Pecos, to protect the pass if need be, and by his presence keep the people of Pecos subdued.

During the second week of September the General's cavalcade came into view. Arellano and his men welcomed it with great joy. The General paid a visit to Pecos, and was politely received by the people, for he knew what he knew, now, and they realized it. He then pushed on rapidly to the river, and the soldiers of his party mingled with Arellano's, and the General talked with his officers, and on reaching Alcanfor everybody had something to ask and to answer. Those starved for news were fed by those who had meagre news to share, and most of that outrageous.

What was King Tattarax like: Montezuma?

They saw a chief, an old naked wretch with white hair and a copper bangle around his neck, that was his whole wealth, and they were not even sure he was King Tattarax.

And the canoes with golden eagles? The gold bells in the trees? The wagons full of gold?

No gold anywhere.

But the Turk said?

The Turk was dead, garrotted one night in silence in the tent of Captains López and Zaldívar, and buried in a hole already dug for him, before anybody woke with the morning watch.

But why?

Treachery. He lied and lied. He plotted the destruction of the whole army from the first. Going east through Pecos, he arranged with the people to lead the army astray and exhaust them and remove them from food supply, so their horses would die, and if they straggled back from the plains, the Pecos warriors could easily dispose of them in their weakness.

But Pecos? Why would they agree to this?

Bigotes. The iron collar and chain, the dogs that bit him when ordered to. Cacique's captivity.

But the country? The wealth?

Immense plains, people with grass-roofed huts, people who ate meat raw and carried a freshly butchered cow-gut around their necks from which they drank blood and stomach juice when thirsty, people who did everything with little flint knives set in wooden handles, who sharpened the blades rapidly against their own teeth, like monkeys that put everything to the mouth.

And the Turk knew all the time there was nothing else?

He must have known, though he kept saying to the end that just a way farther there really was the other great river, with all its gold and silver and jewels and royal splendor. But then, he had said that about every place at which they had stopped, and where they had found nothing.

Why was he not killed much sooner then?

The General was partial to him. Everybody knew it and resented it. Finally, of course, the General ordered the execution himself.

How miserable. And there was nothing else in the country of Quivira?

Big wolves, and white-pied deer, and rabbits that a man on foot could never catch but that never moved from the path of a horse, so that you could lance them from your saddle with no trouble. And grapes grew there, nuts, mulberries, and plums like those in Castile. As for riches and comforts and fine living—when you got off your horse at the end of a hard day and had to get some supper to satisfy your hunger, you cooked whatever you had, and you cooked it on a fire made of the only thing to be found, which was cow droppings. That was Quivira.

12.

Prophecy and Retreat

The Turk lied and died for it, at the hands of outraged Europeans. But it was more than individuals, it was two kinds of life that told on the one hand, and punished on the other. The quest for wealth led to different answers in each case. To the Indian, wealth meant all that both pueblo and plain offered—rain and grass and primal acts of work and of the fruits of the earth only sufficient to sustain life equally for all. To the Spaniard it meant money and all that lay behind it: to purchase instead of to make, and of the world's wealth, all that a man could possibly gather and keep far beyond the meeting of his creature needs. The logical extension of the Indian's view would in time produce the wealth sought by the Spaniard, but only through work and cultivation of the humble stuff of the earth. But the Spaniard's hope had a simple logic that ended with the ravishment of wealth already existing in forms dependent upon civilization for their pertinence—gold and silver instead of grass and rain.

The General went among his people hiding his disappointment as well as he could, and giving them heart against the problems of the winter by a promise of renewed hope. Now that he knew the plains so well, and would not have to count upon treasonable Indian guides, he would lead the army out again in the spring, for it was entirely possible that by going just a little farther to the east, the rich kingdoms would at last appear before their eyes.

Some of the soldiers could kindle to this hope; others could not. It was going to be another cold year, the food stocks were not any too full, and the silent towns of the river no longer supplied clothing, even under force. Even keeping warm by fire was not easy. The General wrote to the Emperor Charles about Tiguex and its problems. Of all the lands he had seen, he wrote on October 20, 1541, "the best I have found is this Tiguex river, where I am camping, and the settlements here. They are not suitable for settling, because, besides being four hundred leagues from the North sea, and more than two hundred from the South sea, thus prohibiting all intercourse, the land is so cold, as I have related to your Majesty, that it seems impossible for one to be able to spend the winter here, since there is no firewood or clothing with which the men may keep themselves warm, except for the skins that the natives wear, and some cotton blankets, few in number."

(Eighteen years before, far away at the mouth of the same river, another captain-general had concluded that the river lands he saw were not suitable for settling, either.)

The winter garrison was increased by the arrival of Captain Pedro de Tovar and a small force from the base camp far away in Sonora. He brought letters, including one that announced to Captain de Cárdenas that his brother in Spain was dead and that he had succeeded to titles and properties at home. There was also news of disorders and rebellions among the detachment at Sonora. Tovar's party looked about eagerly for the treasures of the northern conquest and, finding none, could not hide their sharp disappointment which was like a reproof to the long-disillusioned garrison. But Tovar's men kept their high spirits, for they could hardly wait until spring, and the second march into Quivira, with all its promises of adventure and wealth. The garrison let them hope. For the present all suffered together from cold and hunger and lice. Try as they would, they could not rid themselves of the lice. Some people were colder than others, for the distribution of Indian garments when they could be had was not always fair. The soldiers said the officers took more than their share, or gave more than was just to those whom they favored. Yes, and certain ones were excused from sentry duty and other hard jobs. All of this in the face of Quivira, the famous swindle. It was a hard winter in the soldier's heart as well as in his stomach and on his shivering skin. When Captain de Cárdenas, with permission, departed on the long trip home to assume his inheritance, and took with him a few who were no longer able-bodied fighters, there was many another soldier who would have gone too, but did not ask, for fear of being thought cowardly. Bad feeling ate at the core of the command. If things went wrong, who was responsible? The General himself, no matter how much he had once been respected and loved.

But as winter wore on the General once again was setting things in motion for the return to Quivira. Few of the soldiers wanted to go. Most of those who were eager to go were officers. Preparations went ahead with commands given by enthusiastic officers to men in low spirits.

Christmas came and went, with the friars leading in the observance of the Feast of the Nativity.

The army had time on its hands, and all sought diversion as they could. The General liked to ride. He had twenty-two horses with him, and often went out riding with one of his close friends. On December 27, 1541, he took riding with him Captain Rodrigo de Maldonado, who was the brother-in-law of the Duke of Infantado. Riding side by side, the two officers were soon in a race. The General's horse was spirited. The contest was lively. The General was leading. Suddenly his saddle girth broke. He fell. As he struck the ground, there was no time to throw himself out of the path of Maldonado's horse, or for Maldonado to check his mount. The Captain tried to jump his horse in order to miss the General, but one of its flying hoofs struck the General in the head.

The garrison was horrified at the calamity. They took the General to his quarters and laid him in bed. He was close to death. How could it have happened? The saddle girth, long among his effects, must have rotted without anyone's knowing, the servants or anyone. For days his life was given up for lost. When at last he began to recover, and was able to be up again, they had to give him bad news.

Captain de Cárdenas on his way to Mexico to sail for Spain, had returned in flight to the Tiguex River with news of Indians in rebellion in Sonora, and Spanish soldiers stationed there dying from arrows poisoned by the yerba pestifera of that land. The homeward path to Mexico was endangered.

The General turned faint at the story and took to his bed again.

And there he had time for a terrible reflection.

He spoke of how a long time ago in Salamanca his mathematical friend had prophesied for him that he would one day find himself in faraway lands (which had come true), and that he would become a man of high position and power (which had come true), and that he would suffer a fall from which he would never recover (and was this coming true now?).

He spoke of his wife and children, saying that if he were to die, let him be with them.

The doctor taking care of him repeated outside what he had heard in the sickroom. Those who meant to return to Quivira were angered at the thought of giving up the expedition, and the doctor carried to the General reports of what they said. In his weakness the General was pressed by all—those who wanted to go to Quivira, and those who longed, like him, to return to Mexico. He kept to his rooms, saw few people, and sent word that if, as was claimed, the army wanted now only to go home, he must have proof of this will in a written petition, signed by all their captains and leaders.

This was given to him, and he hid the folded paper under his mattress. If enemies should steal his strongbox to recover the paper and destroy it for bad ends, they would be fooled. The General then sent forth an order announcing the return of the entire army to New Spain.

But once the decision was made to abandon the poor realities of Tiguex and the vision of Quivira, some officers changed their minds and proposed compromises. Let the General go with sixty men, leaving all the rest to make a colony. But few of the bulk of the army would agree to this. Then let the General take the main body and leave sixty men here until the Viceroy could send reinforcements. But the General disapproved all such suggestions, and held legal proof in the petition which all had signed that his order to retreat from the hard country was by the agreement of all. Somehow in spite of the guards posted in his quarters and outside, an attempt was made to rob him of the petition. The thieves got his strongbox, but not the paper, and only knew afterward where he had kept it.

Visions were lost, and fealties broken, and as the army came to readiness to depart in April of 1542, the dissident officers showed disrespect to the General and carried out his orders with poor grace, if at all. He relied on the common soldiers to sustain him, and they did, and all that remained to do before he led the army home was to take leave of his friends and counsellors, the Franciscans, who were not going with him.

During the season of Lent in 1542, Fray Juan de Padilla preached a sermon at Mass attended by the army. In a time of penance and rededication he spoke of his duty, based on Scriptural authority, to bring eternal salvation to those whom he could reach. Amidst the sorrows and furies of life in the kingdom of these lands, there had been small opportunity to go among the people and preach the word of God. Now that the army was returning home, it was his firm decision, and likewise that of his fellow Franciscans, the lay brother Fray Luís de Escalona, and the oblates Lucas and Sebastián, to remain here in the service of their Divine Lord. They would live among the Indians and convert them and give them peace. He declared that he had received permission from the General to take this course, though such permission was not necessary, as he drew his authority from the superior of the Franciscans in Mexico.

The soldiers listening to him knew well enough the images of the land he chose for his own.

Fray Juan was going back to Quivira, where he had been with the General. Indian guides from the plains would return with him. One of the army's Portuguese soldiers, Andres Do Campo, volunteered to go with him too, and a free Negro, a Mexican Indian and the two oblates. The General gave them sheep, mules and a horse. Fray Juan carried his Mass vessels.

Fray Luís de Escalona chose Pecos for his mission. He owned a chisel and an adze, and with these, he said, he would make crosses to place in the towns. He was not an ordained priest, and so could not administer the sacraments, except, as he said, that of baptism, which he would give to Indian children about to die, and so send them to heaven. Cristóbal, a young servant, volunteered to stay with him.

In their blue-gray robes, the little company of Franciscans set out for the east, escorted as far as Pecos by a detachment from the army. At Pecos, Fray Juan and his companions took leave of Fray Luís and advanced into the open prison of the plains.

A few days later a handful of soldiers went back to Pecos from Tiguex to deliver some sheep to Fray Luís, to keep as his own flock. Before they reached Pecos, they met him walking accompanied by Indians. He was on his way to other pueblos. The soldiers talked with him, and hoped that he was being well treated and that his Indians listened to his word. He replied that he had a meagre living, and that he believed the elders of the pueblo, at first friendly, were beginning to desert him. He expected that in the end they would kill him. The soldiers saw him as a saintly man, and said so many times. They never saw him again, or ever heard of him further, or of Cristóbal, his servant.

In the battles of Arenal and Moho the army had taken many Indian prisoners. The General now ordered these released. It was his last official act as lord of that river province. Early in April, 1542, the command was given to begin the long march down the river to the narrows of Isleta, and there turn west over the desert to retrace the trail to Mexico. Aside from a few Mexican Indians who decided in the end to remain in the Tiguex nation, the expedition had lost in its two years of movement and battle and privation no more than twenty men out of the whole fifteen hundred.

Travelling at times by litter, the General left behind him a vision changed and gone like a cloud over the vast country of the Spanish imagination in his century. A faith of projected dreams and heroic concepts gave power to the men of the Golden Age, a few of whom found even more than they imagined. The General, like many, found less. Having searched for the land of his imagining, and not finding it, he could have said, as Don Quixote later said, ". . . I cannot tell you what country, for I think it is not in the map. . . ."

The army, as it descended into Mexico, began to disintegrate. Officers and men fell away as it pleased them to find other occupations at Culiacán, Compostela, and all the way to the city of Mexico.

In due course reports of the expedition went to Madrid and came before the Emperor. The royal treasuries had supported the expenses of the undertaking. On learning of its outcome, Charles V ordered that no further public monies were to be allocated to such enterprises.

As for the governor of the Seven Cities, the Tiguex River and Quivira, the Emperor received another report during a legal inquiry a few years later. The Judge Lorenzo de Tejada, of the Royal Audiencia of Mexico, wrote on March 11, 1545:

"Francisco Vásquez came to his home, and he is more fit to be governed in it than to govern outside of it. He is lacking in many of his former fine qualities and he is not the same man he was when your Majesty appointed him to that governorship. They say this change was caused by the fall from a horse which he suffered in the exploration and pacification of Tierra Nueva."

13.

Lords and Victims

If the early governors of the river came to poor ends, they were not alone in their last bitterness at the inscrutability of strange lands, the resistance of betrayed natives and the ingratitude of governments. There was hardly a conqueror for the Spanish crown who after his prodigies (whether of success or failure did not matter, for the very scale of colonial operations was prodigious in itself) was not stripped of power, or tried, or impoverished by fines, or imprisoned, or subjected to all these together. What amounted each time to a passion for probity in the crown's affairs reached out to take hold of the adventurous lords of the conquests—but only after they had done their grandiose best or worst.

Of the administrators of the Rio de las Palmas, two were saved by death—Garay in the terrible mercies of Cortés, Narváez in the tempests of the Gulf.

Of the others, Nuño de Guzmán died first, in 1544, in Spain, penniless, while attempting to defend himself against grave charges of maladministration. Cortés was in Spain at the time and, hearing of the trials of his old rival who hated him, offered him money. In bitter pride the offer was refused.

The years between 1540 and 1547 Cortés passed in Spain on the profitless enterprise of trying to recall himself to the memory of a king who as a matter of policy preferred to forget him. If the Marquis of the Valley of Oaxaca was a great man before whom a hemisphere had trembled, he was yet not so great a man as the Emperor of the Holy Roman Empire and King of Spain. In vain Cortés submitted plans for new conquests, petitioned, presented himself at court, reminded the currents of cold air about the throne of what he had accomplished. The court officials were sensitive members that extended the monarch's capacity to know; and in just the same relation carried as in gelid nerves the monarch's messages to enact. Cortés never reached the Emperor—until one day as the royal coach was passing through the streets he detached himself from the crowd and before he could be prevented threw himself upon it, clinging to its leather straps, at last face to face again with the source of power or misery.

"Who is this man?" inquired the king who years before had seated him at his right hand, had ennobled him, and had known him well enough to deprive him of power.

"I am the man who brought Your Majesty more kingdoms than your father left you towns," cried the desperate old conqueror.

The embarrassing scene ended quickly. The coach jolted on. Cortés fell back among the street idlers. However much longer he might live, he had come to the end. On December 2, 1547, in the village of Castillejo de la Cuesta, near Seville, while on his way to embark again for Mexico, he died at the age of sixty-two.

And in Mexico, where out of all his preferments he was left with only his membership on the city council, the Captain-General Francisco Vásquez de Coronado lived for twelve years after his return from the river. He was tried on various charges of crime and error in the conduct of his command, but was absolved, and the attorney for the Crown was enjoined by the court "to perpetual silence, so that neither now nor at any time in the future may he accuse or bring charges against him for anything contained . . . in this our sentence." The judgment was handed down in February, 1546.

In the following year an amazing creature appeared in the streets of Mexico City. His hair was extraordinarily long, and his beard hung down in braids. What he had to tell soon became news everywhere. He was Andres Do Campo, the Portuguese soldier from the Tiguex River who had gone to the plains with Fray Juan de Padilla when the General turned toward home. For five years he had struggled to return to Mexico. One year he spent in captivity, the rest in wandering ever southward. He could speak of having witnessed a martyrdom, for five years before, when the Franciscan's party were come to the land of Quivira, they encountered Indians who made it plain that they were going to kill the hardy priest. Fray Juan ordered his companions to retire out of reach of danger. They fell back to a little rise of land, and watched what followed. Falling to his knees Fray Juan began to pray, and prayed until pierced with arrows he fell dead upon the earth. His companions were permitted to return and bury him where he fell. Ten months later Do Campo and the oblates Lucas and Sebastián, escaped with two dogs. On their backs the fugitives carried wooden crosses with which to invoke grace for themselves and for the Indians whom they met in their travels. Their dogs hunted rabbits for them. Somewhere near the site of Eagle Pass they came to the lower reaches of the same long river in whose pueblo valley far away they had spent two wretched winters. Making their way southeast across Mexico, they reached the coast, and the town of Pánuco, and civilization.

The General must have heard the story, for it was discussed widely. It was the last report of his venture, and it reminded its hearers of the tales of Núñez Cabeza de Vaca, by which the venture had been conceived.

Some years later other news of the river was talked about in Mexico. A certain group of twenty ships had left Veracruz for Cuba and Spain with the spring sailings of 1553. They touched at Havana and sailed again, but were blown from their course by a furious storm that drove them almost all the way back across the Gulf of Mexico.

Only three of the ships ever got to Spain, one returned to Veracruz, and the remainder were lost at sea or wrecked on the Gulf Coast. Three hundred survivors, including five Dominican friars, found themselves ashore without food and poorly clad. They started to march on foot to the south following the coast, hoping to reach the Pánuco and safety. To protect their large company of men, women and children the only arms they had were two crossbows. Indians soon discovered the toiling procession and followed it making little attacks. Crossing a stream, the fugitives lost their crossbows, and now the Indians knew the strangers to be defenseless. Two days later they captured two Spaniards and took away their clothes, sending them back naked to their friends.

What did this mean? Did it mean that the Indians, naked themselves, resented anyone else clothed? The Spaniards thought so, and in confusion and desperation all stripped themselves naked and left their clothes for the Indians to find. But the sacrifice of modesty was useless, for the attacks continued, and many people fell from Indian arrows, illness, despair, until there were only two hundred left. They came along the coast to the mouth of a large river. It was the Rio de las Palmas. On the near bank they found a canoe and used it to help ferry some of the company across, while the Indians attacked in great fury. It was a running fight which continued on the other bank, for the Indians crossed over also leaving many dead and wounded Spaniards behind.

Among these were two badly wounded Dominican friars, Fray Diego de la Cruz and Fray Hernando Méndez. They saw the party vanish along the misty beach to the south and resolved to recover from their wounds and remain on the River of Palms to find and convert the Indians who lived on its banks in little villages. When they could, the two friars returned to the northern bank of the river to start their mission, but Fray Diego could not go on. He lay down in weakness. Fray Hernando gave him the Last Sacraments and, when he died, buried him on the bank of the river, and went on his way.

Up the river he met another survivor, a man named Vásquez, and later the two met a third, a Negress. In spite of her shame at their common nakedness, they joined forces and went along the river digging for roots. Fray Hernando was growing weaker from his wounds, and they fed him what they could, but he died and they buried him. The Negress was killed by Indians. Vásquez left the river to overtake his retreating companions.

Meanwhile the two Dominican fathers were missed among the party of exhausted and hurrying Spaniards along the beaches. The other three friars turned back to find them, accompanied by two sailors. They returned to the cross of the river, found the same canoe as before, and climbed in to paddle upstream. Coming to two small islands where they would feel safe resting for a while, they touched shore on one to land, when the islands sank with commotion, capsizing the canoe and throwing the men into the river. They then saw with astonishment that the islands reappeared, and were two whales, which swam down the river toward the sea. The Spaniards swam to another island which was real, and on it fell exhausted. The next day they contrived a raft out of driftwood, crossed to the south bank, and set out from the Rio de las Palmas to overtake the party moving south on the shore. After they joined their countrymen, all faced another hard Indian attack in which many more were killed, including two of the three remaining Dominicans. The remaining one, Fray Marcos de Mena, survived to reach Mexico City, and to tell this tale.

If the General heard it, it was the last story he ever heard out of the wilds. He had never regained his health, and he died an old man in his forty-fourth year on the night of September 22, 1554, and was buried in the church of Santo Domingo in the city of Mexico.

14.

The River of May

In the autumn of 1568 the Rio de las Palmas was crossed somewhere in its lower reaches near the sea by three destitute men who were walking to the northeast. They were David Ingram, Richard Browne and Richard Twide, English sailors who had come to the New World with the fleet of Captain Sir John Hawkins. At Veracruz where six English ships had put in for refuge from storm and a haven for overhaul, they had done battle with Spanish vessels in the roadstead. Only two English ships escaped. One, captained by a certain Francis Drake who would richly fulfill a later opportunity for revenge, sailed directly for England. The other, under Hawkins, overloaded with survivors, bore north along the Gulf Coast and at their own request landed one hundred and fourteen men on the beach thirty miles above Tampico, and then stood out to the long voyage across the Atlantic.

The shore party were attacked by Indians, and presently divided, one group going north, another south. The northern marchers lost more men through attack, and others through faintness of heart that made some turn back to overtake those moving southward, and still others who abandoned themselves to the countryside. The three who came to the river referred to it as the River of May, where "the ground and countrey is most excellent, fertile and pleasant," more so than country they had already crossed, "for the grasse of the rest is not so greene, as it is in these parts, for the other is burnt away with the heate of the Sunne. And as all the Countrey is good and most delicate, having great plaines, as large and as fayre in many places as may be seene, being as plaine as a board. . . ."

They examined trees and bushes, identifying many, and tasting the bark of one which bit like pepper, and seeing "a great plentie of other sweete trees" to them unknown. Of all, the fruitful palm tree yielded most interest, for it carried "hayres on the leaves thereof, which reach to the ground, Whereof the Indians doe make ropes and cords for their Cotton beds, and doe use the same to many other purposes." Further, "The which Tree, if you picke with your knife, about two foote from the roote, it will yeelde a wine in color like whey, but in taste strong and somewhat like Bastard, which is most excellent drinke. But it will distemper both your head and body, if you drinke too much thereof. . . ." The palm tree gave not only drink but meat, since "the branches of the top of the tree, are most excellent meat raw, after you have pared away the bark." Finally, the useful and beautiful tree could save life, for "Also there is a red oyle that commeth out of the roote of this tree, which is most excellent against poisoned arrowes and weapons: for by it they doe recover themselves of their poysoned wounds."

As for "Tempests and other strange monstrous things in those partes," the sailor saw it "lighten and Thunder in sommer season by the space of foure & twentie houres together," and concluded that the cause for this was the heat of the climate. They saw "Furicanos," and "Turnados," with "a Cloud sometime of the yeere seene in the ayre, which commonly turneth to great Tempests," and again, "great windes in maner of Whirlewindes."

They crossed the great River of May whose gulf land they saw so clearly, and went on their way until a year after the beginning of their misadventure they arrived at New Brunswick, having walked the whole shape of the American coast from Mexico east and north. In 1569 they were safe again in England.

15.

Four Enterprises

For nearly forty years after Coronado's retreat no organized Spanish entries were made into the country of the Rio Grande. As Garay had abandoned the river at its mouth, so Coronado had abandoned its pueblo valley. What these explorers knew about the river was not lost, yet neither was it part of common knowledge. The river had to be discovered over and over again. From time to time little streams of information came out of the blind north country along Indian trails and aroused speculation as though no Spaniard had ever been there before. No comprehensive theory of the river's course was yet held; but Indians told of how the big Rio Conchos, flowing northeast from the Mexican Sierra Madre, made a junction—La Junta de los Rios the Spaniards called it—with the long river whose valley twisted and turned and led northward to the pueblos. The Conchos suggested a new route to the north, more direct than the wide swing westward up the Mexican coast and across Arizona to approach the river from the west as Coronado had done; and finally like all roads it called to be taken. From 1581 to 1593 four small expeditions went to the river from the vast empty highlands of Northern Mexico.

Marching northward along the Conchos, three Spanish Franciscan friars, nine soldiers and sixteen Mexican servants arrived on July 6, 1581, at the junction with the Rio Grande, which they called the Guadalquivir, and also the Rio de Nuestra Señora de la Concepción. The founder of this expedition was Fray Agustín Rodríguez. His squad of soldiers was commanded by Francisco Sánchez Chamuscado. They were on their way to convert the pueblos in the north. Guided by river dwellers they marched northwest following the valley, and turned with it northward, coming at last among the nation of towns that Coronado had known as Tiguex. One of the friars, Juan de Santa Maria, who was an adept in astrology, there resolved to return to Mexico with reports of what the party had seen; and despite warnings of his comrades departed alone for the south.

The rest of the company explored the land east of the river, passing through Pecos to the buffalo plains and returning; visiting the salines east of the Sandia and viewing the rosy stone town of Abo; and marching to the west past Ácoma as far as Zuñi, where a December snowfall forced them back to the river. There the two other Franciscans declared they would stay to preach the word of God. A handful of Indian servants elected to stay with them at the pueblo of Puaray, not far from Coronado's capital of Alcanfor. Chamuscado gave them a few goats, horses and articles of barter, and left them there. With his reduced party he went down the river retracing his course. He was sixty, an old man, exhausted and ill from his hardships. He never reached his home in Santa Barbara near the headwaters of the Conchos, but died a few days' journey from it.

In the following year another small troop took the same passage up the river. This party of thirteen soldiers and various Indian servants was commanded by a merchant of New Spain, Antonio de Espéjo, who was a fugitive from justice under charge of having murdered one of his ranch hands. Its real authority was its spiritual leader, Fray Bernardino Beltrán. Their mission was to bring aid to the two friars who had remained the year before at Puaray, and to look for the astrologer, Fray Juan de Santa María, who had never arrived in Mexico. Coming on December 9, 1582, to the Rio Grande, which they called the Rio del Norte, for the direction of its source, and the Rio Turbio, for its heavy flow of mud, the soldiers were welcomed by people who greeted them with odd, sweet music, which they made with their mouths, and which sounded like the tones of flutes. Along the river Espéjo came upon the memory of Núñez Cabeza de Vaca who with his one black and two white companions was still spoken of among the little towns of willow switches, mud and straw above the *junta de los rios*. The river flowed in silence even in its larger passages. Some of the inhabitants went naked with

strings tied upon their prepuces. Other peoples farther north were fully
clothed.

The soldiers proceeded up the river in December 1582, passing
crosses that still stood since the year before. On occasions Indians whom
they met sat at night around a great bonfire and clapped their hands in
music, while some rose to dance in pairs, fours or eights. In curiosity
and delight the Indians touched the soldiers with their hands, fond-
ling them, and their horses. Gifts were brought to the travellers—food,
blankets, hides. Tanned deerskins reminded the soldiers of soft Flemish
leather. The Indian weapons were wooden clubs and "Turkish" bows,
both fashioned from mesquite. The soldiers made new stocks for their
harquebuses of the same wood.

Wherever they stopped the Spaniards erected crosses, and took
possession of the lands of the river with properly notarized documents.
After turning due north on the river, they met an Indian who told them
that one of friars of the year before had been killed (was this the
astrologer on his way alone to Mexico?) and that the other two still
lived (and were these the two left at Puaray in Tiguex?). Coming into
the country of the three-and-four-storey pueblos, they marvelled at their
size and permanence after the half-dugout, perishable houses below them
in the valley. At Puaray, not far from Coronado's old headquarters of
Alcanfor across the river, they learned the worst. The two missionaries
had been slain, presumably for their possessions—the goats, the horses,
the little metal hawk's-bells, the beads, and the red caps, of barter.

Espéjo and Fray Bernardino had completed their mission, but like
all of their kind before and after them, turned to explore the lands east
and west of the river. Near Pecos, they found that Fray Juan was indeed
also dead. He had been murdered before the expedition of the year
before had even left the pueblo valley. They went on to the plains and
saw the buffalo herds, and they returned to the river, crossing it and
marching to the west. They saw Ácoma, and beyond, in the pueblos far
from the river, they found that Coronado was remembered, and in one
of them, Espéjo came upon an old, small travelling chest and a book
that the General had left there. They collected mineral specimens from
mines even farther west, and turned back to the river, where since their
passage the towns had become rebellious.

Espéjo met his own battles, too, in the upriver pueblos, and with
spirit. "The Lord willed this that the whole land should tremble for
ten lone Spaniards, for there were over twelve thousand Indians in the

province with bows and arrows. . . ." declared his chronicler, and yet when reports came of Indian peoples waiting to attack the travellers, ". . . trusting in God we always marched to the place where we were told the largest number of people awaited us." Espéjo was obliged at one point to burn a town and execute by the garrote sixteen Indians, not to mention those who burned to death. A soldier reflected that "this was a strange deed for so few people in the midst of so many enemies." He knew too what it was to come before a walled town and find it empty, its people immured in the mountains, full of distrust and fear.

In Indian grottoes or caves the soldiers saw prayer sticks with feathers and bits of cooked meat and concluded that there the Devil came to take his ease and feed himself and speak with the Indians. Once they saw in a cage what looked like a Castilian parrot. They noticed that the women of the river were whiter of skin than the Indian women of Mexico, and that the pueblo people did not stink like Indians met with earlier. They remarked much "game of foot and wing, rabbits, hares, deer, native cows, ducks, geese, cranes, pheasants, and other birds," and spoke, like connoisseurs, of "good mountains," and Espéjo euphorically cited "millions of souls" for conversion.

When they turned toward home, the company divided and followed two routes. Fray Bernardino and one group went down the river as all had come. Espéjo and his soldiers returned to Pecos and marched southward along the Rio de la Vacas, which was the Pecos River. Indians whom they met told how this River of Cows joined with another large river flowing eastward which in turn formed a junction with a large river flowing from the north. They knew then that they were once again near the Rio del Norte and its meeting with the Conchos. Turning west they found the river and were given a joyful reception by the people, who performed dances, and fed the soldiers with a feast of green corn, cooked and raw squashes, and cat, and other river fish. The welcome was so friendly that the soldiers put aside arms and armor, going about "almost in shirt sleeves." On August 21, 1583, they came to the *junta de los rios,* where people of another town greeted them warmly, and gave the news that Fray Bernardino and his party had already passed safely by there. The river was now too high to ford. The soldiers rested there for three days, and all traded for blankets, buffalo robes, and Indian bows reinforced with rawhide, and received supplies of squash, beans and corn. Those Indians, thought a soldier, were "fine and elegant people who would readily accept the Holy Faith."

On the twenty-sixth the little troop started homeward up the

Conchos into Mexico. They had failed of their first purpose, but once again knowledge of the river and its lands went to the authorities in New Spain, who noted among other details that Espéjo spoke of a kingdom of New Mexico, which in honor of his native soil he preferred to call New Andalusia.

Again the country of the north, New Mexico in particular, emerged in both fact and dream. Coronado's failure was forgotten, his hope remembered. Explorers were still talking of the vast river (the Mississippi) beyond the plains, adding now that it was salty, and spoke of a great lake with canoes whose prows carried decorations of "brass-colored" metal. The South Sea (the Pacific) was assuredly rich in pearls. New Mexico, as it lay between all these promises, must be worth the labor, the distance, the danger, to colonize as a base of operations. The government in Mexico City was besieged with applications to forward to the Crown, each begging for the honor and opportunity of leading a colony to New Mexico, and serving God and the King at private expense as governor and captain-general, and signed with piety, humble duty and rubric, duly notarized. Strict laws governed the terms by which a colony might be launched forth. Applicants made elaborate cases for themselves. All papers went to Madrid to pass over the worktable of King Philip II to await, sometimes for months, his personal attention. News of his pleasure, coming by sea, subject to the winds, could be hurried or delayed, or lost in disaster. The applicants could only wait.

But seven years after Espéjo with his soldiers marched down the Pecos on his way home, another, and much larger, procession followed it to the north. Acting apparently in good faith under the colonial laws which with certain requirements allowed any governor to settle lands already discovered, Gaspar Castaño de Sosa came to the Rio del Norte near the site of modern Del Rio in September, 1590, with one hundred seventy people, a long supply train, and two brass fieldpieces. The company were the whole population of the mining town of Almaden, now Monclova in Nuevo Leon. Castaño de Sosa was lieutenant governor of his province. At the river he found no settlements. He camped for three weeks in the low sandy hills and heavy greenery of late summer along the banks. On the first of October he started out again, following the south bank until near Eagle Pass he found the ford, crossed over, and went upstream to the Pecos. The canyon of this tributary was too deep to follow from this point to the north. He forded it, marched on to the passes of the Davis mountains, and found the Pecos again in its high plains character, and followed it to the pueblo of Pecos where he halted toward the end of December. His supplies were depleted, the weather was bitter, and it was time to be made welcome, but the people of Pecos were defiant before his resounding overtures of colonial kindliness. Night fell before the negotiations were completed, and when day came again, the colonists saw that the town had been silently abandoned during the dark. Entering in, Castaño de Sosa found rich supplies of corn in the storage cists of the cellular houses. Taking what they needed, the invaders went on their way westward to the Rio Grande del Norte. Once again the river towns submitted to Spanish expeditioners, let them have food, clothing, watched them raise crosses, saw them go exploring east and west of the river. Now and then there was hostility—at a parley before a pueblo, a soldier of Castaño de Sosa's company spoke out for peace, at which an Indian came forth on his terrace, with throngs of his own people clustered about him on the rooftops, and in a gesture small in size but great in power, threw a pinch of ashes at the soldier. At this, as on a signal, the other Indians raised their voices in imprecation, and the soldier departed.

Near the pueblo later called Santo Domingo the new colony made its capital in camp. Castaño de Sosa, sure of his governorship now, sent couriers with news of his march and achievement to the Viceroy at Mexico City, to claim that what no one had yet done, he had succeeded in doing. In his river capital there were men, women and children, domestic animals, a government, a new land—in fact, a colony. Farms must come, he saw Indians growing cotton and several kinds of beans. In reporting to the Viceroy, he was complying with one of the most important requirements of the laws of colonial administration. Knowing its importance, he had been careful to acquaint the Viceroy of all his plans even before leaving Almaden. His report of later progress could only improve his position with the Viceregal Court. With it he sent requests for reinforcements—more soldiers, more families, more supplies.

Meanwhile, at his river outpost Castaño de Sosa was scrupulous to enforce all regulations protecting native peoples. Many of his followers wanted to use their superior armaments and habitual sense of command to despoil the Indians of property and require labor of them. The leader refused to approve such plans. As a result his life was in danger from his own people. A plot to kill him was exposed. He gave any man or woman freedom to return to Mexico as they liked, but he would remain. The cabal died away. He went to Pecos again for more corn from the stores. He explored his country north on the river, and west, and returned to his capital which was no better fed or clothed or protected against all strangenesses than Coronado's Alcanfor. There he had news of a Spanish detachment marching up the river and went out rejoicing to meet his reply from the Viceroy—the reinforcements, the honors, he must have.

What he met instead was a warrant of arrest at the hands of an officer, Juan Morlete, who came to take him prisoner and to disband his colony. His report to the Viceroy from the river had been the first word of his adventures, his presumptions, to reach the government. The law was plain. He had entered the north without a royal commission, such as even then many great captains were hoping to receive from the King. They had been waiting for it, and would be waiting for it, for years. Castaño de Sosa's disgrace was inescapable. Captain Juan Morlete led him down the river. His people were dispersed—Thomas and Christopher, two Mexican Indians, remained at Puaray to live, the rest straggled back to old homes and lost satisfactions. Castaño de Sosa was entered into the infinitely slow mercies of viceregal justice, which was merely a lever touched by the royal hand in Madrid.

> The King: to the president and oidores of my royal audiencia which resides in the City of Mexico in New Spain: I have been informed that Gaspar Castaño . . . entered New Mexico with a company which he collected upon his own authority without order or license to do so. This having come to the attention of yourself, the viceroy, and you learning that those men had committed many disorders and abuses and had taken certain Indians as slaves, you sent in pursuit of them Captain Juan Morlete, who entered New Mexico and took prisoners Captain Gaspar Castaño and his companions. Since it is just that such a bold and dishonorable act should be punished, I command you to . . . proceed against them judicially. . . . Dated at Madrid, January 17, 1593. I THE KING.

Castaño was tried, found guilty, and exiled to China.

In the same year, two officers led a small detachment of soldiers on a mission to subdue Indian disorders in northern Mexico. The task accomplished, they were supposed to return south to their home garrison; but across the deserts of northern Mexico was the river, and up the river was what so many had gone for—Coronado, Chamuscado, Espéjo, Castaño —and the two officers proposed to their men that they too, though without orders, enter the north. Some of the men refused. Others agreed, and followed Captain Francisco Leyda de Bonilla and Captain Antonio

Gutierrez de Humaña along the Conchos, up the Rio del Norte, and out
of living knowledge. Word of their defection was circulated; they were
famous deserters, lawbreakers. Their capture or voluntary return was
awaited with all propriety. They would not be forgotten by the courts.

The courts, in fact, also remembered Castaño de Sosa and his case.
Before a final decision was made in respect to applications before the
King for the governorship of New Mexico, the case of Castaño was revived. Reconsideration of all its aspects led to a reversal of the earlier
verdict. He was exonerated and ordered home from exile to become the
first royally authorized governor of New Mexico. His recall went to
China, where it arrived too late. He had been killed shortly before
while dealing with a mutiny on a Chinese junk.

So through many weighings, intrigues, hesitations and refinements
of policy, the question of the colony for New Mexico aged with the last
decade of the sixteenth century; until the decision was finally made, the
captain-general named once and for all, the expedition authorized, and
the northward toil undertaken over a new route to the river in 1598.

16.

Possession

Late one morning in April, 1598, a party of eight armed and
mounted men came to the river from the south through heavy groves
of cottonwoods. They were emaciated and wild with thirst. On seeing
the water they lost their wits, men and horses alike, and threw themselves into it bodily. The current was swift. Two of the horses thundered
too far into the stream and were carried away and drowned. Two others
drank so much so fast that, as they staggered to the bank from the
shallows, their bellies broke open and they died.

The men drank and drank in the river. They took the water in
through their skins and they cupped it to their mouths and swollen

tongues and parched throats. When they could drink no more they went
to the dry banks and fell down upon the cool sand under the shade of
the big trees. In their frenzied appetite for survival itself, they had become bloated and deformed, and they lay sprawled in exhaustion and
excess. One of their company, looking upon himself and them, said
they were all like drunkards abandoned on the floor of an inn, and
that they looked more like toads than like men.

Numbed with simple creature pleasures they took their ease in
the shade. In the bounteous trees overhead many birds sang. There were
bees in the wildflowers of spring, and the surviving horses grazed in
near-by meadows. The river looked calm and peaceful. All such sounds
and sights were deeply restful to the squad of men. Their clothes were
ragged, their boots were worn through, and their bellies were hungry;
for they had come for fifty days through deserts with thorns, mountains
with rocks, and nothing to eat but roots and weeds. For the last five days
they had not had a drop of water. In finding the river, they not only
saved their lives; they fulfilled their assignment—to break a new trail
to the Rio del Norte from the south, that would bypass the Junta de los
Rios, to bring the colony directly to its New Mexican kingdom with
one hundred and thirty families, two hundred and seventy single men,
eighty-three wagons and carts, eleven Franciscan friars, seven thousand
cattle herded by drovers on foot, and all commanded by the Governor,
Captain-General and Adelantado Don Juan de Oñate.

The little advance detachment was headed by Vicente de Zaldívar,
sergeant major of the colony, and nephew of the Governor. Among his
seven men was Captain Don Gaspar Pérez de Villagrá, from Salamanca,
a former courtier of King Philip II, and a scholar with a classical education who later wrote the history of the colony's first year in thirty-four
rhymed Virgilian cantos. When they set out on their mission Villagrá
said they were all without scientific knowledge of the heavens by which
to set their course. He doubted if there was one among them who, "once
the sun had set, could with certainty say, 'There is east, there is west'."
They marched with hunger and thirst and once were captured by Indians
who freed them unharmed having enjoyed their fright. But with the next
dawn the eight Spaniards charged the large camp of their tormentors
from all sides, firing their arms, and scattering all but a handful of
Indians, whom they captured, holding two as guides, releasing the others.
Now they also had rations—venison, badger, rabbit meat, along with
herbs and roots. They moved on to the north, again running out of
water. The guides brought them to six shallow water holes where all

horses and men drank selfishly and greedily but one—Zaldívar, the leader, who waited till all were done, at the risk of there being no water left; then last in turn by his own choice, he drank his fill. Advancing over a plain where they could see far, they asked the guides where lay the river they sought? One did not understand. The other smoothed the ground and at once drew a circle, and "marked the four cardinal points . . . the two oceans, the islands, mountains, and the course of the river we sought. He seemed to act with the knowledge and experience of an expert cosmographer. As we watched him it seemed as though he was tracing the Arctic and Antarctic seas, the signs of the Zodiac, and even the degrees and parallels. He marked the different towns of New Mexico and the road we should follow and where along the journey we should find water. He then explained to us the direction we should take and where we would be able to ford the mighty river." It was reassuring to have such a guide; but by the next day the Indians had escaped and the Spaniards were adrift in the desert, "trusting in God to bring us with safety to the river's shore." There was always too much water or too little. They passed through a whole week of uninterrupted rain; and then there was thirst again, like that of the last five days that brought them to the river.

But now they rested and recovered their strength. They fished in the river, and shot ducks and geese, and on April 20, saw with pride and joy the best results of their efforts, for then arrived the mounted vanguard of the main body, led by the Governor. The wagons and the herds were following more slowly. That evening the trail blazers and the Governor's great cavalcade celebrated their meeting with a feast. They built a roaring fire, and in it roasted meat and fish. Afterward there were speeches. The Sergeant Major described the adventures of his little party. The Governor then rose to tell of all that his people had endured, and they listened thirstily to his accounts of their heroism, and knew all over again the burning days, the cold nights, the thorns, the hunger, the fear, the bewildered privation of children, the courage of women, and the power of prayer to bring them rain when they were parched. At the end of his speech, the Governor was pleased to make them all a gift which only he could make. It was a whole day of rest in which all might do as they wished, to recover themselves before the journey up the river was resumed.

On April 26 the rest of the expedition arrived. All were reunited, and moved together up the south bank of the river a few more leagues.

There was a sense of great occasion in this arrival and encampment at the Rio del Norte. The wastes of northern Mexico were behind them all now, and the path to the north was more familiar from this point on. To select the ford to the north bank the Sergeant Major detailed a party of five men, all good swimmers. They found a shallow wide place, and returning to make their report met with an Indian encampment where four friendly Indians agreed to return with them. The Governor received the Indian visitors, gave them clothes and many gifts to take back to their people. It was not long before the Indians were back again, with many of their friends, bringing fish in quantities, which were welcome for the celebrations and feasts that were approaching. The river flowed through the gates of the kingdom of New Mexico. The army would enter through them only after suitable observances.

Under a river grove they built an altar. There on the morning of the last day of April in the presence of the whole army and the families, a solemn High Mass was sung by the Franciscan priests. Candle flames dipped and shone in the dappled shady light under the trees that let moving discs of sunlight in upon the gold-laced vestments, the bent heads of the people, their praying hands. At Mass the Father Commissary, Fray Alonso Martinez, preached a learned sermon.

After Mass came an entertainment. It was a play composed for the occasion by Captain Don Marcos Farfán de los Godos, who came from Seville and in his forty years had seen much of the theatre. He understood the drama as a habit of occasion, a proper part of any festival. He was a man of good stature, with a chestnut-colored beard, and his sense of amenity was becoming to a soldier who was also a colonist. His play, hurriedly prepared and rehearsed, showed how the Franciscan fathers came to New Mexico; crossed the land, so; met the poor savages, so; who were gentle and friendly, and came on their knees, thus, asking to be converted; and how the missionaries then baptized them in great throngs. So the colony showed to themselves a great purpose of their toil. The audience adjourned in high spirits to prepare for the next episode of the celebrations.

Men with horses now went to mount, and came in formation shining with arms, armor and all their richest dress. The rest of the colony took up formal ranks, and when all was ready the Governor came forward accompanied by the crucifer, the standard-bearer, the trumpeters and the royal secretary of the expedition to perform the most solemn of acts.

All knew what a great man the Governor was. He was supposed to be one of the five richest men in Mexico. His father the Count de

Oñate had been a governor before him—in New Galicia. During the four years of preparations, delays, starts and stops which the expedition had already endured, they said the Governor had spent one million dollars of his own fortune, for salaries, supplies, equipment, and running expenses. The Governor was magnificent on both sides of his household, for his wife was a granddaughter of the Marquis of the Valley, Cortés, the conqueror; and the great-granddaughter of the Emperor Montezuma himself. Her father was Don Pedro de Tovar, who had gone and returned with Coronado. As a child she must have heard him tell of his adventures in the north. All such great connections were matters of pride to the colony, but since opinion was always divided in human affairs, there were those who had heard things. They said the Governor had squandered and mismanaged his great patrimony so that he actually owed more than thirty thousand dollars, all of it borrowed in bad faith, with the creditors evaded by tricks ever since. Everybody knew he was only a private individual, and thus had no place in the government to command respect for him. How would anybody obey him? In fact, once before, leading soldiers, he had been treated disrespectfully and disobeyed. Would anybody but wastrels and thugs enlist to go with him? But for all such opinion there was plenty of the opposite, which held that the delays and frustrations that had so many times during the past four years prevented the Governor from actually marching forth with his army had come from the Devil, whose purpose it was to prevent the colony from going to convert the heathen Indians, and it was plain that those who worked against the Governor worked for the Prince of Darkness. Many said that nobody was better fitted for the command than the Governor, with his virtue, his human understanding and the nobility of his character; his efficiency and his place in the affections of the soldiers; and the fact that he was the son of his father, who was the beloved "refuge of soldiers and poor gentlemen in this kingdom."

When he now came forward to face the army and with them all to signalize their common achievement, all hearts lifted to him in unity. He was a fine-looking man in middle life, wearing one of his six complete suits of armor. He held many closely written pages of parchment on which were written over three thousand words of solemn proclamation. Bareheaded, in the presence of the cross and the royal standard, he began to read aloud.

He invoked the trinity in "the one and only true God . . . creator of the heavens and earth . . . and of all creatures . . . from the highest cherubim to the lowliest ant and the smallest butterfly." He called upon the Holy Mother of God and upon Saint Francis. He set forth the legal basis of his authority, and declared, ". . . finding myself on the banks of the Rio del Norte, within a short distance from the first settlements of New Mexico, which are found along this river . . . I desire to take possession of this land this 30th day of April, the feast of the Ascension of Our Lord, in the year fifteen hundred and ninety-eight. . . ." He commemorated the Franciscan martyrs of earlier years up the river, and showed how their work must be taken up and continued. Turning to other purposes of his colony, he listed many—the "need for correcting and punishing the sins against nature and against humanity that exist among these bestial nations"; and the desirable ends "that these people may be bettered in commerce and trade; that they may gain better ideas of government; that they may augment the number of their occupations and learn the arts, become tillers of the soil and keep livestock and cattle, and learn to live like rational beings, clothe their naked; govern themselves with justice and be able to defend themselves from their enemies. . . . All these objects I shall fulfill even to the point of death, if need be. I command now and will always command that these objects be observed under penalty of death." Mentioning the presence of his reverend fathers and of his officers, and the name of the King, he declared:

"Therefore . . . I take possession, once, twice, and thrice, and all the times I can and must, of the . . . lands of the said Rio del Norte, without exception whatsoever, with all its meadows and pasture grounds and passes . . . and all other lands, pueblos, cities, villas, of whatsoever nature now founded in the kingdom and province of New Mexico . . . and all its native Indians. . . . I take all jurisdiction, civil as well as criminal, high as well as low, from the edge of the mountains to the stones and sand in the rivers, and the leaves of the trees. . . ."

He then turned and took the cross beside him, and advancing to tree he nailed the cross to it and knelt down to pray, "O, holy cross, divine gate of heaven and altar of the only and essential sacrifice of the blood and body of the Son of God, pathway of saints and emblem of their glory, open the gates of heaven to these infidels. Found churches and altars where the body and blood of the Son of God may be offered in sacrifice; open to us a way of peace and safety for their conversion, and give to our king and to me, in his royal name, the peaceful possession of these kingdoms and provinces. Amen."

And the royal secretary then read his certification of the deed, and the trumpets blew a tremendous voluntary, and the harquebusiers fired a salute together, and the Governor planted with his own hands the royal standard in the land near the river.

17.

The River Capital

Four days later, on May 4, the army arrived upriver at the ford discovered by the five swimmers a week before. There the river flowed from between two mountains whose flanks it had for aeons worn away in its search for the sea, still so distant. All went to work to get the train across. The ford was close to the site of modern El Paso-Juarez. The most noble youth sweated himself like the commonest half-breed, hauling at the heavy carts, calling to the cattle, riding back and forth from dust to dust on each side of the river. A man's worth was in how much he worked when the time came. The Governor's nephews, Juan and Vicente de Zaldívar, were among the worthiest.

Once across on the left bank, the colony moved on to the pass through the mountains, which they called now the North Pass, El Paso del Norte. Wandering Indians watched them, Mansos, naked and passive, but known to be capable of great ferocity. They had no fixed dwellings or planted fields, but ate berries and whatever they could catch that jumped or ran, such as toads, lizards and vipers, and other animals, all of which they ate raw.

The colony moved safely on with all its burdens on pack animals and in the two-wheeled wagons. The wheels were made of cross sections of cottonwood trunks, joined by a pine-log axle on which rested the wagon bed four feet square. The wagon sides were made of slender branches lashed upright. The shaft of the wagon was of pine, and to it were chained the yokes of the oxen. There went all the household treasures and trifles, the possessions that meant personality and home and ways of doing things, from sacred images to dishes to books and clothing, whether humble or grand.

A servant of one of the officers was in charge of his master's arms and wardrobe, which included a captain's lance of silver with tassels of gold, yellow and purple silk; three suits of armor; three Madrid harquebuses, with powder horns, firelocks, and bullet moulds; three sets of buckskin armor for horses; a sergeant's halberd with yellow and purple velvet tassels; a Toledo sword and a dagger inlaid with soft gold, with silk belts; four Cordovan leather saddles; a bed with two mattresses and coverlet, sheets, pillowcases, pillows. The Captain owned a suit of blue Italian velvet faced with wide gold lace; another of lustrous Castilian satin, rose-colored, with a short gray cloak trimmed in long silver and gold fringe, and rose-colored silk stockings and striped rose-colored taffeta garters; another of straw-colored Castilian satin, slashed over crimson Castilian taffeta with matching garters and stockings; another of purple Castilian cloth with cape, garters and stockings to match, all trimmed in gold; another of chestnut-colored London cloth embroidered in silver; another of flowered silk from China, tan and green, trimmed in gold; two doublets of soft kid leather decorated with gold and silver lace; another doublet of royal lion skin with gold and purple braid and buttons to match. The Captain had a gray rain-cloak, and two Rouen linen shirts with collars and cuffs of Dutch cambric, six handkerchiefs of Rouen linen, eight pairs of linen drawers with socks (plain), six pairs of Rouen linen drawers (trimmed), eight pairs of Cordovan leather boots, four pairs of sole leather and buckskin boots, four pairs of laced gaiters, fourteen pairs of Cordovan leather shoes, white and black. He had three hats, one black trimmed around the crown with a silver cord, with purple, white and black feathers; another gray with purple and yellow feathers; and the last of purple taffeta with blue, purple and yellow feathers and trimmed with gold and silver braid. For riding (he was a captain of cavalry), he had four pairs of spurs, two for short stirrups, two for long stirrups, and some Moorish spurs with silken tassels and cords. And to house himself and his establishment in camp (he had a wife and family and two young Spanish servants, and thirty war horses) there were fifty yards of striped Mexican canvas for a tent, with all the gear with which to set it up, including forked stakes.

The train stretched out for nearly four miles along the road it was making as it went. Drovers and mounted soldiers did their best to keep the animals, the carts, the walking people closed up in manageable formation. It was often hard to do. Animals strayed. Horses would run away and their soldiers grumbled at continuing on foot. The Governor had much to think about on the route. The Viceroy was known to be against him. When the expedition found its settling place, it was possible that another man might arrive by the fleet (for surely the river in the north was near enough to the sea for shipping to ply between New Mexico and Acapulco as all the best cosmographers believed?), and would produce a royal commission to take over the governorship. But perhaps not, if all went well in the meantime. If, for example, there was much of interest discovered east and west of the river, and if there were many conversions, and if the renegade explorers, Bonilla and Humaña, were at last found and captured, and returned to the proper authorities to be punished with "pain of death or mutilation of members," as the familiar legal expression put it. It was one of the duties specified in the Governor's commission that he find and capture the two deserters believed to be "in that country . . . wandering about there."

He hoped also to find one if not both of the Mexican Indians, Thomas and Christopher, who had remained along the river when Castaño de Sosa's column returned to Mexico.

Leaving the North Pass behind them the Governor's train marched up the wide flat valley where they met wandering Indians who lived a carefree existence, "far removed from the bustle and hurry of our great cities," and a former courtier noted that the Indians were "ignorant of court life." Soon they heard that the first of the river towns lay ahead. The Governor sent a detachment under Captain de Aguilar to scout the town, with orders, under penalty of death, not to enter the town for any reason whatsoever, but to see it from afar and return to report.

At a point sixty miles above the North Pass, the army came to the great westward turn in the river caused by the end of a mountain range. It was the same place where Nuñez Cabeza de Vaca had turned west. The river could not be followed in its valley there, for on the east bank mountains sloped almost directly into it, and on the west bank the land fell to the river in such a repeated tumble of gullies and arroyos, with rising and falling hills between, that no road could be made over it with the tools and equipment owned by the army. And where the river went west, the army wanted to go north. There was only one thing to do, which was to leave the river and continue overland on the northward course, and presently—ninety miles upstream—the river would be accessible again. For all the intervening distance, bare, high and abrupt mountains separated the travellers from the river, and their course would lie over a desert plain flat enough for the carts and wagons.

Just as the colony was about to leave the river and enter the journey over the north-lying desert, Captain de Aguilar returned to report to the Governor.

He had seen the town?

Yes.

How far away was it?

About ninety miles—near the end of the desert passage.

And there were people?

Yes, he talked with them.

Talked with them?

The Governor was enraged. Did the Captain disobey orders and enter the town, then?

Yes. He had done so.

The Governor stormed on. Did the Captain not suppose that the Governor had full and sufficient reasons for giving orders not to enter the town? It was a known habit of those Indian people to gather their possessions and abandon their towns when they heard of an army's approach. Such behavior would defeat the Governor's purpose. If they now through the Captain's disobedience had news of the approaching caravan, a proper beginning for the colony might be impossible. The Captain's grave offense must not go unnoticed. The Governor hardly pausing to catch his breath commanded that he be executed at once, for outright disobedience to orders.

The sentence aroused the colony. The Captain's men came to plead with the Governor for his life. The Governor listened to all who asked to be heard. Had he been hasty? But he was not entirely alone in his decision. Juan Piñero, an ensign of the army, who had gone north with the Captain, stated that he for one had wished to obey the Governor's orders exactly. He had been overruled, and he now repeated that the orders should have been obeyed. He would not plead against the punishment. But in the end the Governor yielded to all the others and spared the Captain.

But he felt obliged now to take a mobile and light detachment of thirty horsemen and go ahead himself, to meet the Indians in the pueblos, and pacify them, and keep them in their houses. He gave command of the army to a senior officer and by forced marches crossed the desert passage leaving the army to follow him in its trudging.

They made their course by the stars at night. The desert was bounded on east and west by long mountain ranges between which the river had once run. In the summer daytime the heat was great. Mountains seemed to waver on their bases in the desert shimmer. A knife, a sword, any metal thing, or even leather, if it was shined and hard-finished, was actually too hot to handle if exposed to the sun. The mountains between the desert and the river held the colors of dead fire—dusty reds, yellows, clinker purple, ash violet, and burned blacks; and at sundown for a few moments seemed to fire alive again on the surface as once they must have been fired within.

On May 21, Pedro Robledo, one of the soldiers, died and was buried near the end of the mountain range on the west, which was named for him. Two days later the Governor's party was in distress from lack of water. They had advanced only six leagues since the twenty-first. Man, horse and dog (there was a little dog travelling with the party) searched for a water hole in any likely place. On the twenty-third the little dog disappeared and awhile later returned to his soldiers. They took him up and spoke to him, but he had already answered them, for all his paws were freshly muddy, and there must be water near-by. Everyone looked again, and the dog helped, and presently Captain Pérez de Villagrá found a water hole a little way toward the mountain barrier of the river, and soon after that a soldier named Cristóbal Sanchez found another, and all drank, some too much, including the Father President Fray Alonso Martinez, who drank until he was ill. They named the place Perillo Spring, after the little dog, and marked it for those following. It was for generations the only place where travellers could find water in the whole desert passage between the outlying mountains. Later Spaniards named the ninety-mile desert the Jordada del Muerto, the Dead Man's March—the name by which it was finally to be known.

Where the river came back from the west and joined the north-ward route, ending the Dead Man's March, the Governor found a good campsite. In honor of one of his Franciscan chaplains, the place, and the mountains that rose above it, were given the chaplain's name—Fray Cristóbal—when on a later passage he died near there.

And north of there on the river's west bank clear in the diamond sunlight was the first of the towns. As the Governor approached with his men the sky went suddenly black with clouds. How could it be, when a moment ago the sky was clear? A torrent fell on the instant. The soldiers trembled. There was no shelter. They prayed. It was certainly the Devil who had done this, to keep the army from its good task. Hail followed the rain and wild shattering thunder. Lifting their crucifixes the friars

replied to the storm with the terrible prayers of exorcism. What happened instantly was almost more fearful than the storm. The sky cleared,
the rain stopped, the clouds vanished in silence, and the sun shone forth.
As the soldiers rode forward to the pueblo they saw that the Indians too
were amazed at the sudden end of the tempest.

The Indians came out to meet them, took them into the pueblo,
gave them rooms, food and comforts. Seeing the crucifixes on the long
rosaries of the friars the Indians took them up and kissed them. On the
walls of the little cubed rooms the soldiers saw paintings of the Indian
gods—gods of water, mountain, wing, seed, all fierce and terrible. In
honor of the day, for it was the Feast of Saint John the Baptist, June 24,
the Governor ordered a military display and sham battle. He divided the
command into two sides, both mounted, and put his nephews Juan and
Vicente in charge as opposing leaders. The brothers gave a brave show,
and all handled their horses with skill and their weapons with dexterity.
Indians watched. There was much meaning to the tournament.

When it was over the Governor went among the soldiers speaking
about the games. Presently three naked Indians came up to him, and
one declared loudly, in Spanish:

"Thursday, Friday, Saturday and Sunday!"

What was that?

The Governor and all others were astonished. As a soldier later
said, it was like hearing the serpent bark like a dog, after the defeat of
the Tarquinians, in Roman history.

The Indian would not repeat what all were sure he had said, and
therefore the Governor had him and his companions seized. Then, ter-
rified, the Indian spoke again.

"Thomas and Christopher!" he shouted.

What?—And by much questioning with signs, and indications
upon the ground, the soldiers found that he was telling them of two
men named Thomas and Christopher who lived at a town two days away,
who had been there for seven years, ever since the last time the valley
had seen men with horses, armor and guns.

This could only mean the two Mexican Indians who had stayed
behind after Castaño de Sosa. The Governor needed them as interpreters,
for they could speak Spanish, and having lived in the pueblos they must
now speak Indian languages. Their capture was essential to his mission.
He took leave of this first town and hurried north with his cavalcade
to look for Thomas and Christopher two days' journey away.

On the following day he came to Puaray and with all his men

was hospitably received. They were conducted into the pueblo where passing through a room they saw something that made their hearts turn over. It was a wall painting which had been lately whitewashed, as though in hasty response to a warning. But the effacement was not complete, and the Governor and his men could see that the mural painting represented the murder with stones and arrows of two Franciscan fathers. Now it was plain that seventeen years ago Fray Agustín Rodríguez and Fray Francisco López had died there in that fashion. With his eye the Governor warned his people not to give any sign. They accepted rooms for the night, but did not sleep, and late in the darkness while the whole pueblo slept, the Spaniards led by the Governor withdrew in dead quiet.

Early the next morning at the pueblo which the Spaniards named El Agua de Santo Domingo they met the Indians as friends and asked if Thomas and Christopher were here.

Yes, they were here, but still in bed.

Just where?—and the soldiers found them, brought them to the Governor, and they spoke freely with him.

They said they were Christian Indians who had come from New Spain with Castaño. When he was taken away, they had stayed here of their own will, were now married to pueblo women, and were happy. They could speak the Mexican, Spanish and the local Indian tongues. From that time on, they belonged to the Governor, and played a vital part in his government, for through them he could now make his way into the understanding of the people of his river.

At Santo Domingo the Governor received seven chiefs representing thirty-four pueblos. With fuller communication achieved through Thomas and Christopher, a solemn ceremony was held in the great kiva of Santo Domingo in which the chiefs swore allegiance to God and the king of the Christians on the seventh of July.

The Governor moved upriver again, and on the eleventh arrived near the two pueblos of Yuque and Yunque which faced each other across the river just below the confluence of the Chama with the Rio del Norte. These were the same towns seen fifty-seven years before by Captain Barrionuevo of Coronado's army. From the nearer one of these pueblos —the one on the east bank—the people came out to give their submission to the Governor, and peaceably evacuated their houses to let him and his soldiers move in. In memory of the first Spaniards who had erected the cross there years before, the Governor named his town San Juan de los Caballeros, and designated it as his capital.

Captain Vicente de Zaldívar, the Sergeant Major, was sent downstream to meet and escort the heavy train of the wagons and the cattle to the new capital, while the Governor with a small party rode to the north as far as Taos, and to the east as far as Pecos.

At Pecos a man was brought forward who could speak in a sort of Spanish. His name was Joseph. After a few words he struck deep into the interest of his hearers. Another mystery of the north was partly solved as he talked. Five years ago Joseph was taken from the Rio del Norte with other Indians to guide some Spanish soldiers eastward to the plains. He spoke the names of Captain Francisco Leyda de Bonilla and Captain Antonio Gutierrez de Humaña.

The Spaniards quickened at this mention of the deserters, the leaders of an illegal entry, whom it was the Governor's assigned duty to arrest, and for whom he had been looking ever since his arrival in New Mexico.

But go on: where were they now?

Joseph continued. They had gone together eastward, and for six or seven weeks travelled past pueblos, rivers, great herds of buffalo, until one day Gutierrez de Humaña turned on Leyda de Bonilla and killed him on the plains.

So: Gutierrez de Humaña was not only a deserter but also a murderer. What else?

After that, the party came to a large river, and there Joseph and five other Indians ran away and tried to go back to the Rio del Norte. He alone got back, and then only after a year's captivity by plains Apaches.

And Gutierrez de Humaña and the rest of his soldiers?

They had never returned from the plains. There were several possibilities. They might be living there as conquerors. They might be captive slaves of buffalo-hunting Indians. They might be dead.

Joseph, after his escape, hearing that there were other Spaniards on the river, went to meet them, and there, at Pecos, found them. The Governor was glad to take him into his service as interpreter, guide and geographer. Turning back to the Rio del Norte, the Governor's party crossed westward and explored the Jemez province.

In his absence from the capital, other soldiers, with fifteen hundred Indians, undertook to build the first municipal works—an irrigation ditch —for the river city of San Juan. At that point the valley was wide, with many grand steps in the land rising away from the river, through river terraces of pinkish sand, and Indian-colored foothills carved by the wind into fantastic shapes, and high flat mesas, to mountains whose forests turned the clear air blue as smoke. The river course was edged with trees.

Here on August 19 the wagon train arrived to be reunited to the Governor and his command, and to stay on the river as no colony had yet stayed. They brought more than their lashed and lumbering cargoes to the capital high on the river, more than their toiling bodies. They brought all that had made them, through the centuries. If their heritage was a collective memory, it remembered for all more than any one man could know for himself. It shone upon their inner lives in another light than the light of the material world, and in countless hidden revelations suggested what brought them where they were.

18.

Collective Memory

i. sources

Brown plains and wide skies joined by far mountains would always be the image of home to them, the image of Spain, that rose like a castle to inland heights from the slopes of the Mediterranean, and gave to the offshore wind the fragrance of ten thousand wild flowers that mariners smelled out at sea.

The home of the Spanish spirit was Rome. When Spain was a province of the Caesarian Empire her promising youths went to Rome, to make a name for themselves, to refresh the life of the capital with the raw sweetness of the country, and to help form the styles of the day in the theatre, like Seneca of Cordoba, and make wit acid as wine, like Martial of Bilbilis, and elevate the public art of speech, like Quintillian from Calahorra, and even become Emperor, like Trajan, the Spanish soldier. Rome gave the Spaniards their law; their feeling for cliff and wall, arch and cave, in building; and their formal display of death in the arena, with its mortal delights, its cynical esthetic of pain and chance. Martial said it:

> Raptus abit media quod ad aethera taurus harena,
>   non fuit hoc artis sed pietatis opus. . . .

A bull, he said, taken up from the center of the arena rises to the skies, and this was not act of art, but of piety. . . . It remained an act of passion when Spanish piety turned to Christianity.

It was an empowering piety that grew through fourteen centuries, the last eight of which made almost a settled condition of life out of war with the Moslems of the Spanish peninsula. It was war both holy and political, striving to unify belief and territory. Like all victors the Spaniards bore lasting marks of the vanquished. Perhaps in the Moors they met something of themselves, long quiet in the blood that even before Roman times flowed in Spanish veins from Africa and the East, when the ancient Phoenicians and the Carthaginians voyaged the Latin sea and touched the Spanish shore and seeded its life. From the Moslem enemy in the long strife came certain arts—numbers, the mathematics of the sky, the art of living in deserts, and the virtue of water for pleasure, in fountains, running courses and tiled cascades. That had style: to use for useless pleasure in an arid land its rarest element.

Hardly had they made their home kingdom secure than the Spaniards put themselves and their faith across the world. They fought the infidel wherever they could find him, they ranged toward the Turk, and the Barbary Coast, and for them an admiral mercenary in 1492 risked sailing west until he might fall over the edge of the world and be lost. But however mockingly he was called a man of dreams, like many such he was a genius of the practical, and as strong in his soul as in his heart; for he believed as his employers believed.

ii. belief

They believed in God, the Father Almighty, Creator of heaven and earth; and in Jesus Christ His only Son their Lord, Who was conceived by the Holy Ghost, born of the Virgin Mary, suffered under

Pontius Pilate, was crucified, died and buried. He descended into hell; the third day He rose again from the dead; He ascended into heaven to sit at the right hand of God the Father Almighty from thence to come to judge the living and the dead. They believed in the Holy Ghost, the Holy Catholic Church, the communion of saints, the forgiveness of sins, the resurrection of the body, and life everlasting. Amen, they said.

So believing, it was a divine company they kept in their daily habit, all, from the monarch to the beggar, the poet to the butcher. The Holy Family and the saints inhabited their souls, thoughts and words. They believed that with the love of God, nothing failed; without it, nothing prospered. Fray Juan of the Cross said it for them:

> Buscando mis amores,
> Iré por esos montes y riberas,
> No cogeré las flores,
> Ni temeré las fieras,
> Y pasaré los fuertes y fronteras.

Thus seeking their love across mountain and strand, neither gathering flowers nor fearing beasts, they would pass fortress and frontier, able to endure all because of their strength of spirit in the companionship of their Divine Lord.

Such belief existed within the Spanish not as a compartment where they kept their worship and faith, but as a condition of their very being, like the touch by which they felt the solid world, and the breath of life they drew until they died. It was the simplest and yet most significant fact about them, and more than any other accounted for their achievement of a new world. With mankind's imperfect material—for they knew their failings, indeed, revelled in them and beat themselves with them and knew death was too good for them if Christ had to suffer so much thorn and lance and nail for them—they yet could strive to fulfill the divine will, made plain to them by the Church. Relief from man's faulty nature could be had only in God. In obedience to Him, they found their greatest freedom, the essential freedom of the personality, the individual spirit in the self, with all its other expressions which they well knew— irony, extravagance, romance, vividness and poetry in speech, and honor, and hard pride.

If they were not large men physically, they were strong, and their bodies which the King commanded and their souls which God commanded were in harmony with any task because both God and King gave the same command. It was agreed that the King held his authority

and his crown by the grace of God, communicated to him by the sanction
of the Church. This was clear and firm. Thus, when required to serve
the King in any official enterprise, great or small, they believed that
they would likewise serve God, and had doubled strength from the two
sources of their empowerment.

But if the King was divinely sanctioned he was also a man like
all; and they knew one another, king and commoner, in the common
terms of their humanity. To command, to obey; to serve, to protect—
these were duties intermixed as they faced one another. The King was
accountable to the people as well as to God; for they made the State,
and the State was in his care. *Del rey abajo ninguno,* they said in a
proverb, Between us and the King, nobody. So they spoke to him in
parliaments. Representative government began with the Spaniards. All,
noble or commoner, had equality before the law. They greatly prized
learning and respected those who owned it, such as lawyers. Indeed, the
law was almost another faith, with its own rituals and customs, and even
its own language, closed to uninitiated eyes and ears. Learning being
scarce must also have seemed precious, and beyond the grasp of many a
hungry mind. Yet with other peoples of the Renaissance, the sixteenth-
century Spanish had intimations of world upon world unfolding, and
they could not say what their children would know except that it would
be greater than what they the fathers knew, watching the children at play
with their little puppets of friars made from bean pods, with the tip
broken and hanging down like a cowl, and showing the uppermost bean
like a shaven head.

iii. the ocean masters

The year after the astounding first voyage of Admiral Christopher
Columbus came the Bull of Pope Alexander VI giving the King and
Queen of Spain for themselves, their heirs and successors, all the lands
of the New World known and still to be known. Given the unexempted
belief of all civilized society in the reality of the Pope's spiritual and
temporal power, this was an act of unquestionable legality. (In making
his proclamation at the Rio del Norte, the Governor cited it, outlining
briefly the divine origin of the Papacy through the story of Christ.) Thus
the Americas came to belong to Spain, and to reach those lands she

became a great sea power, for a time the greatest in the world. Schools of navigation and piloting were founded at Ferrol, Cádiz and Cartagena. Universities maintained professorial chairs in cosmography. The great lords of Spain were given command of the fleets that plied to the Indies, though some had no qualities for the ocean but rank and magnificence, like the old marquis, a certain governor of the Armada, who through gout could not take off his own hat or feed his own lips, but had to have his courtesy and his food handled for him by servants. But still the Spanish sailed, and sailed well, and their fleets were prodigious at their greatest, like the one that bore the King to marry the Princess of England—gilded carving on the stern galleries, and sails painted with scenes from ancient Rome, and fifteen thousand banners at the masts, and damask, cloth of gold and silk draping the rails, and the sailors in scarlet uniforms, and all the ships standing to one another in such perfect order as to remind those who saw it of the buildings of a city, and the music of silver trumpets coming from the ships as they sailed.

To recruit the Indies fleets, a public crier and his musicians went from town to town, mostly in Andalusia that bordered on the sea. The drums rolled in the plaza, the fifes whistled a bright tune, calling a crowd. Then the crier bawled out his news. He told the sailing date of the next fleet, how great the ships were, some of one hundred twenty tons burden and sixty feet long, how skilled the captains, what opportunities oversea awaited the able-bodied young man between twenty-five and thirty years of age with a taste for adventure and good pay. And many a youth saw in his mind the great lands lifting over the ocean, with their Amazons who invited and broke men, and the golden treasuries waiting to be shipped home, and shapeless but powerful thoughts of how a fortune waited only to be seized, and a fellow's excellence recognized, his body given content, his pride matched with hazard, his dearness to himself made dear to all whom he should newly encounter. Many answered the fifes, the drums, and the crier. But if the recruitment was not great enough under the regulations which forbade signing on heretics and foreigners, then the merchant marine took on Jews, Moors, Frenchmen, Italians, Englishmen, Scotchmen, Germans, for the fleets had to sail and men had to sail them.

They sailed twice a year from Seville, in April and August, after three inspections held in the Guadalquivir. Crewmen signed on in the ship's register, took an oath of loyalty to the captain or the owner, and were bound for the voyage. Some were paid by the month, some by the mile, some with shares in the cargo. A sailor could not go anywhere without the commander's consent, and unless in port for the winter could not even undress himself without permission. If he did so, he was punished by being ducked in the sea three times at the end of a rope from the yardarm. The crew's rations left them hungry enough at times to catch rats and eat them. The ship provided beef, pork, rice, fish, spices, flour, cheese, honey, anchovies, raisins, prunes, figs, sugar, quinces, olive oil and wine, but in poor quantities, and very little water. The officers fared better, dining apart.

The passengers prepared their own meals out of the stores they had brought along, mostly hardtack and salted beef. They were almost always thirsty. Some slept on deck, some in little cabins five feet square, on mats stuffed with a thin layer of doghair, and under a blanket of worked goatskin. Below decks all day it was nearly dark. They could hear cockroaches and rats at restless work, and feel lice multiplying. There was no place in which to walk around. They could only lie down or sit, day and night. In storm the alcázar at the stern swayed as if to fall off the ship, and the blunt prows under their heavy castle shook like shoulders burrowing into the deep. The pumps at work spewed up bilge water as sickening as the air below decks, and all remained above whenever possible—the pilot navigating, the captain inspecting the artillery and other defenses, the master of the treasure that was packed in the hold, the cargo-master, the barber-surgeon, the caulker, the engineer, the cabin boys, the seamen.

But on busy days when the weather was blessed, the company was busy with interests. So long as they lasted uneaten, cocks were set to fighting on deck for an audience that took sides and made bets. A young fellow would become a bull and another would pretend to fight him with cape and sword. Clever people got up plays and gave them. Others sang ballads to the music of the vihuela. Others read poetry aloud or improvised rhymes about the people on board. There were always some who brought the latest books printed by the Crombergers of Seville, and sat reading by the hour. The fleet might be becalmed, and then boys and men went over the side to swim near the ships. And when the wind came alive again, the painted sails swelled out, and the hulls leaned, and their sodden timbered breasts pushed heavily against the waves, while the cabin boy sang out the devotions of praise and thanks, "Amen: God give us a happy voyage, may the ships make a good passage, captain, master, and your lordships, good day my lords, from stern to prow," and at evening they cried, "Evening chow, ready now," and "Long live the King of Castile on land and sea," and all bowed and said "Amen."

So they sailed and were sailed, taking two to three months to come to New Spain, where, like Juan Ponce de León, when he saw Florida, they said, "Gracias le sean dadas, Señor, que me permites contemplar algo nuevo," giving thanks to God that He granted them to see the new.

And some amongst them feeling if they could not speak the wonder of the New World, where dangers and hardships in the end bound them more closely to her than easy victories ever could have, exclaimed in their hearts, with love, in their various ways, "Oh, Virgin of the World, innocent America!"

That the Spaniards take her lawfully, with care, and with conscience, the Spanish kings of the Golden Age worked without cease.

iv. the king and father

Not all Spaniards had seen the King, but in every large company there was always one who had seen him, or knew someone who served him closely, and remembered much to tell. Anything they could hear of the King was immensely interesting and important. He was their pride even as he was their master. He commanded them by the power of God, and yet as they were so was he, a man, their common image, but with the glory and dignity of the crown over his head, and so, over theirs. What he was had greatly to do with what they were, as in all fatherhood. So, his image passed through them to the Indies, wherever they went, beyond cities and maps, however far along remote rivers. Even the gossip about great kings created the character of their subjects.

King Charles, who was also the Holy Roman Emperor, lived and worked in hard bare rooms with no carpets, crowding to the fire in winter, using the window's sunshine in summer. The doctors of medicine stated that the humors of moisture and of cold dominated his quality. His face was fixed in calm, but for his eyes, that moved and spoke more than his gestures or his lips. His face was pale and long, the lower lip full and forward, often dry and cracked so that he kept on it a green leaf to suck. His nose was flat and his brows were pitted with a raised frown that appeared to suggest a constant headache. He held his shoulders high as though on guard. He would seem to speak twice, once within and fully, and then outwardly and meagrely. But his eyes showed his mind, brilliant, deep and always at work. He loved information for its own sake, was always reading, and knew his maps well. They said he saw the Indies better than many who went there, and held positive views on all matters concerning the New World and its conquerors.

But if his opinions were strong, so was his conscience. He said once that it was his nature to be obstinate in sticking to his opinions. A courtier replied that it was but laudable firmness to stick to good opinions. To this the Emperor observed with a sigh that he sometimes stuck to bad ones. Much contemplation rested behind such a remark. He was in poor health for most of his life, and as a result considered himself in many aspects. In his young days he was a beautiful rider, with his light legs and his heavy lifted shoulders. He once liked to hunt bear and boar; but illness and business put an end to it. He worked all day and much of the night, until his supper at midnight, at which he received ambassadors, who were amazed at his appetite. Matters of state went on even then, by candlelight, as the platters were passed, and the baskets of fruit, and the water bowls. He wore his flat black cap, his black Flemish velvet doublet and surcoat with the collar of Germany-dressed marten skins, and his chain of the Golden Fleece. The letters of Cortés from New Spain had good talk in them, and the Emperor later had them published in print.

Whether or not America, so far away, was a matter of policy instead of feeling, Charles required justice for the Indians of the New World. Before 1519 he was sending people to the Indies to study and report to him upon the conditions of the natives. Uppermost was his desire that their souls be saved through Christianity. It was of greater moment that Indians became Christians than that they became Spaniards. So as the conquerors made cities in the New World they made schools, colleges and universities for the Indians, in which to teach them—often in Latin but more often in the Indian tongues which the friars learned rapidly—salvation in Christ. The Emperor held that through such salvation all else of life must naturally take its course and would come. He strongly supported the missioners in the Indies, and inspired them and many laymen to build the Church in the New World even as ominous cracks ran up its walls in the Old.

But from the first, and increasingly, another spirit worked against the Indians. The military, the landowners, the civil officials believed that conversion was a proper thing, but once out of the way, let the natives be useful to them in labor and arms. But the priests meant what they preached, just as much as the men of the world meant what they ordered. Both said they served the Crown as it desired to be served. Both appealed to the King.

His Holy Caesarian Catholic Majesty (for so he was addressed in documents) wished to know an all-determining truth. Was the Indian a man, as many claimed? Or was he an animal, as many others insisted? Could he understand Christianity? Did he deserve better than the yoke of slavery?

Commissions investigated, passions rose, and humanity triumphed. The Cardinal Adrian in Spain preached that the Indians were free and must be treated as free men, and given Christianity with Christian gentleness. The Emperor acted, and the laws for the Indies were decreed in that spirit. The Crown gave its approval to the ideals of the missionary priests who ever afterward, over new land, went with the armies not only to convert but to protect Indians.

When he left Spain for Germany, and after his retirement from the throne in mid-century, the Emperor kept the problem in mind, for he wrote to his son Prince Philip to caution him that he must be vigilant to prevent oppressions and injustices in the Colonies, saying that only through justice were sound business and prosperity possible. It was a cold and impassive statement of policy, but in it (as in the brilliant black and white flash of those eyes in his pallid face that found it so difficult otherwise to express itself) true humanity shone behind expediency.

When the Emperor abdicated to become a country gentleman at Yuste near Placencia, there was still much to hear about him, even as he invented ways to pass the time. He made a garden. He designed and fashioned mechanical works, including a hand mill to grind meal, and a marvellous set of little clockwork soldiers that performed military drills. Visitors brought him watches and clocks upon which he delighted to work. The joke went around that one time when he complained of his food, he was told by the majordomo that the only thing that would please his palate then would be a stew of watches. He laughed heartily at this.

From his early days in the Italian campaigns he loved the arts of music and painting. In his military travels, even to Africa, he took along his choir—the best choir in Europe—and pipe organs. His ear was true, he remembered music as well as he did facts, and he loved to sit and listen to a French air, *Mille regrets*. At Placencia he had his nine favorite paintings by Titian with him.

With a few guests in his party, he would go wandering through the woods with his harquebus in hand, watching for game. But the joy he took from this sport in his old age was more that of watching birds, and little animals, and their quick mysterious commerce, than that of killing them. He would shoot now and then, but his friends said that the pigeons pretended out of courtesy to be frightened of his blasts, and perhaps he was an old man hunting for life, not death.

But his piety kept death before him. He was read aloud to from the *Confessions of Saint Augustine,* and he could nod in recognition of anybody who turned sharply away from the great world to lead a modest life of outer trifles and inner mysteries of faith and conscience. It was talked of everywhere, for thousands were there, when he had a Requiem Mass sung to rehearse his own funeral. It was just as though it were the actual funeral. There before the altar was the catafalque swept in black draperies and silver lace, with thousands of candles burning at all the altars and shrines, and the prelates and priests singing the pontifical Mass, and the Emperor's wonderful music in the stalls with the organ, and there in the middle of it wearing a black mantle was the Emperor himself, praying for the repose of his soul before it left his body.

The Spaniards knew the same thing in themselves—the strength and the countenance to stare upon contrition and death. For, in their belief, what could anyone do enough to mortify himself, if he was to be worthy of salvation by the sufferings of the Son of Man upon the cross? The Emperor had a flail with which he would whip himself so hard that the thongs showed his blood. After his death it became known that in his will he left this flail to his son Philip, for him to prize all his life and in his turn to pass on as a beloved heirloom, a relic of the blood of the father. . . .

Philip II spared himself no less, and left his image no less in the Indies, though in somewhat different manner. People missed the occasional humor and grace of the Emperor, even though under him they had had to work just as hard as under his son. But there was as it were a darkening of life that came when the Emperor retired and, dying in retirement, left all power to the new King. But the King demanded more of himself than of anyone else. New Spain and all the other Indies became greater, quieter, richer, and as the conquests receded, the work of government grew enormously. The whole world wrote to Spain. Her ships carried not only the treasure of the New World, they took also reports, contracts, budgets, petitions, court records, confidential intelligence, complaints and all manner of papers to Madrid. And there, the

King himself read them, all of them, and marked his wishes upon their margins.

Secretaries came to him in the morning as he dressed, and after dinner at midday, and again to spend the long evening, while he dictated, initialled, weighed, decided; held in abeyance, revived for discussion, or postponed again; examined for policy or referred for further study dozens, and hundreds, and tens of thousands of papers through a lifetime of late-working nights. Besides all that, there were the endless committees to receive, who sat through hours of giving all aspects proper consideration. Minutes of such meetings were kept, and, doubling the ecstasy of administrative indulgence, could always be referred to later. It was a poor business if anyone sought to relieve the King of any small details of his official burden. Some of the best men in the land were called to court for appointment to important posts, and then denied the use of their faculties of originality and initiative. No detail was too small to interest the King. If he was King and was to sign, then what he signed must be exquisitely proper; and he would put all the power, weight and style of his office into a debate upon the nicety of a word to employ in a certain phrase to be written down in a state paper. He would refuse to be hurried, but would spend himself twice over on a matter rather than settle it out of hand. Don Pedro Ponce de León (he was Governor Oñate's most serious rival for the appointment) wrote to the King from Mexico asking for the command of the entry into New Mexico to colonize the Rio del Norte, and as the ocean passage of letter and reply would take eight months more or less, he expected to hear nothing for a while. But time passed, and no answer came to him from the King, whereupon he wrote again, begging in all respect for a reply to his earlier petition. The reply when it came said, "Tell him it will take a year to decide."

There was much to decide at home. The King saw with sorrow the disorderly and frivolous nature of the populace, and, asking less actually of them than of himself, issued decrees of prohibition upon conduct, possessions and belief. It was unseemly and therefore forbidden by royal edict to wear luxurious dress; to live amidst lavish surroundings; to use private carriages or coaches except under certain stated conditions; to employ courtesy titles; to seek education beyond the frontiers of Spain; to open the mind to the inquiries of science; or otherwise fail in proper humility and self-discipline. It was a grief to Philip that despite his endless efforts to guide his great family of subjects in ways of piety and decorum all manner of license grew and continued. Rich and clever people found ways to evade the laws, while poor people could not even qualify under them to commit the crimes of indulgence they forbade. Orders might come in a stream of papers from the palace, but Madrid remained a mudhole, the filthy streets choked with carriages and palanquins, bearing rich ladies who accosted men unknown to them, and of whom they invited proposals of shame. How could this be in a land where women were previously sacred and guarded within the family walls as the very Moors had done before them?

How could it be when any man worked so hard that he should be visited with so many sorrows and reverses? The King bent his head and spoke of the will of God. There were endless tales of his natural piety, that sustained him in the hours of humiliation that came to Spain. The Dutch wars went against the Spanish forces. They were defeated in France. The English under an infidel Queen broke Spain's greatest fleet and a year later raided, burned and robbed Cádiz, Spain's richest city. Spanish ships were attacked homeward bound from the Indies. The King suffered all with courage, determined to be an example to all in adversity, that they might keep their faith. He declared that it was better not to reign at all than to reign over heretics. Of these there were not many, then, and those few learned or vanished, though the question remained whether the delicate seed of faith that could grow to such mighty power could truly prosper through the habits of brutality of all agencies of discipline, such as the army, the constabulary, the office of the Inquisition, and the law courts alike. And still the King worked, writing orders to govern how many horses and servants a man could maintain with seemliness; how funerals should be conducted, and how weddings; what public amusements might be countenanced and what not. And while he slaved at concerns so alarming and dear to him, there went unanswered pleas from his ambassadors overseas and viceroys desperate for Crown policies ("tell him it will take a year"), and groaning supplications from fiscal officers who expected mutinies unless the armies were paid.

How could a man's goodness be so crushing?

Those who saw him come to the throne saw his father's son, in the tall forehead, the vivid black and white eyes, the lower lip permanently outthrust. Even then, as a young man, there was no mark of humor in his face, which was furrowed beside the nose and under the cheekbone. Yet it was a head of grace and distinction, lean above the ruffed collar of Brabant linen, and the puffed doublet worked in gold. His beard and hair, that had a little wave in it, were a golden brown.

And then those who saw him long later saw a heavy face, with sallow color, and sacs about the eyes, now smaller and heavier-lidded. His dress was different, he wore a tall black cap and black garments relieved only by the starch-white of his collar. His spirit was heavy, too, and sallow, if souls had color. The feature most unchanged in his face was the deep cleft between his eyes, that made a scowl of abnegation natural to him in youth when he first renounced so much for himself, and that cut deeper in age, when he renounced so much in their own lives for others.

An image of his quality was the palace of the Escorial which he built on the sweeping plain outside Madrid, below the mountains. It was as big as a palisaded mesa. The plain was as barren as a desert. In New Spain and New Mexico was much country of which that was the miniature. The palace rose in a great square of ochreous gray walls. It was so vast that human silence seemed a very part of its design. What no man could see but which the profuse flocks of little martins and swallows could see as they circled over it was that within the great square stood inner walls, crisscrossing one another in the form of a gridiron or grill. It was believed that this was built in imitation and endless reminder of the grill upon which St. Lawrence met his death. Thus Philip could have constant point for contemplation. Within the palace the long corridors that followed the lines of the grill were low and narrow, showing the bare granite of their walls. The floors were of unfinished stone. Coming in from even a hot summer's day the courtier met indoors the chill of the tomb. The palace was so made that a great portion of its internal volume was taken by a dark church whose dome and towers rose above the enclosing walls. The King's own bedroom, a cell, was placed so that he could look out from it through an indoor window and see the Mass at the high altar, which was just below. Church, monastery, palace and tomb, that tenebrous heart of the Empire expressed in all its purposes the sacred and profane obsessions of the King its builder.

And if the monarch had his palatial rack designed after a saint's, the soldiers, the traders, the shopmen, the scholars, the voyagers of Spain each had his Escorial of the soul, where to endure the joys and the pains of his spiritual exercises he entered alone and in humility.

Perhaps the deeper a man's humility in the privacy of his soul, the more florid his pride in public. All Spaniards, high or low, could use a spacious manner. Its principal medium was the Spanish language. Not many could read; but all could speak like lords or poets. The poorest soldier in the farthest outlandish expedition of New Mexico might be a chip floating beyond his will on the stream of history, but still he could make an opinion, state it with grace and energy, and even, in cases, make up a rhyme for it. He spoke his mind through a common language that was as plain and clear as water, yet able to be sharp as a knife, or soft as the moon, or as full of clatter as heels dancing on tile. Like Latin, from which it came, it needed little to say what it meant. It called less upon image and fancy than other tongues, but made its point concretely and called forth feelings in response to universal commonplaces rather than to flights of invention. With that plain strength, the language yet could show much elegance, and such a combination—strength with elegance—spoke truly for the Spaniards and of them. The Emperor once said that to speak to horses, the best tongue to use was German; to talk with statesmen, French; to make love, Italian; to call the birds, English; and to address princes, kings, and God, Spanish. In the time of Cicero the Spanish town of Córdoba was famous for two things, its poetry and its olive oil. He said the poetry sounded as though it were mixed with the oil.

v. arts

A passion for study filled the century of the Golden Age. In Spain, thirty-four universities were at work, and others were founded in the New World within a few years of the conquest. The German Jacob Cromberger and his sons established their printing house at Seville in 1500, reading became an indispensable part of living, and all because a complicated machine held together many rows of reversed little metal letters and pressed them into damp paper, again and again, until many copies of the same words and ideas were at hand. Because her language went everywhere with Spain's power, printers in Italy, France, the Netherlands and the Indies printed books in Spanish.

Everything found its way into print, even the ballads that previously passed through generations by word of mouth. People made them up in inns and on travels and marching in wars, telling droll stories or love stories or wicked scandals, and the rude narratives were sung wherever somebody had an instrument to pluck. Seeing how such efforts looked in print, men of letters began to write ballads in the style of the old popular ones, that had gone always changing as one man's memory revised the residue of another's. The new poetic ballads sang of the courts of chivalry; imaginary histories that revealed Spanish ideals of noble kingship, knightly valor, reverence for womanhood and death to monsters. True histories were also written in rhyme, long chronicles of heroes, as when Captain Pérez de Villagrá, the alumnus of the University of Salamanca, sat down to write the history of Oñate's first year on the Rio del Norte, he wrote it in heroic verse. The Spanish world grew not only in range but also in meaning as the people saw its likeness in all that was made by writers and artists.

As his father the Emperor admired Titian of Venice, so King Philip admired and employed Domenico Theotocopuli, known as The Greek, who came from Greece by way of long studies and labors in Venice and Rome. He was a learned man and a pious one, and for the Escorial and churches elsewhere he painted many pictures that swept the eye and mind of the beholder upward to heaven. Often even the very eyes of the kings and saints he painted were gazing heavenward and shining with great diamond tears of desire, and seeing them so, the beholder cast his desires upward also. The skies of his pictures of martyrdoms and sufferings and triumphs were like the skies of Good Friday afternoon, torn apart and blowing aloft in black and white clouds through which the Spanish temperament could see the immortal soul of Christ as it flew to His Father from the cross. The Greek painted many likenesses of people of circumstance, who without their starch and black velvet and swords, their armor and ribbons, or their violet mantelletas and trains, would have looked very much like everybody else in the Spanish populace, even those on the northern river of the latest and farthest Crown colony. All countenances which he limned were grave and melancholy, even that of the Madonna in the Nativity. The Spaniards were a people who did not often smile, but more often laughed outright or possessed their faces in calm, when most faces look sad. The Greek was much seen at Toledo, where he painted the town many times, making odd changes in exactly how it looked, yet by so doing, making the city's image combine with the beholder's feeling to produce a rise of the soul.

It was the same rise that Spaniards knew from music in the High Mass, when the dark high vaults of the church where candlelight never reached would be filled with the singing of choirs, plain, without instruments. They heard the masses composed by the great Tomás Luís de Victoria of Ávila, and Cristóbal of Morales, and Francisco Guerrero. The voices of boys came like shafts of heaven, and in the polyphonic style,

the voices of men rose under them and turned with melody, and the
two qualities met and divided, the one qualifying the other, now with
one long note held against several notes in a figure, again with highs
against lows, and again with syllables against whole words, and loud
against soft, so that in heavenly laws known to music alone an experience of meaning and delivery struck all who truly listened, and the
stone arches and the drift of incense and the possibility of divinity in
mankind and the Mass at the altar all became intermingled with the
soul that rose. How, lost in dark choir stalls under lofting stone, could
boys, having yet had so little of life, strike so purely to the darkest self
with their shining voices that seemed to come from beyond all flesh?

And there was other music that used the very flesh itself, spoke
to it, enlivened it, cozened it with coarse jokes, and pulled its nose and
made the hearers laugh and clap and stamp their feet. It was heard at
the inns, in public squares, and in the theatres, when ballads were sung
or skits and plays given by actors and dancers. They came out on a stage
bringing sackbuts, or dulcimers, harps, lutes or vihuelas, or combinations
of all these, and struck up a tune to which they sang a story with many
verses. They plucked, beat, blew and nodded together, and often repeated
with each verse a clever effect in which one musician gave a little variation at the same place each time, so that the audience listened for it
in following verses. Such players entertained anyone who called for them
and displayed a coin. They went from one tavern to another, ready to
stand in a half-circle facing a table and play to a private party much to
the advantage of any others in the place. Their music went with the
Spaniards wherever in the world they might go.

If popular balladry was the poor man's comfort, there was much
to sing about as the world moved and poor times befell Spain in her
might. Great fortunes shrank, and the high state of many nobles lost
its quality because it could not be paid for, and wage earners found their
coins worth very little, and poor people lived always hungry. It was
the very outpourings of wealth from the new world that caused such
trouble. When so much more gold than usual came to be circulated,
each little coin or bit of gold spent in trade was worth much less than
usual, as gold itself became too common. In giving civilization to the
New World, Spain seemed to give up its own strength as the new land
found the lusty power to grow by itself. In the home kingdom, while
all graces were maintained, the substance behind them shrank, and for
great numbers of Spaniards the graces which they aired came to be
pretensions and little else.

vi. style and hunger

And yet there was that in the Spanish spirit which made of each Spaniard his own castle, and it was very like them all that as the wealth that sustained public nobility began to shrink, and as every hidalgo by birth disdained to reveal his poor estate, so many another man who had no title or claim to nobility adopted the airs and styles of the hidalgo, until the land became a parade of starving lords, real and false, who the lower they fell in worldly affairs, the more grandly they behaved. Going hungry, they would loll against a wall in public, picking their teeth to convince the passer-by that they had just dined on sweet carrots and turnips, sharp cheese, pungent bacon, fresh eggs, crusty roast kid, tart wine from Spanish grapes, and a covered dish of baked gazpacho, that was made out of wheat bread, olive oil, vinegar, onions, salt, and red peppers hot enough to make the eyes water.

There was little else for such a gentleman to do. If he had talents that could be employed, there was hardly anybody to pay him for them. He was a man of honor and to make a living could not stoop to improper ways, which no matter how hard the times seemed always to prosper. If his shanks were thin and bare, and his sitting bones almost showed in his threadbare breeches, and his belly was puffy with windy hunger, then he still had his ragged cloak to throw about such betrayals. Within his cloak he could stand a noble stance, and at a little distance, who was the wiser? As the proverb said, "Under a bad cloak there may hide a good drinker," which gave comfort to fallen swagger; and to comfort the dream of impossible valor, there spoke another proverb, saying, "Under my cloak I kill the king."

But no patch ever failed to show, however lovingly stitched, even a patch on a man's pride. To cloak his spirit, the mangy gentleman had another sort of possession left to him from his better days. This was the high thought of chivalry, that gave to human life, all human life, so great a dignity and such an obligation of nobility on behalf of all other persons. There was a poor sweetness in this extravagant spending of spirit, that the more a man lacked simply to keep him alive, the more he disdained his own trouble and grandly swore to demolish the trouble of another. In his ironic self-knowledge the Spaniard knew such men, and smiled at the antic capers they cut in their hungry pretensions. And yet he bowed to their spirit which stated that "he is only worth more than another who does more than another." It was no surprise to him that a champion should vow the rescue of anyone in distress, without reference to rank or station. If there were different levels of life, then one man in his own was worth as much as another in his, and was free to state as much, and act accordingly. And as every soul originated in God, and so was equal to every other in worth, so its offerings on earth deserved succor without discrimination. The Spaniard knew that the grandeur of God did not disdain the humblest surroundings, and could say with Saint Teresa of Ávila, *Entre los pucheros anda el Señor*—God moves among the kitchen pots.

But all came back to hunger. Private soldiers who went to the Americas were experienced in that condition. It was a marvel how far they could march, how hard they could fight, and how long they could cling to unknown country on empty stomachs. Nuñez Cabeza de Vaca, Coronado's soldiers, Castaño de Sosa pillaging at Pecos, Zaldívar crawling over deserts toward the river, all gnawed on tradition when rations were low. Certainly the adventurers did not enlist for the pay, for the pay was meagre and always in arrears, even that owed to the commanders in silver-gilt armor. Nor did they venture forth for commerce as it could affect the ordinary individual, for the risks were too great for uncertain profits, and in any case the Spanish gift for business fulfilled itself not in the largest but in the smallest affairs, face to face with another man. For the pleasures of business were firstly social—little exchanges of desire and deceit, indifference and truth, the study of human nature, the flourish of bargaining, the satisfaction of the righteous swindle, in buyer and seller alike. Nor was it inordinate love of adventure that took Spaniards past oceans and shores, and up the river, for adventure could be had anywhere, even at home. Perhaps more than any one other motive it was a belief in their own inherent greatness that took the men of the Golden Age to their achievements in geography and colonization.

For to them it was finer to make greatness than to inherit it; and after they made it, they could in all justice cry with the True Chronicler of the conquest of Mexico, "I say again that I—I, myself—I am a true conqueror; and the most ancient of all . . . and I also say, and praise myself thereon, that I have been in as many battles and engagements as, according to history, the Emperor Henry the Fourth." In such spirit, what they did with so little, they did with style.

vii. the swords

Even the swords that were extensions not only of their right arms but also of their personalities came out of humble means through fire and water to strength and beauty. Ovid sang the praises of Toledo blades, the best of which were made of old used metal, such as horseshoes. The Spaniard's sword was born at nighttime, through fire, of a river and the south wind.

In the city hall of Toledo the master steelworkers—Sahagún the Elder, Julian del Rey, Menchaca, Hortuño de Aguirre, Juanes de la Horta—kept their metal punches when these were not in use to stamp the maker's name on a new blade. Every blade had its *alma,* and this soul was the core of old iron on whose cheeks were welded new plates of steel. Standing ready were the two gifts of the river Tagus that flowed below the high rocks of Toledo. These were its white sand and its clear water. The blades were born only in the darkest nights, the better to let the true or false temper of the steel show when red-hot; and of the darkest nights, only those when the south wind blew, so that in passing the blade from fire to water it might not cool too rapidly as a north wind would cool it. The clumsy weld was put into the coals where the bellows hooted. When it came red-hot the master took it from the fire. It threw sparks on meeting the air. Casting river sand on it which extinguished the sparks, the master moved to the anvil. There with taps of hammer and sweeps of the steel against the anvil he shaped the blade, creating a perfectly straight ridge down the center of each side, until squinted at endwise the blade looked like a flattened lozenge. Now the blade was put again into the fire and kept there until it began to color again, when the master lifted it into the darkness to see if it showed precisely cherry-red. If so, it was ready for the river. There stood handy a tall wooden pail filled with water from the Tagus. Into this, point down, went the blade for its first immersion. To keep the exact right time for each immersion, and to bring blessings, the master or one of his boys sang during the first one, "Blessed be the hour in which Christ was born," and then the blade was lifted out. Heated again, it was returned to the water, and they sang, "Holy Mary, Who bore Him!" and next time they sang, "The iron is hot!" and the next, "The water hisses!" and the next, "The tempering will be good," and the last, "If God wills."

Then once more the blade went to the fire, but this time only until it became dull red, liver-colored. Then with pincers the master held it by the tang which would later fit into the hilt, and had the boy smear the blade with raw whole fat cut from the sac about the kidneys of a male goat or a sheep. The fat burst into flame. They took the blade to the rack and set it there against the wall point downward. The fat burned away, the blade darkened and cooled through several hours. In daytime they sharpened and polished it, and if it was to bear an inscription, it went to the bench of the engraver, who chiselled his letters on one of the flat faces, or perhaps both, spelling out a pious or patriotic motto, like one on a sword found in Texas not far from the Rio Grande, that read, on one side, "POR MY REY," and on the other, "POR MY LEY," thus swearing protection to king and law. The hilt, with guard and grip, then was joined to the tang, and those for plain soldiers were of well-turned iron, but without inlays of gold or silver, or studdings of smooth jewels, or wrappings with silver-gilt wire that variously went onto the swords of officers and nobles.

And at last the maker sent for his stamp from the city hall and let his device be punched into the blade at its thickest part near the guard, and the proud work was done, and the Spanish gesture could be sharpened and elongated across the world.

viii. soul and body

Both within the Spaniard and without him lay the country which Lope de Vega called "sad, spacious Spain." If Spaniards enacted their literature, it was because, like all people, they both created literature and were created by it. So it was with memories and visions in the colony of the river wilderness. Their hopes of what to be were no less full of meanings than their certainties of what they had done, and both found their center of energy in a moral sense that gave a sort of secret poetry to the hard shape of life. The Spaniard was cruel but he loved life, and his melancholy brutality seemed to issue forth almost involuntarily through the humanitarian laws and codes with which he surrounded himself. If his nature was weak his conscience was strong, and if he sinned his first act of recovery must be to recognize his guilt. When one of the most brutal of the conquerors of the New World was dying of wounds given to him by Indians he was asked where he ached, and he replied, "In my soul."

So the baggage of personality brought by the colonists told of their origin, their faith, the source of their power, the human types by which they perpetuated their tradition; and forecast much about how they would live along the river.

But in that very summer of 1598 when the newest colony of the Spanish Empire was settling on the Rio del Norte in northern New Mexico, the Empire was already ailing. Its life stream carried human tributaries to the river, but already at its source, in Madrid, the springs of Spanish energy were starting to go low. It was an irony of history that just as the American continent was being comprehended, the first great power that sought it began to lose the force to possess it. It would take two more centuries for the flow to become a trickle that barely moved and then altogether stopped. But the Spanish effectiveness in government, society and commerce began to lose power in the New World with the failure of life in the last of the kings of the Golden Age.

Laboring inhumanly to govern his world-wide kingdoms for goodness and prosperity, Philip II left them a complicated legacy of financial ruin, bureaucratic corruption and social inertia. After a dazzling conjugation of *to do,* the destiny of Spain seemed to turn toward a simple respiration of *to be.* One was as true of the Spanish temperament as the other.

If Philip left to his peoples anything in the way of a true inheritance, one that expressed both him and them, and that would pass on through generations, it was his example in adversity, his patience facing a hideous death, and his submission to the will of God.

He lay through the summer of 1598 in the Escorial holding the crucifix that his father the Emperor had held on his own deathbed. The son in an agony of suppurating tumors repeatedly gnawed upon the wood of the cross to stifle his groans. His truckle bed was run close to the indoor window through which he could look down upon the big altar of the Escorial church. In the early mornings he could hear the choir singing in the dark stalls and watch the Holy Sacrifice of the Mass performed for the repose of his soul whose liberation was nearing. But it came slowly. On August 16 he received the pontifical blessing from Rome. A fortnight later he took the last sacraments, and afterward spoke alone to his son and heir on the subject of how reigns ended and crowns passed and how instead came shrouds and coarse cinctures of rope in which to be buried. For days and nights the offices of the dying were chanted by priests in his cell. If momentarily they paused, he whispered, "Fathers, continue, the nearer I come to the fountain, the greater my thirst." Before four in the morning on September 13 he asked for a blessed candle to hold. Its calm light revealed a smile on his face. His father's crucifix was on his breast; and when he gasped faintly three times, and died, and was enclosed in a coffin made of timbers from the *Cinco Chagas,* a galleon that had sailed the seas for him, the crucifix was still there. By his will the blood-crusted flail left to him by his father now passed to the new ruler, King Philip III. In the austere grandeurs of such a scene the deathly luxuries of the Spanish temperament, as well as the dying fall of the Empire, found expression. At San Juan de los Caballeros, in the valley of the Rio del Norte, near the junction with the Chama, where willows and cottonwoods along bench terraces of pale earth all imaged the end of summer, the Crown's new colony was at work on a matter of enduring importance to their settlement. By order of Governor de Oñate they were already building their church.

19.

Duties

It was a dry summer. Late in August, 1598, the Governor was at his mess table one day when he heard unearthly wailing from many voices. He sent an officer to inquire who returned to report that the Indians were making lamentations to their gods because there had been no rain, in spite of the many dances for rain that the pueblo had performed during the summer. It was already very late, and the crop of corn would wither and die and the people would hunger unless rain came. Through four centuries it was a familiar condition along the river in certain years.

The Father President and his assistant Fray Cristóbal spoke to the Indians and calmed them, saying that he and his brothers would offer prayers to God that rain might come and the corn be saved. An officer heard the promise, and sarcastically remarked that the Indians ceased their frightful wailing immediately, "like little children who hush when they are given the things they have cried for." All the rest of the day, and that night, and the following day, the Indians watched the sky, which was "as clear as a diamond," until suddenly it rained. Torrents fell. They were moved and awed. The corn was saved.

But the Indians were not the only residents of San Juan who showed dissatisfaction and fear on occasion. Some forty-five soldiers and officers, including Captain de Aguilar who had once had his life spared by the Governor's clemency, felt aggrieved on several counts. The Governor was aware of their feelings. They had come expecting to get rich, and they were not rich. He said, with his heavy irony, that they expected to find whole platters of silver lying on the ground waiting to be picked up. Failing that, they were not even allowed to take what they liked of the Indian properties, or do as they wished with the Indian persons. They were disgusted with the country, or, said the Governor, "to be more exact, with me," and they resolved to mutiny and desert the colony, stealing slaves and clothing in their flight. The plot failed. The Governor put Aguilar and two soldiers in arrest, and condemned them to die by the garrote. It was a shocking event with which to begin life in the new capital, and once again, as at the entrance to the Dead Man's March, down the river, the Governor was entreated to pardon the condemned.

Life was as easily spared as taken. He consented, ordered a week of jubilee, and work on the church was hastened, and on the eighth of September, the first Mass was sung before San Juan's own altar. The heads of all the pueblos had been invited to the celebrations. A messenger had visited them all in their provinces, carrying with him the Governor's diary, which the Indian chiefs acknowledged as his emblem of office—the pages bearing the marks of his own hands. All had accepted the Governor's invitation but the chief of Ácoma, who chose to be represented in another way. He sent spies who lost themselves among the other Indians but saw everything.

The colonists gave a new comedy specially written for the feast (was Captain Farfán at work again?) and a mounted tournament was staged, and bullfights, and a pageant and sham battle representing the wars of the Moors and Christians, in which brave salvos of firearms were discharged, concluding with a "thunderous discharge of artillery"—but all with gunpowder without shot.

The Ácoma spies watched. How was it that though the soldiers fired, nobody fell and died? The firearms of the white men, though noisy and smoky, must be harmless. It was useful to Ácoma to know this. . . .

On the following day, September ninth, a solemn event was celebrated in the church. The Governor rose to address the chiefs of the Indian provinces. Behind him were the Father President and the other priests. As the Governor spoke the royal secretary noted down his words.

He spoke of his love for the Indian people, and came to them with a grave duty. He must tell of his Divine Lord, and the rewards of heaven, and the punishments of hell, that came to all according as they chose well or ill in the life of the world. But man needed guidance and was provided with God's ministers who could give it. To receive it, all must swear allegiance to the royal crown, and could never after withdraw. Many benefits of body and spirit would come to those who swore. Would they swear?

The Indian leaders would swear.

The secretary then prepared the necessary papers, and all were appropriately signed "amid great rejoicings."

Now the Father President came forward and proposed their salvation to them, in the name of "Christ, God and man, who died and was buried for the redemption of mankind." Would they be saved?

They considered, and presently gave their answer. First, they desired to be instructed in all he had proposed; and second, if they liked what they learned, they would gladly follow his teachings; but third, if they did not like them, it would not do to be forced to accept something they did not understand.

The example of the apostles was before the Franciscans. It was enough. The Father President, Fray Alonso Martinez, rededicated his brother Franciscans in their calling, and assigned to them one by one the parishes over which each would preside. He called them forward in turn:

"Father Fray Francisco de Miguel"—and to him gave the province of Pecos that lay beyond the mountains to the east, and included forty towns, the roving peoples of the cow plains, and the great salines where the Indians went for salt;

"Father Fray Juan Claros"—and to him, all the towns of the Tigua language along the Rio del Norte to the south in number close to sixty;

"Father Juan de Rosas"—the province of the Keres language, on the river and westward, excepting Ácoma, which was assigned to another parish;

"Father Fray Cristóbal de Salazar"—the Tewa towns to the north;

"Father Fray Francisco de Zamora"—the province of the Picuries, and Taos, and the river towns to the north, together with the Apaches north and east of the snowy mountains;

"Father Fray Alonzo de Lugo"—the Jemez province of nine towns and all the Apaches west of the river;

"Father Fray Andres Corchado"—the city of Ácoma on its rock, the Sia province, and the towns of the Zuñis and Hopis far to the west.

Each was to go alone with only Indians to his parish, which was so vast that it could contain mountain, desert and river, all three; and so far from the comfort of familiar life and reassuring knowledge common to all, that a journey of many days by horse or weeks on foot would be needed to bring the priest from his parish to the capital.

They prayed at San Juan, received their commissions and, guided by Indians who had attended the Governor's convocation, went forth into wilderness through their own human trepidation empowered by that which was greater than both.

Four other men left the colony soon after. They were horse thieves and deserters, unreconciled since the Aguilar mutiny. The Governor could not countenance insurrection and the loss of horses. He sent two captains, Pérez de Villagrá and Márques, to arrest the fugitives and bring them back. Expecting them to return in a day or two, the Governor waited at San Juan. But they did not come. He busied himself with organizing an expedition to go east to the buffalo plains, under the command of Vicente de Zaldívar, with "many droves of mares and other supplies," which departed on September sixteen, to look for all that nobody before them had ever found. September passed, and the first days of October, and still the fugitives had not been returned in arrest. The Governor could wait no longer. He was ready to go forth himself to visit the salines east of the mountains, and then turn west across the river and explore possible trails to the South Sea where there were certain to be pearls. He left orders. Pérez de Villagrá was to overtake him after arriving at San Juan with the prisoners. Juan de Zaldívar would stay at San Juan in command until his brother Vicente returned, and then turning over the command to him, would set out with a mounted squad and ride to meet the Governor in the west.

The Governor left San Juan de Nuevo Mexico (as he headed his letters) on October sixth.

20.

A Dark Day in Winter

The Zaldívar brothers were reunited on the eighth of November, when Vicente returned to San Juan after fifty-four days of travel to and from the buffalo plains. He had seen nothing that earlier travellers had not seen, but he was the first to try to capture the buffalo herds into cottonwood corrals which he built near a river. He could not take the cows and bulls, but calves were captured. He thought to domesticate and raise them. But they all "died of rage" within an hour. He brought none back.

Juan now set about arranging to leave with thirty soldiers to reinforce the Governor in the west. In a few days Captain Márques returned to the river capital from his long expedition with Pérez de Villagrá to overtake and bring back the four men who had stolen horses and flown in September. He was alone, for down the river at Puaray on the way back, he and Villagrá, coming home together, had met young Francisco de las Nievas, who said that the Governor had been there only the day before on his way west from the saline provinces. Villagrá believed he should join the Governor without delay, and saying good-bye to Márques, had struck westward alone across the river from Puaray to pick up the Governor's trail, going by way of Ácoma.

And the prisoners? Where were they?

Márques shrugged. Two had escaped. He and Villagrá had trailed the other two almost all the way to Santa Barbara on the Conchos River in Mexico, and on finding them, had taken such action as had seemed in the judgment of Villagrá, who was in authority, to be suitable. They had executed the prisoners, cutting off their heads, and dutifully had made haste to return, themselves, to San Juan. Captain Márques took up new duties under Vicente de Zaldívar at the capital.

In about the third week of November Juan took leave of his younger brother. Both wore beards the color of chestnuts. Juan was twenty-eight, Vicente twenty-five. Juan was the taller of the two, but both had good stature. They were from Zacatecas in Mexico. At the head of his thirty troopers Juan rode out and down the river. They were on their way to find the Governor in the western wilderness.

Cold was coming down the river from the northern mountains. Huge geese went south in great high flocks, making their hornlike calls that came muted to earth. Faster little ducks went plummeting south too, landing at times on the river like bullets, and talking in circles, and rising away again. Soldiers shot them as they could, and feasted the home garrison. On some mornings there was snow on the riverbanks, which made the brown water look darker than usual. Winter wood was being gathered to burn in the pueblo rooms, whose thick walls could hold cold or heat for so long. The river cottonwoods were heavy gold, keeping their leaves, and the bare willow groves looked from a little distance like smoke. Winter was coming and even in so open a valley cutting through such vast plains, there was a sense of days closing in, and vistas, as November passed and early December came crisply along in golden chilly days, so far away from other homes in other winters.

One day—it must have seemed ever afterward a dark day no matter what the weather—there returned to San Juan from a forced march on spent horses three exhausted soldiers who had gone out a few weeks before with Juan de Zaldívar. Vicente received them and stood as they told sorely what they knew. He was dazed. He crossed his arms on his breast and bowed his head; and then he groaned and began to sob.

The soldiers said that on December first they arrived with Juan de Zaldívar at the base of the rocks of Ácoma, under a cold, cloudy sky. The rock mesa was nearly four hundred feet high, from afar it looked like a palace, a fortress, a city, all of it; only on coming near could you see that the city was on the very top, a line of low clay houses against the sky. The walls of the mesa were cliffs, in all places but one, and there a trail led up through slopes of sand and finally it too became a cliff with toeholds cut in the stone. The Indians could swarm up and down the difficult approach like monkeys. They all came below to welcome everyone on that first of December, and when Zaldívar asked for food, they said that if he camped here below that night, he and everyone could ascend in the morning, and would be given provisions. So the soldiers made their camp and slept in peace.

In the morning they went up. It was awkward. They had to hang their swords behind. Armor was stiff and heavy to climb in. They were laughing and wheezing by the time they got over the edge and walked about on the high island of dusty red stone surrounded by an empty valley. They saw that Ácoma was made not of one rock but two, separated by a chasm of varying width. Down below they could see the horses and the squad of soldiers left to guard them. They looked like toys. The men on the rock turned and went into the town, guided by a chief, Zutucapan, who was all courtesy. Food, their needs, he indicated, would be taken care of at various houses, there, there, and there—and Zaldívar sent soldiers separately to the places indicated.

And as soon as they were separated, the soldiers were lost. A fearsome cry sounded over the stone plateau. It came from Zutucapan crying for battle. The Indians began to gather in menace. Zaldívar yelled with warning and encouragement to those few men remaining by him. They sprang their swords (". . . the tempering will be good . . .") and Zaldívar called out asking if they should retire to the plain below and later inflict punishment for treachery. One soldier objected. He said he would be glad to take on the Indian mob alone, and after he had disposed of it, see that the soldiers could then in their own good time leave the rock. There was a dead moment of wonder and indecision. It was a fateful pause. The Indians poured out of their housetops and streets and closed in. Zaldívar keeping the peace cried to his men to take aim but hold fire. But the Indians flew arrows, lances and even their wooden clubs at Zaldívar's small band, and the soldiers at his order fired. In another moment the fight was joined. Over a thousand Indians broke upon the soldiers in wild combat.

It lasted three hours.

Zaldívar was prodigious. His men fell wounded and dead and three jumped from the cliff and were killed and all fought who could in hand-to-hand combat, and one soldier with his belly ripped open as he died cut his enemy's body awide with his dagger so that the two men fell with their entrails mingling. Zaldívar fell three times only to rise and fight, until he fell forever, when the Indians stormed upon him and destroyed him obscenely. There were five soldiers left on top then, and seeing that Zaldívar was dead and mutilated they battled their way to the edge of the island and jumped out into the air, whether to live or die they didn't know.

One died striking rocks as he fell. The other four landed hundreds of feet below in long sand drifts against the base of the island. From the camp came the guard who had remained with the horses, and three soldiers who had already escaped from the rock. They revived the four who had jumped and all hurried to the camp. They made quick decisions. The survivors were divided into three parties, one to hurry westward to inform the Governor; one to take advice to the isolated fathers in their lonely missions to return with speed to the capital; and one to ride hard to San Juan de Nuevo Mexico to tell the colony.

Vicente de Zaldívar was in command at San Juan. He received the names of those killed at Ácoma. He went to the families and told them and comforted them. He ordered Requiem Masses for the faithful departed. The colony on the river was in mortal danger, and all knew it.

Presently came home the soldiers who had left Ácoma to over-take the Governor. They had not been able to find his trail. It was of the first importance that he hear immediately what had happened. Vicente de Zaldívar sent a new detachment to find him at all costs. They rode out immediately heavily armed. Nobody knew if the revolt would spread. The garrison at San Juan lived at the alert waiting for the Governor.

He arrived four days before Christmas with his troops, including Pérez de Villagrá. The Governor already had the news. The soldiers from the capital told how they had met him returning from his western explorations in a pleased frame of mind. In spite of having had reason to suspect disloyalty if not treachery at Ácoma on his way west in November, he had planned to spend the night there homeward bound. But the messengers with their awful news had saved him. In the open land by his camp they gave him a description of the massacre, for some of them had been there. He listened on horseback. When they were done, he dismounted and went to his knees and prayed aloud. Then in grief he walked to his tent, leading his horse, and ordered Pérez de Villagrá to make a rude cross of lashed branches. This was taken into his tent, where he asked to be left alone.

In the morning he ordered a formation and came out to speak to the men. His eyes were swollen and his face was haggard from lack of sleep. He had prayed all night for wisdom and guidance in the danger about them. Facing the soldiers he tried three times to speak, but could not, until at last he was able to say that they had all suffered a terrible loss in their comrades, who died martyrs. He spoke of dangers to come that must be met bravely, and he invoked their faith by saying that all knew it to be true that the more they suffered the greater would be their heavenly reward, and he placed all trust in God. He lifted up the soldiers' hearts.

With that he gave marching orders and the exploring party turned toward the capital. It snowed. They drank melted snow from their helmets. It was hard marching in December on the friendless plains.

When he arrived home the Governor found all turned out to wait for him. They were weeping. He went to them, and in silence embraced each one of his people. He then led them into the church where he greeted the friars with his embrace, and the Father President led the priests who chanted in chorus the Te Deum Laudamus in thanks for the Governor's safe return with his men.

The city of San Juan de Nuevo Mexico was in the form of a great square with four gates at which sentinels were now posted. All people carried arms. The Governor retired to his quarters and did not put away his belt and baldric, his sword and dagger, all night. He had a heavy decision to contemplate. Its basis in law was already, at his request, being considered by the Father President and the other friars.

21.

The Battle of Ácoma

He received their official opinion on the following day.

"What conditions," he had asked them, "are necessary in order to wage a just war? In the event of such a war, what steps may be taken against those warred upon and against their possessions?"

In reply to the first question the learned friars made several points.

To begin with, there must be authority to wage war, as in the cases of popes, emperors and kings, *and those acting in their stead.* The Governor was a delegate of the Crown. Plainly, he had authority.

And then there must be a just cause. The friars listed "to punish those who are guilty of wrongdoing, or have violated the laws of the land," which clearly covered the crime of treacherous insurrection. The friars added that the final just cause for war was to establish peace, "for peace is the principal object of war." The Governor could feel that he had more than one just cause.

Moreover, they stated, war must be waged with good faith, and without covetousness, malice, hate, or ambition for power. The Governor examined his conscience.

As to the second question, though several points were analyzed, the pertinent one seemed to be that about war against wrongdoers, and the opinion declared that "they and their possessions are at the mercy of their conqueror according to the laws of the land," and could be "treated by divine and civil law, as law and justice require," but any punishment visited upon the vanquished must be taken "to carry into effect the requirements of justice." The Governor noted this respect for due process.

Finally, said the friars, "as the purpose of war is to establish peace, then it is even justifiable to exterminate and destroy those who stand in the way of that peace."

The Governor could hear his duty clearly. If he had known doubt before he knew none now. He ordered public proclamation in the capital that "war by blood and fire" was declared against the Indians of Ácoma, and announced that he would himself lead the punitive army. Immediate protests of concern for his safety made him change his mind about taking personal command, and instead he named Vicente de Zaldívar to lead the return to Ácoma.

On the same day—December 22, 1598—a Requiem Mass was held for Juan de Zaldívar and all who had died with him. The cold, narrow, dark, clay church above the riverbanks resounded with the offices of the dead. It was, the church, as plain as a coffin and the spirit of all there that day filled it with fierce thoughts and prayers upon the reality of death.

But three days later came the great feast of Christmas, and the birth of life and purity in the world. All worked hard, and rededicated themselves in the midst of hazard, loneliness and loss; and resolve grew with the preparations for war.

Seventy picked soldiers made up the army against Ácoma. Each had his coat of mail, double strength. They had shields which when not in use hung from the shoulder. The lancers carried many designs in their tall weapons. Some had points called partisans, like sharp leaves facing both ways. There were glaives, which carried a plain, long knife with a sudden curve at the tip like an eagle's beak. The halberds had

an axe facing one way, a steel beak another, and at the very top, a long
sharp point. All these the soldiers polished and tightened and sharpened. The firearms were taken apart, the springs tested, oiled and reassembled. Some musketeers carried the harquebus, others the petronel,
which was fired with its butt against the breast. Colonel de Zaldívar
had two pieces of brass artillery to take with him—culverins with the
Spanish Crown engraved above their touchholes. The artillerymen polished them inside and out until they shone green with the blue sky.
Gunpowder was sifted and spread thin to dry in the sun. The heavy
fixed maces and the morning stars from Germany with a spiked ball
hung by a short chain from the mace-staff were scrubbed with river sand.
All riding equipment was inspected, repaired with rawhide thongs, and
inspected again—bridles, reins, saddles, stirrups. The horses had heavy
steel breastplates, and these were burnished. Every man's knapsack was
filled with his issue of emergency rations, gunpowder, bullets. With so
much at stake, proper preparation was essential. As the men worked day
by day, after Christmas, and into the New Year, they came to love their
weapons and equipment. They worked as absorbed as children in ritual
play. Their common purpose, their similar tasks, the buried excitement
of awaiting danger, made them happy in a way that they could never
expose. They were soldiers getting ready for a soldier's job.

By order of the Governor all men went to confession and communion before leaving with the army—all but one, "who, despite the
urgings of his commander, would have nothing to do with the holy
sacraments." He was called "an abandoned wretch."

On the morning of January 12, 1599, the army against Ácoma
left the capital on the river. It took nine or ten days to reach Ácoma.
On arriving, Vicente de Zaldívar was under orders to call upon the
Ácomese for peace and submission. If these were denied, he was to
attack. It would take nine or ten days for news to come back to the river
after that. The Governor and the colony could only wait, hope and
pray as January passed.

On the night of the twenty-first while the Governor was in his
quarters at San Juan disturbances broke out among the Indians in the
twin pueblo over the river. Sentries reported hostile announcements.
Defiant reports came of how all the pueblos of the river country were
marching in arms to destroy the Spanish colony. The Governor personally took charge of doubling the sentinels on guard, with a captain
at each of the four gates to San Juan. Fires were lighted to see by. It

was a cold night. The army must have just about then come to Ácoma, for they had left nine days before. Here on the river, and there far to the west, were they all in danger tonight?

The Governor making his rounds saw the rooftops of his own town full of people who should be inside. Who were they? He sent two officers to find out. They returned to report that the roofs were thronged by the wives, the mothers, the widows of the colony, under the leadership of Doña Eufemia de Sosa Peñalosa, wife of the royal ensign. They had all decided that they must in the common peril help their soldier menfolk to defend their common home, the capital city. The Governor was touched at such spirit, and confirmed Doña Eufemia's command of the roofs. The women of the garrison "walked up and down the housetops with proud and martial step."

The vigil lasted all night, but no attack came, then, or in the days following. It was hard to wait and to wonder, but they could do nothing else at San Juan, though a curious thing happened in the late afternoon of January twenty-fourth. A very old Indian woman came to see the Governor and was admitted. She was accustomed to the respect which her people always gave to the aged and the ancestors, and she expected it from the Spaniards. She had something to tell the Governor and she told it with gravity. She made references to distance, westward, wide country, vastly high rock, so, long and sheer. Her little crabbed hands whirled in gestures of battle and strife one against the other. The war at Ácoma. The soldiers with brave swords, the Indians with arrows, the air full of fury. The battle came and went. It lasted three long days. It was over just today, she said. There was much death amidst the Indians. There came smoke, the town was burning. There was a vision in the air. Quiet came. The soldiers were victorious. She nodded many times, nodding with her whole drawn, eroded and folded person in emphatic confirmation of what she knew and told.

The Governor thanked her and dismissed her. Her recital hardly allayed his impatience to hear what really had happened.

But at last nine days afterward, the quartermaster Diego de Zubia came riding to San Juan from the battle of Ácoma with information and two prisoners. The prisoners he put into a kiva under guard and went to report to the Governor. He announced an overwhelming victory at once. The details followed.

Late in the afternoon of January twenty-first the army was greeted at Ácoma by fearful sights and sounds. On the rock overhead, the Indians, men and women, were naked, figuring obscene gestures, and shrieking like devils out of hell. Vicente de Zaldívar sent the secretary and Thomas, the interpreter, to demand peaceful submission and delivery of the murderers of December, only to be greeted with vileness and scorn. Night falling, the army camped below the rock while Zaldívar completed his battle plan. When the sun rose on the morning of January twenty-second he took eleven men unseen to one of the rocks of Ácoma while the rest of the army marched in plain view to the other announcing their attack. The Indian defenders swarmed to fight the main army, while Zaldívar and his little squad scaled the far rock to gain an all-important foothold. Four hundred Indians discovered them and attacked them with stones and arrows, but without driving them off the cliff. Zaldívar called on his patron Saint Vincent and gave battle. Soon he saw an Indian dressed in his brother Juan's clothes, and in valorous rage he killed him with one blow. The army at the other rock, and other soldiers on the ground far below, attacked with all their power so that the Indians found themselves defending three fronts. Many Indians were killed by fire from below, and fell from the edge of the island "leaving their miserable souls up in their lofty fortress." The battle raged all the first day and was ended only by the cold January nightfall, with Vicente down on the ground in camp again, making plans for the second day, while his squad retained their safe position on top of the first rock. The army once more confessed to the chaplain, all but the "abandoned wretch," and received communion from the Father President before sunrise on the second morning, January twenty-third. A large force then went to the first rock, scaled the cliff and were received by the soldiers on top. The pueblo on the islands looked deserted. Thirteen soldiers carrying a heavy timber to bridge the chasm between the rocks advanced and crossed, and pulled their bridge with them to use again farther ahead. The Indians then broke from hiding to attack. The rest of the army saw their comrades cut off from them beyond the abyss. Captain Pérez de Villagrá superbly ran, leaped the chasm and heaved the great log up, restoring it as a bridge, upon which the soldiers crossed to the reinforcement of their fellows, while the trumpeter blew his trumpet and all felt great new strength. A harquebusier, firing wildly, shot four times through the body of his comrade the "abandoned wretch," who then called for God's forgiveness and heroically made his way to the camp below, where he confessed to the Father President and died. The two brass culverins were brought up, and each was loaded with two hundred balls and fired into a front of three hundred Indians who were advancing, and did fearful damage.

A squad of soldiers went behind the battle and set fire to the city of Ácoma, so that smoke and flame rose to obscure the sun. Peace demands were made repeatedly by the attackers and refused. Some Indians in despair threw themselves from the rock, and others walked into the burning houses to die, and others hanged themselves. In the third day an Ácoma ancient came forward walking with a staff, pleading for peace, offering the surrender for his people, which was accepted by the Colonel. Zaldívar asked what had happened to the bodies of the soldiers murdered in December, and the old man led him to the place where all had been gathered and burned in a savage funeral pyre. There Zaldívar prostrated himself to weep and pray, saying to the soldiers with him, "Here is another Troy." He raised a cross at the site. After the surrender of every Indian was certain, the soldiers saw the women of the pueblo rush forward with sticks and fall to beating a dead body that lay on the stone until it was a mound of formless flesh. They explained in their rage that they were punishing Zutucupan, the treacherous chief who had led the Ácomas into the terrible revolt from the beginning. Finally as the stillness of the third evening came, the Indians asked the soldiers who was the mighty warrior who rode to battle above them in the sky, mounted on a white charger, carrying a fiery sword, wearing a long white beard, and accompanied by a maiden of heavenly beauty, robed in blue and crowned with stars. Hearing this Zaldívar and his men made the sign of the cross and declared that their arms had been triumphant through the support of Saint James of Compostela on his white horse, and of the Queen of Heaven herself. Colonel de Zaldívar shortly afterward sent the news of all these events to the Governor at San Juan by his courier the quartermaster Diego de Zubia, who reported thus. Zaldívar, the army and their captives would arrive in a few days.

Governor de Oñate could be proud and thankful. The victory was prodigious—seventy soldiers against thousands of Indians on their rocky fastness. He marvelled. Almost a thousand Indians were killed, and only two soldiers. And the city burning, and the vision in the sky? The Governor regarded all Indians, including that old woman who had come to him on the twenty-fourth, as superstitious creatures. How had she known on the very last day of battle what the courier took nine days to bring him? The Indians believed all old people wise unless crazy. Who knew?

He thanked the quartermaster, who mentioned the two Indian prisoners whom he had brought and who were now detained in a kiva at San Juan.

Who were they and what were they about?

Zubia explained that he had taken them as they were fleeing Ácoma. They told him they were Indians from elsewhere who had been attacked and robbed by the Ácomas. They asked him for food and help. He gave them what they needed and they were now awaiting attention in the kiva.

The Governor made inquiries. Friendly Indians reported to him that the two men in the kiva were not fugitives from Ácoma at all, but were actually two Ácoma Indians who had not surrendered. An extraordinary affair followed, a miniature of the battle of Ácoma itself. The two in the kiva when asked to come out refused. For three days they threw stones at all who tried to reach them. They lurked in the dark kiva emanating baleful energy, like wild animals dangerously trapped. Finally their bodies yielded but not their wild spirits. They asked for daggers with which to kill themselves, as they disdained to surrender to the Spaniards. The Governor and his Indian friends besought them to come out and be baptized. The reply came in vile abuse from the dark round cave. The Governor shrugged, and ordered then that instead of daggers, ropes be thrown to them, with which if they chose they might hang themselves. Silence followed for some time. The soldiers stood listening in the bright sunlight while mortal exasperation gathered its powers out of sight in the kiva. At last there was a sound, the scratch of body on packed clay, and the two emerged wearing their nooses already around their necks. Permitted to pass, they went to a sizable cottonwood tree like all those that cast shade by the river. In and out of sunlight they climbed to a topmost branch where the golden winter leaves quivered about their dry brown bodies. Knotting their ropes to the tree, they were silent, and after that they stared at the Governor and the others who watched from below. Finally one of the Ácomas spoke. With pride and scorn he declared that the two of them would die and dying would leave the soldiers free to ravage the land. "Our towns, our things, our lands are yours," he said bitterly, and promised vengeance, if anyone could ever return from the dead. And with that, he and his comrade dropped from their bough with the spittle of fury on their lips. They hung swaying and ugly with bent necks and swollen faces as they died.

Looking up in awe and fascination, the soldiers, the Governor, witnessed there in the river cottonwood at San Juan the end of the battle of Ácoma.

22.

Afterthoughts

Though there were afterthoughts that wanted expression in the official terms of legal government, and found it. The battle, the war was won, but the Governor set about confirming the gains already made in his province by civilization as he represented it. If he re-examined the legal opinion of December twenty-second, he found full justification to punish the leaders of the insurrection, so long as "divine and civil" law were properly administered. It was therefore with every proper observance of the Spanish passion for legality in its finest details that he ordered a trial at the pueblo of Santo Domingo down the river of those captives brought from Ácoma by Vicente de Zaldívar.

The prisoners were charged with killing eleven Spaniards and two Indian servants in the massacre of December; and further charged with refusal to submit peacefully, deliver the murderers, and accept due punishment when the army went in January to Ácoma to accomplish these ends.

The trial was held in early February, 1599, with the Governor presiding. It was a medium through which the Spaniards heard once again the chronicle of Ácoma treachery and Spanish valor. The prisoners—a throng of them—had no advocate. Witnesses described known perfidies. The corporate indignation of the stronger of two societies energized itself emotionally. Who could doubt that punishment—any conceivable punishment—paled beside the acts that cried for it? Virtue was not a strand of life interwoven with evil. It was a dogmatic posture which for its own protection could justly resort to any devices of pain and mutilation. The law took for granted in the last year of the sixteenth century that acts of crime done by a human body called for the breaking of such a body in degrees varying with the offense. Such degrees could hardly be arrived at without due process of law, and the Governor heard the witnesses one by one as they came in their soldierly leather, steel, feather and linen and wool to speak. The testimony was all in by the eleventh, and on the twelfth of February, the head of the government was ready to respond with the sentences, which would be properly recorded and notarized.

The Governor ordered that: all male Ácomese prisoners over twenty-five years old be condemned to have one foot cut off and to give twenty years of personal service (assignments to be made later); all males over twelve and under twenty-five years of age, to give twenty years of personal service; all females over twelve years of age, to give twenty years of personal service; and two Indians from the towns in the far west who had been captured at Ácoma, to have their right hands cut off and to be sent to their western homes to warn others of the power that dwelled upon the river.

The expression "personal service" with its limitation of term was preferred to the term slavery. Among the assignments made later was that of sixty girls of Ácoma who, escorted by Captain Pérez de Villagrá, were sent to the viceroy in Mexico for distribution among the convents, to be educated and converted, in alien peace. Pérez left in March, 1599, bearing a letter to the Viceroy from the Governor, asking for reinforcements in men with families "who are the solid rock upon which new republics are permanently founded," and arms, and ammunition; while the colony got on with the spring planting.

23.

Exchange

With each day that passed the colony more deeply established its roots, bringing new ways to the Indian people, and in turn acquiring from them some of the old habits of living along the river.

The river lands met now a new use on a larger scale than ever before. The Spaniards set their cattle, sheep, horses and goats out to graze on the slopes of the valley above the irrigated fields—the slopes where storm water ran, and according as it was detained by vegetation made great or little damage in the face of the earth. Nobody could see in the first years or even generations, as the grass came back every spring, whether or not there was less of it showing each time; and whether gullies formed and grew faster than before. It was an immemorial process, the grazing of animals, and the land had always fed them. There were no thoughts of river life and valley character and land use as related to one another by all the fateful possibilities that lay within change wrought by man.

Vásquez de Coronado had brought his sheep along to be eaten. Oñate's sheep gave not only mutton but wool. Indian weavers prepared the wool just as they had their cotton and used the same looms and methods with the new material. New garments began to appear among the Indians, which could be acquired by the Spaniards in turn through sale or force.

Foods were exchanged. The Indian chocolate, that had come from the Aztec, and the tomato, were already in the Spanish household. Indian hunting drives to the foothills after piñon nuts brought a rich little nibble to the colonists. On such expeditions they saw many piñon trees ruined by the heavy antics of bears—the silver-tip, the brown bear and the black bear—who loved to gather the clustered nuts but broke whole limbs away doing it. In return the Indian farms came to plant new foods brought by the colonists—wheat, oats, barley, chile, onions, peas, watermelon, muskmelon, peaches, apricots, apples and certain varieties of beans. The irrigated fields of both Indian and Spaniard showed new plants. The honey of the Indians was "very white," as the Governor wrote to Mexico. He detailed much of the wild life, the vegetation, the untouched mineral riches of the land; and he found the Indians much like those of Mexico in coloring, disposition and all but speech.

Colonists went looking at their new land. They saw the abandoned cliff cities west of the river, and came upon the two stone panthers in a mountain shrine above the Rito de los Frijoles. The carved animals were four feet long with tails two feet longer than that. They were crouched as if to spring. A circle of large rocks surrounded them. Traces of red ochre showed on the cats' heads—devotional signs made by Indians. The Spaniards watched how the Indians fished, using long nets of yucca fibre stretched from bank to bank across a shallow place. Great hauls were taken, most of them thrown away. So too the Indians killed game far beyond their needs. The soldiers marvelled at the quantity of deer in the country. They would capture fawns and train them to pull little toy carts for the Spanish children. Later, grown deer were broken to harness and used to draw full-sized vehicles. Indians now had wheels to use. The vast land began to lose its secrets. The Governor thought there were about seventy thousand people in the pueblos.

As to where they were, the people of the river colony had firm notions. They thought it was nonsense to say, as some people said, that the New World had been peopled in the beginning by a landing of King Solomon's armada on the coast of Peru. Such a theory was held by certain scholars, but it was demolished by others who pointed out that King Solomon sailed from the Red Sea on a cruise of three years, from which he returned with gold, silver and ivory. There were neither elephants nor ivory in Peru. What seemed plain was that he had actually been in the Orient, China. As for where the earliest people came from—somewhere in the north there was a strait, and they came across it from China. China, Japan Island, India, were not far distant in the seas to the west, and only awaited the discovery of suitable harbors on the coast of New Mexico for the birth of lively overseas trade. The Governor had a clause in his royal contract granting him the right to bring two ships annually direct to New Mexico. He looked forward with confidence to trade with China, so close in the west, and with Mexico and Peru to the south. He saw world enterprises centering upon his city of San Juan on the river. Already capital of so much land, who knew what remained to be brought loyally to it? The western sea shored along the provinces of "the Californios." Reports compared the climate there to that of New Castile, and added further that "their states are the best managed of those thus far discovered," resembling, indeed, "Roman republics." In the summer of 1600 Vicente de Zaldívar led a troop of soldiers to find so promising a sea. On his way out he marched first to the saline pueblos beyond the mountains east of the river, to gather provisions for his journey. At one town where he asked for maize and beans the Indians gave him stones. He sent word of this to the capital and went on his way.

The Governor acted upon his message. Taking fifty soldiers he went to the transmontane pueblo, gave battle in which six Indians died, and later hanged two chiefs. He then burned part of the town, but in a manner "tactful and gentle," and returned to San Juan.

Zaldívar was home before autumn to report that though he had come within three days of the sea he had not been able to reach it through hostile Indian country and high mountains. It was a setback for an impatient Governor, who had problems of discipline to contend with besides. During that autumn two captains of the army were murdered—Aguilar, who had twice made trouble for the Governor, and Sosa Albernoz. There was talk. The Governor was supposed to have ordered the killings.

But Christmas came and with it a new train from Mexico. It arrived at the capital on Christmas Eve bringing new families, new soldiers, six new friars; quantities of arms and ammunition; blankets and clothing, and shoes for everyone. Bonfires of celebration were lighted, and there was music and singing, and at midnight everyone went to Mass to give thanks. With his new resources the Governor could now plan to explore in strength his lands to the east and to the west.

Once again Quivira glowed in the civilized mind. Joseph, the Indian who had escaped from Bonilla and Humaña on those same plains, beguiled the Governor as the Turk had beguiled Vásquez de Coronado. It had long been a common form of Indian politeness to say that which the hearer would like to hear, the truth to the contrary notwithstanding. By his questions a Spanish general could kindle the answers he longed to receive. Gold, like this? Silver? Cities? A great house, a palace? Bounty in all things? Joseph had much to promise, and recited his wonders, ending with an account of a city he himself had not happened to see, but which he well knew from descriptions by other plains people—a city nine leagues long, two leagues wide, filled with marvels. There wasn't a city in all Spain as big as that. The Governor commanded that preparations be launched for his entry into Quivira in the springtime.

But once again his peaceful purposes of acquisition were interrupted by calamitous news, when three soldiers came home to San Juan to say that two of their comrades had been killed by the same insolent Indians over the mountains to the east. Zaldívar once again led a punitive force against the guilty pueblo. The Indians massed at Quarai, one of the three large towns in the saline district. A battle of five nights and days followed before the town, deprived of its water supply by the soldiers, surrendered. Forty soldiers were wounded. Zaldívar had an arm broken and carried two wounds besides. Nine hundred Indians were killed. Their town was burned and two hundred prisoners were taken to the capital. Two months behind schedule, the Governor marched for Quivira with nearly a hundred soldiers, and pack animals, and cottonwood carts, in June, 1601. His sense of high fortune was at its fullest.

Crossing the vast eastern land would be like the act of rolling up a map after it had served its simple purpose.

24.

The Promises

Close to eight hundred people were left at the river capital. Not long after the Governor's departure they began to air certain disagreements.

First of all, the friars spoke out against the cruelties shown by the Governor to the Indians, and the robberies of Indian food, clothing and other possessions which many of the colonists seemed to consider privileged acts. Certainly no firm action against such unjust behavior was taken by the government. The Indians were close to starvation because the colonists had despoiled them of so much food. It was not to be condoned. Better no city, no province at all, than one so godless.

Other complaints came from other sources. There were charges of misrepresentation of the whole nature of New Mexico and even of the purpose of the expedition. Where was the quick return in wealth and personal fortune that all had believed in? A man put all he owned into a venture of this sort, and he deserved a proper return on his risk and his investment. What did he get here? He owed something to himself and his family. Back in Mexico, they had at least had a home of their own and something to eat.

Many men disdained to work in the colony to develop its modest but life-sustaining yield. They had come to make a fortune, not an irrigation ditch, a bean patch or a slaughter pen.

It appeared to the majority that one after another, the Governor's explorations up the river, west of the river, east of the river, all founded on promises, showed nothing in the end but battle and burning pueblos. He himself seemed disappointed, but that helped nobody, for his temper only grew shorter, his rule more strict, and his methods more cruel. (After all, if what was going around was true, *somebody* had ordered the assassination of Aguilar and Sosa Albernoz.) Perhaps he was desperate to prove his whole venture a success. The question remained as to how long others should be expected to pay for things as they were.

In July a mass meeting was called at San Juan to give all such opinion a chance to crystallize. The Governor had his defenders who pointed out the happier facts overlooked by the discontented—there was plenty of food if farmers farmed, the plains were stocked with buffalo if hunters hunted, wheat and corn crops of the year were excellent.

Very well, cried the opposition, if the colony could be sustained on its river, then let the Governor stay at home, keep his soldiers here, and work hard to develop the new city where people could live decently. All those forays over the country brought nothing, took away man power, interrupted family life, and led to conflicts with the Indians.

The Governor's supporters picked up the attacks of the friars and flung them back. If the friars stormed over the treatment of the Indians, some of the friars themselves were not doing their whole duty in their far-flung missionary parishes. Let them go back to their outlying pueblos, and do their work, and then talk.

The debates were full and bitter, and out of them came two documents. One, representing the great majority, filed fifty-seven charges against the Governor. The other, signed by his supporters, defended him. Both papers were sent by courier to the Viceroy in Mexico, and through the remaining weeks of summer, all but a small part of the colony made ready to take the road down the river to Mexico and older homes. At the end of September, 1601, they departed. Their journey took them two months, and as they arrived home at Santa Barbara near the head of the Conchos River in Mexico, the Governor was approaching his capital from yet another crossing of the plains of Quivira.

He brought a meagre return for all his pains. In his fifty-nine days of travel he saw nothing that had not been reported before. He learned one thing he was eager to know, and that was the fate of Humaña, the murderer, and his fellow deserters. Indians far eastward told how the Spanish renegades had been captured, surrounded with fire on the plains, and burned to death. *Pace*. For the rest of it, spirit and courage had run out of Oñate's men, who hearing warnings of hostile Indians in vast numbers farther east presented a written petition to the Governor to turn homeward, as the "horses and mules were tired out and exhausted." The petition bravely went on to say that in any case, "the chief purpose of our journey had been achieved," which was merely to learn "the wonders of this land," so they could be reported to the King in Madrid. The wonders were now detailed in terms not of gold, silver and jewels but of soil and innumerable cattle, yielding suet, hides and tallow. Confronted by homely realities, the Governor assented. Turning homeward, his party had to battle an Indian ambush. Many soldiers were wounded, many Indians killed. One Indian was taken prisoner, assigned the name Michael, and carried back to New Mexico to "give information." He made a map of Quivira and described its treasures. Once again an Indian talked about gold in the east and Spaniards listened. But they continued westward toward the river. There remained little else to say of the plains, except that "the carts went over the country . . . very nicely," which would interest anyone who had not heard that the plains were flat.

And now arriving at San Juan on November twenty-fourth the Governor found his capital deserted by all but a few loyal families and officials. His lieutenant governor was still there, and the Father President. As to the others two months gone he could hardly believe his ears. In rage he commanded Zaldívar to ride out with a troop, overtake the deserting colonists and return them to San Juan for punishment. He filed legal charges against them. It was all useless. The Mexican authorities ruled that the returned colonists need not go back to New Mexico, though the colony as presently constituted was to be continued.

The Governor found himself with a skeleton town, a mere cadre for an army, and a waning reputation. His fortunes were reversed. He had promised wealth out of the north, the east and the west. Only the west remained. There beckoned the pearl fisheries of the Californios of which Indians gave reports, and the harbors for the Orient trade, where surely the Governor's own ships could unload treasure. These things had to be real. He proceeded in the certainty that they were. But to make them come true, he would need more people—soldiers, and pilots, and men with special skills; and he would need money and supplies. There was small chance that the Viceroy of Mexico would grant him what he asked. There remained only one to whom to turn, and in 1602, from the little clay hive on the banks of the Rio del Norte in remotest New Mexico, the Governor sent Vicente de Zaldívar, who had never failed him, to the great city of Madrid across the ocean to see the King.

Zaldívar pursued his mission in the chambered perspectives of the Madrid government. He asked for four hundred soldiers, a detachment of skilled shipbuilders to construct vessels for the New Mexico-

Orient trade, a money loan, and men with families. Papers passed from the Council of the Indies to the Casa de Contratación, and the four hundred became forty, and difficulties developed about ocean passage for men with families, and affairs sometimes required reconsideration. Meanwhile, in secret, the Crown had ordered an investigation into the charges brought against the Governor. The very existence of the colony trembled in the balance. Now it was abolished by royal decree, and again it was confirmed. Zaldívar returned to his uncle empty-handed. The reduced colony and the small army then were made to serve one more reach that never found its grasp. In the autumn of 1604 the Governor led a detachment westward determined to find pearls and harbors. He returned to San Juan in April, 1605, having reached the Gulf of Lower California at the mouth of the Colorado River. It was his last expedition and like his others it was a failure, in terms of what he sought.

In the following year King Philip III instructed the Viceroy in Mexico to order all exploration to cease in New Mexico. It was a profitless region and the colony was a poor enterprise—though it should not be abolished. "And," continued the royal letter, "you shall, with tact and discretion, cause the said Don Juan de Oñate to be recalled for some sufficient reason, as seems best to you, so that he may come without disturbance; as soon as he has come you will detail him in the City of Mexico, disband whatever military force he may have, and appoint a satisfactory governor, discreet and Christian, to govern what has been discovered in the said New Mexico, and you will endeavor to maintain it in justice and peace, and to protect and treat with kindness the native Indians, providing them with religious fathers to instruct them, and if any of these wish to go into the interior of the country to teach with Christian zeal you will permit it, so that fruit may be drawn from it and by this means certain information of what is to be found in that province may be had without recourse to arms. . . ."

There were delays, suspicions, acts of obedience and revolt and again submission, but the end so inexorably spelled out by the royal letter came to pass. The Governor left San Juan forever. Going south to oblivion he suffered yet one more blow from the hard country of his lost dominion. As he crossed the Dead Man's March with his little company, he encountered Indians who gave challenge. In the skirmish that followed a young soldier was killed. He was the Governor's only son. The father buried him there and moved on to Mexico and the courts. Behind him, up the river, his colony survived him. In 1610 a new governor took the capital away from the river to a mountain plateau to the east, where he founded Santa Fe. The period of exploration after treasure was at an end. Another motive began to know its own full expression.

25.

The Desert Fathers

An early Franciscan on the river said that its human life seemed to show on a map the shape of a cross. The upright stem, north and south, was the river itself along which clustered the great house-towns, and the arms reached east and west to settlements of other Indian people. It was an approximate image, but it expressed the dedication of the friars to their inner and immaterial motive. Their spirit and their flesh were one in purpose. They came to take nothing and they brought with them nothing that could be measured. Like the founder of their order, Saint Francis of Assisi, they could have said that they "had been called to the way of simplicity," and that they always "wished to follow the 'foolishness of the cross,'" by which they meant the innocence that made worldly men smile. Certainly it was the act of a fool, in terms of shrewd mankind, to go into barbarian wilderness at times alone and unprotected to preach the love of Christ. The Castilian Saint John of the Cross said, "Where there is no love, bring love and you will find love." The martyrs of Puaray, and Fray Juan de Padilla in Quivira, had made their ultimate demonstration. "They killed him," said another Franciscan of Fray Agustín Ruíz, "and threw his body into the Rio del Norte, which flows along the edge of this pueblo." And at Taos, when Fray Pedro de Ortega came to offer his faith to the Indians, he was refused a place to live, and to eat was given tortillas made of corn meal and the ground-up flesh of field mice, mixed with urine. These he ate with words of relish, remarking that for "a good appetite there is no bad bread." The Indians marvelled. "They go about poor and barefoot as we do," said Indians elsewhere, "they eat what we eat, sit down among us, and speak to us gently."

In one respect the Indians and the friars were close together from the beginning. Both had profoundly religious character, and saw life's essentials best explained through the supernatural. But as the friars believed that their faith enclosed all faiths and purified them in the fire of divine love, until God's relation to man shone forth in the image of Christ Who was the Son of Man, so did they think to bring love to replace the fear that animated all objects, creatures and forces in the Indian's pagan world. The gift they sought to give the Indian was the sense of his individual human soul, and the need, and the means, of its salvation.

But if the friar in himself was poor and managed with very little, his work in the aggregate required extensive organization. The friar's immaterial mission was enclosed in a system that rested on a rigid hierarchy and showed itself in massive monuments. At the pueblo of El Agua de Santo Domingo, that stood on the banks of Galisteo Creek a short way east of the river, the Franciscan order established the religious headquarters of the whole kingdom of New Mexico. There resided the Father President, and there he held his yearly chapters when all his friars would come in from their lonely posts in the outlying missions. Santo Domingo was a little Rome, the seat of an authority that bowed to no secular power in matters of the spiritual welfare of men and women. In the mountains to the northeast was the new political capital of the colony at Santa Fe, founded in 1610, after Oñate's recall. Between the river pueblo and the mountain capital much was in dispute throughout the seventeenth century and would be composed only in slowly gathering tragedy.

Meanwhile the work of the religious reached into the river towns to the north and south; into the pueblos of the west, and to the saline towns over the eastern mountains. Nominally, even the Apache nations who roamed the plains and alternately traded with and attacked the settled pueblo people were part of a missionary parish. The Apaches, wrote a Father President in his report, "are very spirited and belligerent . . . a people of a clearer and more subtle understanding, and as such laugh at other nations that worship idols of wood and stone. The Apaches worship only the sun and the moon. . . . They pride themselves on never lying but always speaking the truth." It was an optimistic vision of mass murderers of whole towns. To such peoples went "missions of penetration," consisting of a travelling friar who preached, converted where he could, and if he lived, returned to Santo Domingo, or to the settled "mission of occupation" to which he was assigned; for many of the outlying missions in Indian towns were organized as field headquarters from which faith and civilization were carried to other towns that had no permanent pastor. Such other towns were designated *visitas*.

Fifty churches were built in New Mexico by twenty-six friars in the first quarter of the seventeenth century. First came the word of God and the conversion of the Indians; and then, with no other power but example and patience, the solitary Franciscan father led his parish-ioners in building a church. In choosing the site for his church he considered many things. He looked into the hearts of the Indians and seeing all that mankind was capable of in good and evil, he felt that a church surrounded by the town was subject to being overwhelmed from within. He looked at the country beyond the town and he saw that the strongest fortress should stand first in the way of invaders. Considering ceremony, he saw how a church must have approaches for processions, and remem-bering functions, he knew it must be close to community life. Accord-ingly, at the edge of the pueblo he marked out a site for the church where it could stand by itself, yet be tied to the walls of the town.

He had large papers scratched with drawings. The people looked from these to his face and then to the straggled marks on the baked ground. He was all things: architect, engineer, carpenter, mason, fore-man, building master to apprentices who themselves were masters of a building style. He did not scorn their methods or their designs. He saw their perfect economy of material and purpose in what they built. Remembering vast vaults of stone, the flutings of arches and echoing heights, sombre color in glass and every intricacy of grille and recess and carved screen, he saw that reduced to essentials, even the great churches of Europe and Mexico had a plain strong purpose, which was to enclose the attention of men and women in safety and direct it toward the altar. Here were wanted walls and roof as soon as possible. They must be made of materials already used and understood by the people, and to them must be added new methods understood by the friar. He had with him, assigned by the Father President at Domingo, and paid for by the King of Spain, ten axes, three adzes, three spades, ten hoes, one medium-sized saw, one chisel, two augers, and one plane; six thou-sand nails of various sizes, a dozen metal hinges, two small locks, several small latches, and one large latch for the main church door. With him, too, he brought the principle of the lever, the windlass and the block and fall. Out of his belief and his technique, combined with native materials and the Indian's reproduction of earth forms in building, a new style was ready to come, massive, stark, angular, and powerfully expressive of its function.

Until they worked under Spaniards, the Indians built their walls of puddled clay and rock. Now the first lesson of the friar was to teach the making of adobes—earthen bricks. Clay was disintegrated rock. The adobe was a restoration of clay to coherent form—a sort of return to rock. With their new hoes, people went to work mixing water and earth in an excavated tray. Only Indian women did this work, for as theirs was the ancient task of enclosing life so they had always made the dwelling rooms of the family. Men, as craftsmen of arms and tools, learned carpentry, and made wooden molds after the friar's instructions. Into the wet clay, straw was mixed as a binder, and the clay was then pressed into the molds to take the shape of large bricks. A brick weighed sixty pounds, and measured ten by eighteen by five inches. It was about all the load a man or woman could carry over and over, as the rows of drying bricks grew longer.

Sometimes foundations were dug and filled with loose stone footings, sometimes the walls rose directly from unopened ground. The walls were deep—six to nine feet thick, and one side wall was several feet thicker than the other. The people wondered why this was as the width was marked out on the ground, and as the walls rose they discovered why, but meanwhile the dried bricks were brought by a long line of workers, and laid in place. The entire pueblo worked on the church. While women mixed earth, and men molded bricks, other men and boys went to the mountains to bring back timbers. With rock and chisel they shaped these. The friar drew patterns for them to follow and out of the wood came beams, corbels, door panels, doorframes, window embrasures. If someone knew where deposits of selenite or mica were to be found, men were sent to bring in a supply so that thin layers of the translucent mineral could be worked into windowpanes. The days were full and the walls rose slowly but all could see progress, and it made them one in spirit. The church was from twenty to forty feet wide, and sixty to a hundred feet long. Its ceiling was to occur at about thirty feet. On one of its long flanks, against the thicker of the two walls, were laid out living quarters for the friar and his Indian staff in a row of little square rooms with low roofs. These formed one side of a patio, the other sides of which held more rooms or a covered cloister. In certain towns the walls of the convent quadrangle took in a round sunken kiva previously used by the Indians. Rooms in the patio were planned for teaching classes, for cooking, dining, and storage of grain and other supplies.

Nowhere in the church or its convento was there a curved wall line, or arch, or dome. As the walls rose to their limit, the purpose of the wider wall became plain. Down on the ground the great tree beams were about to be hoisted up to span the church. Their weight needed a heavy support, and the dozens of men on top of the wall working to bring them up needed room to stand. The wide wall made a fulcrum for the great levers of the beams, and served as a broad platform on which men could work. Scaffolding was little used. Indians had ladders by which to enter their houses and kivas from the roof, and these were put to work too in acts of building. As the church walls achieved their height, carved wooden corbels were laid into the bricks to support cross-beams. Oxen dragged one timber at a time to the base of the walls and men hauled it upright, tipping it against the massive fulcrum at the top, and laying it across the nave. Such beams, or vigas, were of unequal length. Their ends projected beyond the walls and were often left so. Now between the beams were placed branches of uniform size to close the ceiling, and above these rose the parapet of the walls high enough to hide a man. Crenellations were let into the parapet for sighting with musketry or arrows. Over the whole roof went load after load of loose earth, which was packed down by feet, and hardened by water and sun.

The river churches followed two designs. One was that of a long narrow straight box; the other that of a cross, with shallow transepts. Where transepts occurred, the builders lifted a higher roof over them and the sanctuary in a gesture of grace; for where this higher portion rose above the long nave, they placed a clerestory window reaching the width of the nave that took in the light of the sky and let it fall upon the altar, while the rest of the interior remained in shadow. The only other occasional windows were two or three small, high openings in the thinner of the long side walls.

Entering by the main door anyone had his attention taken to the altar by many cunningly planned devices of which the first was the pour of wide and lovely light from the clerestory whose source was hidden by the ceiling of the shadowy nave. The builders used the science of optical illusion in false perspectives to make the nave seem longer, the approach to heaven and altar more august and protracted. The apse, tall and narrow, tapered toward the rear wall like the head of a coffin. Where there were transepts, the body of man was prefigured all-evidently—the head lying in the sanctuary, the arms laid into the transepts, and all the length of the nave the narrow-ribbed barrel and the thin hips and the long legs inert in mortal sacrifice. Many churches added one further symbol and illusion: the rear wall of the sanctuary was built upon another axis than that of the nave. It suggested two things— the fall of Christ's head to one side as he hung on the cross; the other, a farther dimension to the house that honored Him. All such variation of symmetry, and modulation of perspective, combined with inexact workmanship and humble materials, resulted in an effect of spontaneity and directness, like that in a drawing made by a child to fulfill a great wish. The wish, the emotion, transcended the means, and stood embodied forth in grave impersonal intimacy.

Over the adobe texture was placed by the women a plaster of mud. They applied it with the palms of their hands and sometimes smoothed it with a patch of sheepskin bearing fleece. The outer walls in time bore the same marks of the weather as the ancient natural forms of earth all about—little watercourses that ran making wrinkles which when dry came to resemble the marks of life in an old sun-browned face. And yet with even such sensitive response to the elements, an unattended adobe building weathered down only one inch in twenty years. In any proper town the walls were replastered after every rainy reason. The walls were renewed so long as human life used them. Some stood for centuries after being abandoned, and still stand in part, above talus of their own yielding as they go ever so slowly back to the earth.

The interior walls received a coat of whitewash and on this in pure colors the people painted designs, as though they were decorating great unrolled surfaces of clay pots. Scrolls, parrots, columns; flowers and cornstalks; symbols of sun, rain, lightning, thunder and the oblique slantings of terraced forms that took an impression of the landscape receding from the river. Many of the frescoes had not only an Indian but also a strangely Byzantine air, as though a new hybrid culture must turn back to relive all the stages of its various influences.

Finally, before the front of the church a walled enclosure was completed where the blessed dead could lie, and where, against the façade an outdoor altar could be set in a sort of atrium to accommodate large crowds on feast days and Sundays.

From a little distance then the finished building gave its purpose with hard grandeur in its loom and weight, its grace of plain angular shadow, and the wide sunlight on its unbroken faces, where the shadows of the vigas bladed down the walls making a sundial that told not hours but centuries. The whole mission with church, convento, cloister and walled burial field seemed like a shoulder of earth emerging out of the blind ground as a work of living sculpture. To see the true beauty of those structures it was necessary first of all to love and to believe in their purpose.

With the establishment of the "missions of occupation" came the need of a train to bring supplies from Mexico every three years. An invoice of 1620 showed aside from common tools and builders' supplies a variety of foodstuffs, clothing, and articles of religious use. The Father President at Domingo received for distribution many boxes of salt pork, cheese, shrimps, haddock, dogfish; lima beans, lentils, frijoles; rosemary and lavender; white sugar, salt, pepper, saffron and cinnamon; preserved peaches and quinces and sweetmeats; noodles, Condado almonds, Campeche honey, Castile rice, cloves, ginger and nutmeg; and wine, olive oil and Castile vinegar. On his lists he checked frying pans, brass mixing mortars, tin wine vessels with pewter dishes, and leather wine bags. To clothe his friars he noted Córdoban shoes, Mexican sandals, leggings, kidskin hats with cords, sackcloth and Rouen linen in bolts, and to work these materials, papers of pins, sixteen hundred needles, twenty-four pounds of thread and fifty-two pairs of scissors. To take the missioners on their visits he issued travelling bags for bedding, and leather saddle-bags and saddles and heavy Michoacan cloth of tents, and tin boxes in which to carry the Host. For the infirmaries he checked one hundred and seven Mexican blankets.

To furnish the altars he distributed frontals of Chinese damask, with borders of brocatel and fringes of silk, and lined with Anjou linen; figures of Christ on crosses four and a half feet high; pairs of brass candlesticks and snuffing scissors; an octagonal wooden tabernacle over six feet tall lined with gold leaf and its panels painted in oil with sacred likenesses; several large paintings framed in gold; a pall of red damask edged with brocade; vessels of tin, silver and copper for water and wine; and handbells for the consecration. He bestowed silver chalices lined with gold plating, and gold patens, and bound missals "recently revised," and tin chrismatories, and processional candelabra of gilt wood, and choir books, and a brass lamp. For sanctuary floors he sent Turkish carpets. The Father President assigned vestments to the missions—chasubles, stoles, maniples, dalmatics and copes, of various materials: velvets from Granada and Valencia, brocades from Toledo, enriched with designs by the embroiderers whose craft came long before from the Netherlands; "small shirts of Chinese goods to be used as surplices" by altar boys; and for the friars albs and surplices of Rouen linen and lace.

He gave them rosaries and breviaries and little iron molds in which to take the wafers of the Host. For the towers he sent bronze bells, and for High Mass sets of musical instruments—flageolets, bassoons and trumpets; and incense, and wax, and four quires of paper, and oddments like a gross of little bells, and macaw feathers, and twelve bundles of glass beads, and ecclesiastical certificates on which to record the large stages of life, and twelve plowshares with steel edges to help all become self-sustaining on their riverside fields. The Father President's catalog was a history in itself.

And when the mission was built and furnished it was both fortress and sanctuary. When outside its blind heavy walls a wind rose, there within were peace and security, where the many candle flames never wavered as they shone on flowers of colored paper. "It all looked very holy," remarked a friar of such a church in 1634. And yet, if he knew Spain, and its sacred treasures, he perhaps looked upon his mud walls and his rough-chiselled timbers and bitterly told himself that here he had contrived no beauty or splendor, remembering such an altar vessel as the monstrance of Toledo that took nine years to fashion out of three hundred and thirty pounds of silver, until it was eight and a half feet high, with two hundred and sixty small statues amongst jewelled pillars, so that in its exposition the Blessed Sacrament appeared to hover in midair surrounded by a shining cloud. He could only say to himself that there was work to be done as well as possible with the materials at hand. Ending his day only to dedicate the morrow, he recited the prayer written by his founder Saint Francis that said ". . . grant that I may not so much seek to be consoled as to console; to be understood as to understand; to be loved as to love; for it is in giving that we receive; it is in pardoning that we are pardoned; and it is in dying that we are born to eternal life."

And when the morrow came, there were many tasks to guide. The convento and the church were staffed by Indians—a bell ringer, a cook, two or three sacristans, a porter, two boys who kept order in the friars' cells, some women to grind corn, an old man who scratched at the beginnings of a garden within the clay walls of the patio. Without seeing themselves so, the Franciscan priests of the early river were great artists of community life. If they desired to bestow and maintain the standards of civilization in their wilderness, they had first to show the Indians the whole image of the cultivated life that came from Europe. Many of the friars were extraordinarily versatile, and most of them were wholly without that pride of learning which in the universities and coteries of the day often allowed both the scholar and his knowledge to die unused by life. The friars put their learning to work.

Lessons were organized and conducted with discipline. At dawn every day but Sunday the bellman went to ring the church bell for Prime. The pupils, young and old, came to the classrooms which they at once swept out. They then took their places and the pastor came to teach.

He was quick at languages, and for immediate understanding of the Indians, learned the native tongues rapidly, and taught the Christian story in the people's own words. The earliest book to be printed in the New World appeared in Mexico in 1539 under the imprimatur of Zumárraga, the first Bishop of Mexico. It was a catechism in Spanish and Nahuatl. Some of the friars came to the river after preaching for years in Mexico in the native dialects. Once having reached the understanding of the Indian, they developed it with classes in many subjects. They first taught Latin, so that the responses at Mass and vespers could properly be made. Eventually they taught Spanish so that daily life might link the wilderness people to the all-powerful source of national life in Madrid. The Indians learned to speak and to write in those new ways, through which such amazing information came to them. The past found a way to exist in the Indian mind.

Along with words, the Indians learned music. Boys were formed into choirs and trained in the sacred chants of the Church. In one pueblo, out of a thousand people who went to school the pastor chose and trained a "marvelous choir of wonderful boy musicians." In another, the singing boys "with their organ chants . . . enhanced the divine service with great solemnity." Winter and summer, in the river dawns and twilights the heavenly traceries of the polyphonic style rose to the blunt clay ceilings of the coffinlike churches; and the majestic plainness of antiphonal chants echoed from sanctuary to nave as the people together stolidly voiced the devotions composed by Fray Geronimo Ciruelo and shipped north to the river in 1626. A little organ with gilt pipes went to Santa Fe in 1610, and a few decades later eighteen of the kingdom's churches had organs. The friars taught how to play them, and how to make and play stringed musical instruments, and flutes, and bassoons, and trumpets, after the models shipped in from abroad. On great feast days, the level Indian voices were enriched by ardent stridencies from pierced cane, hollowed gourd, and shaped copper. A tradition lasting centuries had an imitation of nature at work in the worship of the Mass. From the choir loft over the main door of the church came first softly then mounting in sweet wildness the sounds of a multitude of little birds calling and trilling in controlled high spirits. On the gallery floor a dozen little boys lay before pottery bowls half-filled with water. Each boy had a short reed pierced at intervals which he fingered. He blew through one end while the other rested in the water, from which rose the liquid notes of songbirds adoring God. At the elevation of the Host or other moments of high solemnity it was proper on great feast days to fire a salute of musketry amid the rolling of the bells.

The Franciscan school taught painting. Indians learned not so much how to hold a brush or use color—they knew that—as how to see, look, formalize a representation. A whole new notion of what the world looked like came to the Indians; yet without greatly affecting their decorative styles, for they continued to draw more the spirit, the idea of a subject, than its common likeness.

Joy and laughter were praised by Saint Francis, and there was no reason why the river fathers should not by these means as well as any other reach into the minds and hearts of their taciturn children. The Spanish delight in theatre, scarcely a hundred years old, was already a deeply rooted taste; and the friars, like the lay colonists, gave plays on suitable occasions. In the pueblos, the comedies were meant to instruct as well as entertain. Ancient Nativity stories were acted out by well-rehearsed Indians, who took the parts not only of the Holy Family and their ecstatic attendants but also represented a little party of Indians in their own character. When in the play it was asked who were these strangers come to attend the birth of the Infant Savior, the answer said that they too were men for whom the Son of God was born on earth that He might save them. A dignifying love reached out to the Indians in the audience. Sometimes the plays were hilarious, and all could laugh at the embarrassments and defeats cleverly visited upon Satan, whose exasperation would know no bounds. Any play telling the story of people brought a sense of community and self-discovery.

The Franciscan teaching turned everywhere, lifted up the soil, planted new seeds, and put the soil back. Among the first new crops was one directly related to the Mass. Cuttings of fine grapevines were brought across the sea from Spain and sent up the long trail from Mexico—a light red grape and a purple one, from which the fathers made sacramental white and red wines. New fruits were set out in orchards—peaches, apples, pears, plums, cherries, quinces, figs, dates, pomegranates, olives, apricots, almonds, pecans, walnuts. Later when the missions rose by the river at the gateway to Mexico, lemons and nectarines were planted to thrive in the mild winters, and oranges, which had first been planted in the New World by Bernal Díaz del Castillo landing with Cortés. Together with the fields of newly introduced vegetables, the orchards were irrigated from the river with improved methods long known to the friars from their Mediterranean culture. With the foundation of horses, cows and sheep brought by the colony, the friars taught the Indians how to herd and how to breed the animals for improvement of the stock. There were workable resources in the kingdom observed by the well-educated priests, who said that with patience and labor much could be done with the ores in the mountains. The treasure hunters had come and gone, unwilling to work for what they wanted. New Mexico was officially reported as a poor country. But a Father President of the Franciscan province in 1629 disagreed: "As for saying that it is poor, I answer that there nowhere in the world has been discovered a country richer in mineral deposits." He listed the very localities of the river kingdom where he had seen deposits, and went on scornfully to say that all such news meant nothing to the Spaniards in Mexico, who if they had merely a good crop of tobacco to smoke were content. It seemed odd to him that they should be so indifferent, when Spaniards "out of greed for silver and gold would enter Hell itself to get them."

But the chance and toil of the freight trains to and from Mexico could not be lightly ignored. The regular service to supply the missions was established in 1617. Trains left for the north every three years, and took the better part of a year to complete the journey. Escorted by a handful of hard soldiers and driven by Mexican Indians about thirty cottonwood carts drawn by oxen came over the gritty trail in movements as slow as the high turns of astronomy by which like ships at sea they made their course. They passed among enemies and at the Northern Pass came to the Rio del Norte, whose source, they said, was at the North Pole. This was easy to believe, in the absence of maps visualizing the unknown country above New Mexico, for the river had an arctic character, "during the months of November, December, January and February . . . frozen over so solid that iron-bound wagons, heavily laden," crossed on the ice, and "vast herds of cattle" went over it at full gallop. "To the same extreme," they noted, "this land suffers from the heat during the months of June, July and August, for even in the shade of the houses tallow candles and salt pork melt."

The freighters saw the Manso Indians about the river at the Pass, who ate their fish and meat raw and bloody, not even cleaning the entrails, but devoured it all "like animals." With mineral powders of different colors rubbed on their nakedness they looked fierce, despite their "good features." As the years passed, and the trains came and went in their crawling regularity, these people about the ford at the Pass came to know the Franciscans and in them grew the desire to be Christians. In time they were taken farther north on the river, near to the Piro pueblos which were the first of the river towns reached by northbound travellers, from Nuñez Cabeza de Vaca to the supply trailers of the seventeenth century; and there they found their mission. It was the policy of the religious province wherever possible to bring together compatible Indian peoples, the better to instruct large numbers, and to insure common defense. Pueblos grew. Ways were traded. New dimensions of human life reached out from the river. Tucked away in the lumbering carts were richly printed little gazettes and random news sheets from the printing shops in Mexico. So came news of the great world, the gossip of government and religion and solemn bulletins in science and philosophy, to the remote fastnesses of spirit and education in the river kingdom of the north.

Knowledge, a full mind, made a companion in the empty wilds when the friars went forth from their clay citadels to preach among the Indians far east or west of the river. They might be accompanied by a dozen soldiers "more," as a Father President said, "for the pious sentiment of not abandoning such a sacred enterprise than for protection or defense, which would have been very limited considering the large number of people they were to meet, all as skilful at arms as they were tenacious in their wars." The friars, he said, "know much hardship in crossing the river each time their ministering demands it, since the river is very swift and subject to bad floods." But all was endurable in the natural world for the sake of that which came to pass in the spirits of those whom they sought in simplicity and love. An Indian cacique came to a father missioner bringing him a marvelously tanned buffalo hide. Unfolding it, the friar saw a painting that showed a green sun and a gray moon, and above them each a cross.

"What does this painting mean?" he asked, and the cacique replied,

"Father, until now we have not known other benefactors greater than the sun and the moon. They light us and warm us, and make our plants produce and the flowers germinate. Thus because of so many benefits we have worshiped them as the arbiters of our lives. But since we heard you tell us who God is who created the sun and the moon, in order that you may know that we now worship only God, I had these crosses, which are the emblem of God, painted above the sun and the moon."

And there were other simple evidences of the new reach of spirit and understanding. If once the Indians were creatures of blind destiny denied by fear the state of the responsible individual, they now had an instrument of self-knowledge and mercy and they used it serious as children. "When they come to confession," wrote a pastor, "they bring their sins, well studied, on a knotted string, indicating the sins by the knots. . . ."

Again, encouragement of their efforts seemed to come in "a very special manner" to the laboring friars in 1629. Its awesome source was in itself enough to overwhelm them with a renewal of the humility that was their spiritual food. One day in the church at the ancient pueblo of San Felipe on the west shore of the river below a dark mesa, Father Fray Cristóbal Quirós was busy baptizing a large group of Indians. He was an old man, though his tonsure was not gray, and his long face had a ruddy complexion. The stone baptismal font stood at the rear of the nave to the right of the main door. Many Indians crowded into the door but hung back in diffidence from taking their proper places. The throng grew. The old priest would have them come forward to help him expedite the ceremonies. They hardly moved until suddenly there was a surge in the crowd and each row turned around to see who pushed. Even the people in the last row turned around, for they had felt the push harder than anybody. When all saw that no one was behind the rearmost people, who yet were thrust forward by an invisible force, they laughed out loud, and continued to push those ahead of them until all were in their places and old Fray Cristóbal was satisfied. Though mysterious and amusing, the incident by itself would not have seemed significant. But other interesting events followed.

On July 22, 1629, at the pueblo mission of Isleta fifty Humanos Indians appeared on what had been for several summers an annual excursion. They invariably brought the same request. Would not the fathers come to their country east of the river over the waste of plains, and convert them to the Christian faith? Summer after summer the request was received with a stir of interest. It was odd that those people should come from so far away, already aware of Christianity. Yet each year the fathers had to deny them what they asked for, because so much work for so few priests was already called for in the river kingdom. The Humanos presently would go away unsatisfied. It was sad for all. They were so persistent. They were so ignorant and so hopeful.

A few days later in July, 1629, the first supply train in four years drew into view through the glassy curtain of the river heat, and with it arrived thirty friars. They brought letters and news from Spain, and fresh supplies of food, and holy oil for the tin chrismatories, and many other supplies, and reinforcement in their persons for the field forces of the missions. And they brought an interesting assignment from Don Francisco Manzo y Zúñiga, the new archbishop of Mexico. It was a professional matter, and the newly arrived religious settled down with their hosts to discuss it fully.

It seemed that for the past several years, there was much talk in Spain of how the Reverend Mother Superior of the Discalced Nuns of the order of Saint Francis at Agreda, on the borders of Castile and Aragón, had been miraculously transported over and over again from Spain to New Mexico to preach the Catholic doctrine to the savage Indians. Her name was Mother María de Jesús, though in the gossip that aroused such interest everywhere she was more commonly mentioned as María de Agreda. Her whole family were widely known for their unusual piety. On a single day in 1619, she and her mother entered a convent, and her father and two brothers took their first vows as Franciscan friars. She became abbess of her convent in Agreda at the age of twenty-five. Her leadership was exemplary, and under her rule the convent became fervent and prosperous. People said she was planning to write an extraordinary book, to be called "The Mystical City of God, A Divine History of the Virgin Mother of Christ." In it she was to give detailed accounts of her puzzling visits to other kingdoms, including Spain's farthest colony on the Rio del Norte. How could it be? She never left Agreda, yet was able at the same time to be in a far corner of the earth. The Bishop of Viseo in Spain heard of her aetherial journeys. Learned theologians spoke of "bilocation," a miraculous faculty with subtle distinctions as to whether it was the physical body that was transported, or the spiritual essence, which then projected the image of its body's likeness María de Agreda spoke of being transported to the Orient, and to New Mexico, which she visited as often as four times in one day. She gave descriptions of her visits—how she spoke to the Indians in their own tongue, though at home in Spain she could not speak a word of theirs; how she was lifted and taken by angels; how the people needed instruction and of what kinds of country and customs would be found by the missioners when at last they went among them. The whole affair was fascinating, even though as usual in newly reported supernatural matters the Church preserved an official skepticism pending further investigation. News of the marvellous mother superior came to Mexico, and the Archbishop now wished to know whether in the country of the Rio del Norte there had been any evidence of her visits, or "flights," as they were spoken of.

The pueblo friars looked at one another and racked their brains. To men of their fervid belief, whose very canon of faith proclaimed the possibility of the miraculous, it was an exalting thought that they and their works may have been visited by Divine Favor through the occasional presence of the zealous nun. And yet nobody could recall out of the dangers and labors of every day a bit of evidence that she had indeed been with them. If only they might see her, speak with her, ask her what of the river kingdom she had observed, to test her knowledge! The matter must be deeply looked into. What had the Archbishop written? The Father President Alonso de Benavides had the paper in his own hands: ". . . do hereby urgently recommend this inquiry to the reverend custodian and fathers" of New Mexico "in order that they may carry it out with the solicitude, faith and devotion as the case demands, and that they duly inform us concerning its results, so that they may be verified in legal form." The whole thing deeply stirred the religious New Mexicans. They had never before heard of Mother María de Jesús, or suspected the existence of her influence.

But a thought struck them. What of the pathetic trudging visits, summer after summer, of the Humanos people from far over the plains? Why had they come back faithfully after so many discouragements? Was it possible—who could dare hope so—was it even likely that they had been inspired by someone from far away? The fifty Humanos petitioners were still lingering in the pueblo of Isleta before setting out in disappointment once again for their homeland. The pastor of Isleta, Fray Estevan de Perea, sent for a group of their spokesmen. They came where he and the other friars now sat in the common room of the convento.

Why, asked the pastor, had the Humanos come year after year to ask with such insistency for baptism?

The Indians pointed to a painting that hung on the wall of the refectory. It was a portrait of a famous old nun, Mother Luisa de Carrión, in the full habiliments of her order.

"A woman in similar garb," they said, "wanders among us over there, always preaching, but her face is not old like this, but young."

The inquirers leaned forward with quickened interest. But why, demanded the pastor, had the Humanos never mentioned this before?, and they replied,

"Because you did not ask us, and anyway, we thought she was around here, as well."

It was astounding. It demanded action. The religious community immediately decided to send two friars from the river province to the Humanos kingdom. Without delay, Fray Juan de Salas and Fray Diego López set out with the Humanos for the east. In a week or two they were back to call for more workers, "as the harvest was great." They told how crossing the plains of the Apache buffalo country they travelled one hundred leagues by the time they came among the Humanos nation. There the people came forward in procession to meet the friars, calling aloud for baptism. They carried a large cross garlanded with wild flowers. Mothers with babies at their breasts held the infants aloft and begged that they be baptized too. The friars were enchanted. Where had the people gained knowledge of the cross? The Indians replied that the same young woman in nun's robes had told them how they must go in procession to meet the friars, and herself had helped to decorate the cross with its garlands. For several days the friars prayed with the people about the cross which they set in the ground. There was more to hear about the visitation. To the Indians she was flesh and blood like another woman. They all saw her, though this joy was denied to the friars. The Indians told how she taught them in their own language, and reproved them for laziness that they did not go more often to seek the priests of the Rio del Norte. The friars were moved. What was known of this matter in Spain now began to be supported by what was becoming known of it in this last wilderness of the New World. One day while Fray Juan and Fray Diego were with the Humanos, messengers from two other Indian nations to the east arrived asking for baptism. A white woman, young, pretty, in gray, black and white robes, with a blue cloak, had been among them preaching and urging them to seek the desert fathers. It was bewildering. The Franciscans made ready to return to the river to ask for more help in the great task. The Humanos chief begged that before they went they would bless the sick. Two hundred invalids were brought to the cross, and the friars told the other missioners at Isleta on the river how they had immediately arisen, "well and healed."

There was much to report to the Archbishop of Mexico. Fray Alonso de Benavides, the Father President of the river province, resolved to go to Mexico, and—there was much other administrative business to justify the decision as well—even to Spain, where he hoped to obtain permission to pay a call upon Mother María de Jesús himself. To his brothers on the river he would report the outcome as soon as possible.

He left New Mexico in the summer of 1629, in time to make the spring sailings from Veracruz in 1630.

It took nearly two years for his report to come back to the river. Affairs of the church and the government moved slowly across time and distance. But at last it came. Fray Alonso submitted his findings in detail, in a letter written at Madrid on May 15, 1631.

"Most dear and beloved father custodian and other friars of our father, Saint Francis, of the holy custodia of the Conversion of Saint Paul in the kingdoms and provinces of New Mexico," he wrote, "I give infinite thanks to the divine majesty for having placed me, unworthy as I am, among the number enjoying the happy good fortune of your paternities, since you are so deserving of heavenly favor that the angels and our father, Saint Francis, aid you. They personally, truly, and actually carry the blessed and blissful Mother María de Jesús, discalced Franciscan of the order of Concepción, from the town of Agreda, which is in the limits of Castile, to help us with her presence and preaching in all these provinces and barbarous nations."

Having first stated his tremendous conclusion he went on to the absorbing details. He arrived in Spain on August 1, 1630, and in due course was received by the Bishop of Viseo, who at the moment was governing the Franciscan order. They exchanged their knowledge of Mother María de Jesús. The Bishop had been familiar for years with the matter, had been to see her, and only looked for confirmation of her claims. Fray Alonso told him of what had occurred in New Mexico, which seemed to supply it. The Bishop authorized him to go to Agreda, there "to constrain the blessed nun through obedience to reveal . . . all that she knew about New Mexico." He kissed the bishop's ring and by the last day of April, 1631, was in Agreda, where the Mother Superior was waiting.

She could not, he thought, be as old as twenty-nine. Her face was beautiful, white except for a faint rosy tinge. She had large black eyes under heavy, high-arched eyebrows. Her costume consisted of coarse gray sackcloth worn next to the skin, and over that a habit of coarse white sackcloth with a scapulary of the same stuff. She wore the white cloth tucked up so that much of the gray showed. Around her neck was a heavy rosary. At the waist she wore the Franciscan cord. Her face was framed in a winding of white cloth over which she wore a black veil. To her feet were tied hemp sandals. Her cloak was of heavy blue sackcloth. If her eyes were darkly calm, her mouth had a little smile of sweetness and humor. She talked freely.

She said that all her life she had suffered for those who did not know God, especially the heathen peoples whose ignorance was not their own fault. She had had made known to her in revelations all those lands which did not know God. To them she had been repeatedly transported by her guardian angels, whom she identified as Saint Michael and Saint Francis of Assisi. As for New Mexico, she had been expressly called for by the custodian angels of that kingdom, who had come to get her by divine command. She went there the first time in 1620, and continued to go ever since. On some days she went three or four times in less than twenty-four hours.

So much for the general claims. As to particulars, she said that when Fray Alonso himself had gone to baptize the Piro pueblos, she had been there. She recognized him now.

On another occasion somewhat similar, she said, when a father was baptizing Indians in a pueblo church, the people all crowded about the door. With her own hands she pushed them on. They looked to see who was pushing "and they laughed when they were unable to see who did it." She described the officiating pastor—an old man but without gray hair, who had a long face and a ruddy complexion. It was a clear description of Father Cristóbal Quirós, who was known to all the province.

She told in detail about how Fray Juan de Salas and Fray Diego López went from the river to the Humanos nation, and said that it was she who had sent the Indians to fetch them. She described the two priests, and declared that she helped them herself in their work. When the messengers came to them from the other tribes farther out on the plains, it was because she had sent them. Her descriptions of the country were so accurate and detailed that they recalled to Fray Alonso much that he had seen and forgotten.

Fray Alonso asked her "why she did not allow us to see her when she granted this bliss to the Indians?" and she "replied that they needed it and we did not, and that her blessed angels arranged everything."

He then asked her "most earnestly" if she would not make herself plain to the friars still in New Mexico, and "she promised that she would ask God, and that if He granted it, would do it most willingly." Fray Alonso wrote that he trusted that "by the time this letter reaches the hands of your paternities some of you will have succeeded in seeing her." They could not say that they had.

She went on to tell of other savage kingdoms which she had

visited, and of dangers, conversions, and martyrdoms. She herself, in her other person, had been martyred "and received many wounds, and her heavenly angels crowned her. . . ."

When the interview was over, Fray Alonso showed her what he had written down of their exchange, and asking her whether it was the truth he "invoked the obedience from our most reverend father general that I carried for this purpose." Her confessor was also present and he called down upon her the same powerful sanction. In her own hand she addressed to the friars of the New Mexican river a confirmation of all that Fray Alonso had put down in his notebooks. ". . . I saw and did all that I have told the father," she wrote, and in a final summation of his view, the priest declared, "She convinced me absolutely by describing to me all the things in New Mexico as I have seen them myself, as well as by other details which I shall keep within my soul. Consequently, I have no doubts in this matter whatsoever."

In her written statement to the friars, Mother María de Jesús spoke gently of the nature of the Indians, and of the measures to be taken for their salvation. It grieved her to see them "continue in darkness and blindness and . . . deprived of the . . . immaculate, tender and delightful law." The friars must work tirelessly, and in their work must be aided and protected by "soldiers of good repute and habits, men who forbear patiently the abuse that may come upon them." All must "exercise the greatest possible charity with these creatures of the Lord, made in His image and likeness with a rational soul to enable them to know Him." It was a view of the Indian that was by no means universally held. But she was firm. "God," she wrote, "created these Indians as apt and competent beings to serve and worship Him. . . ."

When Fray Alonso asked her whether in the river kingdom of New Mexico all were "proceeding in the right way" in the work of conversions, she replied that "everything was pleasing to our Lord, as it was all directed to the aim of the conversions, which is the greatest charity." But she also said that she had taken it upon herself to pray for "the peace and harmony between the governors and the friars . . . so that friars, governors, Spaniards and Indians together and in harmony may worship and praise the Lord. . . ."

With those words, and in her baffling knowledge of the river kingdom of the seventeenth century, Mother María de Jesús de Agreda went to the heart of a problem that was charged with passion and violence.

26.

The Two Majesties

For in the seventeenth century the river colony was like a man in whom raged opposing desires, good and bad. These forces contended so long and so hard that they nearly tore apart forever the social body in which they were inescapably joined. The body and the soul were at war—life temporal and life spiritual. In her cry for harmony Mother María had fearfully seen who were the contenders. They were the governors at Santa Fe, with their corrupt little garrisons and their comic vanity and their bald cleverness at scraping private gain from the impoverished province; opposed by the friars in their fortress-missions, with a grim strength of spirit, and arrogance on behalf of Almighty God, and certain convictions as to human nature which keeping faith they could not recant. With but a few brief peaceful interludes the struggle raged for seven decades, and was resolved only in a disaster which falling equally upon both contenders was the bitter product of their strife.

In a certain sense the conflict was an outgrowth of the Spanish character. The agents of both civil and religious government used to speak of "the two Majesties" in whose name all affairs were conducted; and they meant God and the King of Spain. The Spanish character in which these two majesties were polarized was able at times to be furiously partisan. The armored captain-general saw himself as the inhabitant and example of that majesty which had created the New World under Charles V and Philip II. The friar in his proud rags no less strongly saw in himself the representative of a divine prototype, his Lord Jesus Christ. But each believed not only in his own majesty, but also in the other's, so that the internal conflict was complicated; and yet each claimed the superior right and glory of his own motives, and was obliged to illustrate them in physical acts which often took hard effect upon many human beings outside the quarrel—the Indians.

Behind the open strife between church and state in the river kingdom lay the whole Spanish conquest, with its mixed motives. These were never more bluntly exposed than by the old warrior of Cortés, Bernal Díaz del Castillo, when he said, "We came here to serve God, and also to get rich." If these purposes were equal, they became less so as Spain's red and yellow royal colors moved northward on the map of the New World, until on the Rio del Norte a bare subsistence for the colony was to be had, while the harvest of souls among the Indians was almost inexhaustible to those who believed in its actuality and desirability.

The fight between governors and friars in the river colony revolved around a number of issues, all of which had to do with limits of authority, but one rising above the others related to jurisdiction over the native peoples. It was an issue so sharpened by prejudice and conviction and inherited attitudes that it too struck more than merely the local factors, and reached back to the earliest thoughts about the Indian —his nature, his purpose and his right. The struggle between the body and the soul of the colony was essentially about human relations.

What was an Indian? The question had been asked so long ago as the reign of King Ferdinand, when the Laws of Burgos, regarding Indians, were enacted in 1512. The Emperor Charles V saw it raised again, and serious debate was carried on as to whether an Indian was an animal or a human being, or if a mixture, just how much of one and which nature dominated to what extent. Possibly, thought some philosophers, he represented neither man nor animal but some intermediate species. Or if Indians were animals, then as such, they might enjoy the faculty of reason in various low degrees. The question was, how much, if at all? For the purposes of inquiry, some even supposed that the Indian might be a rational being, though barbarian. Where had the Indians come from, anyhow? It was a striking possibility that they had wandered into the New World as descendants of the lost ten tribes of Israel. But if thus they were human beings, how was it that they seemed to be indifferent to the mining of gold, which was assuredly a human preoccupation, and preferred simply to eat, which was both human and animal? Further, if they were human beings, were they free or slave? It was all a most involved and serious question, and it was endlessly explored in written works and before boards of inquiry and courts of law. What lay at the heart of it was whether or not the Spanish conquest, in its treatment of Indians, was just. It was not long until the various speculations crystallized into two opposing views, held with vigor on the one hand by the Spanish civil powers and on the other by the Church. The Crown, to its credit, required full examination of its own conduct of the conquest in respect to the Indian, but it was forced to do so by the impassioned outcries of the clergy on behalf of the despoiled native. Mercy and protection for the Indian might be translated into law (and they were) but established attitudes were hard to change.

For the Spanish civil view of the Indians, brutally clear in the colonization, was that they were as different from Spaniards as monkeys from men. They were miserable, glum, vicious and lazy. They could not read or write, they had no laws, or private property, or respect for human life. Their religion was idolatrous and obscene. They practiced incest and sodomy. They were so thick-skulled that if a soldier struck one of them on the head with his sword, the tempered steel of Toledo would be dulled. It was absurd to imagine that such a creature was capable of living in freedom. Even if he were sentimentally called a man, it would be far more suitable, as a Spaniard said, for him to live as a slave man than as a free beast. Aristotle's *Politics* was quoted to prove that some men were slaves by nature. If all this was true, how could anyone hope that the Indian any more than another beast of burden could be saved? That was how most of the colonial administrators, and military officers, and landholders felt about the matter.

The Church felt differently. Even if all such charges against the Indian were true, they could be nullified if the Indian were educated, trained, given freedom, and brought to Christianity. The champion of this view was a Dominican friar who as a young propertyholder had seen both sides of the conquest in Cuba in the early sixteenth century. He was Fray Bartolomé de las Casas, later Bishop of Chiapas. He himself had owned Indian slaves, whom he used for the working of mines on his land, even after he had taken holy orders. But preparing a sermon to deliver on Whitsunday in 1514, he came upon the text in Ecclesiastes that read, "He that sacrificeth of a thing wrongfully gotten, his offering is ridiculous, and the gifts of unjust men are not accepted." His thoughts were sober and long, but they led him to the inevitable conclusion, and he announced "that everything done to the Indians thus far was unjust and tyrannical." The remainder of his life was given to the cause he proclaimed, which repeatedly took him from the colonies to the Court of Madrid and back. He faced powerful adversaries, but the Emperor Charles ordered that he be heard, and Spain listened to the conscience of the conquest.

Aristotle, he conceded in the context of his times, might be right about the condition of natural slavery; but if they existed, natural slaves were few in number, and were to be regarded as mistakes of nature rather than as an order of beings. No, all the peoples of the world belonged to mankind; all had understanding and free will; all had the same senses, and were equally moved by the objects of these, took comfort from goodness, felt pleasure with happy and delicious things, and regretted and turned from evil. All men and their nations no matter how barbaric or corrupt were capable of improvement and susceptible of acquiring the virtues of domestic, political and rational man. The way to such human achievement was not through armed conquest; but through peaceable preaching of the love of God and the brotherhood of mankind. The way to imperial conquest was not by war but by peace.

No enduring society could be built upon the shaky foundation of the Spanish treatment of Indians. Its chief feature was the *encomienda* system, or provision of guardianships by which each Spanish landholder had "commended" to him the Indians who lived on his land. He was to be responsible for them, in their spiritual and physical welfare. In return, their work was owed to him and their defense of the land. Ideally the design was that of a family, which was what was intended when Pope Alexander VI deeded the western hemisphere to the King and Queen of Aragón and Castile. But in practice the guardians were slaveholders and the entrusted children of the wilds were slaves. From the days of the earliest conquerors onward—beginning with Columbus himself—the persons and products of the Indians were considered practical spoils of conquest. Forced labor in pearl fisheries and mines and farming fields and domestic life and concubinage and armed forces was the lot of the Indian wards. As early as 1509 the Church asked that Indians not be required to serve their guardians for longer than a year or two, instead of for life. The Crown so ordered, but the order was flouted, and before long new regulations were won by the landholders that permitted guardianships to descend by inheritance, with the practical result that not only the current generation of Indians but even future ones must know bondage.

In 1520 the Emperor Charles issued a memorial requiring that the Indians be treated as free men, and in 1523 he directed Cortés to assign no more Indians to guardianships. Neither proclamation had any practical effect, and in 1526 the guardianship system was legalized for Mexico with the provision—meant to be ameliorative—that no guardian might receive more than three hundred Indians. The colonists pressed at every opportunity for laws that gave them complete and perpetual jurisdiction over the native peoples. Government officials—even, it was whispered, some in the Council of the Indies itself—took bribes to influence policies in favor of the slaveholding class. To protect their material holdings, the lords of the Indies used their consciences loosely, and took comfortable refuge in theories of Indian inferiority. Las Casas gave them no rest. He wrote, he spoke, he memorialized the Crown. The Emperor had already proved himself sympathetic to his views. The issue was the liveliest one of its time, and decades later its energy was to reach even the remotest colony on the farthest river of the Crown's dominions. Throughout the Empire, in spite of royal and even papal declarations of policy, the protective laws for Indians remained only ideal and never knew the simple reality of obedience. But the agencies of human charity never ceased to do their duty.

If the arguments of Las Casas, "Apostle to the Indians," carried much weight with the Emperor Charles it may be imagined how thoughtfully he took notice of a bull, *"Sublimis Deus,"* which was issued by Pope Paul III in 1537, at the very height of the controversy. The Pontiff was explicit in the utterance of his exalted conclusion: "The sublime God so loved the human race that . . . all are capable of receiving the doctrines of the faith." Lest anyone might choose to exclude certain types from the human race, he thundered on saying that the Evil One himself had inspired those who, "to please him, have not hesitated to publish abroad that the Indians of the West and the South . . . should be treated as dumb brutes created for our service, pretending that they are incapable of receiving the Catholic faith." It should have made the enslavers of the Indian tremble. The Pope proceeded: "We . . . consider, however, that the Indians are truly men and that they are not only capable of understanding the Catholic faith but, according to our information, they desire exceedingly to receive it. . . . We declare . . . that, notwithstanding whatever may have been or may be said to the contrary, the said Indians and all other people who may later be discovered by Christians, are by no means to be deprived of their liberty or the possession of their property, even though they be outside the faith of Jesus Christ: and that they may and should, freely and legitimately, enjoy their liberty and the possession of their property; nor should they be in any way enslaved; should the contrary happen it shall be null and of no effect." Having thus laid the foundation for granting legal personality to the Indian, Paul III concluded that august and compassionate charter by declaring that "the said Indians and other peoples should be converted to the faith of Jesus Christ by preaching the word of God and by the example of good and holy living."

How in the face of such a document, and against his known piety, the Emperor could increasingly make legal concessions to the big and little estateholders of the Colonies it was hard to understand. Under the law itself the encomienda system grew worse instead of better, and the whole vast spectacle of abuse and injustice in the New World was more than a devoted follower of Christ could endure. The Holy Father's intention in giving the new lands and their peoples into the care of the Crown had been betrayed. The conquest instead of being a glory to God was a fulfillment of evil. If the encomienda system was inevitably the accompaniment of conquest, then there was but one thing left to do, and Las Casas demanded that it be done. He called upon the Emperor to order a halt to all further wars and conquests in the Indies, so that the existing evil of Indian bondage might at least grow no greater. On April 16, 1550, Charles V to the astonishment of the world commanded that all conquests in the Spanish empire be halted until a royal board of inquiry, composed of church doctors and political scientists, could propose an acceptable scheme of waging war and conquest with justice. There was splendor in this act, and its extreme simplicity could come only from an absolute morality. Right and wrong was the issue, and not even vast expedients and material commitments—on a scale of continents—were to justify an improper humanity.

But as before, the fiery ideal was lost sight of in smoky argument. Old abuses gradually crept forward again, though a framework of regulations for the conduct of wars of conquest was set up requiring that commanders must have the approval of proper ecclesiastical authority before opening battle against the Indians. (Hence Oñate consulting his chaplains for official opinion before moving against pueblos.) Colonists were to be responsible for the welfare of their Indians, and must explain to them the advantages of coming under the government of the Crown— think, they said, of the new things brought by the Spaniards: horses, cows, silk, iron tools, firearms, wine, oil, roads, wheeled vehicles, and the supreme gift of the Holy Faith. If the Indian worked for the Spaniards, they would see that he was fed and clothed, and he would give them his labor and the products of it. If asked to work on the land, the colonist, like Cortés, would reply, "But I came to get gold, not to till the soil like a peasant."

After over half a century of debate and legislation, the Indian laws of Philip II were in practice even less protective than those of his

father the Emperor. The moral force of the clergy had resulted in a
great statement of principle; but the heavy inertia of those men who by
their courage and ambition had continued the conquest was more powerful than any ideal. With their methods of gunfire and slavery, the practical men of affairs prevailed over the friars' promise of peace and prosperity through the word of God. The result was unceasing strife, and a
slow process of organic death for the empire and its most outlandish
colonies, where even so, the claim could be made in good sense that
in their daily living, the Indians in pueblos were closer to Christian
simplicity and perfection than many a Spaniard, who ravaged them in
the name of the Two Majesties. Las Casas saw the Indians as compact of
all virtues. They are "more delicate than princes and die easily from
work or illness. They neither possess nor desire to possess worldly wealth.
Surely these people would be the most blessed in the world if only they
worshipped the true God."

On the regal and viceregal level the view of the Indian was
beneficent and gentle. Mendoza, the first viceroy of Mexico, advised his
successor in office to accept neither one nor the other extreme opinion
as to what an Indian was. "Treat them," he declared, "like any other
people, and do not make special rules and regulations for them. There are
few persons in these parts who are not motivated, in their opinions of
the Indians, by some interest, whether temporal or spiritual, or by some
passion or ambition, good or bad."

Few on either side of the controversy were as wise as he; and on
the river in New Mexico where the struggle over the Indian went on at
a lower level, fury replaced amenity, and poverty settled its dust over
the meagre stakes.

For it had been a long time since New Mexico was hopefully
regarded as another treasure house, and all large-scale exploitation of its
resources by the Crown had been abandoned. The kingdom was regarded essentially as a missionary field. The civil authority, the armed
garrison, were to exist primarily to protect the friars at their hazardous
work, whose object was the peaceful conversion of the Indian. But the
position of the Indian under the guardianship of the encomienda was
poison at the heart of the province; and with their attitudes of mind
inherited through history the governors who favored the Indian civil
system and the friars who abhorred it must only come to blows. Carefully
as it was worked out through experiment and altruism, imagination and
a royal sense of honor, the legal frame of the occupation of the colonies
could not stand against the force that worked to tear it down. This

was, once again, the Spanish character. "Spaniards always end by devouring their institutions with the acid of their corrosive individualities."* The two governments of New Mexico—the provincial majesties of the Church and the State—poured forth streams of accusations, complaints, scandals against one another to the viceroys of the seventeenth century in Mexico. These mostly had to do with circumstances of the Indians, though side issues were often too outrageous to miss. The freight wagons crawled out of Santa Fe on their triennial voyages to Mexico City bearing packets of official letters wrapped in antelope skin. Often by the very same train the friars and the governors dispatched their dossiers against each other. Personalities changed, governors came and went every three years with the supply trains, and new fathers president were assigned nearly as often. Details varied, and the scenes of conflict, but the bitter lack of harmony continued from about 1613, shortly after the establishment of Santa Fe as the civil capital, until the eighth decade of the century.

The deeply rooted disagreement in policy broke into the open in May, 1613, when Governor Peralta sent a squad of soldiers to Taos to collect tribute owed by the Indians under the official encomienda. Fray Isidro Ordóñez, the Father President, was in Taos at the time. He came out of the pueblo, dispersed the Indians who were waiting to deliver their levy, and commanded the Governor's troops to return empty-handed to the capital. The Governor was outraged and when he persisted in his orders, Fray Isidro invoked against him the terrible wrath of excommunication, calling him "a heretic, a Lutheran and a Jew." Peralta was at that time beginning the construction of the Palace of the Governors in the new city of Santa Fe, which had been established on the site of a long-abandoned pueblo. Indian laborers were used in the work. Fray Isidro denounced the Governor for using the natives as a press gang, and the Governor on meeting the friar later on during the summer fired at him with a flintlock pistol, missing him but slightly, and hitting another friar and a civilian. For this Fray Isidro demanded that the Santa Fe town council arrest the Governor, but to no avail. The Governor's chair was thrown out of the parochial church. When it was certain that news of the squabble must be sent to the Viceroy in Mexico, Fray Isidro promised to excommunicate anyone bearing dispatches for the Governor, who then moved to go to report in person, and started down the river road. At Isleta he was captured by agents of the Father President who threw him in chains into a cell at the convent of Sandía. Fray Isidro was

---

* Salvador de Madariaga, in *Rise of the Spanish Empire*.

for the moment triumphant. His position was particularly strange since there was some question as to the validity of his appointment and his credentials as Father President. Some of the friars under him were in revolt against him. None was permitted to leave the kingdom, and Fray Isidro's furious dispatches describing his own hardships of spirit and person went to Mexico by fast courier. The Governor escaped from Sandía and returned to Santa Fe, only to be clapped into prison again on reduced rations. His friends were powerless, and the state of the province was critical, for under what purported to be a royal order Fray Isidro had published permission for all colonists and soldiers to return to Mexico if they wanted to do so. As a result the Spanish lay population of Santa Fe dropped to forty-seven persons, and the continued life of the colony was precarious.

In May, 1614, a new governor, Admiral Bernardo de Ceballos, arrived to take office. Peralta was sent on his way south. He was ruined, and even the last legal recourse that might have proved him right in his report to the Viceroy was snatched from him. At the Perillo Spring in the Dead Man's March, he was once more confronted by Fray Isidro's partisans and robbed of his papers before being permitted to proceed to his obscure fate in Mexico. But a refugee friar managed to reach Mexico in the same year, and there he made charges against the Father President. The Viceroy acted at once to appoint another friar already in New Mexico to succeed Fray Isidro, who was recalled to Mexico City to face the Holy Office of the Inquisition.

The whole affair was all too typical, with its angry challenges of authority between the two majesties, its infinitely laborious intrigues across desert kingdoms and quires of parchment, its squalid local reprisals. The Indians strove to keep their ancient ways of life while submitting to the physical and spiritual demands of the warring powers, and the colonists subsisted on their national traditions while watching the energies that might have worked for peace and plenty spend themselves in ceaseless recrimination. One after another, the successive regimes in the Governor's Palace and the Chapter House of Santo Domingo poured forth for vice-regal consumption the accounts of each other's infamies.

Governor Eulate, cried the friars, in 1619 sent permission to the Indians to revive the pagan religious practices which the friars had worked hard to supplant with the rituals of Christianity. It was an official act designed to divide the allegiance of the Indians from the friars who lived and worked among them. The same governor, against the royal edict that prohibited governors from engaging in trading enterprises, raised livestock to be exported at profit to himself. Another governor closed the river highway to friars who wanted to send little herds of sheep to be sold in Mexico for "ornaments, decorations for the churches and other necessities." When they protested to him, the governor replied "that churches with decorations and costly ornaments were not necessary; that a few huts of straw and some cloth ornaments, with spoken [as against sung] Masses, were ample." He did not or would not understand: the friars pleaded that "these things are what we have the most care for, and procure at our expense and labor, for, if precept and virtue teach these natives, they are all influenced as well by the decency, ornamentation, and ritual of the churches." The governor cared as little for the health and safety of the Indians. From the rich salt lakes beyond the eastern mountains of the river, the native people were forced to bring like beasts of burden great cargoes of salt, and this, wrote the friars to the viceroy, "has occasioned among the natives serious illnesses and convulsions, some of them being permanently incapacitated . . . both on account of the haste and the misfortunes attending their departure, and because of the long distance which they carried the salt." By 1630 the garrison at Santa Fe had again increased, and two hundred and fifty soldiers were paid, declared the father president of the time, through a levy on the Indians of a yard of cotton cloth for each Indian house and a bushel of corn.

Against these and other abuses the friars pleaded with the King to command relief. The guardianship system was wholly corrupt. Royal decrees specified that no Indians could be given in encomienda until after baptism. And yet, "even before the pueblos are converted, the governor himself gives them out in encomienda without notifying the father president or the viceroy. Even before they are converted and baptized, when they are only pacified, they constrain them to pay tribute and do personal service, taking them far from their pueblos and treating them badly. As a result, the heathen Indians who have not yet been converted or even pacified say that they do not want to become converted, or even pacified, that they do not want to become Christians, in order not to pay tribute or serve. They have even been sent to be sold as slaves in New Spain. . . . They escape these and other abuses as long as they remain free and do not become Christians." And the friars, in whom the justice of Las Casas was still alive, prayed the King to order that "the Indians of New Mexico be not given in encomienda by the governors of New Mexico until five years after the whole pueblo has been baptized."

Every request they made of the King revealed a new abuse.

Pray, let the King order that no landholder or any other Spaniard be allowed to live in the Indian pueblos "without the consent of the Indians themselves." If every Indian house had to pay the governors a cotton blanket and five bushels of corn per year, let the king issue orders against charging the tribute against individuals who lived in, or moved into, the house. Let Indians move freely to whatever pueblos they chose to live in, and not be bound to the land where they were discovered. Command that Indians who are officials in their own pueblos be excused from personal service, and prohibit the practice of taking Indian boys and girls from their homes on the pretext that they are orphans and must be given care, which invariably is seen to be for what it is, the position of slaves. Indians captured in wars should not be sold far away as slaves, but should be given to the convents for teaching faith and industry. Grant that the royal power move against the way Indians were forced off their lands. Order that the governors be required to obey the decree against raising of cattle to be exported for their private gain, a practice bad in many ways. To drive the cattle to Mexico, the governors "send along the best Indians of the land who then are left stranded because the distance is so great . . . and unable to return to their country and homes." And others connive to send cattle with the governors' herds, "and in particular female cattle, whereby the land is impoverished." It should be ordered that the right of sanctuary in the churches be respected. "This will afford some protection and relief to the helpless Spaniards who live there as in a walled prison." And the friars looked to the future of the kingdom and requested "that if anyone should wish to found at his own cost a town at the pass of the Rio del Norte, which is midway to New Mexico," the viceroy should be given power to encourage this, for "that pass is extremely important, both for keeping open that trail and for the conversion of the many savage nations in that region. Your Majesty would be greatly benefitted by the foundation of such a town and by the production of the mines and farms that may be established there."

The complaints of the clergy went up through the years like sighs. A state official at Santa Fe travelled to the Apache nation to buy buckskins for the governor. He informed the Indians that his father had begotten a son among them and he wished to do the same. The Indians withdrew and discussed his statement and came to understand what he wanted. Accordingly, at four in the afternoon they erected a tent for him, made it comfortable with skins, and seated him on a new hide spread out. "Then they began their wedding dance as they call it, and when it was finished they brought to him a young maiden, and he admitted her and slept with her. In the morning the Apaches came and seeing that he had known her, they anointed his breast with her blood." It was—but only to the Indians—a marriage contract.

Another civil official "of large body, coarse, and somewhat brown," came one time to the pueblos over the mountains to the east where Indians in the choir were assembled to sing the High Mass. For this by his order they were to be given fifty lashes each, and "the poor things have not since then dared to take part in any sung Mass, wherefore the divine service has been impeded." In the pueblo of Quarai the same man was once sitting in the very cell of a friar who was making him a cup of chocolate when the Indian officers of the pueblo came in to say that they were sorry to see their pastor go out alone to the wheat fields to reap the harvest singlehanded. They asked for permission to help him. The visiting official flew into a rage and ordered the Indians "not to reap the wheat nor serve the father, for if they did he would give them one hundred lashes; for such," he roared, "was the command of his governor. . . ."

Anything was to be expected as the governors and their men worked to discredit the clergy and the church. At a western pueblo certain captains from Santa Fe spoke to the Indians. "One of them went out proclaiming that the people should come together, for he had some things to tell them which were very sweet, very pleasant, and very much in accord with their desires." Nobody knew what was said to the Indians, "but from that time they did not ring the Ave Maria, or the evening bells, nor did they attend the teaching of the doctrine or the choir, but acted as if they had never been converted. . . ."

Another officer went to a pueblo, assembled the people, and insisted to the Indians that they make charges against their priest, who was ninety years old. An Indian woman finally rose to state that he had violated her. The Indians burst into roars of laughter, jeering at the name of the priest, who was ordered to pay the woman a fine of a piece of cloth worth a dollar. Someone went to the friar's cell where he had remained reading his breviary during the scene, and asked why he did not come out to defend himself. The old man replied "that it was of more consequence to him to continue reciting the divine office . . . than to notice all that."

There seemed no end to the irresponsibility of the governors. There was one who sent all his troops to capture slaves whom he could sell. "The army went away at the time when the corn was maturing, and there are eight hundred and forty fields left to go to ruin without their owners, at the mercy of bears and other wild beasts, which constantly destroy the crops." This occurred at a time when the "poor kingdom" had just been through a serious famine during which Indians had to live on grass seeds and harmful herbs, and everybody in Santa Fe ate "bran, quilites, green barley, and other herbs which they happily were able to find."

One of the charges made most bitterly by the friars was that more than one governor since Eulate did his utmost to revive the pagan dances of the Indians. The friars believed these to be diabolic in their nature, and believing so, were compelled to suppress them at all costs. The Indian communal dance, they said, consisted first of an invocation of the devil in unknown tongues during which he was offered the fruits of the earth; and second, of a growing frenzy so that "they appear beside themselves, though no drinking has taken place whereby they may have become intoxicated. Sometimes they go from this dance and enter any house they wish, and take pleasure from any Indian woman they desire— even," they said, daughters, mothers, sisters, "no attention being paid to relationship." No wonder it was a shock to Fray Salvador de Guerra, pastor of Isleta, to see his people performing the dances from which he had believed them converted. Not being able to make them desist in any other way, he "went throughout the pueblo with a cross upon his shoulders, a crown of thorns, and a rope about his neck, beating his bare body, in order that they might stop the dance." When he reached a certain part of the pueblo "they came after him weeping, and saying they were not to blame, because the governor had commanded them to do as they were doing."

What could be hoped for from such a ruler, who was heard to declare loudly in the corridor of his palace at Santa Fe that "if it were not for the necessity of upholding his dignity as governor, he would himself go out and perform the dances, and for a little he would do it anyway"? When assured that the dances were superstitious, he replied that he could see no superstition in them, and he doubted whether anyone else could either. If any could, let them say so. After all, the Indian chorus in the dance sang "something which sounded like 'Hu-hu-hu.' "

"Look here," said the governor, "this dance contains nothing

more than this 'Hu-hu-hu,' and these thieving friars say it is superstitious."

The friars looked around and "knew from the faces of those who
were present that they were much affected by this action, but offered
no opposition to it because the speaker was their governor and captain-
general." And so the authority of the kingdom was torn apart over yet
another issue, and the Indians were offered both restraint and license,
and the dances went on in the earthen plazas along the river, and at
Pojuaque they danced at night so bedevilled and rapt that when the
horses of some Spaniards stumbled over them they did not feel it, and
at Taxique in the mountains when the snow was heavy on the ground
the people went to the church roof to dance and the Spanish mayor
went to the priest and mocked him, asking how it happened that he
had ordered the Indians to "dance the catzinas on the roof of the
church. . . ." It was a curiously prophetic episode, for centuries later
the modified Indian dances were to be approved by the pastors, and on
occasions permitted in the very churches; and it also recalled how in
the fourth century, Priscillian the Heretic introduced dancing into the
services of the Church, with lasting effect, for even centuries later the
Dance of the Seises was still given before the high altar in the cathedral
at Seville.

In the long roll of the contentious governors, Peralta, Eulate,
de Rosas and Mendizabel were the most reckless in their hatred of the
other majesty until the arrival in New Mexico in 1660 of Governor
Diego Dionysio de Peñalosa Briceña y Bertugo, who from the first
moment in his new kingdom showed himself master of a particularly
malicious style in government. He sent word ahead that all settlers
for fifty leagues around must come to meet him at Senecu, the first pueblo
on the river above the Northern Pass, and accompany him from there
to Santa Fe. Some two hundred colonists responded. As he approached
the pueblo and convent of Senecu, the friars there paid him due cour
tesies of an official nature. The bells pealed and the pastor in canonicals
accompanied by a crucifer bearing a large cross went forth to meet him
at the gate of the holy field of the cemetery. The new governor halted his
cavalcade to berate Father Fray Benito de la Natividad for not having
advanced down the road six miles to receive him. "What ridiculous pretensions for his reception!" exclaimed the priest in a protest to the
authorities in Mexico. From Senecu the governor proceeded up the
river in a royal progress, pausing at the convents with his huge court to
be fed and entertained and bedded without remuneration to the

frantic clergy, who having no resources equal to such privileged invasion, cried out that his vanity "exhausted the convents through no fault but his own, for they were ruined by such great expense."

The new administration was off to an unhappy start. Peñalosa, once installed in Santa Fe, commanded that from each pueblo convent a trumpeter must come every week to the capital to "play for him in his palace when he eats or rises, using for his own ostentation that which the clergy employ" to dignify the church services in the missions. His incumbency was one long scandal, public and private, and he enlivened it by new hostilities against the Church. In his clay palace, ruling a province suffering from famine, drought and rising threats of Indian aggression, and supported by a half-intimidated, half-cynical official circle, he was heard to murmur grandly that he had "secret instructions from the Duke of Albuquerque to put the clergy to the garrote, or hang them, and haul their corpses away ignominiously on pack saddles." A friar went to Taos to rebuild a church that had been destroyed and whose pastor had been murdered. Peñalosa appointed as governor of the pueblo the same Indian who had murdered the priest, and decreed that under penalty of death no Taos Indian was to help the new pastor to rebuild the church. The pastor was forced to resign and work elsewhere. Even though Taos was readily accessible from Santa Fe by the river road, Peñalosa never visited that most important of the northern pueblos.

All the familiar issues between the two majesties reappeared under Peñalosa, and the father president Fray Alonso de Posada, who was also the resident commissioner of the Holy Office of the Inquisition, opposed him with increasing vigor throughout the three years of the administration. In 1663 the climax came. Francisco de Madrid, captain of the governor's cavalry, appeared at the church capital of Santo Domingo one day bringing two prisoners, Don Pedro Duran y Chavez and his nephew Cristóbal, on the way to Santa Fe. They installed themselves in the convent that fronted on the plaza of the pueblo. Seeing that his guards were inattentive, Don Pedro told one of his Indian servants to take him up and carry him into the pueblo church where he hoped to enjoy the right of sanctuary. The Captain saw too late what had happened. Reluctant to violate the church on his own responsibility, he sent a courier to the Governor asking for orders. As soon as possible additional troops arrived from Santa Fe with an order to take Don Pedro from the church. Having demanded the keys from the pastor, after Mass on Sunday, August 23, 1663, they entered and took the refugee by force. Word of the outrage came to Fray Alonso who was at Pecos. He called upon the Governor to release the prisoner, threatening him with excommunication if he refused. The governor was heard to say that "he recognized no judge in this country who could excommunicate him, neither ecclesiastic, bishop, nor archbishop," and in his most florid style added that "I was a cleric in my own country, a padre, and I married when I was ordained as subdeacon, and I sang and intoned nicely a gloria, a credo and a prefacio." His next move was to gather up the father president at Pecos, remove him to Santa Fe and make him a prisoner in the palace. He then looked about to find witnesses to justify his actions.

But none came forward. The city—it was then the only Spanish city in New Mexico—and the river missions stirred with excitement. It was unheard of, to throw a prelate and a commissioner of the Inquisition into jail. Peñalosa searched for a diplomatic formula that would allow him to climb down with dignity. Surely the friars would petition him to free their president, whereupon he would do so with clemency? But the clergy kept an offended silence. Finally desperate, he wrote in October to the pastor of Isleta, asking him to call. With a show of diplomatic mediation, the incarcerated commissioner was released, and promptly made charges to the Holy Office in Mexico. Peñalosa decided to vacate his office voluntarily, and returned to Mexico, where the Inquisitors dealt with him in an exhaustive inquiry. He received the heaviest sentence ever imposed by the Inquisition in the New World—he was ordered to perform an act of faith by walking, bareheaded and barefoot, in a penitent's robe, and carrying a lighted green candle, through the streets of Mexico City; to pay a fine of five hundred pesos and all the costs of the case; to be ineligible ever to hold political or military office; to perpetual banishment from the New World; to make various holy devotions for one year; and to quit New Spain within a month. In the end the Inquisition had to lend him the money to pay for his passage to Europe, where he sought the ear first of Charles II in England and then of Louis XIV in France with a traitorous scheme to conquer New Spain.

If such were highlights of the religious case against the governors, equally profuse and even more violent charges were made throughout the century against the friars. In their hatred the governors accused the protectors of the Indian and of the common colonists of every conceivable crime. The quarrel was morally unequal, for the clergy in their ire were motivated in behalf of the human conscience; while the governors in their attacks upon the only valuable possession of the friars—their purity of purpose and repute—were moved by an exasperated venality. A governor stated that some of the friars he knew were "sailors, artillerymen, and men of ill-repute, engaged in evil pursuits; they took the habit in order to go to the provinces of New Mexico. They served no novitiate, and were without religion, which they did not understand." They "took holy orders only to avoid work and live with greater liberty than in worldly pursuits." The town council of Santa Fe in 1639 charged that the friars exploited the Indians for their own rich gain, and caused anguish to the Spaniards by refusing them the sacraments, even in Lent. ". . . On the doors of the churches there are posted more excommunications than bulls," and ". . . the worst thing about it is that usually they take action against the governors and justices . . . and since all the religious belong to the same Order, quarrels or contentions with one mean trouble for all. . . . Thus the royal jurisdiction is much humbled and violated and the few inhabitants who uphold their governor, besides suffering poverty greater than that of Haman, are afflicted and snubbed and addressed by the religious with ugly and insulting words, and even forbidden to fight in the field."

The issues complained of by the friars were reinterpreted by laymen. To keep the Spaniards from "holding or establishing farms, under the excuse of protecting the cornfields of the Indians [the friars] find sufficient reason for interfering with the Spanish inhabitants, even though the latter settle two or three leagues away from the Indian pueblos. . . . When they can do no more they even burn the farms, as they have done in some cases." Let the Viceroy "consider, for the love of God, that this is a very poor land, with few people, and that the measures were taken in passion and with great harshness." The maintenance of civil order was impossible if the clergy were able to harbor criminals in the sanctuaries of the chapels, which were becoming "asylums and refuges" for "delinquent." The convents, declared the councilmen, maintained large farms and herds, and the Indians were abused by being put to work with them, and the pastors in their stables kept "three or four saddle horses very daintily, for they are quite valuable and are taken to be sold in New Spain." Worst of all, and almost incredible, was that the clergy "hold most of the arms that there are in the country, for they have armor for the horses, leather jackets, swords, harquebuses, and pistols," and the council begged that these arms be ordered turned over to the governors to issue in times of trouble, "for there are none in the storehouse." Did a friar steal most of a shipment of iron intended for horseshoes? Did he sell a herd of oxen intended for the use of Indians in tilling their fields? Were even religious articles meant for the chapels sold for private gain by the Franciscans? The councilmen bitterly said so.

Some of the charges made by the officials were appalling. At a certain pueblo the resident friars took much cloth and other tribute from the people, who sent a delegation to complain to the authorities. Upon their return the pastor had them brought before him for questioning. He then went to their houses and searching them found "some feathers, or idols"—the usual Indian katchinas. He flew into a passion and confronting his people again he sent for turpentine, threw it upon them and put the torch to them. Many people were badly burned. One died of the effects. The resident friars were ordered to Santa Fe to be disciplined by the father president. But soon they were again in favor and assigned religious duties.

The indictments streamed on—friars whipped Indians; sometimes cut off the hair of Indian women; put prisoners whom they detained into a little cell "not even large enough or decent enough for a good-sized pig"; were frauds, hypocrites and drunkards. As for Indian dances, the friars were willing enough to let them be danced if they needed the Indians to sow the fields or do other jobs. Most fervently of all, the civil charges complained of religious abuses by the friars. They refused confession at a whim, excommunicated for nonreligious reasons, suspended the saying of Mass thus anguishing many more persons than the one or two they meant to deprive, and again, "would say Mass in the house of any mulatto or kept woman, according to their pleasure." The laymen repeatedly begged that clergy be sent to them who would restore the sacraments of which they were deprived and of which they felt such profound need. The faith itself was never threatened; only its priesthood, whom the governors chose to judge by its least instead of its most worthy members. Even a certain friar said to one of the governors, "Sir, the ignorance of these fathers is immense. God take me away from here." But this governor was a poor witness, for like all the others who accused the friars of heinous deeds he was himself a man of low character.

So in bitter animation of the whole tiny society, the two majesties took issue for generations over the prerogatives of the soul and of the civil power. Against the sparse and lonely background of the narrow river valley, the Indians in their towns, far from the great world, were the victims of a divided authority which they had never invited over them. The stalemate between church and state, with its postures of mutual defiance, was symbolized in a story believed in 1660. Told that the father commissary of the Holy Office of the Inquisition was coming to arrest him, Governor López de Mendizabel "said that before that commissary could seize him, he would hang him to a tree (indicating with his hand a tree which was there). Then, though the sky was serene, clear and without clouds, a little cloud came up with a tempest and a ray of lightning fell, which reduced the entire tree to ashes. . . ."

27.

The Hungry

Trouble of another kind, vast and impersonal, came to the whole river kingdom and its outlying unknown lands and peoples in the middle of the seventeenth century. The plains Apaches and Comanches roved under the weather, obeying its great movements like shadows obeying clouds. Where the grass was ripe the cows went, and the Indian rovers followed to hunt and eat them, and to pick berries and herbs that prospered as the grasses did, when the rains fell on all things and made life. All depended on the rains. The plains people had no storage. Their food grew before them, and they took it, and used it, and moved on to the next living supply.

In the land of the pueblos, and farther south, below the North Pass, where the river turned east and south for its last thousand miles, were people who planted crops and harvested them, saving against the future what they did not need each year. The lower river people were seen in 1653 by Captain Alonso de León who with thirty soldiers came to the river from the settlement called Cerralvo in the province of Nuevo León. He was under orders to find the mouth of the Rio de las Palmas from its inland approach. Since the efforts of more than a century before no foreign travellers had sought the lower river. De León came to its bank a few hundred miles from the sea and followed its course toward the mouth. He passed through a green land, saw many fish in the river, and found many Indian settlements whose people were friendly, unlike "their forebears, who killed a large number of Spaniards who attempted to settle in that country" generations before. Life seemed abundant on the River of Palms, which once again had been discovered.

But in the middle decades of the century a vast restraint of nature came upon the whole Southwest, plain and river alike, and brought suffering for people. It was drought. In the long valley of New Mexico the Spaniards recognized drought when it came, for the rivers of Spain mostly went dry in summer, and the white riverbeds and the gray grasses and the staring empty sky and the winds that hauled away the surface of the land and the endless question waiting to be answered out of the hot light of day were doubly familiar to them where they now lived. The river Indians knew it too and eyed their storage cists whose seed corn, held sacred for planting, would be eaten only in desperation. In the farms of pueblo and encomienda alike lay the hope of the future—feed for the cattle, crops for the people, seed for the next year.

With the plains Indians the problem had a different solution. Their roving life reached in an immense crescent from the unknown lands north of the river to the low gulf lands of the east and south. In the long years of drought the plains cattle and the people alike had little food. They had to forage far and wide for what had failed them in their own sweeping country. The great crescent contracted. The hunters turned to the river, where in its northern reaches lived people with stored food, and where across its long southeastward passage were increasing settlements of farmers and cattle raisers from New Spain. The Apache and Comanche raids, always a sporadic menace to the river dwellers, grew with each passing year of the drought.

In 1660 war parties of the plains people crossed the southeastward river and struck at the frontier posts of New Spain—Cerralvo, Saltillo and Monterrey, even going as far inland as Chihuahua and Cases Grandes. They drove off herds of cattle and retreated swiftly to the plains. The widely separated towns took joint action to punish the raiders, and by October, 1663, an expedition was ready to leave Monterrey with a hundred men, eight hundred horses, eighty loads of flour and other provisions. Under the command of Sergeant Major Juan de la Garza the volunteer army marched to the river, which they called the Rio Bravo, and crossed near the site of Eagle Pass. They found the enemy Indians defensively gathered in a ranchería, and battle followed, in which a hundred Indians were killed and a hundred and twenty-five men, women and children were captured. Six months after they had set out, the soldier-farmers returned to Monterrey. Many of their prisoners were sent to work as slaves in the mines of Zacatecas.

Two years later the pattern was repeated. The Indians came, plundered, retreated, and again the towns mustered a force to overtake them, this time with the help of three hundred Bobole Indians of Coahuila. Seventy-five miles north of the Rio Bravo the fight was joined. An old Indian woman played a flute to hearten her tribesmen. The Indian allies of the Spaniards begged for permission to capture her and eat her. Their request was not granted. But at night, when the battle was over, and the Indians were defeated without loss to the Spaniards, a captive boy was taken by the Boboles, sacrificed and eaten—"a matter which could not be remedied."

So the necessities of defense took the first Spaniards to the river in its southeastward inland stretches, showed them the country beyond it to the north, and acquainted them with the Indians who lived along it on both sides. In the years following, another necessity brought repeated delegations of Indians from the plains river to the northern settlements of New Spain. Like the Humanos to the north, they came asking for conversion, remembering the appearances among them of a woman in a blue cloak. Their appeals were finally heard by Fray Juan Larios, who came from Guadalajara to Coahuila and spent three years among the Indians south of the river. In 1673 he went home to recruit missionary help and returned with two other friars, one of whom, Fray Manuel de la Cruz, in the following year crossed the river alone to reconnoiter the opportunities among Indians in the northern plains. Once again Indians asked for instruction, but nations beyond the river were not always at peace with one another. The little frontier outposts in Mexico, with their armed garrisons, were creeping nearer to the river where it cut its long way through harsh highlands, and now the missionary purposes and those of civil government combined to make a reconnaissance in force. Under orders of the governor of Coahuila, Lieutenant Fernando del Bosque set out with an observation party on April 30, 1675. With him were Father Fray Juan Larios and Father Fray Dionysio de San Buenaventura, ten Spaniards, two Indian chiefs and twenty-one Indian allies. The company was augmented later by another hundred Indians recruited as they went north.

They crossed the high wastes of northern Mexico where the pale ground was dotted with dusty scrub groves of mesquite. Encountering Indians almost every day they made addresses, took possession and planted crosses, duly notarizing these actions. They passed over many little rivers, some dry, some flowing, and arrived on the eleventh of May, 1675, at a "very copious and very wide river," nearly four hundred yards across, bordered by "fine pastures of green grass . . . which the Indians said was called the Rio del Norte." A scattering of people lived there in grass huts. They searched for a ford and found none, and finally crossed at a place where the river had three channels, the first of which was as deep as the "hind bow of the saddle," and the second of which, too deep to ford, they managed with an improvised raft. In artless words that caught the picture of how the river looked in countless places, the Lieutenant spoke of "willow and osier brush on a little island which is in the middle," and said that the banks of the river were "very pleasing, and it had many fish, such as catfish, *piltontes,* very large turtles, and eels." He claimed the river for the Crown, named it the San Buena Ventura, and planted a large cross.

Two days later the scouting party moved inland going north and east. Once again they passed among little scattered nations of hunting Indians, and promised them baptism when they should have learned their prayers, and set up crosses, and saw the buffalo which gazed at the people sidewise "like wild hogs, with hair abristle," scolded tribes that would not befriend one another and ordered them to settle together in peace which they promised to do. The Lieutenant made notes of the country and its products. In a certain encampment on the sixteenth of May an Indian "made a demonstration" and brought him "a Spanish boy apparently about twelve years old, with a black streak on his face running from forehead to nose, and one on each cheek, like o's, and many rows of them on the left arm and one on the right." Questioned, the boy replied that his mother had raised him, and had given him to the Indians years ago. As far as he knew, he came from near Parral, in Mexico. His Indian masters said that "although they loved him like a brother," they would give him up to the Lieutenant who could take him home to his relatives. Asked if there were any other captive Spaniards, they answered that there were none at present, though years ago a boy prisoner had been killed with arrows, "praying till he died," and that a girl prisoner, after dying the same death, had been left where she fell, and for two years her body did not decay and no animals touched it. "In view of this, they took it and carried it to a cave, where it now is; and (said) that it has long hair; and that this is the truth."

On the same day a portable altar was set up, the small bell was rung, and the first sung Mass was held in the Indian wilderness above the southeasterly river in Texas.

By May twenty-ninth, the combined military and religious expedition was again on the Rio de San Buena Ventura, returning to Mexico. In June Bosque submitted his report with his recommendations. He proposed three settlements, widely separated, with four friars for each group, and a district garrison of seventy soldiers, for it would be impossible "for any officer of his Majesty to keep them in order and under instruction unless he has forces for it, although he may have to use much love and blandishment when having to correct them, for since they are vicious people and not habituated to labor to sustain themselves, they will return to their natural habits, and greater damages will result," such as the murderous and thieving raids over the river of the 1660s.

It was not long until four mission outposts, with their protective garrisons, were established in central Coahuila which though not on the river itself worked to educate and stabilize the Indians on both sides of the river frontier.

Far to the west and north, the same vocations were already implanted. At the Northern Pass of the river in 1659 "a church of branches and mud and a monastery thatched with straw" had been erected on the south bank of the river where the Mansos Indians lived, and where the supply trains between Mexico and New Mexico made a station on their long hauls north and south. In 1668 a new church was completed. At its ceremonies of dedication, a group of Indian women were baptized at one door and a group of men at another. Entering, then, the men and women were married before the altar during a nuptial Mass. The church was named Our Lady of Guadalupe of El Paso. It stood on a slight eminence about a mile from the south bank of the river. The heavy beams for its ceiling were brought from mountains far away, and were richly incised, and set upon corbels that were beautifully scrolled. Above the beams ran the ceiling in a herringbone pattern of peeled sapling branches. The Indians stood and gazed at the length of the ceiling and felt a mysterious joy in the perfect regularity and repetition of the polished timbers, in so high and so wide and so long a place. The thick walls were plastered inside and out. Before the church the dead were buried. About its walls in the open wilderness the living came together and made houses—the first wholly Spanish town on the river. For its first decade the settlement existed almost entirely to meet the needs of the mission—its irrigated fields, vineyards and pastures. These, like the whole land, suffered in the drought. It was a small settlement referred to as The Pass, and roads drew toward it from all directions. Of these the one most travelled was that which connected the two Mexicos, old and new, north and south. In the 1670s the town grew, and parish books recorded weddings, baptisms and burials of Spanish settlers. Friars on ecclesiastical business from Santo Domingo up the river brought news of the capital, where the small garrison was helpless to control the local Indian aggressions that broke out in widely separated places like fires kindled on dry wooded mountainsides by the pitiless sun, which as they burnt out left an acrid trace in the air like a troublesome reminder. Travellers from the south told of the settlements in Coahuila and Nuevo León that reached nearer and nearer toward the river to bring conversion and peace where starving atrocity roved. Every traveller could recite more calamities than joys.

It was possible that only an epidemic of smallpox in 1641, in which many thousands of Indians had died of the imported disease, prevented a general uprising of the native peoples against their new masters who quarrelled so bitterly among themselves. There were whispers of revolt among the Piro pueblos, who were conspiring with the ancient Apache enemy to turn against the settlers. Soldiers went out from Santa Fe to put down the disturbance. There were skirmishes and a few were killed. The Apache had entered the pueblos as a confederate. Withdrawing, he was like the fox who had been guest in the farmyard. He knew his hunger and he knew where to take his fill.

The great Piro pueblos of the Salines province stood in a long line below the fine sweeping eastern approaches to the Manzanos mountains east of the river. They were cities of stone. Behind them rose the mountains whose air, sweetened by the moist breath of forests, was a living blue. Before them to the east stretched golden-grassed plains where no natural barriers divided them from the country of the hunters. Twenty miles away in a straggling line thirty miles long from north to south lay the shallow white lakes of salt which gleamed amid low crusty dunes. The three southernmost of the saline pueblos—Quarai, Abó and Tabira (the Gran Quivira)—had the largest churches of New Mexico. These like the towns they served were made of the native sandstone, ranging in color from a gray rose at Quarai, to a deep coral at Abó, and at Tabira a speckled gray and tan like the skin of a rattlesnake. The friars went to these towns in the 1620s, made their conversions and led the people in building the missions. Each church and its convent were made of millions of pieces of shaped sandstone, set layer by layer in earth mortar. The thick walls, heavily buttressed, had almost no outside windows. In a great square growing from a side wall of the church were enclosed the living quarters, the storerooms, the patio and the corral of the mission, with no separate outside gate. At Tabira the livestock was driven along the interior cloister to reach the corral. Light entered the rooms from the patio, and in the center of the patio as if to be enfolded by the teaching of the church was the sunken kiva for the male cults of the pueblo. It was a kiva without the supernatural shipapu, or passageway to the nether world, such as the kivas of the ancients always had.

Large· as they were—the nave at Quarai was one hundred two feet long and fifty-seven wide—the churches were built with false perspective so that the nave would seem even greater. White plaster with colored decorations made the interior brilliant. Light fell upon the altar from a transverse clerestory window above the transept. Wooden beams, altars and corbels were carved and painted and touched with gilt. The ceiling was between thirty and forty feet above the floor. The Indians had never seen any such building: its size, its hinged doors, carved woodwork, staircases, balconies, windows, bell towers, enclosed fireplaces and chimneys; though into it went ancient devices of their own, like the ceiling with its willow wands reaching from beam to beam, and its open-hearth fireplaces in the convent kitchen, where on earthen ledges rested the table service and cooking pots. These were assorted. There was one Indian ware of the red clay found right outside the building, and there was another of pale clay decorated in black also made at home. There were rich pots from the river, brought in trade, done in black, red, and tan. From Mexico there was flowered Majolica ware and from China there was porcelain, jade green on one side and white on the other, brought north in the mission freight trains. The water for such establishments flowed in stone-lined ditches from springs or seasonal pools that lay outside the walls. In the years of drought these sources dwindled, and at Tabira Spaniards noticed that Indians saved their own urine for use in mixing plaster.

But however primitive that life, it was complete; and however isolated from civilized delights it knew a natural one in the space and color of its setting, with blue quiver of mountain air, pale gold of prairie grass, sparkle of dense cottonwood groves, and far away the pearly clouds and their wandering shadows on the plains, where hidden in space lived the quick and starving enemy. The people of Tabira looking south from their hill could see fifty miles away in its ever-changing atmosphere the range of the Sierra Blanca. There lived the Mescalero Apaches, an interior pocket of menace quite as grave as that of the eastern plains.

To those Saline pueblos, reaching from Tabira in the south to

Taxique and Chilili in the north, came drought and the threat of famine. They had no spare stores to use in trade when the inquiring Apaches came to see them. The Apaches might withdraw in peace once or twice; but as the dry years pressed hotly upon the whole kingdom they came again when the meagre harvests were ready, and stole what the towns needed to live on through the winter. They came and went, relenting long enough to let the townspeople get their hopes up and set another year's planting; and then at the ripeness of corn and fruit, they struck once more. They could lay siege to the towns by bracketing water supplies until tribute was forthcoming. Any Christian Indian venturing beyond his walls was walking into his death. "The whole land is at war with the widespread heathen nations of Apache Indians," wrote a friar in 1669, "who kill all the Christian Indians they can find. . . . No road is safe; everyone travels at the risk of his life." From the forests in the mountains about the pueblo of Taxique the Apaches would burst forth and capture Christian Indians and carry them off to their own distant encampments. "There they build a great fire, near which they bind the person whom they have captured; they then dance around him, cutting off parts of his body, which they cook and eat, until they entirely consume him, cutting him to pieces alive." More than one kind of hunger was fed but not appeased.

As the murderous raids continued, there were only five Spanish soldiers at each frontier station to combat them, and any soldiers on a mission went armored with leather shields and rode horses wearing armor. As they marched in 1668 they saw innumerable Indians "lying dead along the roads, in the ravines, and in their huts." In one pueblo more than four hundred and fifty died of hunger. A friar reported that there was "not a fanega of corn or of wheat in the whole kingdom." Indians and Spaniards alike fought starvation by eating leather. Taking hides and even the straps off their carts, they soaked and washed them, rolled them in corn meal, and toasted them in the fire, or boiled them with herbs and roots. In 1671 "a great pestilence carried off many people and cattle," and in the following year, with the province at its weakest, the Apaches struck again and again, taking away cattle and sheep until hardly any were left to the Spanish population that numbered less than twenty-five hundred.

Against such privations and dangers the stone cities of the Salines could not prevail. In the early 1670s their people crept away forever leaving their magnificent churches, their clustered houses and their lyric fields. The rust-red city of Abó was pillaged and the convento

burned. Fray Pedro de Ayala was stripped naked, tied with a rope around
his neck, viciously flogged, and finally killed with a blow from a stone
axe. He was left with his body intact and surrounded by dead white
lambs and his sex covered, a seeming respect that astonished the defeated
Indians who crawled back after the battle and saw him so, for they
knew "the ferocity of these Indian barbarians, who kill one another for
a piece of meat. . . ."

The refugees from eastern pueblos went through the mountains
to the river where some settled among kinsmen at Socorro and Senecu,
and others fled downstream to El Paso. The Salines cities were never
really inhabited again. The winds took them and the earth rose slowly
about them. The ceilings of the great naves fell. The walls in a shudder
that took centuries crumbled from the top. Weeds grew high on the
exposed masonry filled with clay. Above the common, mounded grave
of each town loomed like a sepulchre the great fragment of its church.

But even where they sought sanctuary by the river the transmontane Piros were not safe. In 1675 the Apaches streaked out of the
mountains on the twenty-third of January and attacked the pueblo of
Senecu. The pastor, Fray Alonso Gil de Ávila, showed himself in a
window holding a crucifix. He was killed by an arrow in his heart, and
more than half the people died that day. The remainder fled up the
river to Socorro. Senecu was never resettled, though the Father President
at Santo Domingo drew up plans for the reoccupation of all the Piro
towns. There was no possibility of military protection from Santa Fe.
In 1675 the government could hardly have been more disorganized under
the forces of disaster, physical and spiritual—drought, famine, Indian
atrocities, on the one hand, and on the other, a breakdown in moral
authority resulting from the long quarrel between the two majesties.

Though the quarrel had been left passive ever since a strange
event given credence in the middle 1670s. One day the Blessed Virgin
Mary appeared in a vision to a dying young girl and cured her, saying,
"My child, go and tell everyone that the kingdom will soon be destroyed
because of the lack of reverence shown to my priests. . . ." Miraculously
cured, the girl told her story, and fear seized the province. A special
Mass was sung, and the civil majesty ceased its attacks upon the friars.
But the damage was long since done, and the Indians in their impas-
sivity seemed somehow alarming, and now and then their open return
to communion with the superstitious powers of their ancient days affected
the settlers. There was an odd strength to the Indian attitude and belief.
Most fearful of all was that which defied understanding.

The Spanish governor, trying to undo the effects of earlier permissions by his predecessors, ordered the Indian rituals and incantations discontinued, and sent his cavalry to take prisoner as many of the pueblo medicine doctors as possible. Forty-seven were arrested and dragged to Santa Fe, where they were charged with witchcraft and sorcery—a crime so serious that even the Spaniards were tried for it whenever it appeared in their own life by the Holy Office of the Inquisition. Three of the Indian doctors were hanged and the others were severely whipped and jailed. Bitterly the river towns from which they came spoke against such action. They felt their own sacred forces to have been profaned, and without their doctors of magic they were defenseless against the invisible powers of evil. Once willing to come like children to Christianity, in fact, to ask for it, now in consequence of corruption and persecution within the Spanish vision of life they were clinging more fearfully than ever to their ancestral explanation of the world.

Seventy Indians from the Christianized pueblos of the Tewa nation on the river came to Santa Fe to see the Governor. They demanded the release of their doctors, and declared that unless this were granted, their people would abandon their towns and flee to the Apaches, or together rise up and make war upon the colonists. The Governor yielded. With his twenty-five hundred colonists, he could not hope to prevail for long against an angry pueblo population of between sixteen and twenty thousand. The liberated doctors returned to their towns. Among them was one from San Juan named Popé, whose bitterness was as great as that of his fellows, and whose strength was greater. With a fiery vision burning in his mind he returned home making threats and summoning powers. What he saw for the future did not seem so difficult to bring about.

Santa Fe, the capital, was the only Spanish town in the kingdom other than the tiny post on the overland march at El Paso. It lay in a wide shallow cup among mountains and it drank from a little creek that flowed west to the Rio del Norte thirty miles away. It was not a river town, it was a mountain town, and all its relation to the actual river life was administrative. A plaza twice as long as wide lay east and west. Clay houses were scattered close to the plaza, where the Palace of the Governors on the north side was the center of all office and authority. This was a long low building between towers, in one of which was a chapel, in the other a powder magazine and a prison. The official residence and offices were between in the long low rooms with connecting doors. Behind the Palace was a garden with a well, and beyond this, the cavalry horses were stabled, and the state coach was kept, and the guard was quartered. Cultivated fields stretched away to the north beyond the buildings. To the west of the Palace were the barracks for the garrison. On the east side of the plaza stood the parish church and convento of Saint Francis, in whose tower was the voice of the colony, ringing for daybreak, for Mass, for noon, for evening vespers, and for jubilation when appointed, and for sorrowful news in affliction. Across the creek to the south stood the chapel of Saint Michael surrounded by fields.

Each house was set in its farm field. Plows now and then turned up reminders of how people long ago had lived there in an ancient pueblo, and had breathed the delicious air, had raised their faces to the golden sunlight's vast clear jewel, and had known the unspoken joys of nature's beauty. For the rest, life was different, it meant to be better, it could hardly have been more severe, and its troubles of body seemed to produce there as well as everywhere in the kingdom trials, and even absurdities, of soul.

For the evils of superstition were not invited by the Indians alone. In Santa Fe private sorceries ate away at the edges of society, and scared people, and made them gossip and doubt. No force seemed absent from the hungry little colony that could help to disunify it and promise its destruction, if not yet from without the human spirit, then in time from within. When Indians worked as house servants, they brought into the Spanish mind much of their view of life, including their constant commerce with the occult. Spanish women implored Indians to bring them love potions. One such feared to lose the love of the man with whom she lay illicitly, and begged an Indian for "some herbs" which would cause her lover to "love her very much and never forget her." The Indian agreed, "but first he desired to speak to her privately." They went away together to the garden and there the Indian spoke to her, but nobody ever knew what he said. Presently they returned, and much later it was known that "the Indian gave her the herbs, that he is now dead and that the woman is now married to the same man."

The same Indian failed another supplicant. A certain Spaniard asked for herbs that would make the Governor like him very much, and was given them. Not long afterward the man was arrested by the Governor who threatened to have his throat cut. The prisoner sent back the herbs to the Indian with the message that "he was a dog of an enchanter, that there his herbs were, and that they had no effect at all."

Love and success, health and the recovery of lost articles and magic protection—all the immemorial desires ached again and were approached through sorceries. A Spanish official living in a pueblo heard that his ten-year-old son Francisco went with his young uncle to the kiva where several Indians let them in. There the young man pricked himself with an awl but without any effect. At another time in the presence of the boy and two women, he had stabbed himself with a dagger and a knife, but without making wounds. It was astonishing and frightening. Asked for an explanation, the young uncle said that at Mass one day while he was up in the choir loft, a German trader from Sonora who travelled with the supply trains had come up the stairs and had written something on some slips of paper. These, said the German, if you ate them, would make you "invulnerable for twenty-four hours." The young man at once swallowed one and could not then hurt himself with a blade. The papers read:

$$\text{"+ A.B.V.A. + A.D.A.V. +"}$$

The Spanish official was horrified and hastened to the Father President at Santo Domingo to denounce the German sorcerer, who was arrested after further testimony and charges, and imprisoned for trial. After several months in jail he escaped with the aid of an Indian, and fled south on the river road. Five soldiers were sent to pursue him and his accomplice. The case was closed with the report of one of the pursuers. Near the spring of El Perillo in the long desert passage separated from the river by mountains they found a dead roan horse tied to a tree. Near it were a pair of blue trousers and a blue doublet lined with otter fur. A little farther away they came upon hair and bones—the bones had been gnawed by animals—and the soldiers identified the remains as those of the German witch, and said they supposed he had been killed by the Indian who was travelling with him. And now they named the desert passage after the lost German—the Jornada del Muerto, the Dead Man's March. The whole story was a parable of moral confusions as they showed in the actions and the guilts of the Christian, the heathen, the Spaniard, the Indian.

But if the Indian failed in his grasp of Spanish and Christian civilization, who was to blame but the colonizer himself? "It is a shame," wrote a friar, "to see how we tell them one thing and then do the opposite, and the poor ignorant Indian sees very well what I do and forgets what I say." It was again the voice of the Spanish conscience, accusing its own "base sinners and their bad example." The hour was late, in the river kingdom of New Mexico in the 1670s, for its salvation through the spirit. The two majesties of God and King could only look desperately for aid on the physical level, and were lucky enough to find a good man in a hard job who saw what was needed and did his utmost to get it.

28.

"*This Miserable Kingdom*"

He was the Father Quartermaster of the Franciscan province of New Mexico, Fray Francisco de Ayeta. In 1674 the supply system dating from 1609, whereby freighters took contracts to operate the wagon trains, was ended, and the religious establishment on the one hand, and the civil power on the other, were obliged if they needed supplies to go in their resepective persons to fetch them. Every three years the Crown granted alms to the missions, by which was meant an aggregate of money, foodstuffs, livestock, and various matériel. Fray Francisco came with the cargo to Santa Fe in 1674 on the first of his several trips. The oxen, mules, wagons, carts and all travelling gear now belonged to the Franciscan Order. In the hard times which he found prevailing in the kingdom, much of what he brought was needed for distribution to relieve the suffering population outside the missions. He was shocked by what he found, and his energies of mind and body—both exceptional —began to work first on understanding the serious problems all about him, and next on their relief. It was fortunate that he was so robust for his age, that his nature was generous, and that with his gifts as a bookkeeper he combined a sense of humor. Such qualities were crucially valuable in the midst of the hardships of the trail and of the land at its end. "This miserable kingdom!" exclaimed the governor's papers again and again in communication with the viceregal offices of Mexico City.

Fray Francisco de Ayeta brought his train up the valley road in the dry summer. His only reliefs were the little pauses he would make— like all voyagers—at the haciendas along the river, where each clustered around the life of a family that had chosen to live away from the mountain capital of Santa Fe. Each was a walled sanctuary against the dangers of distance and unconverted Indians. Widely separated from its nearest neighbor, the estate had to be self-sustaining in all things. Owners, relatives, servants, Indian slaves, all lived like one family, taking life itself from the river water, and insuring it in the tending of farm fields and animal herds. Constant vigilance was the price of bare survival. Yet with the graces of bounteous shade from cottonwood groves, modest satisfaction in daily work, and faith in Providence, the haciendas seemed to have much to offer the infrequent passer-by, as he came to one after another in the long valley where the scattered pueblos were the only other dwellings. The valley of New Mexico was separated into two districts, as seen from Santa Fe. These were called the Rio Arriba, the Upriver—above Santa Fe; and the Rio Abajo, or Downriver—below Santa Fe. Coming north the wagon train entered into the Downriver district where most of the haciendas were strung out, and Fray Francisco broke his journey at many of them. There were the establishments of the matriarch Doña Luisa de Trujillo, and of Don Alonso García, the lieutenant general of the kingdom, and of the Gonzales Bernal family who called their place Bernalillo. The train rested at Don Cristóbal de Anaya's place, which stood near the river in a narrow part of the valley where the desert heights crowded close, and went on to the estate of Captain Agustín de Carbajal and his wife Doña Damiana Dominguez de Mendoza, who had a grown daughter and several sons. Farther along were the houses and corrals of Pedro de Cuellar.

The Father Quartermaster saw that life in such places was in danger now from many forces. One was the drought. One was the intermittent threat of the Apaches. One was the gossip going around that made much uneasiness over the other Indians in the pueblos, who here and there and in ways hard to define portended trouble. A number of families—he eventually heard of forty—talked of banding together for the purpose of quitting the northern river altogether, and returning to Mexico in a spirit of outright failure. Such a movement, if it gathered momentum, might lead to the abandonment of the whole province. And yet who could blame those who felt undefended, hungry and at the mercy of the merciless sky?

In 1675 at San Juan pueblo the Indian doctor Popé, ever since his release from punishment and prison at Santa Fe, did his best to make trouble among the other Indians whom he exhorted to rebel. The Spanish authority of San Juan watched him narrowly, and curtailed his doings until in exasperation he moved to Taos to continue his campaign. He had ominous information to give to the Taos people. It was his distinction that extraordinary powers had been revealed to him. He was able to say that Montezuma, their ancient war god, in his other-kingdom of Po-he-yemu, was gathering all his forces to lead the Indian people in revolt against the Spaniards. Popé was in direct communication with him through three spirits of the underworld who regularly came to him in the kiva and told him what to do. He could tell their names. They were Caudi, Tilini and Tleume.

Rumors of such machinations came in driblets to the Spaniards through Christianized Indians, and caused uneasiness, and yet with a garrison of only ten regular soldiers in the capital, what could be done, even if volunteers took up arms? There were precious few arms to wield. The Indians were superstitious. Popé was a disgruntled hothead. Perhaps it would rain, and all would be well. . . .

Arrived at Santa Fe, Ayeta saw how in places the walls of the Governor's Palace were falling down and how the main entrance leading through a covered passage to the patio had no doors. He heard how five whole settlements had been destroyed by Apaches, and churches burned, and their sacred images profaned. Friars had been murdered at their altars. The contempt shown for the friars through so many years by the local government was ripening in bitter fruit, for the Indians in general seemed to have lost all respect for the teachings which they had once so hungrily and so simply taken. It was an appalling situation, and Ayeta must have wondered how it happened that nobody, from the Governor down, had made vigorous moves to save it. He would soon return to Mexico. Let him present to the Viceroy a clear picture of what was needed to save the province from utter collapse. He was empowered to act for the colony, and with his creaking vehicles and his trudging oxen he went slowly, but with rapid thoughts, back to the source of power.

In early September, 1676, he made his petition, supporting it by scholarly references to earlier royal decrees pertaining to the frontier, and arguing with a show of reason on behalf of an issue vital to his emotion. It was all precarious. If he asked for too little—which might be easy to get—life itself might be the cost in New Mexico. If he asked for too much, the mind of government would decide that any real need hidden beneath extravagant demands was not worthy, and he would get nothing. On September twenty-second he was informed that he would receive almost exactly what he asked for, and this on the authority of the Viceroy, without reference to the Crown in Madrid. The memorandum provided for fifty soldiers to guard the frontiers; eight women to accompany the train to make tortillas and cook for the men; one thousand horses; twelve men to drive the horses; supplies for the caravan sufficient to last six months; and other miscellaneous provisions. The total cost was 14,700 pesos. He went to work at once to fill the bill.

Man power was the first need. He published calls for volunteers. Enlistments were not forthcoming, and he petitioned the government to fill his lists with men chosen from the usual source. Eventually he was granted forty-seven convicts, who "were condemned to serve His Majesty in New Mexico." They were to receive a pittance as pay, and be commanded by an officer and a sergeant. Freed from jail to march northward for the defense of a threatened province, the criminals for the most part accepted their fate calmly. At the last minute, three young men volunteered, and received sixty pesos each forthwith. On February 27, 1677, with his people and his animals and his cargo, Fray Francisco left Mexico again for Santa Fe. He had his problems on the way. At El Parral one of his convicts, an epileptic, who had repeatedly tried to commit suicide, and who suffered from the grand mal, falling from his cart time and again, finally ran away. At the ford of El Paso where the party was long delayed by flood waters, six convicts assigned to guard duty deserted their posts and ran away and were never heard of again. They stole fifty-seven horses, three harquebuses and six saddles. The Father Quartermaster had been given supplies to last the caravan through a journey of six months, but delays on the way stretched it to nine, and it was November before the train crawled into Santa Fe, to be joyfully received.

In December the whole population was assembled in open meeting to hear Fray Francisco's official report of what he had obtained for them. Governor Antonio de Otermín presided. Fray Francisco reported that he had brought one hundred new harquebuses with locks; one hundred new hilts for swords and daggers; fifty saddles, and a thousand saddle horses (at three pesos each). For the use of the city of Santa Fe, he assigned fifty head of cattle, and one hundred thirty fanegas of provisions, and twenty soldiers whom he armed with twenty leather jackets of six thicknesses and twenty leather shields, and sets of armor for two of their horses. On his way up the river he had paused here and there to relieve suffering by unloading supplies. At the despoiled pueblo of Senecu, where he found an attempt at resettlement, he left four hundred fanegas of provisions, two hundred goats and sixty head of cattle. At Galisteo he unloaded over four hundred fanegas of food, and cut out four hundred goats and sixty head of cattle from the caravan herds to leave behind. What was more, he reported that he had fed the troops out of his mission stores during the extra three months consumed on the journey. To keep his accounts straight, he asked that this be acknowledged, and that general receipts be issued covering all his deliveries. These the Governor was glad to authorize "on common paper because stamped paper is not current in these provinces." Stating plainly that without Fray Francisco's help the soldiery "in the defense of these provinces could not have been maintained," the receipt was witnessed by the clerk of the council, and then the clerk's witness was witnessed by the Governor. In an atmosphere of compliments and thanks and solemn legalities the kingdom took heart from its new resources.

But what were fifty men and a thousand horses and a hundred sword hilts in that land where there were thirty missions to guard, and dozens of pueblos to watch, and cloud-shadowed empires to scan for the Apache marauders who could appear and disappear like streaks of shadow on the plains? What good were so few sacks of grain to farmers who knew that the future depended not on laboriously shipped supplies but on green fields at home every year after rain? What could be done for people who let the walls of their capitol building fall down without repairing them? The drought's vast lassitude seemed to have entered into men and women. Proverbs and prayers—what else was there to try? Fray Francisco was not finished, however. If he had not asked for enough last time, he would ask again. Providence, in which he strongly believed, could operate not only outside but inside a man. Let him not wait and observe, but go to work again in the elaborate and familiar approaches to government.

In 1679 he was again in Mexico City, and again he wrote and wrote. He told the Viceroy what had already been granted, and what had been done with it, and what now remained to be done. He reminded him of how the King had approved the relief granted in 1676, and he told how the savages had been deterred since its application. Fawning almost desperately upon the Viceroy (who was an Archbishop), he recalled to His Excellency His Excellency's gift for seeing "misfortunes before they come in order to avert them." And then he had to say that whatever had been done before, it was not enough. He gave details and statistics, and labored to bring into the remote mind of authority an image of the space, the sparsity of mankind, and the poverty, of New Mexico. "There can be no remedy except to increase the number of people, so that everywhere," he said in dignity and courage, "when the offender arrives he will find the defender."

And then he asked for fifty more soldiers to assign to frontier posts, and fifty to be garrisoned in Santa Fe. He anticipated the recoil waves of such a demand, and cushioned them by quoting earlier decrees of the Crown, variously dated 1602, 1664, 1670, 1671. He was trying to influence bureaucracy with its own methods and styles of argument.

But to no avail.

On May 16, 1679, a reply from the government found his frantic appeals "not sufficiently convincing," and pointed out that only three years had passed since His Majesty had granted earlier aid. In view of this, the new requested relief would, it was feared, seem to His Majesty "to be a useless and unnecessary expense." Fray Francisco's poor wilderness reality had run into abstract policy at the viceregal capital. However, the government mused, when looked at closely, there was one aspect of the matter which might be referred to Madrid after all. The New Mexican requirements were actually in two categories—one, the mission alms which were granted every triennium as a matter of course; the other, the military aid newly asked for, and on which all else seemed perhaps to revolve. Having approved military aid three years before on its own authority, with later approval by the Crown, the viceregal court was at this time unwilling to assume the responsibility for assigning more soldiers and their pay to New Mexico. Still, it would forward the inquiry to Madrid, and leave the decision, this time, to His Majesty.

Fray Francisco was left with only his mission caravan to outfit. He spent the summer buying and packing and loading. Again he hoped to be in Santa Fe in six months, and with twenty-eight wagons and small herds of animals whose count he would increase with purchases among the ranches of the trail, he left Mexico City on September 30, 1679. Heaven only knew what was being done with his petition for armed assistance against the human troubles of the north. He marched without the usual meagre protection himself. Heaven only knew what he would find when he came to the river, after months of travel at the pace of the slowest hoofs in his care.

From Parral, the capital of the province of Nueva Vizcaya south of New Mexico, he wrote to Governor Otermín at Santa Fe by courier to tell him of the failure to get new additional military aid; but assured him that he was coming with full wagons, though slowly. He expected to reach the Rio del Norte in August.

When he saw it from the south bank in that month, the waters were high and he could not cross, but not too high to prevent a detachment of twenty-seven soldiers commanded by Pedro de Leiva to ford the stream and report to him. They had been ordered to meet him and escort him to Santa Fe by Governor Otermín. The cargo was too precious to risk in any way. Too much could befall an unprotected food train. By the muddy river in flood, at the church and settlement of Our Lady of Guadalupe of the Pass of the Northern River, Fray Francisco and his wagons and Pedro de Leiva and his soldiers waited till they could cross to the north together. They were patient, for the rhythm of travel was entirely timed by conditions of nature, and rivers rose when snow melted in far mountains or storms broke on the dry tributaries. They were among friends, for there were several friars and a number of lay families clustered about the big mission. If one day was much like another, that was what their world was made of and they were at home in it.

But early in the morning of August 25, 1680, two Indian couriers appeared at the Pass from across the river, and going to the convent asked for Fray Francisco, and gave him two letters, and reading them he saw that what he had so labored to save, the Spanish world of the Rio del Norte, was lost.

29.

The Terror

He sent for the officers of the escort from Santa Fe. At eight o'clock they appeared in the cell he occupied in the Guadalupe mission. Showing the two letters he told who had sent them. One was from Fray Diego de Mendoza, the pastor at Socorro, up the river, and it enclosed another from a man named Juan Severino Rodríguez de Suballe, a farmer in the Downriver district. Suballe's letter was shocking. The Indians of the pueblos had risen, the farming families of the Downriver were driven away and were coming south looking for safety. Haciendas like those of the Anayas and the Carbajals were destroyed and everyone on them killed. The people from Bernalillo were able to escape and were marching with the rest down the valley. Nobody was left above Sandía, and below Sandía everyone fell in with the refugee column as it passed. Suballe did not know what was happening at Santa Fe, or whether the governor were alive or dead, but he thought it most likely that he was dead. He wrote his letter on August eighteenth at Tomé.

Fray Diego de Mendoza had received it on the twentieth, and immediately forwarded it to Fray Francisco at El Paso. In his note, Fray Diego asked for relief in the way of food and protection by soldiers. He proposed an armed march to Santa Fe "to see if all who are in the town have perished, for it is not right to leave them to their fate." He went on to tell that he knew of four friars already murdered in the uprising, and he wondered about many others. He ended by saying that among the refugees there were many small children, and everyone, women and children included, was travelling on foot.

The officers fingered the letters, and spoke of "the disaster which has threatened so many times." Their families were in the north. None of them knew what might have befallen them. Pedro de Leiva, "General of the kingdom and commander of twenty-seven men" in the armed escort at El Paso, became the spokesman, and asked Fray Francisco for permission to take the letters away and discuss them with the soldiers in a formal meeting, for he recognized "the common desire to proceed juridically." Fray Francisco approved the request. There was much wild feeling and grief, and, as he said later, "The confusion . . . that has passed over my small forces since eight o'clock in the morning of the 25th could not be described on many reams of paper."

At nine o'clock the call for a war council went out. At ten, it assembled, with the soldiery and Fray Francisco attending. General de Leiva read the fatal letters aloud. Discussion followed. The first desire of everyone was to go to the rescue of the refugees on the road, and then of the Governor and all in the capital, if further news should justify it. As far as they could estimate matters now, if everyone north of Sandía was lost, then the Governor and the whole council and thirty-six priests out of forty were dead. This left a vital consideration unanswered: who was the government, and where? Without organized heads, there was no kingdom. Suffering as they were, and hungry for action that would relieve both the victimized population and their own feelings, the little knot of Spaniards at the Pass that day must restore first of all the comfort and the propriety of the Two Majesties, which had come to such grief. Fray Francisco proposed an election to be held the same day in which a provisional governor would be elected, whom he would serve, whoever was elected, as "his Majesty's humblest vassal."

He made his pledge sternly, to set an example, for he saw that there were some who opposed the election "not from dislike of the person elected but for private reasons." He saw jealousy and possibly anarchy looming. "Certain interested individuals" asked why a governor should be elected. Fray Francisco answered them grimly, "in a clear voice, in the presence of all," so that the more who heard him the better:

"So that, in case by some chance any of the same ones who cast their votes should fall short in the duties of vassal and in military obedience, he who may be elected by your honors yourselves may execute the offender summarily, according to military usage and without wasting a great deal of paper in writing, for unless an officer with sufficient authority goes, it will be impossible, in case the governor is dead, to avoid the inconveniences that will arise from every one wishing to be the head."

This appeared to answer the question, and given pause, all agreed upon the proper course, and the election was called for the afternoon.

Then before adjourning, Fray Francisco launched the first of his practical plans to succor the victims. The wagons were to be unloaded immediately of their long-stowed Mexico cargo, and emergency supplies were to be packed in them. Space was to be left for exhausted boys and girls and women to ride in. Two hundred head of cattle were to be driven ahead to afford extra provisions. Forced marches were to be laid out. He would go himself as chaplain and take along four other friars "experienced in hardships." All agreed with his vigorous proposals, and the meeting broke up to set them in motion.

Between one and two o'clock that afternoon a drum rolled and a trumpet flourished, "according to military usage," and the party reassembled for the election. It was quickly over, with unanimous votes for General de Leiva. Fray Francisco sent for a chair, and seated the new provisional governor in it. All then paid homage and swore loyalty. With that, the General was offered "a baton of wood with a blue ribbon as a sign of his election as chief. After making very courteous responses and admitting himself to be the most unworthy member of the group, he received it, in the name of his Majesty, our king and lord, Charles II, whom God keep." By order of the new governor, three volleys were fired.

For the next three days the wagons were unloaded and loaded, and the nature of the first relief debated. The soldiers unencumbered could ride twice as far in a day as the wagons could travel. The first thought of everyone was to rescue the Governor at Santa Fe and put down the revolt by military action. Leiva was to order the refugees whom he met to hurry on to El Paso, sending a small armed escort with them, while he and the rest of his men drove ahead northward for the capital. Wagonloads of relief supplies would go out from El Paso to meet the colonists.

Leiva's soldiery had brought servants and horse-handlers with them from Santa Fe. These—mostly young men—were now armed by Fray Francisco with harquebuses, so that with Leiva's original twenty-seven, and the newly armed fifty-one, the armed force numbered seventy-eight. Fray Francisco provisioned them all "generously, for in such cases niggardliness and calculation are not becoming, and so I gave each one what he asked." One man came back three times, but giving no sign the friar let him have what he took, and reflected, "I acted simply and generously, this being my natural inclination." The soldiers were each equipped with two pounds of powder and a hundred shot. If there was not enough armor to go around for every man and horse, the detachment still had eleven entire sets of armor for horses, and a number of helmets and coats of mail for men. There was a reserve supply of four thousand shot and two casks of powder.

By order of the provisional governor, whom he had sworn to obey, Fray Francisco was not permitted to march with the soldiery, but was to remain at El Paso, for two reasons. One was that he would best be able to succor the refugees as they began to arrive at the Guadalupe Mission. The other was that news of the revolt in the north having reached the local Indians, there was danger of uprisings about El Paso and to the south. If any broke out, General de Leiva thought the Father Quartermaster would be the man to control them. So he stayed behind when the column moved out on August thirtieth. "All are going absolutely raging," noted Fray Francisco. "I believe under God that each one must be reckoned as ten men." All knew in sickening detail what Indian warfare meant. According to what news they had received, many of the officers and men had lost everything in the north—Leiva his wife, three daughters, three sons, eight grandchildren, and a farm; another officer, his mother, three sisters, and much property; another, his wife and children at home. They went over the high waters of the river to take back what was left to them and to avenge what was gone forever.

At the mission, the work of disaster relief went on. The friars and their laymen ground corn, and prepared dried beef, and made biscuits; and as rations for the enemy, they went on making shot. Fray Francisco was everywhere, and his thoughts were far ahead. He saw that there was danger that the colonists, on arriving at El Paso, might not be content to stop there, collect themselves, and undertake what was needed to restore themselves in their kingdom. He feared that they would instead go right on south, through New Biscay, to their old source of life and tradition in Mexico. The entire north would be lost to the Two Majesties. It was a calamitous problem, and its solution was complicated, but he did his best to solve it.

He wrote to the governor of New Biscay, asking for "a dozen vagrants" to help in the defense of the Pass if uprisings occurred. He informed him of the danger that Indian revolt might quickly spread to the south, with the loss of northern Mexico. He wrote to the Viceroy in Mexico City outlining the same argument, and begged that the provisional governor be confirmed in office, so that order and continuity in the life of the kingdom would be assured. He pointed out to the Viceroy that the vital need was to detain and reform the colony at El Paso. The governor must have the authority to command people to stay. If it were not done at El Paso, which was "the key," with "lands and water sufficient for a large settlement," then revolt could be looked for in all the Indian nations about, and all Spain would be lost in the northern provinces There was one difficulty he had to mention—it was a legal one, but he thought it had a legal remedy. El Paso was not in the jurisdiction of New Mexico. If her residents, fleeing south, entered New Biscay across the Rio del Norte, then the Governor of New Mexico would have no authority over them. They would be then under the baton of the governor of New Biscay. It occurred to the Father Quartermaster to propose that the Viceroy issue a decree stating that though colonists from New Mexico might sojourn in New Biscay, they would still be under the legal jurisdiction of the Governor of New Mexico. There was no other way to quarantine the revolt and save the colony. Otherwise, he could promise political, moral and religious disaster. It was a persuasive case and he sent it off with a prayer that the decision would come his way.

His labors cost him peace of mind and health. He said he knew neither what he was saying nor doing. He had no news from the north for days, and then on September eighth he received letters by runner from Don Alonso García, the lieutenant general of New Mexico, who was a resident of the pastoral valley of the haciendas, and from Fray Antonio de Sierra who was travelling with him. Fray Francisco devoured the letters, for they brought more news of the terrifying upheaval in the north.

The news was better than he expected. Governor Otermín was alive, having escaped with a large number of families from the Upriver district, and together they were marching, hungry, in rags and exhausted, down the valley to overtake the families that had fled from the Downriver. Fray Francisco was overjoyed to "taste the sweetness" of this information. The two parties of refugees were referred to as the First Division, which was García's, now waiting for the Governor at Fray Cristóbal at the head of the Dead Man's March; and the Second Division, composed of the Upriver people under Otermín.

The story was enlarged with sorrowful details. The Governor was wounded, along with many of his men. There had been a warning at Santo Domingo on August the eighth, and on Saturday the tenth the rebellion broke into the open in all the northern pueblos at the same time. The Governor and his people were besieged in the palace at Santa Fe, and the town was burned about them by the rebels. Eventually the Governor led his forces in an escape from the palace and began his destitute march downriver. As far as they knew all the churches had been destroyed and their vestments and vessels profaned. The Father President had been killed at Santo Domingo. Only eleven priests had escaped. Three hundred Indians had been killed in battles and the count of Spanish dead now showed seventy-six. Both the First and Second Divisions were desperately in need of food and other supplies, and the Father Quartermaster was begged to prepare relief as soon as possible. The Governor had asked that the request be relayed to him at El Paso without delay.

The whole story was not yet told, and Fray Francisco longed for certain further details and instructions. If there had been some warning given of the impending revolt, how had it come, and what had been done as a consequence? How long was the siege in the Palace at Santa Fe and how had the defenders escaped? How was it possible for all the pueblos to rise at the same moment? What a conspiracy. Who had organized it? If Santa Fe went up in flames was there anything left? If the columns of refugees came down the river how had they managed to travel through Indian country and survive? What was the Father Quartermaster to do to relieve the travellers? Where were they going? Were they going to stop somewhere up the river and "make a stand"? What was the outlook for the future? He wrote to Governor Otermín immediately.

News of the Governor's survival and of the escape of the Upriver families was "very delightful to me," he wrote, "at a time when I and my brothers had been mourning for you." He had never ceased to hope that his patron Saint Anthony "would protect so many poor people . . . from the infernal fury of paganism." As for exactly what he was now supposed to do to help alleviate the tragedy, he wrote: ". . . I find myself confused by not having information of your lordship's decision, in order to know what I ought to do." Once given orders, he was ready to act, for "I have made all arrangements and the wagons are ready to leave." He wished the Governor would come with a guard to meet him so that they could "consult on some matters pertaining to the service of both Majesties," and explained that he planned to leave for Mexico to tell the viceroy and the government what had taken place in the river kingdom, "for not everything should be told in writing, nor is it possible to do so." He added, "I find myself in very poor health," and closed with a solemn assurance: "Your lordship may believe that you are among the chosen."

On the same day Fray Francisco wrote this letter, the Governor with his people arrived at a place near Fray Cristóbal. From there the Governor wrote Fray Francisco further news and asked him to come immediately with the wagons. General de Leiva and his men had met the Governor, and he was sending them back to the Pass to serve as escort to the relief train. The letter took several days to reach the Guadalupe mission. On September sixteenth the Father Quartermaster had his wagons in motion heading up the river toward the ford called La Salineta. He watched them start on their lumbering way, and as he watched he wrote to the Viceroy with the latest reports, announcing that he was sending supplies north, and was going himself. "I shall travel day and night, since for the sake of speed each wagon carries less than half an ordinary load." He was sorry that he could not take all thirty of his carts, but "the men belonging to six of them ran away last night, apparently having little liking for going to war." Alas, they stole some horses as they went. He was prepared to throw his great influence into the struggle to reassure the fugitive colonists, to encourage them to make a halt at a suitable place and preserve the kingdom, and "to placate and persuade them" he was taking in the wagons "a very handsome portion" of goods and provisions. Was this a device? He shrugged. With all sympathy, it was as well to recognize human nature. He glanced up from his pages and saw that the wagons were ready to cross the river, and wrote that he must "go to overtake them," and closed by kissing his

excellency's hands. He sealed his packet, gave it to the courier, sent
him off, and went down to the river to direct a troublesome job.

The river was still in flood from late summer rains, but far
away across its course an urgent need allowed of no further delay. The
lowlands by the river were flooded on both sides of the current. Twenty-
four wagons stood waiting for him. His drivers looked to him for instructions. If the long drought was broken, it was a mercy, though
perhaps one too violent, like many acts of wide nature in that country
of narrow valley, hard desert and bare, cloud-making mountains. The
carts were all but mired and those men riding horses sank in the mud
to the animals' bellies. But the wagons had to move and if nobody else
would move them the Father Quartermaster would show the way. He
ordered six spans of mules to be harnessed to the first wagon, entered it
himself, and taking up the reins drove the mules forward into the
flowing seep of the south bank. The mud dragged at his solid cottonwood wheels. Helped by some Indian swimmers he lurched into the
channel where the sailing heavy current pulled at his cart with wild
power. The mules struggled. Water poured over the bed of the wagon,
and in midstream the wagon stuck. Its high wheels were entirely under
water. It was two o'clock in the afternoon. Those watching saw the
brown ruffled water breaking about the stranded wagon and knew that
the Father Quartermaster was in danger.

At that moment appeared on the muddy north bank a small party
of horsemen. They were thin and exhausted, having travelled from
upriver fifty-four leagues in three days, subsisting off dates of the yucca
palm. They were Governor Otermín, and twelve soldiers, and Fray Francisco's courier. They saw the mules in the river barely holding their
footing on the river bed. The animals would drown there. Fray Francisco cut them loose of their harness and they scrambled for the bank.
He was alone in the flood.

Throwing off their clothes some of the Governor's men swam
out to the wagon and found their precarious footing beside it. They
lifted Fray Francisco out and took him on their shoulders to the north
shore and the Governor. The Two Majesties were united in disaster.
Nothing now concerned them but to work together for the rescue of the
two divisions of starving and frightened people who were coming down
the river. The Father Quartermaster in spite of his narrow escape from
the flood insisted that all the wagons even at the risk of losing some
must attempt the crossing. The Governor proposed instead that supplies
be reloaded on pack animals, and this was done. Men worked all the

rest of daylight swimming horses across with packs on them. In the packs were maize, flour, chocolate, sugar and biscuits. Seeing how the loading went, Fray Francisco said, "I do not know whether gold dust will ever be bestowed in the pockets of the bearers as carefully as were the biscuits." With nightfall a squad with pack mules was sent northward to meet the hungry. The friar's wagon, from the middle of the river, was brought finally to the north shore and its cargo laid out to dry. On the next day another pack train was sent out, and more provisions were brought to the north shore. For fifteen days the Governor and the friar remained in camp there. It was not long until the refugees began to arrive in little groups. Fray Francisco, moved with pity and horror as he saw them, could not find words to express himself at "such great unhappiness and pitiful tragedy, with the need corresponding to the great numbers, and the poor women and children on foot and unshod, of such a hue that they looked like the dead. . . ."

When they had eaten and rested a little the people came to the Father Quartermaster with a petition. His worst fears were justified. Appalled by the disaster that had befallen them, they declared that it was impossible to stay in the kingdom. They begged him as a merciful minister of God to see them on their way south to Mexico. In their misery they were even arrogant. How long could they be expected to sit on the riverbank barely existing on the supplies there?

Fray Francisco's foresight was what saved him, and the kingdom, even as he was wondering what to say to the desperate population. For before they had finished with their appeal to him, he was handed a dispatch from the Governor of New Biscay, written in reply to his report of the revolt and the dangers that followed it. It was "a most strict dispatch." Fray Francisco ordered a roll on the drums, and when all had gathered to hear, the communication from New Biscay was read aloud. It stated that any refugees from New Mexico who passed from that kingdom without a written permission from Governor Otermín would be ordered by all civil officials of New Biscay to return to New Mexico under "penalty of his life and of treason to the king." Any who resisted were to be delivered to the Governor of New Biscay for punishment. The fleeing colonists were trapped. It was a hard condition. But Fray Francisco said, "We have come to the point where we must act or abandon everything." And abandonment, he knew, would "necessarily expose the missions at one blow," not only those in New Mexico, but all other missions already established on the lower river, in New Biscay and in

Sonora. "Thus is seen," he declared, "the importance of maintaining the people at that place as a check, and of controlling them."

For the time being, his energetic grasp of policy prevailed. To gather enough additional supplies soldiers were sent to neighboring settlements to buy what they could. He induced Governor Otermín to ford the river on his horse and inspect the stores at Guadalupe so that he might order proper distribution of what there was there—grain, beef and mutton. Gradually order was restored to the wretched company. The colony took a look at itself in a three-day count during which all passed muster, identified themselves and told off their poor possessions, and those who could signed their names.

Gregorio Valdés "passed muster with five horses useless for service, an harquebus, a sword, a dagger, and a leather jacket. He is married, with two sons, a little girl, and an Indian servant woman. He was robbed by the enemy; and he signed it. . . ."

Sargento Luis Granillo "passed muster with nine very hard-used horses. . . . He is married, without children, and has three grown brothers able to bear arms, but having none, nor any horses. . . . He was robbed by the enemy; and he signed it. . . ."

Captain Alonso del Río, "married and without children, passed muster with three lean and worn-out horses. . . . He was robbed by the enemy; and he signed it. . . ."

Behind their count was the full story of the shock that had struck them all in the events of the revolt, which Fray Francisco heard in detail for the first time from the Governor and others.

For some time there had been no disturbances among the converted Indians or even among the heathen Apaches. Nevertheless, the Governor had ordered repairs on the crumbling Palace at Santa Fe, and the walls were strengthened, the missing gates and doors restored, until the whole government house and its corrals could safely accommodate more than a thousand people, five thousand head of sheep and goats, four hundred horses and mules, and three hundred head of beef cattle "without crowding."

Late in the day of August 9, the Indian governors of Pecos and Taos appeared at the Palace to see the Governor. They told him that they had been asked by Indians from Tesuque pueblo to join in a general rebellion of all the pueblos. They stated that they "now regarded the Spaniards as their brothers" and did not wish to join in the revolt, but came instead to give warning. The Governor thanked them and told them to go home and "remain quiet." He then sent warnings to the officials in all Spanish districts, and especially to the lieutenant general Don Alonso García, at his farms in the Downriver, the district where most settlers lived. He asked them to muster aid and come to the defense of the capital. Many on receiving the message did not put much faith in it. The country seemed quiet in the hot summer.

But the next morning, St. Lawrence's Day, as the Governor was on his way to Mass, a man named Pedro Hidalgo came to him and gasped out a dreadful story. The Indians of Tesuque only nine miles north of Santa Fe had that morning risen and murdered their pastor who said to them just before, "What is this, children; are you mad? Do not disturb yourselves; I will help you and die a thousand deaths for you." They tried to kill Hidalgo himself. He had seen it all. The Indians sacked the convent and drove all its horses and cattle into the mountains. The Governor sent a squad of soldiers to Tesuque to verify the tale and to put down any disobedience there. They returned on the same day to say that the report was true, and that other outrages had happened besides. The pastors of Nambé and San Ildefonso were dead, and whole families in the country places had been massacred, including Doña Petronila de Salas with ten sons and daughters, and the churches had been profaned and the farmhouses robbed.

(Thomé Dominguez de Mendoza passed muster who with his sons was "robbed by the enemy of cattle, houses, crops . . . The rebels killed thirty-eight Spanish persons, all being his daughters, grandchildren, sons-in-law, sisters, nephews, nieces and sisters-in-law. . . . He signs it. . . ." Pedro de Leiva—"The enemy killed his wife, two grown daughters, and two soldier sons, three grandchildren and a daughter-in-law . . . and of thirty servants whom he had, the enemy left him three, robbing him and his sons of all their property. He signed it. . . ." Captain Juan Luís, the elder, "with a worn-out mare and a broken harquebus. . . . He is married, has a grown son without any equipment, two children—correction, three—and a servant. He was robbed. . . . and he signed it. . . .")

Again the Governor sent out warnings and ordered local officials to gather their people together for common defense, and to bring as many as possible to find haven in the Palace. All day word of disaster poured in. Santa Clara had risen, Pecos and Taos too, in spite of the warning from their leaders, and Galisteo and Santo Domingo. Seven friars were killed in those places, and many civil officials and families. No word came from the lieutenant general. The Governor thought he might be dead with most of the residents of the Downriver. To Taos he sent an armed squad to save the residents and the pastors, and also protect the herds of cattle and horses that might be found there. They returned to tell that the Taos and Picuries pueblos, allied with Apaches, had already done their part in the uprising. Three priests were murdered and many families.

It was clear then that the revolt had been planned as a coordinated effort, and the Governor was certain that the Indians meant to destroy every Spaniard in the kingdom. He summoned all who could to come to the Palace. By Monday night, the twelfth of August, many people had come to take refuge from Indians who now when reasoned with said they wanted "to die and go to hell."

At nine the next morning, across the Santa Fe creek in the fields around the chapel of Saint Michael moved what the watchers barricaded in the Palace dreaded to see. Rattling through the cornfields came a painted host, some on horseback, some on foot, making cries for blood. They were armed with native weapons and with Spanish harquebuses, lances, swords and padded jackets which they had taken from the dead. There were dwellings in the fields and these the invading Indians entered and sacked, making barracks of them where they would await reinforcements from other pueblos. One of them was an Indian called John whom the Spaniards knew. The Governor sent an escort of soldiers to bring him to the Palace under safe-conduct. Riding his horse, and wearing about his waist a red taffeta ribbon which had been torn from the missal of Galisteo, he was outfitted with a full complement of Spanish arms. Carrying two crosses, one white, one red, he came to speak to the Governor in the patio of the Palace.

"John," said the Governor, "why have you too gone crazy when you are an Indian who speaks our tongue, who are so intelligent, who have lived all your life in the capital with us, where I placed so much confidence in you? And now look at you: a leader of the Indian rebels!"

"They elected me their captain," replied John. "They sent these two crosses to show you. This one"—the white—"means peace. And the other one, war."

"Well?"

"If you choose the white there will be no war but you must all leave the country. If you choose the red, you must all die, for we are many and you are few. Having killed so many Spaniards and priests, we will kill all the rest."

The Governor spoke to him "very persuasively," saying:

"Now John, you and the rest of your followers are all Catholic Christians. How do you expect to live without your friars? Even if you have committed so many crimes already, there can still be pardon, if you will return to obedience. Now go back and tell your friends, in my name, what I have said, and tell them they should accept it, and go to their homes quietly. And then come back and tell me what they say."

John left and returned. His answer was dishonest, asking that all classes of Indians in the Spanish service be given up, that his wife and children be allowed to join him, and that all Apache men and women who were prisoners of the Spanish be released, as Apaches among the rebels were asking for them. Lacking these things, war would follow immediately. But there were no Apaches among them, and the Governor knew it. John was only playing for time until allies arrived to join him from Taos, Picuries and the Tewa pueblos. The Governor dismissed him to go back and say that unless the outrages in the fields of San Miguel ceased at once, the soldiers would be ordered forth to attack. John went back across the creek with this word, and when he spoke it, the Indians joined in a howl of rage, and rang the bells of Saint Michael's, and blew trumpets, in defiance, and moved toward the Palace.

The soldiers met them in a battle that lasted almost all day, driving them back to the houses in the fields, which were finally burned about them, so that they fled to the foothills. But as they fled, the Indian allies arrived from the Tewas, and Taos, and Picuries, who attacked from another side, and when darkness fell, occupied a high place overlooking the Palace. Many Indian dead lay about. There was one soldier dead in the garrison, with fifteen wounded.

(". . . passed muster with ten lean beasts . . . the enemy killed thirty-two persons of his family; . . . passed muster . . . two sons, naked and without equipment . . . eight more small children; . . . passed muster . . . with twelve children, including four sons of military age, all naked and extremely poor; . . . passed muster . . . the enemy carried off his wife and daughter; . . . on foot, naked, without arms or anything except himself. He signed it. . . .")

On the fourteenth and fifteenth of August the enemy kept to the high ground and the soldiers under the command of the Governor patrolled all day to save the town from being burned. On the following day, Friday the sixteenth, the Indians attacked in a mass of twenty-five hundred warriors, having received more reinforcements during the night. They took positions in all the houses and roads, and in swift moves broke the ditch that brought water from the creek to the Palace, and set fire to the parish church in the plaza and several houses. The garrison made sallies to regain the ditch but failed, and retired within the Palace walls. About noon the Indians swarmed against the Palace chapel with its tower at one end of the building, and tried to burn it. Facing hot vollies from the Spanish firearms in the hands of the rebels, the whole garrison went out to save the chapel, and fought all afternoon. By night-fall almost every soldier was wounded, and when the army barricaded itself once more it was to suffer the first miseries of thirst.

With gunshot, arrows and stones, the Indians attacked on Satur-day the seventeenth, shouting that now there was no hope for the garrison, because the Apaches were coming to join the siege. In one of the Spanish sorties of that day the Governor was wounded, twice in the face by arrows, once in the breast by a shot from a harquebus. Late in the day the Indians took both positions at the gates where the royal brass cannon were trained on the ends of the plaza. To keep these from being turned on their own walls, the Governor ordered a desperate sally to recover them and bring them into the patio. Guarding the cannon all night, the soldiers fought off attacks. The Indians raised a song of victory, believing it all but won. As the Spaniards watched in helpless anguish, the whole town of Santa Fe excepting houses fortified by the rebels was set afire, and pagan chants mingled with the smoke and flame, and the parish church was burned, and its fittings thrown about, and the "whole villa was a torch." The Indians mockingly sang the Latin liturgy.

There was nothing to do on Sunday but make a final effort. After a night of fear and thirst for the thousand people in the Palace where many animals were dead without feed or water, and following Mass at dawn, the garrison in a last show of strength threw itself at the Indians in the streets with resolve to win or lose all. Their spirit triumphed, for masses of Indians, after hot fighting at first, began to break and run, leaving only scattered resistance in fortified houses which were burned about their defenders, who either died or were taken prisoner. Three hundred Indians were dead in the capital after the battles of the week.

Hurriedly the ditch was repaired and water was run into the Palace courtyard for the people and the animals. Freedom was restored —but little else. The city was a ruin. There was no food supply. The Indians had withdrawn but might come again. Nothing had been heard from the Downriver, where the great estates were, whose people would surely have come to the rescue had they been able. Dealing with forty-seven rebel prisoners, the Governor found out that the revolt had been ordered by the gods of Po-he-yemu, who promised to kill instantly any

Indian refusing to join in it. Thus all agreed to destroy all male Spaniards, even to suckling boys, leaving only women and girls. All remaining Spanish men were still to be killed under orders of the powers in the northern underworld. As for the results of the insurrection—the prisoners reported that from Taos to Isleta there was nobody left of the Spanish colony, excepting those who had gathered in the Palace at Santa Fe to defend themselves. The information was officially noted, and the forty-seven prisoners were executed.

At Isleta, as far as could be learned, the families of the Down-river had gathered and fortified themselves. The kingdom was divided in two, and the Governor saw that it was his duty to unite it again. There was no hope of doing this at Santa Fe. After discussions with his clergy and his staff, he resolved for "the better service of both Majesties and the safety of the people, arms, horses, and cattle which have remained where it is not possible to maintain them," to abandon the capital and to march "in military formation" to Isleta. There was nothing to take with them except a trust in Providence, and they left "without a crust of bread or a grain of wheat or maize, and with no other provision for the convoy of so many people except four hundred animals and two carts belonging to private persons, and, for food, a few sheep, goats, and cows."

They came down off the great highlands of Santa Fe on August twenty-fourth and sought the river with its narrow boskied passage below the desert benches, lava flows and mountains that looked down upon it. The country was pale with heat as the fugitives hastened (but nightmarishly at foot-pace) down the river. They were not alone in the land. As they struggled southward, by day and evening, they saw signal smokes on the mesas above the river. They saw lines of Indian warriors drawn up to watch their going. In the dawns the watchers were still there as the column moved starving down the valley. Apart from a few skirmishes there were no attacks; only an alien watchfulness between rock and sky that made them shiver. Among their most grievous losses was the loss of a common ground of understanding between them and the people who had been given to them, and then fought over, in guardianship.

Yet atrocity and delicacy were bafflingly mixed. When the refugees reached the sacerdotal seat of Santo Domingo, they found a common grave holding the bodies of three friars, and signs of fighting all about, and the bodies of five lay Spaniards; but the church, the convent and the sacristy were closed, and on being opened revealed that all the sacred articles were undisturbed—six silver chalices, a hand basin, a salver, seven cruets for wine and water, a thurible, a vessel, a lamp, and "other things of silver." One of the refugee chaplains took possession of these things.

They came to one after another of the estates downriver where in the thick-walled cool rooms still lay the naked dead bodies of families.

(". . . enemy killed two of her nephews, and more than thirty relatives. She does not sign because of not knowing how; . . . a widower with one child three or four years old; . . . robbed of all his property and the enemy carried off or killed his wife, three children, twenty-eight servants, another woman, and a son of his. He signed it; . . . with harquebus and sword. He is more than eighty years old, with a family of nine persons. He signed it. . . .")

During a halt near the hacienda of the Anaya family an Indian escaped from the rebels came to give information to the Governor. Asked why the pueblos had risen, he answered that "they were tired of the work they had to do for the Spaniards and the clergy," who "did not allow them to plant, to do other things for their own needs; and that being weary they had rebelled." As to incidents of the uprising, he spoke of priests who had been killed, churches and homes destroyed, and three Spanish women who had been taken captive—they were of the Leiva family—and used until word came that men from the pueblo where they were held had been killed and wounded in the battle at Santa Fe, whereupon the three women, Lucía, María and Juana, had been killed in retaliation. He himself had had his wife taken away as he escaped to join the Governor.

On the twenty-sixth of August the column reached Sandía. The church was closed. Within, they found wreckage. Everything had been broken and stolen, and the nave piled with straw which had been set on fire, but the choir was all that burned. There were brief skirmishes with Indians at Sandía and below. The column crawled on, longing for the safety of numbers and of the provisions which the Downriver people could surely afford them once they were reunited at Isleta. They saw many estates in ruins on both sides of the swollen river, including that of Don Luís Carbajal on the east bank. When they came upon a mounted Indian in their path, they captured him for interrogation. He was an old man over eighty who came from the place of Alameda. Their hopes sank at what he finally had to say.

First, as to why the revolt had happened, he declared that for as long as he could remember, the Indians had talked bitterly among themselves of what the Spaniards had tried to take from them—the ways of the ancestors, the right ways that had "come up with us," the power and the magic belonging to those "who know how." By these were meant the practices which to the Spanish were sorceries and idolatries, and to the Indians, safety through power and magic. The revolt itself had been secretly talked of for twelve years. What it was moved by went back as early as the first Spanish day in the kingdom. He himself had not taken part in any of the outrages.

Last, as to whether he knew anything of a gathering of Spanish families, soldiers and religious at Isleta down the river, he said yes, some days before a number of friars and Spanish families had come to Isleta, but they had not stayed long. Gathering up everything they could take, they had gone away down the valley leaving the town empty.

This was a hard blow, and perhaps even, in the official view, an act of insubordination had occurred. The Governor pushed on with his party to Isleta, and there indeed found nothing and no one. All that could be done now was to hurry on to overtake the first division before all in the second fell from starvation. The Governor sent four soldiers ahead with a message to Lieutenant General García to halt his march and await the rest of the fugitive kingdom. The Lieutenant General was to return to report to the Governor.

On September sixth García appeared from the south and met the Governor at the farm of the Valencia family, a short distance above Socorro. The Governor ordered him in arrest and gave the signal for legal deliberations to be held. Why had he not come to the rescue at Santa Fe with men and supplies from the Downriver? Why had he left Isleta instead of waiting to determine whether he could help those who might be following? Once again the kingdom, now in its last rags, was torn within. García, experienced in the ways of official life, came prepared to defend himself with thirteen written folios of depositions, properly witnessed. All that he had done he had done according to his best judgment and in the interests of both Majesties. To begin with, he had never received any of the three appeals for help sent to him from Santa Fe by the Governor. The people of his own district had besieged him with cries for help, and he had done his best to bring everyone together for common defense. He and his sons had tried to get word through to Santa Fe but without success. When they heard that everyone in the north had been murdered and the settlements destroyed, he and his wisest advisers had agreed that they must try to save the kingdom by saving themselves, and had gone south along the river. His patriotism had been sufficiently proved in the past. Let him, he petitioned, be cleared of charges and given his freedom.

The Governor studied the case, and in the end was convinced that his lieutenant general had acted properly under the circumstances. He ordered him cleared and released. The march was resumed. García's division was encamped at Fray Cristóbal, on the river, at the northern end of the Dead Man's March, where mountains forced the river to turn west and the land-travellers east.

Later in the same day something was seen on the southern horizon. It was a cloud of dust, and for a little while caused concern; but before long the marchers saw that it was a troop of more than forty mounted soldiers, accompanied by four friars, bringing emergency rations under Pedro de Leiva, now no longer provisional governor. When the two parties met, the soldiers fired their harquebuses in a joyful volley. Together all moved on southward toward Fray Cristóbal and the other division.

A day or so later the Governor received a letter from Fray Diego de Parraga who was at Fray Cristóbal, asking one of two things: either let the Governor send ahead enough provisions for the fifteen hundred people at Fray Cristóbal, for they were starving, or order them to go at once to El Paso without waiting for him. Fray Diego received a sharp reply. Where, asked the Governor, would he get enough food in the desert to feed anybody in addition to the thousand mouths of his own wretched division? Already "straining every nerve" to join the other division and thus provide safety to all in united numbers against the Apaches, how could it be asked now that the first division be allowed to run away—especially, wrote Otermín, when "I am so near to accomplishing the purpose that has brought me, of uniting the two forces. . . . My father, if your reverence wishes to go alone, do what seems best to you, but it is not conducive to the service of God or of his Majesty for that camp to do so. . . ."

At Fray Cristóbal on September thirteenth the forces were united in privation and spirit. The Governor called a council of war to discuss whether they should try to root themselves where they were, but all agreed that in the hardest land in the miserable kingdom they must find nothing but woe, and that the reconquest of the northern river could only be managed after the colony had been reinforced with men and supplies sent from Mexico. While at Fray Cristóbal the Governor received Fray Francisco de Ayeta's urgent request that he hurry southward for consultations, and with his armed escort of twelve men he went ahead, leaving the column to follow to El Paso, where there were food and rest, and where the muster could be taken and concluded.

On October third the rolls were closed when "Juan Sanchez Cabello passed muster on foot with harquebus, leather jacket, and sword belonging to His Majesty. He is married, with a family of six persons. He signed it."

Of the twenty-five hundred colonists and servants who had fled the rebellion, only nineteen hundred and forty-six were recorded on the rolls taken opposite El Paso. Hundreds had already escaped into Mexico undetected. But there was official confidence and pride in what remained, with "a hundred and fifty-five persons capable of bearing arms, including youths who are expert horsemen, and four hundred and seventy-one horses and mules; and there are munitions and provisions of meat and maize." And what if some of the harquebuses are out of repair? "They can be mended, cleaned, and made useful; and although some soldiers are without equipment of arms and horses, they can aid and assist one another in such an important matter in the service of the two Majesties, they being such good servants of his Majesty, deserving, noble, loyal, and zealous in the royal service, in imitation of their ancestors, the conquerors and founders. . . ."

It was a busy autumn at the entrance to New Mexico. On October ninth the Governor moved all his forces to the south bank and settled them in three camps neighboring the Guadalupe mission. The Father Quartermaster moved from camp to camp to say Mass, using a little cart as his church. Everyone thought of the encampments as temporary bases from which one day to undertake the reconquest of the north; but no one could say when that might come, though a council of war decided that it was already too late in that autumn to undertake an expedition. The colony made a town where they were. Its huts were "built in an orderly manner, each one living in the house which he has made with his own hands of sticks and branches," as the Father Quartermaster said. For the time being the kingdom could remain alive at El Paso, which was now more than a village.

But its larger future depended upon powers, resources and decisions in Mexico. Soldiers and arms were needed to establish a fort at El Paso. Legal jurisdiction of a governor over his subjects in another state must be settled. The whole chance for continued existence rested on how clearly the Viceroy and his government could be made to see the true dimensions of what had happened on the Rio del Norte. Once again the Father Quartermaster knew that he must go and work for the miserable kingdom he had already served so mightily. He had told them before, and they had not believed him, but had sent him north with empty hands.

Now in December with a story of shock and blood and horror, he went to renew his pleadings before the impervious bastions of Spanish officialdom. He arrived at Mexico City in January, 1681, and hurried to the government palace. There he was handed a document dated, at Madrid, June twenty-fifth of the previous year. The paper ordered all to be done that was necessary to save the river kingdom. It was the royal reply to his urgent plea of a year and a half ago, when he was moving heaven and earth—but not the Viceroy—to obtain the means to prevent the disaster that he had foreseen, and that had come. The Crown document was issued in the name of Charles II, great-grandson of the selfless procrastinator, Philip II. Four years later, in 1685, in spite of all there was to tell, it had not yet been answered by the viceregal government in Mexico City.

30.

Limit of Vision

The thoughts of the settlers at El Paso could not but turn toward the north. Their hearts ached when they thought of what had there befallen so many whom they loved—little sons and daughters, wives, fathers, grandparents, friends, devoted servants. Remembering life as it had been, they wondered what it was now. What were the Indians doing? What was the present image of familiar and beloved places? Who still lived as captives and what was their lot? The answers lay beyond the limit of vision to the north. Useless to stare at the horizon until the sky seemed to be made of slowly moving motes of dusty gold light. And yet the last thing the majority of settlers wanted to do was return. It was therefore disconcerting when the Father Quartermaster arrived at El Paso from Mexico City in September, 1681, with supplies, a handful of new settlers, and viceregal orders to undertake a re-entry into New Mexico. The Indians were to be punished and reconverted. Information was to be forwarded to the royal offices. Not everyone was as dedicated to duty as Fray Francisco. In Mexico he had been officially thanked "for the kindness and promptness with which he has acted in order to maintain and save the said people." He then was notified of his promotion in the Franciscan Order to the office of Father Quarter-master for the entire western hemisphere, and ordered home to Spain for discussions. It was high recognition of his tremendous labors. But when the Viceroy determined on sending supplies back to New Mexico, it was clear that only Fray Francisco, so well acquainted with the dreadful conditions in the north, could be confidently trusted to control them. He must postpone his sailing to assume his new honors in Spain and go instead to El Paso. The Father Quartermaster replied "that he obeyed with entire willingness that which he was ordered," and added that he he would loyally go north even if it cost him his new office in the end.

With his customary energy and optimism he did all he could to inspire the settlers in their new orders. But even Governor Otermín was without enthusiasm, though he scrupulously carried out every proper detail in ordering the new expedition. He knew that he was poorly equipped for a major military operation. The viceregal government had not sent the garrison to found a permanent fort at El Paso, though it approved the establishment otherwise. The men he had available to him were for the most part untrained and ill-equipped, and many were boys, and hardly any wanted to go. A poor example was set by certain prominent men who failed to volunteer for the march, and refused to accept the royal issue of farming and building equipment which would bind them to the duty of reconquest. Such action unloosed another torrent of legal depositions, charges, defenses. Old sores were raked open —the very ones who now refused to go were those who on the flight south before the storm had clutched their own wealth to themselves refusing to succor their less fortunate fellows. Yet they brazenly demanded royal protection for themselves, their family and their herds. Some had enough cattle to drive off, illegally, many head into New Biscay to be sold for private profit. The animals were so sorely needed to feed the settlers at El Paso that in desperation and contempt the friars bought them and drove them back to the hungry camps at the Guadalupe mission. While the rest starved, such enterprising men now owned "more than they did in the said New Mexico."

Yet somehow the Governor assembled a hundred and forty-six soldiers, a hundred and twelve Indian allies from local tribes, twenty-eight servants, and nine hundred and forty-eight horses, mules and cattle. On November 5, 1681, the silken royal banners were shaken out, trumpets played, and the army crossed the river going north. Without loss of a man, they were back by early February, 1682, with one hundred and three folios of written records of the enterprise.

They found all the pueblos south of Isleta deserted, and many sacred objects partially destroyed. These were gathered up and burned by the Father Quartermaster. As Isleta the Indians were present, and received the column peaceably, coming forth in tears and responding to prayers, and obeying orders to bring forth "the idols, feathers, powders, masks, and every other thing pertaining to their idolatry and superstition" which were "piled in a heap and burned." The Governor sent word ahead by Indian runners to upriver pueblos to stay in their towns and submit. When after two days he received no reply he sent his lieutenant Juan Dominguez de Mendoza with seventy soldiers to investigate, impose discipline, and return to report.

It was a hard winter. Snow and sleet storms swept down the valley. In many a camp firewood was scarce. The troops suffered privation during the whole expedition. Until he reached Cochiti, Mendoza found all pueblos empty except for an occasional old man or woman too feeble to go very far who had been abandoned by their people, and who weeping and bewildered asked for absolution. In the churches there was havoc among the Christian objects, and stores of pagan articles were found in the convent cells. All profaned sacred materials and Indian fetishes were burned. Mendoza's men plundered and burned ten abandoned pueblos.

On the hills signal smokes showed that the Indians were watching the Spanish advance, and at Cochiti, the Indians gathered in defiance. Parleys were opened. The Indians reviled the Spaniards as "horned, bleating he-goats"—a serious insult in Spanish. But gradually the Indian mood softened. A chief came forward and when offered absolution wept for his terrible sins. Plans were made for peaceful return to their pueblos of the Indians who in great numbers had fled to the icy rocks of the mountains. And at last on December eighteenth colonists heard the details of how the revolt had been started, and by whom.

The leader who inspired them all, "who had made them crazy and was like a whirlwind," was the Indian doctor Popé, who had moved from San Juan to Taos, where he talked with the three gods, Caudi, Tilini and Tleume, who had come into the kiva at Taos and were never seen to leave. They ordered him to restore Indian life to the ways of the ancestors, as it had been when all issued out of the sacred entrance lake in the north. Emitting fire from all extremities of their bodies, they told him to make a cord of maguey fibres "and tie some knots in it which would signify the number of days" for each pueblo to "wait before the rebellion." Each knot was a day apart from the next one. The cord was taken to the pueblos by the swiftest young Indian runners. Each pueblo agreeing to the revolt untied its own knot and lit smoke signals and the runners went on to the next. When his son-in-law the Governor of San Juan threatened to reveal the plot to the Spaniards, Popé killed him. Fearing premature exposure from other sources, Popé moved up the date of the rebellion two days and the fury broke out everywhere at once, with Indians crying, "Now the God of the Spaniards who was their father, and Saint Mary who was their mother, and the saints, who were rotten pieces of wood, are dead," and again only the Indian gods lived. The pueblo people were ordered to go to the river and there with the suds of the yucca root to enter and wash away from their skin the touch of baptism, and from their clothes the character of Christians. Popé now lived at Santa Fe in the Palace where he ruled like a governor. The story of the revolt was complete.

Mendoza at Cochiti received agreements to peace pacts from other pueblos. Indians came and wept for the sacraments, and borrowed horses, and gunpowder, and told how in a day or two the pueblos would all be peacefully repopulated. But a former Indian servant of one of the soldiers came to say that all this was deceit. The Indians meant to steal all the Spanish horses, and then at their own convenience massacre the trapped soldiers. The girls of Cochiti were told to go and bathe and scent themselves and on a certain night enter the soldier camp and beguile the men in their flesh until the Indians could come to kill them all. The professions of faith and the tears of penitence were only what the Indians knew the Spaniards wanted to inspire. The whole seventy men were in mortal danger. Mendoza withdrew them and returned to join the Governor in the south.

Through bitter cold and over the riverside country of ruined haciendas Mendoza and Otermín advanced to meet each other, and met in ill will. The Governor believed his lieutenant had not done enough to subjugate the Indians and, above all, had not sent him frequent and proper written reports. Mendoza replied that there had been no time for paper work, and that he stood on his record. The sorry expedition retreated to Isleta. Gathering up three hundred and eighty-five Indians there they took them, restored in faith, to El Paso where the Isletans founded a new pueblo called Isleta del Sur.

The north was still lost. Bitterness and feelings of futility more than ever divided the colony. Even under military discipline the soldiers were lawless. On the winter march to the north and back, though they were ordered to deliver to the Governor all loot or recovered Spanish possessions for proper distribution for the benefit of all, including the original owners, they had taken to themselves whatever they had found, and had kept it "with audacious impudence and effrontery." The Governor hopelessly noted that "this . . . is an offense so general that at present there is no remedy for it." The expedition was a failure. Indeed, its purpose would never be achieved without large forces, said the Governor sombrely, and paid his respects to the fierce individualism of the Spanish character by reporting to the Viceroy that his people "are accustomed to live very much as they please in everything and at long distances from each other—which was the cause of the loss of New Mexico. . . ." He concluded his report with a request for leave of absence to go south for medical treatment, saying, "My health, Sir, what with continuous attacks of headache which I have experienced on this occasion, contracted from the severe cold and extremes of weather in this kingdom, is much impaired and requires some remedy."

His report was grimly reviewed by the viceregal officials. Ignoring the hard conditions under which he had struggled, they found him wanting in proper leadership. The whole rebellion of the Indians, concluded the government in Mexico, rose "from the many oppressions which they receive from the Spaniards." Mention was made of the Indian difficulty in wearing "the yoke of the church." A new attempt at reconquest just now was useless, since the last one was "so unsatisfactory, and the people engaged in it being suspect and discredited, and having little respect and obedience for those who govern them." Governor Otermín's request for leave was disapproved. His term of office expired in the following year, 1683, and his replacement, a veteran of Spain's campaigns in Europe, General Domingo Jironza Petriz de Cruzate, came to preside over local problems at El Paso and to forward the reach of colonial life down the river in its southeastward stretches, where the identity of a people, and a place, called Texas, came to knowledge.

31.

A Way to the Texas

General de Cruzate arriving on August 30, 1683, found his official residence at El Paso to be a twig and timber hut built by the council of Santa Fe. His people were scattered along the river in camps. The land was dry with velvety dust that lay in great flats on the river's south shore. It was sweet dust and when kicked up by hoof or wind put a parched scent in the air, part of the river smell. Sweet under the summer moonlight, too, the dust looked like snow, and cottonwoods made cool sounds and breathed through sparkling leaves. In the wide turn of the valley there were softened signs of the river's old excursions out of its course. Cruzate studied the lie of the land and set about bringing his settlers nearer to the Guadalupe Mission and closer to his government. As Otermín had noticed, most Spaniards preferred to live apart from one another.

Cruzate improved his dignity, buying land from the Manso Indians at El Paso and building a new Government House of earthen brick, containing an audience hall, the secretary's office and dwelling room, a cellar vault for munitions, and another bedroom. Kitchens and pantry formed one side of the patio. Four other adjacent houses belonging to the Indians were purchased and provided a jail, a guardroom and eight bedrooms. To these royal buildings came reports of Indian disturbances in the north Mexico provinces, where the Indian triumphs of New Mexico and the sorry estate of the hungry, poor and meagerly armed colony at El Paso were familiar news. There was occasional talk of reconquering the north, but until the Crown should afford enough soldiers, munitions and pay, even a veteran field commander like Cruzate could not conceive of such a mission. On the contrary, most people still wanted to abandon the kingdom, and said so. And yet the very purpose of the Spaniards in the north was once again underscored when a party of seven people arrived at the Government Houses in El Paso on October 15, 1683.

They were Indians from down the river, the region called the Junta de los Rios, where so many expeditioners from Mexico coming down the Conchos had met the Rio del Norte and turned northwestward to the northern pass. These people came to ask again what they had asked before. Their spokesman was a Mexican Indian from Parral named Juan Sabeata, already a Christian. He asked for missionaries to go among the people of the Junta country, and even beyond, over the river, to the immense plains of the northeast, where lying like a tremendous leaf the land was veined by countless streams that all ran in the same direction toward the sea. He mentioned more than thirty tribes of that land, and the Spaniards understood him to speak of "the great kingdom of the Texas," which was ruled by a powerful monarch. The Texas were farmers, and raised grain in such abundance that even their horses ate it. Quivira, to the north, lay next to them. Once again a colony on the river was tempted and heartened by the glow of fortune, both worldly and divine, over the edge of the eastern world.

The Father President was Fray Nicolás López. While the Governor wrote to the Viceroy of the new possibilities of the Texas, Fray Nicolás instructed Sabeata and the delegates to return to their homes, and there, if they meant to keep faith, to build a church where the fathers could say Mass if they came. If he expected to see them falter, they did not. They went to the Guadalupe Mission, measured it, and left El Paso. Twenty days later sixty Indians were back to say that the church was already going up, and would be ready by the time the father could travel to it. Fray Nicolás clasped his hands together with rapture. They had kept faith and he would go to them. Not waiting for a military escort, he took two of his friars, and on December first set forth down the river, going barefoot on the harsh desert. For thirteen days the three priests, guided by the Indian party, walked along the river, crossing to the north bank at a convenient ford. The river fell lower and lower as they went until toward the end of their journey there was almost no water in it. But where the Conchos entered from Mexico the river sprang back to life again with renewed flow from the great tributary; and similarly the life of faith was redoubled again in the friars when they came to the first Indian town in the Junta country and saw the first church built for their reception. It was built of reeds, and it had an altar the size of the altar in the Guadalupe. A little farther downriver was another basketry church, larger, and equipped with living quarters for the friars.

The Father President and his aides, heartened by such proofs of sincerity, "began at once to baptize the children, because their parents offered them with singular love to our holy faith." Word came from inland towns that there too churches had been prepared. What accounted for all such zeal? Had any friars ever been there before? The Indians replied that years before, at different times, two priests had been to see them and had promised to return; but never had. There had also been visits years ago by a lovely white-faced lady in blue robes who "came down from the heights" and taught them lessons and urged them to ask for further teaching. The old people remembered her and spoke of her. She had come many times; but for a generation now she had not come any more. So once again the missioners encountered the powers of María de Agreda.

Fray Nicolás sent enthusiastic reports to Cruzate at El Paso, and on December fifteenth a military party of twenty-six men under Captain Juan Dominguez de Mendoza rode down the river, joined the priests and went with them among the Texas. Six months later the soldiers and friars were again at the Junta, having been far inland to the northeast. On June 13, 1684, the country across the Rio del Norte, the land of the Texas, was officially and legally taken possession of by Mendoza, for the jurisdiction of New Mexico. He and the Father President were both deeply taken by the lands they had seen, and desired to hurry back to report to the Governor at El Paso, the sooner to confirm the establishment of permanent missions at the Junta, and to colonize New Mexico's vast new Texas possession.

They were unable to return by the river trails to El Paso, for Indians were in revolt along its course. Mendoza and Fray Nicolás and their followers went south in a great arc and approached El Paso from deep in New Biscay. They found the colony harried by Indian threats and divided by opposing desires to retreat and to stay. An Indian uprising had been betrayed and prevented in March, 1684. The frontier was dotted with small outbreaks like fires in dry years, and signal smokes stood inscrutably in the dry skies. Yet in the face of such conditions, and with barely enough resources to hold what they held at El Paso, Mendoza and Fray Nicolás with the Governor's permission were eagerly off to Mexico in 1684 to petition the Viceroy for authority and means to go with cross and banner over the river to civilize Texas.

It was a land for which they longed, ". . . the richest land in all New Spain," said Mendoza, "for it abounds in grapes, nuts, acorns, berries, plums, buffaloes, rivers with pearls [the Concho], and mountains full of minerals." Yes, and "the variety of fruits," cried Fray Nicolás, and the "diversity of fish, the abundance of prairie chickens, quail,

partridges, and especially the grapevines." Mendoza would accept the
governorship, and Fray Nicolás would return as the church father of
the new kingdom, pointing out that he already spoke the local Indian
tongue, "having a very large vocabulary in the said tongue, as had been
legally declared" by those who heard him preach.

And there was another inducement meant in its time to be
irresistibly persuasive. Near the Pecos River, Mendoza and Fray Nicolás
had met Indians—a tribe known as the Stinking Ones—who carried a
painted cross and a white taffeta flag on which, beautifully sewed, were
two blue crosses. It could only have been a foreign flag. It was a French
flag. Somehow into far west reaches of the Texas kingdom had come
evidence that the French were somewhere in its eastern parts.

In 1686 the Spanish Empire was bringing its European resources
of espionage, and its colonial naval and land power, to the job of finding
the French who were rumored to be threatening New Spain from the
unknown country between Florida and the River of Palms. Fray Nicolás
urged that the Texas peoples be taken for Spain before the French might
chance to take them. Acting now, the ingress of the French "may be
prevented with two hundred men," where later it would take "millions"
of pesos to repair the damage. Mendoza for his part announced himself
as "the only one for this affair . . . in order to force out the French
(who may now be settled there), for he is fully experienced in matters
of war, and moreover, is known to be a man of singular good fortune
in it."

It was not to be. The Viceroy, acting more swiftly than was the
custom of his office, analyzed the French menace in dispatches to the
Crown offices in Madrid, and resolved to attack it with expeditions by
sea in the Gulf, and by land, from Coahuila, across the Rio del Norte,
far southeast of the point already established by the El Pasoans as their
crossing.

Between 1685 and 1690 the knowledge of the river in its long
Texas diagonal was increased by many expeditions, on land and sea,
in pursuit of the French to the east. A commission to conquer Spain's
northern American colonies for Louis XIV was in the hands of Robert
Cavalier, Sieur de LaSalle. Another mission was planned for a filibustering attack on the mouth of the Pánuco, where French soldiers would
land and march inland. This latter enterprise was the outcome of
intrigues pursued at Versailles by the disgraced former governor of
New Mexico, Peñalosa, who now styled himself as the Count of Santa
Fe. LaSalle from the north, Peñalosa from the coast, were to combine

their forces inland, and march brilliantly on Mexico City—where the
Count of Santa Fe had suffered such great humiliation—and take it
for the glorious warrior cushioned at Versailles. In the end, though
his scheme was modified to fit in with LaSalle's, Peñalosa did not sail
for his vengeance in the New World. LaSalle alone commanded the
French threat. In 1682 at the mouth of the Mississippi he had already
claimed for Louis XIV "this country of Louisiana" along the Gulf Coast
"to the mouth of the River of Palms."

In July, 1686, an officer of Coahuila, Alonso DeLeón, led a mission
in search of the French colony which, according to Spanish intelligence,
was established somewhere near the coast in the Texas kingdom. He
came to the river by following its Mexican tributary the San Juan, and
marched along the south bank to the gulf. The river was wide, muddy
and swift, but unpopulated until near the coast DeLeón captured
three Indians who had fled their reedy town. They told him there were
other white soldiers living to the northeast, across the river, but could
not say just where. Were these the French? He could not say. After
examining the country of palms at the river's mouth, and recording
the wide lazy issuance of the brown waters into the sea, which was rough,
and the clean beach, and the far tidal marks upon it, he turned south
along the coast. There he saw broken planking, and pieces of mast
timber, and other vestiges of shipping wrecked on the shore, including
cannon wheels, small boats and a corked bottle of soured wine. He
returned to Coahuila by overland trails without proof of the French
occupation. Seven months later DeLeón returned to cross the river
and explore the coast north of the River of Palms, but again without
finding what he sought.

But even in so wide a land, without civilized commerce, news
travelled. Knowing nothing of the Spanish attempts to pierce the distance and discover the French aggressors, the Indians of the Junta
country innocently told of strangers in the East, whom they referred
to as other "Spaniards." The Junta Indians had heard of them while
on trading journeys among the Texas, and told their missionary friar
about them in the fall of 1687. Would he give them a letter to take
to the strangers when next they went to trade? He smiled with skepticism.
Let the strangers send him a letter first, he said. They would bring it,
they said.

In 1688, DeLeón, now governor of Coahuila, was at Monclova
when strange news was brought to him by one of his Indian allies who
had seen a white man across the river in Texas, living naked and

painted as the lord of an Indian nation who paid him royal honors. He gave DeLeón's scout a handful of printed pages. Their text was in French. When DeLeón saw these he acted at once. With a small force of soldiers and a Franciscan chaplain he set out for the river, crossed on May 25, 1688, and sixty miles farther found the man amidst his Indian subjects. He was seated on a throne covered with buffalo hides. Beside him were Indian servants who fanned him and standing about him as his bodyguard were forty warriors. "I am French," he said to his visitors, "Yo francés," and gave his name as Jean Géry. He was about fifty years old. Recognizing the chaplain's calling, he knelt to kiss his robes. DeLeón ordered him politely to return to Mexico with him, and Géry with odd docility obeyed, leaving his subjects behind. Once in Mexico, he was sent to the capital for interrogation.

Meanwhile the government was pursuing the French by sea, but without finding anything except some uncertain wreckage on the Gulf Coast. Late in the afternoon of September 1, 1688, two Spanish pirogues entered the mouth of the River of Palms. There, it seemed to the viceregal view, surely there was where any invading colony would try to settle? But when the Spanish sailors tried to cross rough surf of the bar at the river's mouth in small boats, they encountered angry Indians. The sailors offered them gifts of bread, tobacco and honey, which the Indians threw upon the beach. The shore party withdrew. Heavily armed, another landing party in two small boats explored the river upstream for the next five days. A long drought was again over the river, and the winding stream in the coastal plain was very low. In a penetration of one hundred miles the sailors found nobody but unfriendly Indians who had come to the river's lower reaches in search of seasonal food—roots and shell fish. The sailors returned to their ships and sailed away.

Later in the same month, upstream nearly a thousand miles, the Junta Indians returned home from their next trading journey. Though they brought no letter from the white strangers whom they had spoken of a year before, they came with an animated story of a lively colony in the eastern kingdom. There were wooden houses and enclosures not far from the sea, they said. Other wooden houses sat upon the waters of the sea, though one of these had gone under the sea. The white people wore armor like that of the Spaniards, and traded many of their strange possessions with the Indians for food and skins. They meant to make friends with the Indians, telling them that the Spaniards of New Biscay were bad people whom they would soon go to destroy.

It sounded like definite proof of a French establishment, with a fortress and ships, and the information was immediately forwarded to the Mexican authorities by the friars of the Junta.

Not long after, the friars themselves followed their news to Mexico, for the Junta Indians rebelled. Toward the end of the year Captain Juan de Retana marched for the Junta to subdue the Indians and enlist Indian guides who could take him across Texas to the French colony. Before he could leave for his eastern expedition, Juan Sabeata, the Junta chief, arrived from the east with a tale that changed all his plans. There was no longer a French colony by the sea. It had been wiped out, with massacre and torch, by eastern Indians. Sabeata gave Captain de Retana a few scraps of paper which he had obtained from Indians of the massacre. They were written pages in the handwriting of LaSalle, describing part of his voyage to the Texas coast. One of the pages carried a drawing of a French ship with a French verse on its sail. Retana cancelled his plans and reported what he had heard to his chief in Mexico, sending him LaSalle's manuscripts.

Now armed with the information taken from Géry in Mexico, and with Retana's news, Governor DeLeón marched out for the fourth time to find LaSalle's settlement. Géry went with him as guide. They went over the river on April 1, 1689, crossed many more streams going east, and on April twenty-second (after many false directions given by Géry who they decided was insane), coming downstream along a small creek, they saw at last what it had taken them years to find. It was Fort Saint Louis, empty, silent, charred and strewn with human remains and the wreckage of possessions.

DeLeón explored the coast, and scouted the inland country where he found two survivors of Fort Saint Louis. One of these was Jacques Grollet. The other was Jean L'Archevêque, who in March, 1687, had assisted at the murder of his commander, LaSalle. They were taken as prisoners to give information in Mexico. Before turning homeward the expedition heard the pleas of a Texas chief for conversion. He showed them his altar, with a figure of Christ on a cross, and four painted saints, and a light that he kept burning as in a sanctuary night and day. He had long known the usages of the Christians. Where had his knowledge come from? He replied that though he had never seen her himself, his forefathers had seen her, and had kept her instructions and her memory alive among them. She was a woman in a robe like that of DeLeón's chaplain, over which she wore a blue cloak. The chaplain, Fray Damián Massanet, recognized María de Agreda from the description, for she was now famous throughout the Indies. He promised to return with his brothers and all that would be needed to establish missions in the eastern kingdom. DeLeón led his party back to Coahuila.

He returned in the following year with Fray Damián and a full complement of friars and soldiers. Two missions were established, and for the next few years held the wilderness against rumors of renewed aggressions by the French. Texas became an official province of Spain. Meagre pack trains with a handful of armed guards went back and forth on the long journey from Coahuila across the Rio del Norte. But the tendrils of Spain at their farthest tips received little nourishment from the main source of energy, for Spain was at war with France, and missions without fortresses of soldiers in the wilderness could not long survive. In 1692 and 1693 the Texas missions were abandoned. Yet a way to Texas had been marked out across the river through the hard brush country; and dotted by quill pens in guizache ink on dried skin maps the way remained to be followed again.

An older kingdom, settled for almost a century, and lost for a decade, still called for reconquest. At El Paso, the entrance to New Mexico, Spaniards looked north along their river again.

32.

The Great Captain

In the autumn of 1692 the cold came earlier than usual, and on the plain of Santa Fe smokes from hearth fires stood together in airy columns above the city, where the victorious Indians had lived for twelve years. The palace was partly a ruin, partly a pueblo. All Spanish furnishings had been burned. Rooms had been added, and battlements. Other communal dwellings had been built until there were four, with cells for a thousand people. The church on the plaza and Saint Michael's across the creek were open to the sky. Their doors were long since

burned. Cattle and sheep were corralled within the charred walls of
the churches. The plaza was bare of all but refuse. Spanish trees had
been hauled out by the roots, Spanish flower beds dug up. Orchards
were ruined and fields where once wheat and melons grew, grapes and
any other product of Spain, were long since ravaged, in Santa Fe as in the
river pueblos. Dogs and turkeys wandered freely in the plaza dust. The
city was neither pure pueblo nor Spanish capital, but a heap of occupied
ruins of both kinds of life that told the worst about each. Only the
act of rebellion had been a success for the Indians. Having known a
century or more of a new life, they could never wholly return to the
way of the elders in all the fearful magic of its animal doom. Shreds of
the new life clung, even if they were only the bitterest shreds. The
primal glories of the Indian past, where were they? Under Popé,
governing a pueblo federation, the golden age was supposed to have
dawned. Imitating the Spanish governor, he gave himself state at Santa
Fe. One time with savage hilarity he enacted a furious burlesque
of Spanish manners, religious and official. At the pueblo of Santa Ana
he presided over a feast, with a long table laid in the Spanish style. He
sat at one end as the Governor, and at the other he placed another
Indian as the Father President. From the fouled treasures of a mission
church he sent for two chalices. With one of these, Popé gave a toast,
bowing down the table, and saying, "To your Paternal Reverence's
health." The other Indian rose and lifting the other chalice, replied in
mock courtesy, "Here is to your Lordship's health, my Lord Governor,"
and all roared with laughter. But Popé was a worse tyrant even than
any Spanish governor and by his very pretensions as prophet, a failure.
His promises of rain that would fall on dead Spaniards and live Indians
were lies. The rivers continued to dry up, and if the ancestors came
to show themselves in vast thunderheads over the mountains, no rain
fell from their hands. Popé died but his successor improved nothing.
The Pueblo federation broke up. Rule returned wholly to the separate
pueblos. Neither the old nor the new gave comfort. The Spanish farms
and orchards downriver, the Spanish meadows upriver, were wild and
profitless, except to an occasional Indian who rode by and for his
journey picked a handful of cherries, plums, peaches or apples. The
land and the people were so poor that half the pueblos, undefended by
Spain, were abandoned under Apache pressure against their dwindling
food stores. The baptisms were washed off in the brown river, cribs
of Spanish wheat were burned, pigs and chickens were exterminated,
the many gods were lifted in place of the One, in the plaza of Santa Fe

a kiva was built, and with pity locked in their jaws and in misery under the sun the rebels were left with the forlorn consequences of their triumph.

It was very cold and dark in Santa Fe before dawn on September 13, 1692, and the fields about the town were quiet when suddenly, at something after four o'clock in the morning, the voices of two hundred men rose toward the sleeping walls and together shouted out five times in Spanish, "Glory be to the blessed Sacrament of the altar!"

At once Indians came to the tops of their walls, men and women, youths and children. They peered into the darkness of the fields where the shouting came from. Who was there? they demanded, and a voice answered in the Indian tongue that these were Spaniards, come back to forgive and to resume what was theirs. No, cried the Indians, that was a lie, it was a war party of Pecos and Apache Indians who shouted in the fields. At this the Gloria was repeated, and after a pause, the Indians asked, if it was Spaniards who called from the fields, why they did not fire a harquebus? To this a commanding voice replied:

"Be calm. I am a Catholic, and when the sun rises you will see the image of the Blessed Virgin on my banner."

It was the voice of Don Diego de Vargas Zapata Luján Ponce de León, the new Governor and Captain-General of New Mexico. The banner he carried was the same one that had come up the river with Oñate in 1598, and had gone down the river with Otermín in 1680.

In the darkness the Indians could not be sure, and asked that a Spanish trumpet be played in proof. In answer, the trumpet sounded and a long roll on the military drums. The Indians on the roofs called back that they were ready to fight for five days, and would kill every Spaniard, allowing none to escape next time. Their words stung their own spirits into frenzy. They all turned up their faces and pointed their jaws like foxes, coyotes, wolves and dogs, and beginning to howl in fury, kept it up for more than an hour, while dawn approached, and soldiers went to take up strategic stations at the entrances and corners of the city, and Indians dragged stones to block openings in their walls, and piled others to use as missiles. As the gray light turned to white, and then gold, they could all see each other. At sunrise Vargas, with his interpreter and two officers, rode forward twenty paces and identified himself. Showing the banner with the arms of the king on one side and Our Lady of Reme-dies on the other, he called for peace and promised amnesty. They asked him to remove his helmet so they could see him better. He turned to his arms bearer, and asked for his hat. Then Vargas rode forward, taking off his helmet and the scarf beneath it and showed himself, repeating his promises and invitations.

The Indians were clustered with drawn bows on the roofs. They quickened tensely at every random move made by a soldier. They countered promises of peace by saying that years ago the Spaniards offered peace to Apaches and then killed them. Vargas answered that the Apaches were traitors who used guile to enter in order to kill. He rose in his stirrups and showed a rosary and a cross, and he took his banner and held it aloft. He pointed to his three chaplains who stood with the soldiers. They would absolve the rebels and all would be at peace.

An Indian on the walls acted as spokesman. His name was Bolsa, The Pouches, because of his big cheeks. He said that all the governor said might be true, and yet if they came down, wouldn't the Indians be ordered to rebuild the churches and houses of the Spaniards? If they did not do as they were told, they would be whipped. Didn't they remember? They had not forgotten Xavier, Quintana, and Diego López. Were these men with the soldiers now? Vargas replied that they were not and promised that they would never come back to New Mexico.

In the full daylight the Spanish supply train and two pieces of bronze artillery on carts came over the fields and made camp. Every soldier had strict orders to make no hostile move, and fire no gun, even into the air, unless Vargas gave the signal to attack, which would be the drawing of his sword. Bolsa on the wall declared that those who were to blame for the revolt were all dead. Vargas repeated his pardon and lifted his banner. An armed Indian came forward from the gate in defiance. He refused to give Vargas his hand. Indians on the walls told him to ask for something, and he did so, asking that two friars come inside with him. Hearing him, two Franciscans dismounted and were ready to go but Vargas detained them. Not yet, he said. The friars obeyed him. Spanish sentry calls sounded from the corners of the pueblo.

Vargas turned to see throngs of Indians coming off the heights above Santa Fe, some on foot, some mounted. "Now you will see!" cried the people on the walls. Vargas sent a squad to each side of the town to hold the Indian reinforcements at bay. On the roofs the people dragged up more stones and made their walls higher. They painted themselves with vermilion and called all animal powers to war for them, reviling the captain-general for his pleas and pledges. He called a detachment of Indian allies and soldiers. Pointing to the ditch that took water into the walls he ordered them to break it and divert the flow. It was quickly done. An outcry arose from the walls. Vargas proclaimed that water would be restored, and peace made certain, if the Indians came down to render obedience. He gave them one hour in which to agree, and retired to his camp for a breakfast of biscuits and a drink of chocolate, which was served to all the soldiers.

Vargas was busy for the next two hours. He ordered the two cannon dragged in their carts by mules to a position facing the Palace. Powder stores were brought up to be used as mines against the walls. Indian delegates from other pueblos arrived and were kindly received, promised peace and told to go to the besieged people with calming messages. The soldiers worked mightily at their tasks, and in the face of overwhelming enemy forces, "showed no concern for the risk and danger of their lives." Vargas was proud of them and loved them as a commander loved good soldiers.

There was movement behind the battlements of the Palace. Seeing the artillery now trained on them, all but the archers at the loopholes were leaving the Palace at the rear. An Indian messenger came to Vargas to say that he had done all he could, but without success, and he believed he could do no more. Vargas talked with him at length in the open space before the town. Seeing the two engaged so in conversation, the people began to return to the Palace in wonder. Vargas for the last time seized his banner, his rosary and his cross, and went before the walls to deliver a final exhortation before giving battle.

And now the Indians accepted peace, provided he would pull back his troops to the supply camp, remove his cannon, and come unarmed himself to receive them, who would also lay down their arms.

So the long day of haranguing was over. Two unarmed Indians came forward. Vargas dismounted and embraced them. The Franciscan fathers now went into the Palace. Indians streamed forth to make peace with Vargas, which he "extended to all of them with great love, as I stood there dismounted, embracing them, shaking hands with them, and speaking to them with tender and loving words. . . ." Giving orders that Indians must hang crosses about their necks, and erect a large cross in the patio of the Palace, Vargas some twelve hours after his first call in the fields before dawn retired to camp, leaving soldiers on guard against treachery. But gazing across the fields toward the Palace he made a sudden resolve. "I decided to place some trust in fate," he said, and ordered all soldiers to return to camp, bringing the artillery with them, and leaving the town free and open for whatever the Indians resolved upon. It was a lofty demonstration of good faith. It was supported by good military sense in camp, where Vargas "ordered that tonight the horses and mules be provided with a guard of two squads and that they might not be permitted to separate." Two other squads were armed and at the alert with their mounts saddled, "in case of any sudden attack." Night fell cold on the peaceful reconquest of the capital of the restored kingdom.

Vargas was the son of a great family close to the throne in Spain. From the time of his birth it was taken for granted that he would enter public service, and his career was a pleasant chronicle of progress from one responsible preferment to another. He fought with the Spanish armies in the kingdoms of Naples and Italy, and in 1672, like many another less illustrious scion, turned his ambitions toward the New World, which he entered as a diplomatic courier. In Mexico he filled a succession of political posts, always with distinction and honor. In 1688 he was given the governorship and captain-generalcy of New Mexico by the King, and when talk of a reconquest arose there were understandings that so great a young lord (he was in his late forties) would be willing to outfit an expedition at his own cost, on the revenues derived from his rich holdings—palaces and houses and villas at Madrid, Granada and Mexico City; grainfields, olive orchards, vineyards, pigeon lofts and arable lands at Torrelunga, Buytrago, Miraflores, and Salamanca; the salt works at Orcaña, and the rest. He took command at El Paso in 1691. Facing north, he had the full support of the viceregal government, for it was now understood that New Mexico must be regained on two new accounts—one was the necessity of a northern buffer against the French, or any other power that might look for an easy conquest of a vast kingdom; the other was the rumor that quicksilver existed in rich commercial quantities in a range of mountains called, in a general poetry of the region, the Sierra Azul—Blue Range. Beyond such purposes, there resided always the earnest belief that for their own souls' sakes the apostate Indians must be restored in the Holy Faith.

There had been earlier attempts at a reconquest. While Texas was coming to light across the lower river, the El Pasoans went north in 1687 and again in 1688. The first of these two forays yielded nothing; the second resulted in a pitched battle against the Pueblo of Zia, on the Jemez creek, in which six hundred Indians were killed and the houses were burned. It looked like the beginning of a reconquest, but without additional arms and men to exploit it, the venture had to stand by itself, a futile and costly but proud effort to move against the rebels.

And then before Vargas in his turn could take the river trail he was obliged to remain at the entrance of New Mexico and from there to lead missions of punishment against the Indians of northern Mexico who were in sporadic revolt, and who unsuppressed would be a danger to his base at the Pass and his communications to the rearmost echelon of the colonial command at Mexico City. At last in the summer of 1692 he was ready to go north. Fifty soldiers from Parral were to join him at El Paso, but as the hot months wore on they did not come, and he went without them, leaving orders for them to overtake him in New Mexico. On August twenty-first he led his column of two hundred men, gathered from among Indian allies and Spanish colonists at the Pass, across the river into the silvery wavers of the desert heat. The departure, at four in the afternoon, was ceremonious, with banners shaken out and military music.

Vargas was a tall man. His long hair and large eyes were dark, his face was a long oval with a straight nose, and his mustaches and beard were slender. He wore a morion and body armor. His horse-stained boots were wrinkled up about his thighs when mounted, and folded down below his knees when dismounted. In his luggage he carried court dress of much splendor, including Dutch linen shirts with shoulder-wide collars and long ballooned sleeves; knee-length vests embroidered and edged with gold lace; slashed doublets outlined with fur and tied with ribbons; knee breeches with bullion garters and bows; white silk hose; low shoes tied with double bows of silk ribbons; dark velvet hats crowned with plumes and faced under the brims with ermine; and stiff taffeta baldrics to carry his light dress rapier. These proclaimed estate. Within he carried the essence of it. His mind was orderly, clear and grave. He was without fear of all things short of God. He rode northward into experiences which, however familiar they were to men before his time, were new to him and charged with peril. Many of the soldiers with him were returning to the lands they had fled twelve years before.

They crossed northward along the Dead Man's March, moving slowly because of the dragging pace of the supply train and its animals, and came to the first pueblos, Senecu and Socorro, which were empty. Going up the east bank of the river they passed by the first of the abandoned and overgrown haciendas where the air was hot and sweet with the summer breath of the narrow valley in its wide desert—the smell of warm river mud, and of varnished cottonwood leaves, and of marshy fields busy with droning life in their low air. Vargas at one of the estates left behind him the larger part of the supply train with an officer who was to await the reinforcements from Parral, and moved on through the next pueblos toward Cochiti. There he expected the fullest strength of the Indians to meet him, since all other pueblos were abandoned.

But when on September eleventh he came to Cochiti, it was, like all those towns downriver, empty, and he went to Santo Domingo on the Galisteo creek. It too was abandoned, and only Santa Fe lay ahead. On the twelfth the column with much difficulty climbed an abandoned and eroded path up the escarpment of La Bajada and stood on the wide plain looking toward the Sangre de Cristo mountains at whose base lay the capital. Vargas halted there until sundown, resting his men and animals. He ordered an assembly and spoke to the soldiers of their duty and responsibility in upholding both Majesties in the encounter that surely lay ahead, for Indians from the empty towns behind them must have gathered at Santa Fe. At eleven o'clock he gave the command to move forward in the cold dark night. Later he halted again and designated three o'clock in the morning as the moment to advance against the city. When that time came, he was to be notified by certain officers who would know the hour, "through their knowledge, by the position of the stars." They moved on at three and halted once again to receive absolution from the chaplains. The soldiers were forbidden to fire or make any gesture of war unless they saw the captain-general draw his sword. At another signal, once they had come to the open fields by the walls, all were to cry out the Gloria. Bound together by command, understanding and excitement, the shivering column crept forward to the surprise of Santa Fe and its peaceful recapture after the long day's debate outside the walls.

On guard by the horses in the Spanish camp, the soldiers saw people coming and going all night long at the Palace gates. In the morning, word was sent that the Indians would be given absolution in the patio of the fortified buildings. Vargas laid aside his armor, his rough campaign clothes. His page opened a brass-studded leather trunk and brought out a suit of court dress which Vargas put on. So arrayed "in gala," as he said, but bearing arms, he went to witness the sacrament in the palace. The Indians asked that he come without soldiers, for the women and children were afraid. His officers warned him against going without armor and alone. But he saw the Indians holding bars of timber across the gates, and he went forward unescorted. "So," he said, "I gratified them, so that they would not think that I was afraid," and they lowered their bars, and he entered the patio where he saw that a large cross had been erected. The friars went with him. The people, reassured, in great numbers began to come down from their high roofs on their ladders made of poles. The royal banner was raised three times, and three times the multitude repeated after the captain-general the cry of "Long live the King," and all cheered, and knelt down while the reconquering fathers intoned the Te Deum Laudamus. The absolution, with all kneeling, followed. Santa Fe was again a royal city.

In the next few days, not waiting for the reconquering governor to come to them, the governors of several pueblos appeared one by one at Santa Fe to render obedience. San Lázaro, San Cristóbal, Tesuque, San Juan and Picuries were represented. One of the pueblo lords wore animal skins and around his head a yucca palm bandeau to which a heart-shaped shell was affixed, "all of which resembled a diadem." Advancing toward the Captain-General he three times fell to one knee, "to make three courtesies." He displayed a few Christian objects. Invited into the headquarters tent, he drank chocolate with the Spaniards and was lavished with "affectionate words." On the following day he called again upon the Captain-General with something on his mind. It appeared that his people and certain other pueblos were at war with one another. He asked the Spanish commander to defeat his enemies, among whom were the pueblos of Pecos and Taos. Vargas gazed at him, who was a known traitor, though now restored and absolved. The fifty soldiers from Parral were not yet arrived in Santa Fe. Their presence might tip the scales in any conflict with Indians. Making a sudden decision, and "trusting in Blessed Mary, our Queen, Our Lady and Advocate of Remedies," Vargas promised to march for Pecos.

He waited five days for the Parral company, but they did not come, and leaving orders for them to follow, he set out on Sunday, September twenty-first, and camped that night in an arroyo near Galisteo. As he was mounting his horse the next morning to resume his march, he heard two signal shots, and in a few minutes the guards challenged seven mounted men who rode up with jingling accoutrements. They were the first of the relief party from Parral. The rest were following from Santa Fe. By late afternoon the command was complete. Together, they moved out and marched until ten o'clock at night. Ahead of them was Pecos in the dark.

When they came to it on the following morning, they saw "two curls of smoke" rising above the rosy clay city and when they moved closer they saw that it was abandoned. Vargas remained for five days, scouting the country, and capturing twenty-seven Indians who said only that their people had fled to the mountains and were not ready to make peace. With the captives was another, a Spanish youth, who was the son of Cristóbal de Anaya. He had been held captive ever since the day in 1680 when his father had been murdered at the family estate down-river. He was taken in charge by his uncle, Francisco Lucero de Godoy, who was with Vargas as captain of the artillery, and who now under-took to have the boy taught the trade of armorer. Vargas freed the Pecos prisoners with messages of amnesty. He left the pueblo intact, neither burning it nor sacking its stores of grain, and returned to Santa Fe.

Between the twenty-ninth of September and the eighth of October the army marched into all the northern pueblos and received their obedi-ence, including that of Taos. Ceremonies of rededication to both "the divine and the human Majesties" were held, absolutions granted, and baptisms performed, in peace. At Taos, Indian travellers told Vargas that they had lately returned from the far western pueblo of Zuñi where a council of war had been held with the object of organizing the annihi-lation of the Spaniards. He marched at once for Santa Fe, and left there immediately to make his appearance in all the pueblos not yet visited. Going by way of Pecos, he found now a full population who came out to meet him and to submit, secure in the possession of their city which he had not burned, their storerooms and kivas which he had not sacked. Surrounded by guns and gunpowder, armor and tough horses and an impregnable sense of righteousness, the Captain-General found enough strength aside from these powers to do his duty and fulfill his orders with merciful humanity. It was the strength of a perfect, an unquestioned aristocracy in which official obligation was matched by an imaginative grasp of human nature. He received the submission of Pecos and turned west to the pueblos across the Rio del Norte, where again he entered and left in peace—Zia and Jemez, though at the last of these there were precarious moments when dancing and shouting and arrayed for war the Indians seemed alive with menace under their festive airs. Jemez had attended the murderous council at Zuñi, and Vargas knew it. He entered the milling crowd on foot with only a handful of soldiers, and gravely and calmly ordered the women and children to come down to him from the roofs, and the men to put down their weapons at their feet, and give him their hands, and listen to him, as he walked about among them saying what they must hear and must do. Once again by the richness of his inner powers he prevailed. Jemez kneeled down under his voice, his eye, and his hand.

Now for the march to the far western provinces where revolt was organized, he needed a light force of high mobility. At the end of October the weather was already wintry. His pack train, the people with it, had already suffered from the cold, including many Spaniards and the surviving households who had been freed from captivity in the tour of the pueblos. Facing what was possibly to be his most dangerous march, Vargas yet dismissed his artillery, his wagons and a squad of his soldiers, ordering them to lead the delivered colonists to their kinsmen and friends at El Paso. He gave them meat and pinole, biscuits, chocolate, sugar, tobacco and soap. Then he left them to make their slow way southward, while with his cavalry he rode on to Isleta, which he found empty and in ruins, where only the walls of the church were standing. Turning to the west he left the river on October thirty-first. Far across the wintry deserts were the pueblos in league against him—Zuñi, Oraibi, Walpi—and there too were the mountains where quicksilver was supposed to be seen in an earth called vermilion with which the Indians painted themselves, and "which leaves a purplish luster, greasy and buttery when rubbed in the palm of the hand, and which is good for cold eyes, preserves the condition of the face, and removes the marks of small-pox. . . ."

On December tenth he brought his men back to the river near Socorro. They had marched in blizzards and in thirsty dryness. The western pueblos ready for war had resisted, one by one, but not for long. The Captain-General spoke to them at length, and walked inadequately guarded upon their mesas, and here and there occurred those episodes of suspense in which for a crystalline instant the forces within the Indian mind seemed about to crack toward violence; but piled stones were not hurled, arrows were lowered, and the lonely cry of the Te Deum Laudamus ascended from the rocky plazas in the bitter wilderness.

They hastened south now along the river toward El Paso. Attacked by Apaches, they captured two, one of whom was killed. Vargas intervened before the other was killed, and asked for a statement from him. Had the Apaches entered El Paso to steal and destroy? The Apache replied that during the same moon, "he and a companion had entered and stolen two horses, that this was all he knew." Vargas then turned to his chaplain, asking him to tell the Indian that he should become a Christian and that, after he had agreed, he would be shot. The chaplain talked with the Indian who accepted baptism, and the name of Agustín. In his conviction of performing a virtuous service, both compassionate and stern, Vargas, in the Spanish renaissance, was concerned for the economy, the health, of the soul at the moment of dying. He watched the dealings of the friar and the Apache to their finish, "and this having been done," he said, "I ordered the lieutenant of cavalry to have four soldiers take the said Indian off to one side and shoot him forthwith, giving him a good death." The march continued and on December 20, 1692, after four months in the northern river kingdom, the expedition arrived at El Paso.

What they had accomplished was proudly reported to the Viceroy, and a sample of vermilion earth was sent to Mexico to be assayed for quicksilver. Twenty-three pueblos were pacified and restored to the official faith. Over two thousand Indians had been baptized. No soldier had been killed, and no Indian, other than Apaches. At Zuñi a treasure of sacred vessels and vestments and books belonging to the friars murdered in the great rebellion was recovered and brought to El Paso, and was handed over to the Father President. Haciendas and churches were in ruins, and most of Santa Fe, but with peace restored, there was yet much to rebuild the Spanish kingdom on. Indians could still read and write Spanish, and still knew the responses in hymns, litanies and prayers. Except for the salaries of the fifty men from Parral, the enterprise in all its march of nearly two thousand miles had cost the Crown not a single maravedi. The kingdom now awaited only the return of families, the rebuilding of the capital, the resettlement of the rankly overgrown haciendas. The Captain-General had plans for his second entry into New Mexico.

Vargas's news overjoyed the city of Mexico. The cathedral was outlined with illuminations and bells were rung in all the churches. His report was forwarded to Madrid. Commendations were voted to him, and were sent to him by viceregal courier. The mail also brought instructions for him to return the fifty soldiers from Parral to their home garrison, as he would have no need of them now. One more detail was reported on in the papers that came by official pouch to Vargas at El Paso. "With regard to the matter of the red vermilion referred to in his letter, let him be notified that the examination has been made and that it has been found to have no quicksilver content."

But if one of the purposes of a reconquest was suddenly thus undone, the others remained; and on October 4, 1693, ninety-six years after Oñate's entry, and thirteen after the murderous revolt, the old colony left El Paso for the north. All their difficulties in the undertaking were by now familiar ones, and one by one in laborious and familiar measures they were met. Vargas had asked for soldiers, and had been assigned a troop which brought his armed component up to one hundred men. "You might as well," he wrote in the level tone of his day, "you might as well try to convert Jews without the Inquisition as

Indians without soldiers." The colony embraced a wide range of qualities, from Spanish lords, learned friars, taciturn mercenaries and gently
bred ladies to half-breed Indians, jailbirds under orders, licensed lawyers
and worried merchants; and it included L'Archevêque, one of LaSalle's
murderers, who had come from Mexico to enroll. There were seventy
families, eighteen friars, and many Indian allies. The train included
eighteen wagons pulled by mules and horses and three cannon in carts.
A thousand mules, two thousand horses and nine hundred cattle were
herded along the way. Leaving Guadalupe mission with buccinal music
and flags that bobbed in the air at the rate of a horse's walk, the column
went to the river where they knew much delay and bother in crossing,
but finally crossed and drew away northward through the Pass. A week
later Vargas and his staff left the mission and overtook the column on
the road. With him was his official standard, making its third ascent of
the river. He inspected his people, and rode on ahead with a light escort
to test the temper of the pueblos.

He found that once again all but a few of them were hostile. A
friendly chief offered to help him with messages to Santa Fe. Vargas
rejoined his main column. Thirty women and children had died in
crossing the Dead Man's March. Slowly the remainder advanced to the
heights of Santa Fe and on December sixteenth faced the city. The assembled Indian population awaited him in silence. Fifteen friars chanting
hymns walked into the plaza. Vargas dismounted and followed. As he
passed into the gate he "made due obeisance" to the Indian precincts
he was entering, and those following him did the same—the Spanish town
council of Santa Fe, the standard-bearer and officers. There was a moment
of tension, and then the Father President, "attuning his voice," began
to sing the Te Deum, and the moment broke with relief, and all rejoiced.
Afterward, with the lessons of a century behind him, Vargas proclaimed
that all he came to do was bring Christ to the Indians and not to take
from them anything rightfully theirs. He gave the Spanish city back
to the Spanish aldermen; and then though the ground was covered with
snow, he retired his forces from the city and camped at a little distance
in "a despicable dwelling place" to afford the Indians a reasonable time
to make way for the colonists in their ruined capital.

But the Indians now showed no disposition to move. Twenty-one
Spaniards died of exposure in the snowy campground during the following two weeks, while the Indians were seen to be barricading the walls.
On the twenty-eighth they felt their strength and shouted defiance to
the Spaniards. With weariness and patience in the name of their pur·

poses, the soldiers attacked, and by dawn of the thirtieth were masters of the town. Patience was not to be confused with weakness. Vargas commanded the execution of seventy Indian leaders. The cannon, the animals and the families came into the plaza, and the carts, in one of which was the statue of La Conquistadora, the patroness of the expedition who was returned to her city at last. The Indians fled downriver to the high gravelly benches and the canyon rims of the west side. Their fires burned on the plateau, and smoke talked, and by New Year's Day the kingdom was once again everywhere flaring with promises of war. The Captain-General could count on only four pueblos—Santa Ana, Zia, San Felipe and Pecos. All the rest had to be subdued one by one, in images of violence long familiar in the thin green valley with its tawny wastes beyond—siege assaults, burning rafters, commandeered maize, dried watercourses, hundreds of dead natives, and handfuls of lost Spaniards.

Peace of a sort was restored, and friars moved out to the missions and began to rebuild what had worn so hard in the worst weather between two orders of men. New families arrived from Mexico. The haciendas were resettled, and the first Spanish towns outside of Santa Fe and El Paso came to life in the river kingdom. "With sails full we forge ahead," wrote Vargas to Mexico. Santa Cruz was established with sixty-six new families on April 22, 1695, and more came in May. In the autumn a town took root at the old site of the Bernal family downriver, on the estate called Bernalillo, opposite the long-abandoned and disappearing pueblo of Tiguex where Coronado had bivouacked in hard winter one hundred and fifty-three years before.

The winter of 1695-96 was no easier. War and drought had prevented good crops from being sowed and stored against the cold months. Indians and colonists suffered alike. The friars in the missions felt danger brooding behind the impassive Indian life. They warned Vargas and some even left their parishes to take refuge in Santa Fe. There was a sense of storm building up and on June 4, 1696, it broke with fury: five priests and twenty-one soldiers were massacred when a number of pueblo populations, in a co-ordinated movement, rebelled, burned and outraged their churches, and escaped to the mountains. But if the outbreak recalled the horrors of 1680, it was not so widespread. Pecos and a few other towns were loyal, and warrior Indians from those helped Vargas to suppress the rebellion. The Indian federation was again divided against itself but for the first time the balance of power among them was on the side of the Two Majesties. Vargas moved severely and fast against the miscreant towns. By the end of the year the danger was over. Indians came down off the mesas and mountains to dwell again under the walls of their mission churches, where peace and forgiveness awaited them, and learning. Why, asked the conquerors, why had the revolt of 1696 taken place? and an Indian of Nambé, one of the rebellious towns, answered (and no one knew whether it was the truth or an evasive pretext) that "the sole cause of the uprising of the Indians was the fact that a Spaniard had said, while in Cochiti . . . that the governor of New Mexico had determined that in the month of June of the same year all the adult men of that kingdom were to be killed, reserving only the boys. . . ."

The Pueblo Indians submitted, then, forever. The battles were over between the Spaniards and their Christian wards. Vargas was ready to move into a second term as governor to protect all his people, Indian and Spanish alike, against the enemy who was left, the travelling Apaches and Comanches, and those others of whom rumors now and then dawned out of the east, who were, more than likely, Frenchmen from the lower banks of the river called the Espiritu Santo and, again, the Micipipi.

But his petition to be appointed to a second term in the river kingdom which he had restored to the Crown moved too slowly in the channels of government. In January, 1697, a new governor arrived at Santa Fe, Don Pedro Rodríguez Cubero. Honoring his credentials, Vargas turned the office over to him and remained at Santa Fe to offer himself for the usual hearings required of all outgoing officials. He asked that these be expedited but there were delays. Suddenly, on October second, a squad of soldiers arrested him by order of the Governor and imprisoned him in one of the towers of the Palace at Santa Fe. He was denied communication with the colonists whom he had led and protected. The town council, at the pleasure of the new governor, drew up a heavy bill of indictments against him. If he had any friends left they were powerless to help him. He was fined four thousand pesos. He lost all his property by confiscation. A year passed, and another, and part of another, while he lived isolated in his cell like a criminal. Mexico City and Madrid knew nothing of his condition. No inquiries came from the Viceroy. No one was allowed to see Vargas where he existed in one end of the Palace, while Governor Cubero reigned in the other. People peering in at the Governor's office saw Cubero writing, writing, one official paper after another, almost without cease, like Philip II, while affairs outside were neglected, and the dirt walls of the Palace itself were allowed to crumble. It was whispered that the new Governor was a drunkard. Suspicious of everyone, he was victim of that temperament which fearing to be last respected was first to accuse. In 1700 his treatment of the prisoner finally met open opposition, when the Father President of New Mexico, whom Governor Cubero dared not restrict, went to the Viceroy in Mexico with the story. A report went to the King. Vargas was ordered free to leave Santa Fe without bail. He hurried to Mexico City. There he was heard. His record was cleared. He was reappointed governor and captain-general of New Mexico. He was created a marquis by the King—Marqués de la Nava Brazinas, a title by which thereafter he was known. In July, 1703, he left again for Santa Fe. Cubero, having word of such reversals, announced that he was about to be absent from the northern capital on an expedition against certain Apaches; marched out; and, having allied tact with speed, never came back. The Marquis arrived in November at the Royal City which, with its kingdom, he had won back to security, using the means and laws of his time, according to the powers of his belief. The aldermen of Santa Fe waited upon his excellency's pleasure.

They soon learned it in resounding terms. To the same town council which a few years before had drawn up a bill of accusations against his conduct of official affairs he now made a statement in which he thundered, "It is justice for which I ask." In a single passionate sentence of almost a thousand words he first reviewed his accomplishments and then ticked off the disasters that had befallen the kingdom under his successor and jailer. The Palace and fortress of Santa Fe, restored by Vargas to strength and comfort, was allowed by Cubero to go to ruins, so that the capital was defenseless. The army, once in tiptop condition, was now scattered, indifferent and plagued by desertions. New towns, like Santa Cruz, founded with joy and hope, were unprotected, and therefore abandoned, their crops run to weed, their buildings empty and falling. Why had Cubero treated him and all his works so, "with what intention and malice?" The Marquis did not know. He could only say that it had been the purpose of Cubero to "destroy all I had done and leave no memory of it," even to the dishonoring of land grants already in legal process, and assigning of them to new owners. The Marquis was concerned not only for his own personal redress but for the proper recording of acts of bad government, and the due responsibility for them. Much work had to be done over again. The reasons why must be set down. He asked the aldermen for an endorsement, in triplicate, of all his claims to merit, and of all his charges against Cubero.

They obliged overnight. The Lord Marquis, they said, by his

"ability and resolution" had won Santa Fe and the kingdom from the apostates. He had indeed made the Palace a great fort, and had given his people shelter for their bodies and souls, in house and church. As for Santa Cruz and other places, Cubero had allowed them to go to rack and ruin, a dreadful fact "to be explained by the great enmity and disaffection he has toward the said Lord Marquis, trying by every means to show his malice. . . ." It was all true, as the Lord Marquis had charged, and Cubero, who was now so plainly to be seen as a wretch, "in all the time of his government, was solely occupied in drinking and writing papers with no reason whatever," said the aldermen who had served him earlier, and in "imagining things he had no business to imagine, ascribing faults and crimes to those who had not committed them, like that which he attributed to the said Lord Marquis." The Council could not contain its moral indignation. It was, it said, "sure of the high sense of duty of the said Lord Marquis in the interest of all that was and has been under his charge." It was now their duty, the aldermen insisted, "to give him fully and completely the satisfaction he demands and should have." Bridling with courage, the Council touched upon the charges made against the Lord Marquis, and now flatly declared that "the same were made up, hatched and invented" by the vanished Cubero and his secretary. To the Lord Marquis, then, the Council offered "entire and full satisfaction," signed, sealed and witnessed, with three copies. With these in his pocket, he could now set about his job.

There was work to do on the government houses and on Saint Michael's chapel across the creek. Winter days were clear topaz and nights were cold and brilliant. All was made of earth. Elsewhere he owned palaces, parts of towns, whole lordships where people toiled over crops and enlarged his accounts and supported his noble estate. An altar in Madrid, alive in candlelight with gold and silver, perpetuated his family name, in its place alongside the kings of Spain in history. And yet it was to Santa Fe, lost in the north, that he wanted to return. That was the town where, disdaining armor, he had entered alone in soft velvet, fur and silk, smiling at danger, and declaring, "He who takes no risks to win an immortal name accomplishes nothing." He was most at home where he had most triumphed and most suffered.

The winter months of 1704 went by rapidly. The army was reorganized none too soon. In March came appeals for help, war "with fire and sword," against the Apaches who were sweeping into the central valley farms of the Garcías and the Chaveses, and stealing animals. They came from beyond the Sandía and Manzanos mountains, now around the

northern tip, again through the zigzag canyon that was cut, as though by
tijeras—scissors—between the two ranges, and they struck haciendas at
Bernalillo, Alameda, and below. The Marquis made his plans. Orders
were published on the parade ground in the Santa Fe plaza. Fifty officers
and men from the capital garrison would move out on March twenty-
seventh, to join a selected detachment of Indian allies at Bernalillo on
the following day. The Governor and Captain-General himself went in
command, at the work he liked best, amidst shining arms and armor,
scrubbed saddles, a campaign in the field.

At Bernalillo the troops were mustered and he inspected them.
The Indian thieves had gone into the mountains that lay parallel to the
river. He sent a scouting force to observe them, and received a report
that they seemed to be going under mountain cover toward Tijeras
Canyon, where they would escape through the pass to the great yellow
plain of their cloud-shadowed empire. With the main body he marched
down the river road. On Tuesday, April first, the Apaches were seen
at a watering place at the edge of the Plain of the Inferno, near the
village of Taxique. In the distance gleamed the pale salt lakes. The
Captain-General marched on the following day to join his scouts.
The Apache band were skirting the eastern base of the Manzanos mountains and leaving a clear trail, a fact which was noted in the day's
campaign journal by the Captain-General commanding.

It was the last entry he dictated. In the thin mountain air he
halted. He felt distress in his breathing. He was feverish and in pain.
He was suddenly weak. There was a tightness in his chest. His officers
consulted together and he gave permission to do what they asked. They
took him back to Bernalillo to the house of Don Fernando Durán y
Chaves, the Mayor, travelling slowly. There he went to bed. He saw all
that was done for him, and he knew in a very few days what was coming
to pass. On April seventh he sent for his military and civil secretary,
to whom he gave dictation. Beginning with the words, "In the name of
God Almighty," he commended his soul for a "most clear career of salvation," and his body "to the earth from which it was made." He gave
orders for his funeral, and he divided his arms, his garments of state,
his favorite saddles and other personal objects, between his two natural
sons. With their sister in Mexico City they were to share equally in cash
bequests. His silverware in heavy profusion, bearing his coat of arms,
and his diamond and emerald and pearl jewelry, were to be sold. He
gave freedom to two slaves, his body servants, and a sum of money to
each. He listed debts to be paid. He ordered two hundred Masses for

himself, and three hundred "for the souls of the poor who died in the conquest of this kingdom," his old comrades with whom thus he would be once more united. He signed with the large capitals, the generously spaced light and firm letters of his writing, "The Marquis de la Brazinas." Five officers witnessed the instrument. On the following day, April 8, 1704, he died.

If his wishes were obeyed, a Mass was said for him there at Bernalillo before his soldiers brought him up over the mesa of La Bajada for his last return to Santa Fe, and once there he was laid on his bed "selected as a bier," which was covered with "honest woollen cloth." With military rites he was conveyed from the clay Palace to the temporary clay parish church of St. Francis which stood behind the Palace on the road to Tesuque, close to the north city wall which Cubero had demolished not long before. Two horses, caparisoned in the same woollen cloth, were led before him, while the "title ceremonies and privileges of Castile" were observed over him. He was buried "at the principal altar under the platform where the priest stands." On the day of his funeral fifty measures of corn and twelve head of cattle were distributed for him among the poor of Santa Fe. The earth for which he fought and which he defended was over him in peace, and, in the peace that he had brought to it, the upper river kingdom lived.

33.

Fort St. John Baptist

From high above the map in the last years of the seventeenth century, the way from Mexico City to the Rio Grande was seen as a single stem, winding this way and that around mountains and through valleys and across plains, pausing at watering places and isolated missions with their little forts, touching alive as it went an occasional provincial capital where commerce and religion found rewards, and ending at

Santa Fe. But now at the outset of the eighteenth century a new branch began to grow, reaching northeastward toward Texas and stopping at the southern bank of the river. The northward reach of Colonial Spain took the form of a great Y. No Spanish settlements had been made in Texas since the abandonment of the mission frontier against the French in 1693. But in the Mexican provinces south of the Texas Rio Grande the mission establishments crept closer and closer to the river. Roaming Indians were gathered into villages, converted and taught Spanish ways of work, not only for the peace of their souls, but for the pacification of the frontier. In 1699 Mexico heard that the French were settling colonies in Louisiana. Once again from the east arose the threat that in one or another form would challenge and call forth defensive expansion by the Spaniards for the next century. The mission of San Juan Bautista, first founded on the Sabinas river in northern Coahuila in 1699, was suddenly moved in the following year to the plains of the right bank of the Rio Grande. With it came its Indians, friars and farmers, and in the next three years, with strategic foresight, it was augmented through the foundation of two more missions—San Francisco Solano and San Bernardo—and the establishment of a fortified garrison of thirty troops in a "Flying Company" under the command of Captain Diego Ramón. The whole cluster of barracks, dwellings, Indian huts and three mission churches with their convents was called the Presidio de San Juan Bautista del Rio Grande—Fort St. John Baptist of the Rio Grande. It stood six miles from the river on the vast plain of northern Coahuila, which in dry weather was deep with gray dust, and in wet was a great mire of bottomless mud. Thickets of mesquite forced the road to turn and twist. Underground shelves of porous yellow-gray rock emerged toward the river to make its walls. The fort was placed near one of the river's best fords. It was the way over which most of the expeditions had marched to the northeast since the 1650s, in search of the French. The ford was known for many decades as the Paso de Francia—France Way.

The three missions stood in a triangle a mile or two apart, with the fort in the center. Each had its settlements and its farming fields. San Juan and San Francisco were built of clay. San Bernardo, or Saint Bernard's, the largest, was made of river stone, in massive magnificence. Its largest foundation blocks were cubes of two and three feet cut from the soft yellow-gray limestone that hardened when put into the walls. The scale of Saint Bernard's was grand for its time and place. Baptistry, sacristy, refectory, convent, travellers' rooms, storerooms and corral, grew from one another with uninterrupted walls, and all clung heavily about the main volume of the church. The nave was one hundred two feet long and twenty-four feet wide, except at the cruciform transepts, which reached from side to side for fifty-seven feet. Built with square corners that threw sharp diagonals of shadow on jutting outer walls, the building had many levels of roof and angles of wall. It had a stern splendor, like a monument to the anonymous labor and the tireless belief from which it was born in the river wilderness. Light entered into it in thin rays through small, high, square windows too deep to transit a firearm through more than a narrow arc. But above such weight, such massive secrecy and dedication of its inner life, Saint Bernard's lifted in 1703 a grace new to the river, for with its creation the curve arrived in the Spanish architecture of the Rio Grande. The circle was fragmented and used in the stone arches of the great doorways, the barrel vaultings of the nave and the refectory, and the stone dome of the baptistry. High on the nave were long moldings of carved stone that followed the angles of the walls. The Franciscan style was now formed, and while it spoke with echoes of Rome, Byzantium, North Africa and Spain, it spoke also of the river's rocky walls and ledges, the lateral stretch of plains, and the aboriginal temper it sought to enclose in peace and had to withstand in war. The limestone was pitted. Its colors carried aloft the gray of the plain and the dusty yellow of the mesquite bloom, and even in little fossil shells an ancient undersea white, and all weathered in the speckled richness of tapestry. Across the wastes of Mexico Saint Bernard's high walls and baptistry dome were a signal of haven for wayfarers coming to the wide valley from the south.

A short walk away from the walls was a clear deep pool walled by a little cliff of shelving rock and screened with feathery willows. Into it poured with enlivening voice a pale green fall of water that came over the cliff from a stone irrigation trough above. There missioners and travellers bathed. Canals brought farming water from the river upstream and activated the fields and made a park about the mission. Water entered the plaza of the garrison, and in one corner a pond collected where Indian women washed the soldiers' clothes.

At Fort St. John Baptist in the early eighteenth century all the old tasks of pacifying, teaching and overseeing labor were carried on in all the missions. The friars learned first to speak the Indian languages, and how it hurt the tongue to make it reproduce their clicks, swallowed syllables, and enclosed explosions. With communications established, they had then to explain systematic work to Indians who had never known any. Two soldiers were assigned to each mission to supervise the fields where Indian men learned to plow, Indian women to plant and cultivate. In time Indians were trained to become supervisors. If harvests were bountiful, the common stores held enough food to be distributed to all in bounty. If they failed in dry seasons, and stores were low, Indians ran away, and when overtaken could most readily be lured home again with gifts of Mexican tobacco which the missions kept on hand. From the mission herds a beef was slaughtered every fortnight and all received a share, which was not large, and was quickly gone. In a year of surplus crops, farm products were traded in Mexico for cloth which the friars gave to Indians to clothe themselves.

At morning and evening the mission bell sounded and all came for devotions, followed by religious instruction. Attendance was counted. Only the sick were excused. An Indian otherwise absent was hunted out and taken to the mission graveyard, there to kneel before a cross in penance as an example to others. If he persisted in absenting himself from indoctrination he was whipped in the presence of all the converts. The old life of the plains often called to such a one and he ran away. It called too in hunting season when far over the river in Texas the buffalo were coming south before the continental winter, and Indians were stirred in their old nature and in the nighttime quietly were gone, hollow-bellied with desire for the chase, the kill, the feasts and the orgies of lust that followed in violent satisfaction and gave them animal ease oblivious of sin. Many came back and meeting the mission fathers who had come in search of them fell to their knees and wept for forgiveness and lifted up were accompanied to Fort St. John Baptist where pressing like endless waves the repeated acts of a new way of life prevailed on the frontier shores of Texas.

For even if at the outpost there were hardship and poverty, it was sustained by resources of all kinds deep in the interior. Supplies, armaments, and ideas came from official quarters in Mexico, the sources of which moved forward in settlement as the frontier advanced. Even priests were supplied by colleges that were established far north of the viceregal capital. Many of those friars who came to work at Fort St. John Baptist near the river received their training in the seminaries of Querétaro and Zacatecas. For decades this garrison with its missions was the focus and concentrate of Spanish colonial life on the Texas Rio Grande. It was the foundation of the town long later called Guerrero, thirty miles down the river from Piedras Negras, Coahuila. It was the link between northern Mexico and the immense land of conjecture across the river; the **fort, the hospice, the temple,** and it soon became too the gateway, the trade center, the crossroads and the supply depot when the river ceased being a boundary and became a station on the only way to Texas.

And if this way went northeast, it also went southwest, as the ancient Comanche Trail led out of the buffalo plains to Mexico. The Trail crossed the river at two points, widely separated. One was near the Junta de los Rios above the river's big bend; the other at France Way near Fort St. John Baptist. Other travellers than Indians could use it.

One day in 1704 a young white man twenty-five years old accompanied by a handful of scouts, both white and Indian, appeared at France Way from the Texas side. He saw the stone bulk of San Bernardo in the distance across the river. Going over the river he met Indians and spoke to them fluently in their own tongue. He had trinkets for barter which he showed them. When he came to the mission he presented himself with courtesy. He made remarks about the great mineral riches of Mexico, the mines of Chihuahua and Parral. He had been across all of Texas and had seen no mining country, though he spoke with animation and fondness of the beautiful wooded glades where the traveller could rest, and of the friendly Indians who responded to invitations to trade with him. He had a map of his travels. The Spanish Franciscans examined it. The journey traced upon it started in Louisiana. The traveller believed that peaceful trade should be established between Louisiana and Mexico, through Fort St. John Baptist. He spoke in French. His name was Louis Juchereau de St. Denis, and he had come down the Mississippi from Canada a few years before. He saw bright possibilities of prosperity for himself and his remote settlement in Louisiana. In a sense, he was the future, and the future could wait. His visit was brief. Refreshed by the hospitality of the friars, who at the time were without policy as to what to do with him, he returned with his party to France Way, made the ford and disappeared into Texas.

But Fort St. John Baptist had not seen the last of him, and would not forget what he signified.

34.

Early Towns

Way up the river in the kingdom of New Mexico the haciendas were resettled. Irrigation water once more ran across orchard floors in shady flood, and produce gardens were weeded, and all awoke from the bad dream of the rebellion and the reconquest. New farms were settled about the old ones. Several Spanish families living and working side by side made the pattern of a town, with everything but official organization, armed protection, and the Church. In 1705 the New Mexican governor had the authority to found towns, though in the next century this power was reserved for the home government in Spain. A village was granted in the name of a family at Los Padillas in 1705, on the west side of the river above Isleta, and on April 23, 1706, Santa Fe decreed the establishment of Albuquerque on the east bank amidst deep cottonwood and willow groves on a wide sweep of rich bottom land enclosed by a long curve of the river fifteen miles from the mouth of Tijeras Canyon which cut between the Sandia and Manzanos mountains. The new town centered about the hacienda of Don Luís Carbajal which had been ruined in 1680. If the river Indians were now at peace, the transmontane Apaches were still a menace. With all its other municipal forms the town needed an armed guard, for it was New Mexico's destiny throughout nearly four centuries to live "gun in hand." Albuquerque, named in honor of the Duke of Albuquerque, had its patron saint, Francis Xavier, "the glorious apostle of the Indies," chosen by the governor, who told the King in his report that "as regards land, water, pasture, and fire-wood," the town was in "a good place." The church was already built; it was "very capacious and decent," and the priest's dwelling was nearly finished. The governor contributed vestments, a bell and altar fittings for the church, though chalices and other sacred furnishings were needed, and the King was asked for these. Work had begun on the royal municipal buildings, the settlers' houses were done, corrals were ready and the irrigation ditches already carried water from the river to the fields, which were sown. Thirty-five families, totalling two hundred and fifty people, adults and children, were settled. Everything was "in good order," and there had been "no expense to the royal treasury." It was of great importance to the kingdom to have a new fort "at a middle station along the road on one of the best sites which the said northern kingdom affords."

Soldiers were stationed in presidial squads to protect the new towns. At Santa Fe several Flying Companies of cavalry were garrisoned to take to the field when danger threatened. Bernalillo was already six years old. Santa Cruz upriver was older still. No longer were El Paso and Santa Fe the only two royal towns in the river system. All was in order except that —in a few months—the Madrid government commanded that the Patron of Albuquerque be changed from Saint Francis Xavier to Saint Philip of Neri as a gesture of courtesy to Philip V, the new King of Spain. Otherwise, "the kingdom," said the governor, "has attained the quiet, peace and tranquillity which it now enjoys."

Even the erring children longed to come home. Far to the east still lived most of the Pueblo Indians of San Lorenzo of the upriver country who had deserted their town during the revolt and had sought asylum with the "various heathen nations who inhabit the wide provinces of the plains." But their flight turned into captivity. Ever since the Rebellion they had been held as slaves. They had several times appealed for help from the reinstalled Spanish powers; and now in 1706 their pleas were answered when forty soldiers and a hundred Christian Indians marched to the east as rescuers. Claiming for the Crown all lands they crossed, they came among the heathen tribes, whom they treated "with much affection, flattery and cordiality," and managed to take custody of seventy-four Pueblo men, women and children, including two important chiefs, and to bring them home. Once there, a "ceremony of delivery and reception" was held, the apostates were absolved "with great solemnity and tenderness," and the local chiefs were given their offices again, to the satisfaction of all the kingdom.

In 1708 a new governor was "pleased to take away" the armed garrison at Albuquerque. There were immediate consequences. Albuquerque had been watched from the mountains. As soon as the squadrons withdrew in April, the Apaches came. The royal subjects of the town met to compare losses, and two of them drew up a petition which they presented in person to the council in Santa Fe on the fourteenth. They declared that the plains raiders came every day, even into the very corrals of the farms, and drove off the Spanish livestock with impunity. Seeing that there were no soldiers to prevent them, they could now be expected to fall upon the families and destroy them in their turn. The council was implored to present the case to the governor, that he might restore the Albuquerque garrison.

The old complaint—the governors were "concerned deeply with nothing save their own lawsuits"—was heard again. The missions had begged for help in re-establishing themselves, but without much luck. Mission bells were silent, for the Indians in the revolt had taken the clappers from which to make spear points. The churches, though clean, were bare. The sacred ornaments, vessels and paintings had been burned and never replaced. In some of the poorer parishes the Indians had made crosses and had painted them "according to their own style." In place of silver cruets were others made of clay, and still others of tin. There was hardly a complete set of vestments of one color in the whole province, and even at Santa Fe, Masses for the dead had to be said without a black cope, for the old one there was so worn and patched that it could no longer be used. These were large matters to those who complained of them.

And yet the towns took root, and their spiritual element made a society and a tradition out of life thinly drawn along the river. Los Lunas, south of Albuquerque, was founded in 1716, and, near El Paso, the Isleta, the Socorro and the Senecu of the South, all three founded when the loyal Indians of the upper towns of the same names had retreated with Otermín in 1680, now had their own missions. San Lorenzo, where the refugee governors had maintained their state in reed huts, also had a mission, and all were dominated by the Guadalupe of El Paso. "In these places," said a contemporary account, "Indians and Spaniards live commingled." From the river came the main irrigating ditch which the Spaniards controlled. It had two floodgates which could be opened to release water into other ditches that flowed, at Spanish pleasure, to the Indian fields. The farms were lush. There was "excellent wheat, free of all darnel, and with a remarkably large grain." The fine velvety soil of the south bank had to be plowed extra deep in order to hold up the heavy stalks of maize, for when the hard wind blew, as it so often did in growing season, the clattering plants were uprooted and laid flat on the ground. Beans, chick-peas, and "especially large, white sweet onions" grew well.

Such good things could be shown and handled and believed. Up the river where ice formed every winter, often so thickly that loaded carts could cross over upon it, the mayor and the pastor of San Juan wrote down what happened in the river nature of the early eighteenth century. To the river's banks there would come eagles with white heads and necks, who at sunrise would "perch on the trees nearby. In a little while, circling in the air, they fly to a great height, whence they descend, head downward and wings drawn back, with the swiftness of a shooting star. The noise that they make is so great that it sounds like thunder, and while they are still more than a hundred yards away the ice makes loud cracking noises, and when they reach it a large hole is already open. The eagle enters by it and seizes in its claws a fish weighing four, five, or more pounds, which it eats upon the ice if no one prevents it. The most remarkable thing is that in a short space of time the ice is already closed up." The account was filed away among the official papers of the kingdom, where coming across it later someone added, "Although this note has been copied as a marvelous incident of natural history, we cannot set aside the distrust inspired by the observations of LaFontaine of Grenoble upon the Phoenix, and other fables. . . ." The big sweet onions of El Paso, the fabulous bald eagles of San Juan, both helped to make the river's tale.

35.

Colonial Texas

Like all other frontier commanders, Captain Domingo Ramón at Fort St. John Baptist received in 1713 clear orders from the Viceroy not to admit foreign traders or foreign merchandise into Spanish lands. If any foreigner crossed the frontier he was to be arrested and the Viceroy notified. Mexico City would then decide the disposal of the prisoner. Though France and Spain were precariously allied in the old world through their Bourbon kings, Louis XIV and Philip V, in the new they faced each other across the wastes of Texas as aggressor and defender.

It was a position darkly imaged by the Spanish temperament. The French saw it somewhat differently; or so, with rippling plausibility, they strove to show in the autumn of 1714.

For then there appeared again at France Way out of Texas, bearing information, merchandise and high good manners, the Colonial Frenchman Louis de St. Denis, with three French and three Indian companions. Now ten years after his first visit he was thirty-five years old, and still in love with Texas. He reported to Captain Diego Ramón at Fort St. John Baptist. He was full of stories—his party had set out to buy cattle and other supplies for Louisiana from the Spanish missions that were supposed to be in East Texas, but having heard these were long since abandoned, he had come to the Rio Grande to make his purchases. He had travelled a year and nine months from Mobile. On the way he had been obliged to fight a pitched battle against Indian enemies of the Texas. He had seen a beautiful site for a mission, a fort and a town—the San Antonio River. He gave flourish to his purpose, which, he made plain, was to open trade with northern New Spain. He wanted to draw the two frontiers together, not separate them with barriers. If he was a wilderness master, he was also a merchant of state, and if he was in a position of risk he seemed not to recognize it. He handed his French passport to Captain Ramón, whose orders were clear. Captain de St. Denis and his friends were placed in arrest, while news of their presence on the river went by fast courier to Mexico City.

It was a comfortable arrest, for the prisoners were lodged in the home of the commander. They could easily have escaped, but St. Denis chose not to, saying, "I fear nothing from these people or from Mexico." The post commander's granddaughter, Doña María Ramón, was to be seen. She had been a little girl ten years before, during the ruddy, muscular young Frenchman's first journey to the river. If she saw him then, he saw her now. His captivity lasted several months at Fort St. John Baptist. There were little rides that could safely be taken, from one to the next of the three missions. There were grassy shadows where to lie by the rocky pool with its waterfall near Saint Bernard's. There were dangers to share that like any shared emotion left a certain commitment between people. In March, 1715, the Indians of Fort St. John Baptist revolted. At midnight they attacked the fort, throwing down bars and chasing out horses and cattle, flourishing torches and crying death. The garrison arose to fight. Friars took refuge in the stone granary of Saint Bernard's. Others went for aid from a mission farther inland. Indians set fire to what they could. Help arrived from the south, the revolt was subdued, never to recur, and Captain de St. Denis declared his love to Doña María Ramón, to which her grandfather gave his consent. The prisoner was in excellent favor.

In June a company of soldiers arrived from Mexico to take him and his comrades to the Viceroy. He departed in all confidence, the prospective grandson-in-law of the frontier captain who was duty-bound to oppose the French. He was the smiling embodiment of a force that would not be denied. The Spaniards spoke of him as a menace, and yet with grace submitted to his intention.

He was back in the following April to take his bride at St. John Baptist. After long inquisitions before the viceregal authorities, he ended as a Spanish officer, in charge of supplies for an expedition immediately ordered by the Viceroy. If the French came as traders and as suitors, it was clear that Spain must once again occupy East Texas to prevail against them. The missions abandoned in 1693 were ordered re-established, yet the alarming Frenchman himself who occasioned the move was to serve as quartermaster to the Spaniards on their eastward march. St. Denis faced his loyalties both ways. Through secret letters carried by Indian couriers to the Governor of Louisiana, he kept his own home government informed of his successes, and proposed that France extend the borders of Louisiana to the Rio Grande. The nearer New Spain moved to New France the easier were chances for commerce to sustain the needs of Louisiana. This fulfilled French policy. France inviting, Spain extending defenses, both acted through the imperative medium of St. Denis. He had several weeks with his bride at St. John Baptist before the supply forces, soldiers and missionaries were assembled at the river for the departure to the east.

In March, 1716, the expedition under the command of Captain Domingo Ramón crossed the river at France Way. The ford was unusually easy, as the river was low. Along with arms, building tools, food and sacerdotal supplies, the train carried certain items that had a French air in the wilderness, reflecting St. Denis's accent on trade for his own colonists: silk hosiery for ladies and gentlemen, bolts of laces and ribbons, four dozen pairs of shoes. The train camped on the north bank of the river for a week. A soldier married a girl of a settler's family, and the festivities lasted two days. Fray Francisco Hidalgo, founder of the missions abandoned twenty-three years before, was now joyfully returning to reopen his chapels and see his Texas people again. On March 27 the little army—there were twenty-five soldiers—and all the other company passed in review before Captain Domingo Ramón and his second-in-command, Captain de St. Denis, and with their thousand animals drew away from the Rio Grande over the south Texas plains in the season of wild flowers. The scent of the flowers was aloft in the air for weeks, and the ground exhaling after spring rains was dazzling with fields and meadows and miles of white and pink poppies, blue flax, bluebonnets, magenta phlox, yellow and white daisies, orange gaillardia, in exquisite profusion. The entry was made in peace. Once among the Texas people, St. Denis served as interpreter, presiding over the exchanges between Indian and Spaniard with satisfaction and dispatch. All smoked in turn a peace pipe nearly three feet long. Volleys were fired, the Te Deum was sung, Fray Francisco Hidalgo embraced his children and their new children, and during the first ten days of July four missions were settled in what long later was known as Nacogdoches County. Spain had its living claim to Texas, face to face with Louisiana.

On the journey eastward from the Rio Grande, in slow travel the marchers saw the need of another settlement between the river and the missions nearly a thousand miles away. At a suitable distance from the two ends of the journey, they passed through lush, low-rolling country where a small river wound its way through shady groves and flower-starred meadows. It was a stream that earlier travellers had named after San Antonio. In the following year, at Fort St. John Baptist, the religious and lay powers of Colonial Spain were once again assembling to cross into Texas to found a community, this time on the San Antonio River. Fray Antonio de San Buenaventura Olivares was the chief missioner of the enterprise, and the new governor and captain-general of Texas, Don Martín de Alarcón, was the commander.

Fray Antonio reached the Rio Grande ahead of the Governor. What he found there enraged him. The discipline of the frontier was lax. Indians were insolent and indifferent. After the example of the garrison, they had lost respect for the friars, and even flouted the authority of the troops. Thievery and revolt were everywhere. The corruption of society went right to the top, for the Ramón family, so long in charge at Fort St. John Baptist, gave only nominal observance to the famous regulations against foreign trade, and had actually been enriched by dealing with the French through St. Denis, who had married into the family. To be sure, St. Denis, on appearing for the third time over France Way in April, 1717, had been arrested by his grandfather-in-law, and had had his rich cargo of merchandise impounded; but what good were such measures when there seemed to be evidence that organized contraband trade on a large scale was going on between him and the

Ramóns? Moreover, in spite of the requirement that every Frenchman crossing the river was to be clapped into prison, plenty of them came and went as they liked, and even paused comfortably at the Fort. Three were quite openly digging a mine in Coahuila. St. Denis had been sent to Mexico for questioning again, leaving his goods at the river frontier post.

In August the Governor arrived at the Fort, and conducted a personal investigation into affairs. The French seen there by Fray Antonio vanished, but the Spaniards remaining seemed much influenced by French ideas. The Governor though he was unable to find proof of actual wrongdoing on the part of the Ramón family and St. Denis recommended that they be relieved of their posts. But with an artfulness that recalled the sprightly talents of their French relation, they continued to pursue their double course, and engaged in helping the Spanish Governor assemble his expedition that was to establish San Antonio and to serve as a vital supply link in the chain that would contain the French. The foundation of San Antonio knew another urgent reason: unruly Indians of the Rio Grande were to be moved to the new community, and there resettled about their missions, which would be officially transferred with them.

Burning with zeal and faith in Providence, Fray Antionio tugged at the Governor's establishment to take to the trail over the river. But Alarcón had problems of recruitment, supply and legal authorization that took time to solve. Anxious letters came to the Rio Grande from the East Texas missions, where now the French seemed actually to be hostile to the Spaniards whom they had called to the east for commerce. St. Denis in Mexico, after being questioned and briefly jailed, was at large on bond and free to return to the river to sell his goods. He came, disposed of all his cargo, and returned to Mexico City with money and a plan to arrange a government post for himself. The winter passed, and still the expedition did not leave, and the Two Majesties became acrimonious toward one another, the one over delay, the other over importunity. But finally, on April 9, 1718, Governor Alarcón crossed at France Way, and nine days later, having refused to travel with him, Fray Antonio followed. The two parties followed different routes, through a season of cloudbursts and risen streams, but by May first, they met at the head of a spring creek in "a thick wood of . . . elms, poplars, hackberry trees, oaks, and many mulberries, all of them being thickly covered with wild grapevines," and with proper ceremonies in the following days the town and the first missions of San Antonio were secured. There in the next few years would rise five mission churches, with their cells for dwelling and storing, all made of the rich limestone that lay under the black soil of the grand plain of South Texas, and all beautifully illustrating different graces of the Franciscan baroque style —San Antonio de Valero (the Alamo) with its scrolled façade; La Purísima Concepción with its perfect dome; San Francisco de la Espada with its richly modified Moorish arch at the main door; San Juan Capistrano with its uprolling façade pierced with arches for bells; and San José, with its dome and its carved tower and embrasures and huge barrel-vaulted granary. From the great clay coffins of the upper river, to the mighty walls of St. Bernard's at Fort St. John Baptist, and ending with the temples of San Antonio in their misty meadows, the Franciscan style knew a century of wonderful change that yet expressed unchanging faith.

On January 29, 1719, Governor Alarcón heard a startling piece of news that came wandering overland with whatever traveller might be crossing Texas. It had to do with St. Denis, last believed safely in hand at Mexico City. His money was all spent. The government post he sought had been denied him, and he was in consequence heard to be saying about town that he intended to avenge himself by inspiring a revolt among the Rio Grande Indians. The government heard of his mutterings and threatened his arrest. On September 5, 1718, he vanished, barely escaping a royal order that he be deported with his wife to Guatemala. Had he returned to Louisiana? No one knew in Texas, but the French attitude seemed less inviting.

In fact, the official French policy had never been quite so hospitable as St. Denis had made it seem. So long before as 1715 Governor Cadillac of New France had determined to order St. Denis "to engage all the savages on Red River to oppose the establishment of the Spaniards." And yet they had been established, and with St. Denis's grace. Was it possible that if he had two national policies to dance between, he had also a third which engaged him the most, which was his own? While he could be everywhere, he and his relations grew rich, and to all concerned he could toss what each desired—the Spanish friars their converts, the French settlers their imported finery, the Viceroy of New Spain his fortified frontier, the Ramón family their profits. When he vanished, it was with the effect of broken promises.

In June, 1719, at the Spanish mission outpost of Los Adaes in East Texas, the French attacked. The size of the demonstration—eight Frenchmen made war on a Spanish lay brother and a private soldier and upset the henyard—was less disturbing than its mere fact. The lay brother escaped to the next mission, and as soon as news could travel, the whole Spanish eastern frontier was in panic. St. Denis was blamed for the attack. The missions felt their isolation and insecurity. In the autumn they withdrew to San Antonio, and for the next year all the aching machinery of Spanish viceregal government worked at organizing a return to East Texas. The Marquis of Aguayo came to Fort St. John Baptist in December, 1720, commanding a restorative expedition. There he heard that St. Denis was assembling a great Indian horde to attack San Antonio. Reinforcements were sent ahead, and the Marquis presently followed, but the threatened battle was only a nervous rumor. The Marquis marched eastward, and in August, 1721, at the Neches River a horseman swam his mount across to meet him. It was St. Denis, prepared to observe the peace that had been concluded between France and Spain in Europe. The Marquis agreed, provided France might abandon Texas, and Spain reoccupy it to her former limits. St. Denis withdrew, but reluctantly, somehow preserving intact for as long as he might live his nuisance value as an unsettling presence on the Spanish eastern border.

The flow and counterflow of France and Spain against one another reached from the northern river kingdom of New Mexico out to the north central plains in the same period. Santa Fe heard that the French were intruding westward with Pawnee Indian allies. New France claimed that Spanish forces were mobilizing to march from Santa Fe to capture Illinois. In the summer of 1720 Captain Pedro de Villasur led some of the presidial company of Santa Fe—forty-two soldiers—and a party of settlers and Indian fighters out to the plains. With him was L'Archevêque —the Frenchman who had helped to murder LaSalle—who was now a Spanish subject. Like St. Denis he acted as interpreter between Spaniards and Indians when the two forces met at the North Platte River. The Pawnees were French-trained in the use of arms and tactics. They feigned not to understand L'Archevêque. Negotiations came to nothing. A battle followed in which the Santa Feans were overwhelmed. Only thirteen escaped to return to the New Mexican capital. L'Archevêque was among those killed. It was rumored that French soldiers, disguised as Pawnees, were among the victors, and that to avenge LaSalle they had singled out his assassin. The unsettled plains claimed their dead, but with little to fight over but space, the northern campaigns came to nothing, and hostilities, if not vigilance, died out with the signing of the peace between France and Spain in the homelands.

After the early years of the religious and military missions that crossed the Rio Grande into Texas, the civil authority must follow; and in the winter of 1731 there appeared at Fort St. John Baptist a party of fifteen families numbering fifty-six persons, accompanied by armed escort. These were people from the Canary Islands, removed by royal decree to resettle at San Antonio, there to establish the first civil organization in Texas. They stayed for two days on the Rio Grande. While there one of their company, a little girl of five, died. She was the only casualty of a journey lasting many months. In March all arrived at San Antonio, where the missions and the fort would thenceforth serve a royally chartered city. All the settlers were granted patents of nobility under which they were to enjoy the same privileges, dignity and prerogatives as the Hidalgos of Castile.

Over the river at Fort St. John Baptist went the life stream of Texas. For decades this ford was the beach-head for invasions, the supply depot, the station of reinforcements, the ecclesiastical headquarters, the wayfarer's haven, and the starting point for explorations, like that of Berroterán who was sent northwest along the Rio Grande in 1720 to examine the unknown river country between St. John Baptist and the Junta de Los Rios. In the early half of the eighteenth century Fort St. John Baptist and El Paso marked the extremes of Spanish settlement on the river's lower thousand miles. Between them lived only one other—that of the missions at the meeting of the rivers.

But its life was fitful, now flickering high, again low, for unlike other frontier mission outposts, it had no fort and garrison for its defense. The Indian temper blew hot and cold, and the friars responded accordingly, bringing conversion when it was asked for—and it was asked for repeatedly; and fleeing, often in rags and starving over deserts, when savages backslid. So it was in the time of Fray Nicolás López, the founder of the Junta in 1683, and so it continued to be into the eighteenth century. The Indians were described as "very clever and politic," the country of the junction of the Rio Grande and the Concho was seen as productive and desirable, and the passage of the river there was one of the two grand ways to Texas—as the plains Indians had long demonstrated. Settled missions at that gateway would do much to prevent plundering raids into northern Mexico. The governors of New Biscay and Coahuila sent a number of expeditions (the first of these was that of Trasviño Retis in 1715) to pacify the region permanently, and to bring back information of value to the north Mexican governments. But they sent no garrison to remain. Friars accompanied the march, the missions were reopened, new ones were added, soldiers withdrew, and for a year or two all was well.

And then, usually in the nighttime, with scream and brand, the converts would rise against their peaceful fathers and kill them, or try to, or drive them away. In 1725 two friars were seized and tied. Their heads were to be cut off and the Indians were going to dance about them. Granted time for their own confessions, the missioners gave each other absolution. Suddenly a force of soldiers appeared. They were from Chihuahua. At sight of them the Indians fled. The friars were lifted up and taken to Chihuahua, where their delivery was celebrated with public rejoicings.

In the following year there was talk of establishing a fort with a garrison at the Junta, but nothing came of it, and resident missionary efforts were not resumed. Occasional visits from inland missions during peaceful interludes were all that seemed possible. In 1736 a garrison was stationed in a new fort—the Presidio Sacramento—on the San Diego River that entered the Rio Grande south of the later Del Rio. But with the whole Big Bend in between, it was too far from the Junta to be the source of any protection. Three efforts were made in 1747 to assimilate the Junta into the civilized influence of northern Mexico. Pedro Rábago y Terán led a party from Monclova; Fermín de Vidaurre set out from Durango; and Captain Joseph Idoyaga came with his men from a hundred and fifty miles up the Conchos. They all described the beauty of the confluence, its rich farm lands, the eight Indian villages in the flat valley; and strong recommendations were made again for the establishment of a fort, without which no permanent colonial life could be expected to cling to the river of the Fish Indians, as they were called there.

But government had its maps, and what lay not on the river but beyond it was what induced forts and garrisons and town charters. North of El Paso lay the whole settled kingdom of New Mexico. Northeast of Fort St. John Baptist lay the central Texas kingdom with its steadily developing communities and trade. Both sites called alive important gateway settlements. But across the confluence at the Junta was only the Comanche trail leading to and from the wild plains. Eastern New Mexico and western Texas yet held little but empty wilderness and roving hostility. No garrison was ordered to the Junta for another ten years. There was another immense stretch of the river still unoccupied, hardly visualized, that had to be mapped and settled. It was valley land that reached from Fort St. John Baptist all the way to the river's mouth at the Gulf. Spanish life was pushing north toward the Texas river frontier.

Indian raiders threatened it, in spite of the Spanish settlements in Texas. While in New Mexico, the valley was the road, in Texas the Rio Grande had been known principally by its fords, where colonial life leaped the river and left it behind. It was not until 1747 that the last valley of the lower river came to be understood and used, in a large gesture devised by an able colonizer.

He faced difficulties; but one long familiar to earlier Spanish officers was already ended. "St. Denis," declared a Spanish administrator in 1744, "St. Denis is dead, thank God, and now we can breathe easier."

36.

Mexico Bay

In 1746 Don José de Escandón was corregidor—mayor, or chief magistrate, of Querétaro. For seven years the Mexican government had been looking for the right man to command the settlement of the last Spanish frontier. Several applied for the post, but some were not plausible enough and some were too much so. The Crown weighed all applications, and was not satisfied. A man was wanted who, with a flawless record in public affairs, a history of known piety and a proper family life, could combine large gestures of imagination and of courage. The great conquerors all seemed to love their enemy the wilderness; to understand its dry and poisonous and illimitable reaches. To such men the unknown was an invitation that made their heads swim with desire. They were inclined to simplify their visions, but many of them had the genius to make their visions come true after all. If they could see the *terra incognita* as thought it were on a map, and in the air could trace with a finger just where they would go and what they would do, it was astonishing how often on the land itself they kept their promises.

The great Mexico Bay made a vast crescent, and in the habit of speech in 1746, the term included the wide shore lands that lay inland from the low beaches. For miles from the sea the lands plainly referred to their old life as ocean floors. There were jungles in the southern arc of the crescent and sand wastes on the northern. The Rio Grande flowed into the ocean at the center of the arc encompassing Texas and the Mexican coastline. It was a region that recalled though it did not equal in size the old kingdom of Florida whose western boundary two centuries earlier was the River of Palms. Now with the province of Mexico Bay reaching both north and south of the river, and from the river's mouth upstream to Fort St. John Baptist, the country had to be seen comprehensively, and all its sweep called for sweeping plans to conquer it. On September 3, 1746, the Viceroy of New Spain made his appointment of the commander for the job. He chose the corregidor of Querétaro, who had never applied for it.

But Escandón's record was excellent. He was forty-six years old, a native of Spain, son of a highly respected family. Eager like the conquerors of the Golden Age to create his own glory, he came to the Americas as a youth. He served as a cavalry cadet in Yucatán for six years, fighting renegade Indians and meeting the tentative English thrusts against Mexico made from the sea. Promoted lieutenant, he was transferred to Querétaro for duty against the unpacified Indians of the Sierra Gorda. Local campaigns lasted for years there, with the mountain Indians ensconced in their vast natural castles, and the missions, ranches and towns of Querétaro in periodic danger when the Indians swept down from the heights. At the age of twenty-seven, Lieutenant de Escandón went to Spain to marry. He brought his wife back to his frontier station and resumed his service in the field. In the next dozen years he rose rapidly as an Indian campaigner. By 1740 the Indians of the Sierra Gorda were subdued, largely through his efforts as commander. He was promoted to the post of Lieutenant General, or military governor, of Sierra Gorda, and confirmed his field victories by establishing missions and villages where the Indians, intransigent for two centuries, were now gathered in peace. He was the very officer to understand the problem of Mexico Bay where, noted the government, the Indian nations "live without religion, without fixed habitation, without dress, who like wild and wandering beasts, occupy the coast of the Mexican Gulf, its ports, its famous salines, rich rivers, healthful plains, fertile lands, and valuable minerals. With their murders, thefts, fires, and all kinds of inhuman atrocities, they desolate entire jurisdictions, provinces, cities, villages, and Christian settlements along the southern, western, and northern confines of their haunts. They obstruct the roads, paralyze commerce, and occasion incalculable losses to the royal treasury daily with the increased annual costs involved in the maintenance of presidios and the organization of campaigns."

The Lieutenant General lost no time in organizing his moves upon Mexico Bay. He studied reports and maps. He weighed earlier schemes, and came to his own. He was made a viceregal lieutenant general which meant that his authority was superior to that of the provincial governors and commanders whom he put to work in certain orders that went in many different directions by fast couriers in the autumn of 1746. All of northeastern New Spain came alive with the new enterprise, and provincial governors and frontier garrisons looked toward its realization with the New Year.

For in January, 1747, from seven different posts on the outlying perimeter of the arc of Mexico Bay seven different armed detachments began to move simultaneously toward the mouth of the Rio Grande, which required about a thirty-day march for each. In one great, co-ordinated movement, Escandón brought all of Mexico Bay under comprehensive examination, which, he said, would "cause great wonder to the natives to see Spanish soldiers entering from all directions, before the news of their presence can be transmitted by smoke signals." There were seven hundred sixty-five soldiers in his seven divisions. They reconnoitered a region of almost a hundred and twenty thousand square miles, which Escandón described as "a sort of bag lying between Tampico, Pánuco, Villa de Valles, Custodia de Rio Verde, Neuvo Reyno de León and the Bahía del Espiritu Santo," where stood the farthest Spanish fort of coastal Texas. Two hundred and twenty-eight years after the first attempt to settle the River of Palms—by which was meant the lower Rio Grande—the Spanish power at last embraced all of the river but its source country above New Mexico.

Escandón arrived at the mouth of the river on February twenty-seventh with his detachment from Jaumave, which had begun its march in January. He saw the marshy lands and the palms, and no other trees but willows. He saw how in wide shallow lagoons beside the river the water flowed in and out according to how the wind blew. Upstream the river's meanders could be tapped for irrigation. Wild onions—delicious to taste—grew in abundance. Wild horses and cattle grazed on the seaside flats. On the beach were empty bottles and broken planking cast up from shipwrecks. Escandón saw people—various Indian nations, and one whose people were negroid. Where had these come from? The wild Negroes believed that their ancestors, all male warriors, carrying spears and shields, had come by sea, swimming, or, some said, in boats, and had taken Indian women to wife. Escandón wondered. Perhaps they had come from islands between Mexico Bay and Africa. Perhaps a slave ship had been wrecked and the survivors cast ashore at the River of Palms. Or had they been left behind by the first Spanish ships that had touched the river between 1519 and 1523? Who could say? The beach Indians were friendly, and so were others from the river inlands, who declared that they would welcome the settlement of missions in their country. Gifts were distributed—Spanish tobacco, biscuits, tin jewelry. Escandón and his men built a barge by which to cross to the north bank and sound the river. There was no bay at the mouth, but only a sand bar hardly four yards deep. The stream was so abundant that its waters flowing into the gulf were noticeable for more than a league offshore, and "the waves being unable to thwart them, they maintain their sweetness." If the river had a main channel reaching the sea, there were also others that cut through the low dunes to make little mouths. The river showed change. "I suppose," said Escandón, "small ships could enter the river." But he added that the land was so flat and the banks so low that small protection was offered to navigators.

One of the other divisions in the radial descent upon Mexico Bay started from Fort St. John Baptist, crossed the ford there, and marched to the Gulf along the north bank. They soon came to the end of the river's rocky character, and entered upon the silty lands that went flatter and lower as they marched. The country then as they saw it had little vegetation other than scattered mesquite groves. They said there was little or no water. Nine different Indian nations lived along the river's low reaches and allowed the Spaniards to pass by in peace. Early in March the detachment reached the ocean, following the northernmost branch of the river, which they tried to sound but without success. They reported to Escandón at the mouth of the river's main channel. The co-ordinated expedition was a success, as one detachment after another completed its march and brought its reports to the Lieutenant General. Not a soldier was lost. The vast bag of Mexico Bay was mapped, and the Rio Grande was seen as the central vein for strategic exploitation. Escandón dismissed his divisions to return to their home garrisons, and led his own back to Querétaro, where throughout the summer he worked over his data and wrote his official report and recommendation.

Let the new lands, he said, be settled from the very same frontier forts from which the soldiers of his seven divisions had marched to the river. Offer those soldiers the first chance to become settlers. Give them tracts of land and furnish them with funds up to certain amounts so that in moving and settling they might not suffer undue financial hardship. Choose experienced missionaries to go with the settlers. Do not establish fortresses in each new settlement. Rather let the settlers themselves plant their fields and then defend them if need be; for men with families and fields at stake will defend them with greater devotion than paid soldiers in a frontier garrison, so many of whom were under legal sentences that had to be served in the wilderness instead of in prison. If for the first or second year, while the settlers were putting down their stakes, an armed guard were needed, then a few soldiers might be sent along; but only temporarily. Under these proposals, there were fourteen settlements and missions to be established. Of these, six were to take root along the Rio Grande. The region of Mexico Bay had looked to him like Santander, the province of his boyhood in Spain; and Escandón suggested that the Gulf kingdom be called New Santander. His report went to Mexico City, and there entered into the toils of government. It aroused admiration, his proposals were approved, he was appointed to make good his exploration by undertaking the colonization, and the Viceroy recommended him to the King for some suitable form of royal recognition. He accepted the appointment on June 1, 1748, and immediately sent out word in his famous seven directions to enlist five hundred volunteer families to found the first fourteen towns of New Santander. Seven hundred families applied. Those accepted were given free land, a gift of money amounting to between one and two hundred pesos, and a ten-year exemption from taxes.

In February, 1749, the first of the lower Rio Grande settlers came out of Nuevo León to make the town of Nuestra Señora de Santa Ana de Camargo. Forty families and a squad of soldiers built a town of straw huts thatched with palm leaves on the Mexican San Juan River near its confluence with the Rio Grande. On March third Escandón arrived from the interior where he had already assisted at the establishment of other towns. Two days later Camargo was formally dedicated with Mass celebrated under an arbor. Spirits ran high. The land was good for farming and cattle raising. The neighboring Indians were eager to settle alongside the Spaniards. Wood for building was plentiful up the San Juan. The settlers built flatboats to cross the river. Salt could be had near-by. Two friars were in residence, and a mission was established, and within a few years would have its stone church. Escandón gave the settlers a supply of corn to tide them over until their first harvest, and moved downstream to join another group of settlers from inland posts. With

them on March fourteenth he established the community of Reynosa
on the south bank. He gave them food, farming implements, clothes and
oxen. The pattern of Spanish settlement on the river's last reaches was
being fulfilled rapidly and peacefully. Escandón travelled from one to
another of his new communities watching them come alive all according to his plan. In October, 1749, at Madrid, the King expressed his
approval of Escandón's service by creating him Count of Sierra Gorda,
and appointing him a Knight of Santiago, Spain's highest military honor.
News of such striking royal favor reached him early in the following
year, and he assumed his new style that had been won in the field, far
from palaces and courts.

About halfway between Fort St. John Baptist and the mouth of
the Rio Grande the town of Dolores was founded on the north bank
during the summer of 1750. It clustered about the ranch of Don José
Vásquez Borrego, a cattle raiser who asked Escandón to include him in
his colonization plans. Borrego maintained a ferry service for his own
people and herds, running two flatboats which were attended by four
peons. Down the river in the same summer Revilla (later Guerrero) was
established on the south bank, at the site of the ranch of Don Nicolás
de la Garza. Like Dolores, it was a cattle town, whose herds were grazed
in the vast pastures across the river. Friction between the two towns
occurred now and then as their herds mingled.

Mier near the south bank was founded in 1753, and Escandón
remarked soon that "the entire frontier on the opposite bank of the Rio
Grande del Norte is settled . . ." out of which came the later towns
of Roma and Rio Grande City. On May 15, 1755, on the north bank,
with the benefit of an excellent ford and easy access over flat country
on either side, a handful of families were settled by Escandón, who
named their grant the Villa of Laredo.

And now the lower river towns gradually drew the traffic to
Texas away from the crossing at Fort St. John Baptist. Dolores and
Laredo, with their ferries, Reynosa with its access to the salt deposits
over the river to the northeast, saw more and more of the slow but persistent travel between the older Mexican states and New Santander.
Royal couriers and military inspectors and missionaries went back and
forth over the river on their duties. Wagon trains, cattle herds and
trading convoys chose the more peaceful routes of the river's mild southeast country in preference to the rocky fords, deep walls and Apache
menaces upriver, where in 1749 a priest and his party were murdered
as they neared Fort St. John Baptist. The six lower river towns encour-

aged ranchers to take their headquarters farther into Texas. If the lower river settlement came late, in relation to the old river kingdom of New Mexico, it came fast. The straw huts were soon replaced by earthen houses, stone churches, and plastered walls with carved wooden doors, all squared around a central plaza. Floods rose and towns were removed to safer ground near their original sites—Reynosa and Camargo were moved once, and Revilla three times. Indian settlers took second thoughts and ran away, but were mostly recovered and resettled. Smallpox epidemics struck during the 1750s, there were seasons of drought, and at its best life was hard and meagre. But it was tenacious, and the river was its home. Vast as it was, the province of New Santander had little wealth in the great world's terms of money, purchasable beauty, luxury, or even comfort. Its material values were all reckoned in the earthiest terms— hides, horn, beef, mutton, wool, salt, fish, fruit. Distances were very great, summers were violent with heat, drought or deluge, winters were subject to wild icy storms out of the north. A lower river town made a little geometrized chequer of wall and tower, faintly pink, yellow, blue, white and earthen, at the end of a straggle of road on the river's high bank. For the rest, there was abstract dimension—the plains dimming to sea-blue in a wilderness of light, north in Texas, or south in Mexico, where for all life that came after, the hard, modest toil of the Count of Sierra Gorda remained ancestral.

37.

Forgotten Lessons

Even in the eighteenth century there was but one seaport in Mexico open to ships from the Old World, and that was Veracruz. Every effort was made to exclude trade and traffic from any country but Spain. Spanish America, north and south, tried unceasingly with mission and fort to keep her incredibly extended boundaries everywhere closed. And yet across distance and every imaginable obstacle of geography the immense empire was knitted together by the royal mail service with its couriers. Mail was delivered, however slowly, to any farthest Indian outpost where a Spanish addressee was known by name. To reach the Rio Grande, the post came to Mexico City, and if destined for the lower river towns was forwarded by way of Querétaro or Monclova; and if for New Mexico, by way of Chihuahua and El Paso. With the mail came the news gazettes, late but, for all practical purposes in a limestone mission or a clay fortress on the Rio Grande, absorbingly current. An editor printed in his *Mercurio de México* a notice which begged "the Presidents, Governors, Mayors and other Prelates of the chief towns to let him have the news of their districts, first nights of plays, foundations, origins of miraculous images, and other things worthy of the public light, for him to print it in the coming month," along with the "General News from the Kingdoms of Europe as well as from New Spain." The fringed leather saddlebags were emptied of their consignments of personal and public news at settlements of New Santander; at Fort St. John Baptist where the missions now attended only a handful of Indian families and a constantly dwindling stream of travellers; at the Junta de los Rios, where in 1759 a protective fort was finally established among the missions, and abandoned under pressure from the northern plains in 1767; and at El Paso where life was busy, prices were scandalously high, and the river flooded every summer from May to July.

During the high-water season, traffic for the north forded in peril with the aid of Indian swimmers, or waited among the five towns until the muddy runoff of melted snow from far northern mountains was by. How could melted snow be muddy? they wondered. The river was always muddy. They shrugged. It was its nature, coming through deserts where the earth was loose, and vegetation sparse, so that water rolling over it took along what could be moved. So the riverbed was always being built up by dragged earth, until the river rose above its own walls and fell into new, lower courses, or encountered rock canyons which contained it. There was a dam at El Paso to be rebuilt each year. With willow wands, said a traveller, the El Pasoans made "large cylindrical baskets. These they fill with small stones and gravel and when the flood subsides they roll them into position." Then the less violent flow could be diverted from backwaters into irrigation canals and taken to the Spanish and Indian fields of the south bank. The trade caravans for Chihuahua and Santa Fe crossed in safety, taking to the south such commodities as dressed hides, Indian slaves, peltries of beaver and musk-

rat, woven blankets and rugs, piñon nuts, salt and turquoise; and to the
north, imports from Europe through Spain and Veracruz, and from
China and the Philippines through Acapulco.

Describing the five missions in the vicinity of El Paso in 1764, a
Franciscan inspector called the Guadalupe "the flower of them all, both
on account of its fruits and garden products and of its climate." But all
of the other missions there—San Lorenzo del Real, San Antonio Senecu,
San Antonio de la Isleta and San Francisco del Socorro—had their
gardens and vineyards, their communal orchards and fields. The Indian
farmers, under their Spanish masters, harvested pears, peaches, apples
and grapes. The friars made their own sacramental wine; the citizens
their brandy. Wheat and corn were piled in the granaries, and doled
out to the Indians in lean seasons. Indian servants fulfilled the duties of
bell ringer, cook, porter, sacristans, "grinding-women for the wheat."
The clustered settlements of El Paso were already a busy and strategic
junction point on the traffic lane north and south across the river, "the
great Rio del Norte," which was "a beautiful image of the celebrated
Nile, for if mortals, urged by necessity, are enlisted under the banner
of the waters of the Nile, so also are other mortals for the same reason
settled along the banks of the Rio del Norte."

In "that old and unfortunate province" of New Mexico, as a
Mexican civil servant called it, a census of the mid-eighteenth century
estimated a population of 771 households, comprising approximately
ten thousand people. The greatest towns were Santa Cruz in the north,
Santa Fe, Albuquerque and—the largest—El Paso. In these were con-
gregated rather more than half the Spanish population. The remainder
lived in the river haciendas, now grown from the bosky homes of one
or two families each to clusters of families in a village, where one family
usually dominated with wealth or lineage those others who furnished
labor, servants, soldiery or artisans. These were conservative settlements.
Tradition made them so, and so did the slowness of any vehicle of change.
Above all, the central idea of life was unchanging, as it contained the
society in its explanation of the hard world, and freed in each person his
individual dignity, worth and communication with the divine. The
Franciscan clergy maintained twenty-five missions; though not without
difficulties.

For many churches destroyed in the terror of 1680 had never
been restored, and many of those that had been were still impoverished
and bare. With so little of the world's goods to go round in the "old

and unfortunate province" the missions were often denied their barest needs, and worse, the poorest and most subject people—the pueblo Indians—were exploited for the gain of the official class, from governors at the top to local functionaries at the bottom, who held the whip hand of legal and military force. The lessons in human relations of an earlier century were forgotten; and the old complaints resounded again, as friars who had chosen poverty for themselves cried out against official injustices that befell those who were guaranteed protection by the law of the Crown, which was mocked by its very guardians.

Governors and local officials alike, stormed a New Mexico mission friar in 1750 after forty years of struggle in the river kingdom, "have hated, and do hate to the death, and insult and persecute the missionary religious, causing them all the troubles and annoyances that their passion dictates, without any other reason or fault than the opposition of the religious to the very serious injustices which the said governors and alcaldes inflict upon the helpless Indians. . . ." The friars were able to specify their complaints. In the harvesttime, soldiers came to the pueblos in the guise of traders, bought the whole local crop, ordered Indians to load it and carry it to Santa Fe "where the Governor lives," and paid them, if at all, in little heaps of childish trash—chuchumates, or glass beads, cheap knives, awls, tobacco dregs. In consequence, Indians must hunger and, hungering, go to the mountains after game, or hire out to work on farms, and in any case leave the missions. Spanish officials were still putting Indians at forced labor on building projects, and sending them down to Chihuahua with cattle drives, and causing them to produce blankets and cloth which were taken without proper pay.

As Indian property was stolen, Indian persons were abused. From the river pueblos, five men and five women were designated to go to the Palace at Santa Fe every Sunday. It made no difference whether or not they were enrolled in classes for religious instruction. They had to set out on foot or horseback, and "whether the weather is good or bad, they must be in the Palace on Sunday, to do which they have to cross the frozen Rio del Norte, and this has cost many lives, abortions, and convulsions among the women." When they arrived, the men had to "haul wood and perform other services, and the women to grind wheat and corn by hand." If they were lucky they brought along something to eat, for nothing was given them at the Palace. Mere unkindness was not all. "Such girls as come to this work with their virtue unsullied lose it there, for they are very strongly moved by desire for gain, so that they easily fall. The married women who go there pregnant have miscarriages for the most part, both on account of the excessive labor, and of the long journey. . . ."

The civil authorities permitted buying and selling of Indian slaves. The friars reported that in the case of Indian women or girls, "before delivering them to the Christians who buy them, if they are ten years old or over, they deflower them and corrupt them" with the auction crowd looking on, "without considering anything but their unbridled lust and brutal shamelessness." After such an act the girl was handed over to her purchaser with the remark, " 'Now you can take her—now she is good.' " Once when some friars were talking to the Governor, an Indian woman came to him and accused him of raping her daughter. Hardly noticing her, the Governor interrupted his conversation long enough to direct that the woman be paid off with a buffalo hide he had handy. Even the Indian dead were not sacred. After killing an Indian, "the sergeant ordered him hung up on a plain, where he stayed until the fathers came to take the body down and give it sepulture."

Why was nothing done against such evils? There, said the clergy, "we are coming to the spool on which the thread is wound." For if the Indians were helpless before the material power of the governing class, the clergy were helpless before its cynical reprisals. When friars made complaints to a colonial official, he replied with insults and charges of disturbing the peace. If they were lucky that was all; but all too often they were accused of crimes of which they were innocent, their reputations were destroyed, and false witnesses were paid to appear against them in the inquiries conducted by the Father President, who dared not ignore the formal legal complaints of the civil authority. Justice was corrupted. The law was a private convenience for the magistrate. The only recourse for the guardian priests was to write to Mexico, hoping that their tales would reach the proper listener. For, as a Franciscan said, he and his brothers were "the mystic watch-dogs of the house of God," and if at times they were remiss, they yet awoke when the need for alarm was great, and "now I bark . . . in this paper I make an outcry, and God grant that my barks may reach the ears of the most excellent lord viceroy. . . ." In summary, "the Indians are indulged in their vices, dances, estufas, superstitions, witchcrafts, and idolatries in the mountains, while we receive no favor but on the contrary are interfered with when we try to compel the vicious and rebellious to receive their instruction and catechism. On the one hand"—and here was the heart of the matter—"they give them protection in their disobedience to us, and on the other they harass and oppress them. . . . Now what can we expect . . . ?" The father missioner looked over his shoulder and with a shudder recalled the terror of 1680.

Everywhere on the river the tasks of civilizing and converting the Indians had to be done over and over, often for the very same people. Christianity was not a tradition that struck deeply and sustained itself among them. From one extreme of bloody rebellion to another of trivial but exhausting annoyance—Indian women talked so loudly in church that the Mass could hardly be heard and so they had to be separated by kneeling men—the friars knew every reason for discouragement. But their sense of purpose endured, even in grimly realistic terms. If the lord viceroy is going to send new missioners as requested, let him "for the love of God . . . see that they are over forty years of age, mild and humble, stripped of all property, and that they know how to endure many hardships." The friar who wrote that was a veteran in the river kingdom. "I am sixty-seven years of age, but, judging by the strength that I feel in myself I would say that I have seven and sixty spiritual arms to defend this holy province from so many enemies. They will be conquered, for envy and greed never prevail. . . ."

Rivalry, actually, in his own field threatened the Franciscan. For some time there had been talk of introducing another order of priests— the Jesuits—into New Mexico. Perhaps at first the Jesuits would undertake only certain specified missions. The Moqui Indians of the west were mentioned. But who knew to what such missions might lead? For two centuries the brothers of St. Francis had given themselves to the river, usually alone, and when necessary had walked barefoot into martyrdom. The Jesuits proposed certain conditions to the Viceroy. They even indicated that the Moqui Indians "wanted black fathers to convert them," meaning priests in black cassocks, instead of friars in blue, and would refuse to receive the blue while awaiting the black. It was unsettling, and it brought forth from a Franciscan the sardonic remark, "It is not the color that converts, reverend father, but the substance of the word of God," and the friar added that if the Jesuits came, he would oppose their entrance. But he thought they would not come. If the Two Majesties were again at odds, one of them was not at peace with itself either.

But in another image of life during the decades that bridged the eighteenth and nineteenth centuries along the New Mexican river there seemed to breathe the peace of a long ending. It was an image that presented much of Spain and that modified all things Spanish with the ways of the river land and its earliest Indian people. It was the life of the haciendas in their riverside pastures and classic glades. Spain was far away and had to be imagined, now, instead of remembered. But tradition was strong, even as with each generation it encountered slow change; and in a last golden light the pastoral life of the river kingdom stood clear in all its details of habitation and family, its beliefs, customs, works and ways.

38.

Hacienda and Village

i. land and house

The riverside groves were deep and cast a sweet chilling shade. In their silence, their dampness in the low ground, the composite sound of the river reached far along the cottonwood or poplar aisles. Silky flow could be heard, and little incidents of suck and seep, and the murmur or ducks talking, and the blurred clap of his wings as a blue heron clambered slowly from mud bar to sky. Willow stands made little green rooms open to the air. Cutting through the boskies, the main ditch opened its mouth upstream at the riverbank to take in flow for irrigation. It was a ditch perhaps six feet broad, four feet deep. It had wooden gates and sluices. From its artery ran narrow shallow veins to the various fields. When the light was low and the earth was darkening these little channels looked to hold quicksilver. In full noon, their water was seen to be heavy with mud, brown and sluggish.

But their work was visible in the green of the fields, which gave cool air to anyone who rode by them. Feed for animals grew there, and vegetables for the families who lived beyond the fields that separated them from the river. Orchards lay at the end of the field. Facing anywhere, the immediate land was flat. A few miles away mountains rose up, and against their hazy screens the slim poplars and broad cotton-woods of the foreground were dark. The clear deserts beyond the valley were cooked by the sun to give off an herby sweetness in the air, which travelled to the groves and the fields and, mixing with their blue damp-ness and the rich muddy breath of the river, made an earthy smell that caused a pang of well-being and memory of place in those who now and then inhaled with sudden awareness.

The farms lay in narrow strips inland from the river. The earliest New Mexico grant under title was given in 1685. Where several clustered side by side, there were common enterprises. Cattle and sheep were grazed in the foothills rising away from the bottom lands, and tended for all by herders from not one farm but several. Corrals lay near to the house.

The house of a big hacienda was an image in earth of the family. Through generations it grew as the family grew. Its life faced inward. The outer walls were blind against the open country with its Indian dangers, and were entered by wide covered passageways as deep as a room, and barred with heavy wooden doors that were secured with massive iron locks. Within, the rooms all opened on a patio in which trees grew, that in time towered over the roofs. Where the clay hives of the classic Indian towns grew upward in terrace above terrace, the hacienda, built of the same materials, and using many of the pueblo's details in style and method, expanded along the ground in a single storey. Beginning with one system of rooms about a square patio, the house, as new lives came, grew into another patio, and even another. The walls were often three feet thick, built of massive adobe blocks and plastered with earth mixed with straw. Ceiling beams were peeled tree poles, and between them were laid peeled sapling sticks, often in a herringbone pattern. Windows facing the patio held sections of selenite or small panes of imported glass, and were shuttered with carved wooden panels hung from iron or leather hinges, or upon round wooden pegs fitted into carved wooden rings. The floors were of packed earth. Within the patios, an extension of the roof made a porch on all sides that was supported with wooden pillars and carved, scrolled corbels. In their plan—a succession of squares, either extended in line or grouped in checkerboard—the great earth houses might recall in their humble way the grille of the Escorial Palace.

In feudal containment, the river house threw its high clay wall around all the purposes and needs of its life. There was a great room, or sala, for grand occasions—dances, receptions, family gatherings. A family chapel sat at one corner of the oldest patio, and over its door might be a belfry with a bell from Mexico. Each parental bedroom was also a sitting room with its own fireplace. The kitchen was a long room where the family sat down to meals. Near it were long dark storerooms in one of which meat and game were hung. In another, dried fruits were stored, and piñons in bags, and grain of wheat and corn in jars. Beyond the walls of these rooms, and reached by a heavy rear gate, sparkled a little ditch bringing a vein of water from the main ditch that drank of the river. Rooms for servants ran along the rear. A blacksmith shop with forge, anvil and leather bellows and a tool house with carpentry supplies and hides stood side by side in a work patio, where pens for chickens and sheep, a stable for horses and a shed for milk cows closed the square. The soft lumber of the cottonwood, that yet weathered so well, turning a silvery gray, and drying to hardness, was used for posts, rails, pegs and joists.

The interior walls of the dwelling rooms and the inside patio walls were finished in a glowing white plaster of gesso, or gypsum, which occurred in deposits near the river, as at Cochiti. It was powdered and mixed with water, and applied by the family women with a soft pad of woolly sheepskin, in a craft that was common to the Moors of North Africa, the Spaniards of the homeland, and the Indians of the river pueblos. Around the base of the walls, rising two feet above the floor, a dado was painted with plaster made from the most colorful hue of the local earth—red or yellow or sienna—as a shield for the pure white walls against the dust of the floor. Where black earth could be found, it was mixed with fine sand and moisture until it could be spread on the floors in a smooth thin surface. When it dried hard, it was polished with the bare palm of the hand until it shone again.

In its essential form, the room was simple, and very close to the Indian's. The Indian at first lived on his floor. Later he made an earthen bench that hugged his wall, and if he sat he had his wall to lean against. His very house was his furniture. The humble Spaniard made his earthen bench too, and in using it was tied to his wall. But the rich Spaniard moved away from the wall to the free center of the room, where he placed furniture, which was heavy, dark and formal. Its character reflected his. If he sat in his chair, he must sit bolt upright, for the seat was narrow and shallow, its back straight, its arms high and hard, its legs tall. No matter how rich the materials that shaped it—carved wood, polychromed leather, Valencian velvet, Italian fringe and gold bullion lace, Peruvian serge—his repose was fixed in a discomfort that seemed proper to his decorum. His luxuries, even if he was rich, were spiritual, not material. Even the greatest of his kings had preferred to live and work in a bare stone room, taking little physical comfort in the midst of the magnificence that was his to command. In penance—an opinion that could be detected in many Spanish ways of life—in penance resided virtue. It was only suitable that even wealth brought its discomforts to be suffered in patience.

What grandeurs he allowed himself represented the Spanish colonist's pride more than his joy in luxury. There were beauties to be enjoyed in many of the objects accumulated in the river valley by a patriarchal family, and sentiments to be told over as heirlooms descended. Placed against the stark earthen walls of a valley house, imported furnishings and precious objects even at their richest never seemed out of place. Inlaid woods, gold leaf, velvets, crystal, pure silver, turned the master's rooms, which in form were exactly like those of a pueblo, into the apartments of a Castilian palace. Profuse trade with the Indies brought European articles to New Spain, and some of these found their way to the northern kingdom, where they made references of nostalgia, pride and respect for the past.

In the sala was a pair of Castilian vargueños—Spain's only invention in furniture—which were wooden chests honeycombed with little drawers and compartments, supported by high legs, and carved, inlaid with ivory and nacre, and studded with worked metals. There were tall straight chairs with leather seats, and stiff armchairs in crimson velvet rubbed pale at the edges. A long narrow table, so high that it could not be slouched over, recalling the style and discipline of the monastery, stood in the middle of the room. Along the unbroken whitewashed wall facing the patio windows across the room was a continuous bench made of wall-earth. It was covered with Indian-made blankets. Above it, for its whole length, fixed to the wall, was a strip of Dutch cotton cloth to protect from the whitewash the shoulders of those who leaned back as they sat. At one end of the room was a wide, deep fireplace. Its hearth was made of flagstones. Heavy iron fire tools stood by its maw. In its chimney face there might have been a design of Valencian tiles, showing birds, leaf and flower forms in dark red and white, or an animal drama, such as a wolf eating a rabbit. If the family had armorial bearings, these were displayed in Valencian blue and white tile. Near the fireplace, on the floor, sat a Mexican chest with heavy iron hinges, lock and handles. Its panels were like little scenes in a theatre, painted in brilliant colors, and illustrating stories of common knowledge. Many mirrors hung along the walls, some framed in gold leaf over carved wood, some in tortoise shell and ivory, some in little facets of mirror set in mosaic along the frame. The Mexico-Orient trade brought curious, gleaming fabrics from China, and for its rarity and strange richness of gold and silver thread, a strip of Chinese brocade was sometimes hung flat on the white wall. By daylight the room was cool and dim, for the patio windows were deep and low, and shaded outside by the overhang of the porch. The room was lighted at night by candles, held in iron candelabra, or others carved of wood, covered with gesso, and finished with gold leaf. Everything was always clean.

This was because there were enough servants and because the lady of the house was an energetic and demanding housekeeper. The bedroom that she shared with her husband revealed her duties and her preoccupations. The bed was big enough for two, thinly mattressed, covered with a richly embroidered spread done in native yarns by the mistress who copied flowers off a Chinese shawl, and presided over at its head by a blue and gilt statue of Our Lady of Guadalupe. Clothes were kept in chests of leather studded with brass nails or of carved unpainted wood. Indian rugs were on the hand-rubbed floor. There was a fireplace, and by the window stood a small worktable and a chair where the matriarch spent hours at her work. On the table was her mother-of-pearl needle case. Next to it was a Moorish box of tortoise shell, ivory and teakwood which held her silver scissors, a little penknife, her spools of thread, her gold thimble, and a magnifying glass in a silver-gilt handle. There she embroidered altar cloths, bedspreads, tablecloths, linens, and taught her daughters her skill. If they married, each must know, as she had known, how to work on handkerchiefs with strands of her own hair the name of her husband. They must be able to embroider with beads. She kept little glass phials filled with beads of different colors and with them made scenes, flowers, birds, and sentiments on muslin strips. Vestments had to be embroidered and repaired. There was a rage for poodles in eighteenth-century polite society, for the King of Spain was a French Bourbon and the poodle was a French dog. Ladies—in Mexico and New Mexico—sewed elaborate little backgrounds into which tiny china poodles could be stitched, and the whole framed and displayed in the sala. Callers admired these objects and spoke of them as "very European"—always the highest compliment a colonial could pay. A pair of silver daggers lay on the bedroom table. On the deep window sill were a copper bowl and pitcher, and by them stood a dark blue drinking glass ornamented with golden roses and an inscription in gold that said "My Love." In a corner was a long row of boots belonging to the master, a pair for every task, as they showed, from walking in the river mud, to riding spurred, to dancing in the sala. In the same corner leaned a musket that was always loaded. On a wall of the bedroom hung a likeness of Our Lady of Remedies, embroidered on red velvet in lifelike colors, her robe studded with baroque pearls. She was the patroness of the river kingdom. It was impossible to pass her a dozen times a day without each time in half-awareness wafting to her a thought, a prayer, for protection for the house, its lives, and all its possessions.

The kitchen was in many ways the richest room in the house. Its graduated copper pots, hanging above the fireplace and its iron oven, shone like treasure. On its wooden shelves gleamed rows of dishes and glass. There was blue glass from Puebla—pitchers, mugs, goblets. There were cups and tumblers and vases of glass, milk-white and clear and colored, from La Granja de San Ildefonso in the province of Toledo. There were deep cups and saucers of Talavera pottery out of which to drink chocolate, and large breakfast bowls of the same ware. Porcelain from China, Majolica from Mexico, jugs and bowls from the pueblos of the river stood on wooden shelves or tiled ledges in the kitchen. Wood was used for utensils, too, long trough-shaped bateas, or bowls, in which clothes were washed, or vegetables, or dishes. Large trays and bread plates were fashioned out of cottonwood, and after use were washed and set on edge to drain and dry. From much handling through many years, they were good to touch—smooth, softly polished, and loved through work. The kitchen furniture was not so grand as that in the sala. It was of plainly made, unfinished wood—long table, chairs and benches. Against a wall stood several trasteros. These were tall cabinets with locked double doors whose upper panels were latticed, or pierced in designs, and inlaid with mosaic patterns of common straw that gleamed like gold. Through these openwork panels shone the highlights of the family silver. When the trastero doors were unlocked and swung open, the shelves revealed large silver platters, trays and bowls standing on edge. There were piles of silver dinner plates, and rows of cups and saucers, mugs, pitchers, chocolate pots; knives, forks and spoons. Some of it was made in Spain, and bore Spanish hallmarks; much of it in Mexico. All of it was heavy, almost pure in its silver content and, except for any blazons of arms belonging to the family, plain. Light struck from its surface as from water, with a faint suggestion of ripple that added richness of texture to weight of substance. Though massive, the silver pieces had grace, and though treasured, they bore the little pits and dents of daily use. To eat in the kitchen, off silver—in this were both the Spaniard's earthy simplicity and his pride.

His spirit he took across the main patio to the family chapel, entering through panelled doors that held the carved keys of Saint Peter and the Spanish Crown, side by side, the Two Majesties. The chapel was a small, plain room with an altar at the end. A crucifix of dark wood stood on the altar between candlesticks. The body of Christ was carved to show His agony, with drops of blood in relief and painted red, at brow, side, hands and feet—symbol of a sacrifice never to be forgotten by the family, and lesson to sustain them in their own commonplace daily sufferings. The altar was clothed in a frontal of imported velvet or brocade; or if such was not to be had, in a colcha embroidery done at home, of dyed yarns, representing large flowers, leaves and fruit. The family's favorite saints, in various representations, stood on pedestals or hung on the walls in paintings. To them in mute appeal for aid in particular causes were affixed little votive images called *milagros*. If a hand was injured, if an ear ached, if rheumatism crippled a leg; if a cow was sick; if sheep were threatened by mountain lions, little silver likenesses of these members or creatures were pinned to a saint in perpetual intercession for relief. A thoughtful household obtaining these from Mexico kept a supply on hand in a little velvet-covered casket and produced them as needed. The head of the household conducted family prayers in the chapel, and when the priest came, the altar was dressed with wild flowers and lighted with extra candles, and a set of vestments kept for the purpose was produced, and all heard Mass. Those families who lived near towns went on Sunday to the town church. Albuquerque in the latter half of the eighteenth century was empty all week, but on Sunday was alive with the families who rode or drove from the river farms to attend services at Saint Philip of Neri's.

ii. fashion

They wore their best for such an occasion. Indian servants kept their traditional dress which showed little change since the Spanish colonization, except for woollen blankets which they had learned to make. Half-castes, and the poor soldiery serving time in New Mexico instead of in prison, and an occasional trail-driver, and the valley farmhands, appeared in red, blue or brown suits made of jerga, a coarse woollen serge woven in the province. Their hats were flat-brimmed like those of Cordova. The Spanish cloak was replaced by the Mexican serape, which in turn came from the Indian's shoulder blanket. The men's jackets were long-skirted and full-sleeved, and their trouser legs now reached to the foot, having dropped from the knee. All wore boots. A sash wrapped several times about the waist replaced a belt and held small weapons of blade or barrel. The wives of such humble men wore voluminous skirts of jerga, and shirts as elaborate as they could afford, over which were sleeveless little coats. On their heads and shoulders the women wore shawls, or rebozos, of bright solid colors, which they folded in a large triangle, and whose points they crossed at the throat to be thrown over the shoulders. The shawls were fringed, and the length of the fringe determined the worth of the article, and the wealth, the position, of its owner.

The leading families—those who called themselves *gentes de razón,* "those who use reason," "the educated ones," "the right people,"—had a handsome variety of dress to choose from, with many colors and precious materials. The men wore fine linen shirts and underclothes. Their suits were of velvet, or of thin soft leather, or French serge, heavy with gold or silver cording in elaborate traceries, and buttoned with gold or silver or diamond paste buttons. A skirted coat, a short waistcoat, and long skintight trousers buttoned the whole length of the leg from waist to ankle made up such a suit. With it went small arms—dagger, pistol, short sword; a tightly woven serape large enough to cover the whole body when unfolded and slipped over the head by a slit in the center; and a hat, whether a tricorne edged with ostrich plumage, or a cordovan hat with a high crown banded in many rows of gold lace, either sometimes worn over a silk kerchief tied tightly over the head like a cap, and recalling the scarf worn under a steel helmet.

Women of the rich houses followed the fashion of Spain, which changed slowly, so that even if they were far away in time and distance from Madrid and the court, they were in the style in their tight bodices and long sleeves, their low necks, their pinched high waists and their spreading, shining skirts of heavy silk or satin, over which laces were cascaded and looped. They had a choice of rebozos, whether one of white lace, or one of China silk heavy with embroidered scarlet and yellow flowers and green leaves and blue shading and long red fringe, or one of silk that fell like water in plain solid colors, including black, or finally, one of black lace with its designs like the shadows of rose leaves. From their little ivory and velvet caskets they could choose their jewels—emerald and pearl and amethyst and gold earrings, bracelets, rings and pins; and rose-cut diamonds from Ceylon set in clusters like bouquets; and a Paris-style lorgnette with mother-of-pearl and gold handles with which to follow the Missal and edify an Indian; and gold chains and flexible gold fish and pure gold tassels by the cunning goldsmiths of Germany. If such finery picked up its share of dust in the far valley, still it spoke formally of the proper way to live, wherever.

iii. family and work

For in its own scale the family was as rigid and formal as the court of the King in respect to authority, reverence, and responsibility. So long as he lived the father was the lord, to be obeyed, respected and loved. In turn he must provide the goods of life to those for whose lives he was responsible, and lead them wisely, and guide their work. The mother, in rich family or poor, was the lady of all, and worked harder than any at the endless household duties. Reverence was due to her for she brought life and gave it to the world, and in doing so through the years received wisdom to which all would do well to listen. If her lord died before her, she until her death was the head of the family, and to the love and respect paid to her was now to be added obedience. Her ways were the right ways, no matter what the world tried to teach. She knew them without learning. Often in the colonial family, if the father represented the earth's life and its work of seasons and its secrets of strength, the mother was the fire and the spirit, the divined imagination at the heart of things, which she seemed the older she lived to perceive the more brightly. Her sons and daughters dared to risk humor with her, though rarely with their father. The grandchildren and great-grandchildren—for the families in their homemade sustenances were long-lived—stood in awe of their august forebears.

Relationships were stabilized, and each had its appropriate manner. Matrons of equal age and degree on meeting leaned their faces side by side and each kissed the air murmuring a politeness. Men, in greeting, formally folded each other in their arms, making two quick little slaps on the shoulder. Once a man declared himself *compadre*—"co-father" or fellow godfather—with another man, he was bound in a friendship that had a sacred duty to remain unbroken. A community in which such fellowships were intershared by all the men was certain of its own harmony, for to break it was almost sacrilegious, and could occur only through tragedy or passion.

When prayers in the chapel were finished for the day, all filed out past the senior member of the family who had led the prayers, and kissed his hand, genuflecting, in veneration of age. Arriving in a jolting, heavy carriage slung on leather straps, a great-aunt would come to stay with a rich family. She was received by the assembled relatives to whom she gave the most formal greeting. She stiffly put the tips of her small fingers, heavily jewelled, on the shoulders of each in turn. Her Indian maid followed her from the carriage, and men carried her shallow trunk of tanned rawhide that was stitched together in lozenges and squares, showing red flannel in between. The household soon learned her eccentric custom of crying out "Ave Maria" to anyone who took her notice. Who heard her was supposed to pause, cross his arms, and recite the whole prayer silently. She invited certain ones to join her in a compact of the Ave Maria. Hooking her right little finger in that of her friend, she led in reciting a charm:

> "How many hours has the day,
> Has Hail Mary that we pray."

If she made a compact as *comadre,* or "co-mother," "sister godmother," with another woman, they chanted together:

> "Flower basket, scatter never,
> In this life and in the next,
> We'll be comadres forever.
>
> Tra-la-la and tra-la-loo,
> Whoever becomes comadre
> Divides her heart in two."

To repudiate a shocking statement or action, the cross was invoked by putting the right thumb upright across the right forefinger held level, and saying *"Pongote la cruz"*—"I put the cross on you!"

Children, who wore miniatures of their parents' clothes, early echoed their parents' formality. They soon learned to stop crying over trifles. In their grave dark pearly faces with their large black eyes were reflected the animal repose, the spiritual certitude and the mind's government that so generally marked the temperaments of their elders. These were qualities of order that could be shattered by passion or debauched by folly; but they survived, if not in the individual, then in the ideals of the conservative life he came from, in which the family, however large, remained tightly woven together; and in which a pride of inheritance gave rich and poor alike a dignity becoming to the heirs of Columbus and Cortés and Coronado and Oñate and Vargas whose deeds and graces begot not only kingdoms but characters. In even his simplest acts the colonial Spaniard seemed to proclaim his proud heritage. For his beliefs and ways required a certain accompaniment of style; and in a remote land, poor in itself, style took effort to maintain. Behind the style of the big river households there was much work, for the men out of doors, for the women within.

While children played in the patio, under the prattling cottonwoods, and talked to their parrots, the mother had many tasks to oversee. For her embroidery and knitting, there was wool to be dyed. Favorite colors came in the Mexican trade—reds and blues from cochineal, indigo and brazilwood. But these were scarce, and the old Indian dyes used for centuries on sacred feathers and kachina masks now colored the threads for embroidering bedspreads, altar cloths, upholstery and clothing: yellow from the rabbit brush, blue from larkspur, pink from the tag alder, blue-green from copper ore. Wool from brown and black sheep was used unchanged. With homespun yarns the women knitted stockings, and wove brown and white rugs for the slippery floors. They made toilet soap from animal fats, adding melon seeds, rosemary, wild rose leaves and bran starch, and grinding the whole mixture to paste, forming it in cakes, and setting them in the sun to dry. To make pomade for their hair, they mixed strained beef marrow, powdered rose leaves and rosemary. If their skin was too swarthy, they bleached it with a paste prepared from wild raspberry juice mixed with powdered eggshells or ashes of elkhorns, soaked rice and melon seeds. To hold curls in place, they used thick sugar-water. The women made candles, dipping a long cotton string into melted tallow or beeswax and hanging it up to cool. When it was cool, they dipped it again, and again, until the candle was as big as they liked. In the spring, they gathered up the blankets in the house, heaped them on a cart and drove them to the river to be washed. By the riverside a fire was built, water was heated in big copper kettles, and yucca root was beaten and thrown into a long wooden trough into which hot water was poured. The women, bare-armed and barefooted, knelt by the trough and flailed the water until they made suds. The blankets were then immersed, rubbed and wrung until the country's unfading dye colors came clear again. At the river's edge, while mockingbirds, larks and blackbirds swept above them with excitement, they rinsed the heavy clothes in the current, and then spread them in the meadow grass to dry.

If extra help was needed, women came from near-by families, but never to work for pay. Their men would have been offended to have money offered to their women. When the work was done, and the visitors returned home, they were willing to accept a little gift, of "whatever was handy." This had pride, remembering the pretensions of the starving hidalgos of long ago, and also good sense, if on another day the helpers needed help.

Food and drink took much work to produce. The women made spiced wine, simmered in an earthen pot for a day with spices and sugar, sealed with a ring of fresh dough. Sweet cookies were made with twenty-four egg yolks. On a heated metate stone, dense chocolate was made by grinding cocoa beans, stick cinnamon, pecans and maple sugar—all imported—into a paste which was dried and cut into cakes. Cooked with thick whole milk, these made the black chocolate drink which was served at breakfast, and at four in the afternoon with cookies. The finest tortillas—large, thin, round corncakes—were made from blue corn meal. Three of these, layered with slices of pink onion and curls of yellow cheese and sprinkled with green lettuce and swimming in cooked red chili pepper sauce, made a favorite dish. When men butchered beeves or hogs in the work patio, the beef was cut in strips and dried in the sun, the pork was sliced and soaked in a juice of red chilis sharp with garlic and salt. Pork fat was diced and fried in deep fat to make cracklings which were used in place of bacon. A soupbone was used not once but many times, and was even passed from one poor family to another to boil with beans. Women harvested grapes which they washed, drained in a basket, and hung in a storeroom from the beams to dry into raisins. In the fall, as the Pueblo people had done for centuries, the hacienda women cut up sweet pumpkins and melons, setting the pieces out on stakes to dry. Squashes and plums were dried on cloths spread over the flat roofs. When the cane was mature in the fall, it was time to make syrup, and all helped. Against an outdoor wall near the kitchen was a long oven made of earthen bricks. In its top were six round holes under which a fire was kept hot. The days were often cool and the evenings cold, and as the work was long, bonfires were kept burning to give warmth and light while men with wooden mauls pounded the fresh cane on fat logs, reducing it to a pulp. The pulp was put into a wide barrel, into which a round heavy press was fitted. To the press a long slender timber was attached so that it could rock free like a seesaw. Here now was boys' work, and two climbed on each end of the timber, and as they rode up and down in privileged delight, the press rose and fell, squeezing juice from the pulp which ran through a hole in the barrel's side into a wooden trough. Women took up the juice in dippers made of cut gourds, strained it into clay jars, and set these, six at a time, to boil on the oven until the juice was red and clear. In the bonfire-light after dusk all was animated, purposeful and satisfactory, and when the first jar was ready, a sample of the syrup was passed about to be tasted by those who had helped to produce it.

The great families had Indian slaves. These were housed with the paid servants, and given lessons in catechism, and promised their freedom so soon as they might be, in the judgment of their owners, civilized enough to sustain it. They were allowed to marry, and their children were born free under the law. Female slaves were ladies' maids and kitchen helpers. Male slaves worked in the fields and among the animal herds. So few goods came by wagon train that the province had to sustain itself, and the raising of cattle and sheep, and the growing of food were the main concern of all. Crops, said a Franciscan survey, were "so limited that each inhabitant scarcely raises enough for himself." But by the middle of the eighteenth century there were millions of sheep grazing on the sparse slopes of the watershed. Between two hundred thousand and five hundred thousand sheep were driven every year to Mexico for sale. The grasses struggled for life in ordinary years and in dry years barely showed. The colonials looked at their hills and shook their heads. It was all very much like Spain, a condition of natural life that seemed impossible to govern. The tilted lands were growing more barren, the torrents —when it did rain—swept faster and cut deeper, the earth ran into the tributaries and into the river, piling up silt on the river floor, the river spilled over its old banks and made swamps on good farm land, and a man could only bow his head and invoke patience. Inherited practice had a firm hold upon him, at the expense of understanding the forces that his use of the land released in violence. Rain made grass, and he lifted up his eyes to look for rain. No other answer occurred to him. Animals had to eat. They had to stay on his own range or be stolen by roving Indians. He watched his sheep for signs of rain, for though they rarely gamboled, they would do so if rain were in the air. Before a rain, said the shepherds, a sheep would draw himself up and bleat and shake himself as though already wet. Before a rain, said the cowherders, a cow would throw her hind legs and bawl.

In May men rode out from the hacienda to help with lambing at the sheep camps. There were always goats with the herds, and when the men returned they brought home kidskins of long, silky white hair. These were delivered to the mistress, who had them washed with soap and water. When they were dry, cooked sheep brains were rubbed into the hairless side. Set into the sun, the skins became soaked as the brains melted. Washed again, they were dried and worked by hand until they were soft as cloth and pure white. Some were dyed in brilliant colors and used as little hearthrugs in the bedrooms, to keep the feet warm while dressing and undressing by the fire.

All houses kept horses to ride, burros to carry packs, and mules to pull the massive wagons and carriages. Wheels were greased with a homemade lubricant of fat mixed with pine tar. When a family carriage went travelling, it was accompanied by armed outriders and postilions, not for style but for protection against waylaying Indians.

Where water power could be had from a ditch brought close to the house, a mill was set up in a room twelve feet square. The ditchwater turned a wooden wheel outside the walls, and beyond it fell booming into a pool shaded by willows and huge hairy sunflowers where the youths of the household bathed and swam. Inside the walls an axle from the wheel turned a massive wooden gear that revolved a pole fixed to a grinding stone. Hanging from the ceiling was a stiff bullhide hopper from which grain fell in a steady stream into the hole of the turning stone and was ground against a circular flat stone eighteen inches thick that was bound to the floor, and enclosed in a bin. The meal was taken from the bin, sacked, and sent to the house, where kitchenmaids spread it out on a large white cloth upon the floor. They sifted it through a swiss-cloth sieve that was made to rise and fall on a smooth pole held upright. One sifting prepared the flour for whole-wheat bread; a second, through a finer sieve, for pastries. This work began with a prayer, before the maids loosed their prattle. Later, setting the dough for bread, they murmured the name of the Holy Trinity, and marked the soft loaves with a cross, to insure a good baking.

After the harvest in the fall, and the threshing of beans, peas and grains, orders were given by the master for a wagon to set out for the salines beyond the eastern mountains, where the household would obtain its year's supply of salt. As winter came on, outdoor work lessened, and wandering laborers were seen no more till spring. But others came.

A tailor might stay for weeks, while he made suits for the family men. A shoemaker might appear with his boxes and tools to repair boots and make new ones with tough bullhide for the foot, and fine Cordovan leather for the tops. Now and then a startling creature or two would appear, dressed in wild stripes and shimmering and chiming with jewelry. These would be gypsies—Turks or Arabs—who came selling medals and rosaries which they swore came from the Holy Land. Glaring strangely, they smiled over the secret which all knew they had, which was the power to put evil spells. Apprehensively they were made guests, their holy trash was purchased, and presently they moved on to the mingled relief and regret of the family, who saw so few visitors. An occasional government officer would appear from the Viceroy's court in Mexico on his way to Santa Fe, and make himself at home. He was treated with respect, for Spaniards accepted authority. They might be skeptical and willing to change the authority under which they lived, but authority there must be. Even if the travelling official gave himself airs, which the farther he went from the capital seemed to grow grander, his hosts smiled. Many odd things came with the law, but the law was powerfully implanted in them from long ago, and its flourishes were in fact a pleasure instead of a nuisance. In any case, hospitality to the visitor was a sacred tradition, and every comfort, all exquisite courtesy were his no matter who he might be. And when off the dusty riverside trails there came a guest who brought with him more than his own simple claim as a man, who in fact was a legal and spiritual descendant of the Twelve Apostles, then the household outdid itself.

Three times during the eighteenth century the successive Bishops of Durango travelled from their cathedral city in New Spain to Santa Fe, the most outlandish town in their province. Each moved by heavy carriage, accompanied by baggage carts, a mounted guard and various clergy. The Bishop made use of the hospitality of the great river houses. The chapel was thrown open, decorated and lavishly lighted. His mitre, crozier and cope were taken from their leather hampers, he was vested, he gave Benediction at the altar, and touring the premises, he blessed the house. Children were told off to be prepared for confirmation, which he would administer on his return from Santa Fe. The kitchen buzzed like a hive and steamed like a hot spring. The whole house sparkled and shone. It was like receiving royalty to have the Bishop and his train. Every last finery from the great cities to the south and over the seas was brought out, and every local grace was displayed with anxiety. The Lord Bishop was gratified, and weighed homage for its true value, which was the pleasure it brought the giver, not the receiver. When he entered his carriage again in his worn black with edges of purple, he looked only like a country priest, and when he drove off on his squealing wheels, he left whirling eddies of thought behind him. According to their temperaments, some members of the household, at this contact of the great world, were more content, others more dissatisfied, with the homely labors, loves and beauties of family life in the valley.

In late November the yearly market caravan began to assemble, starting at the northernmost river towns, and coming down the valley to pick up wagons at each stop on its way to Mexico. The wagons were loaded with goods and covered with lashed wagon sheets. The cargoes included woollen blankets, dried meat, tanned buffalo and deer hides, strings of red and green chili. These articles would be sold or traded for products of Mexico, the Philippines, China, South America and Europe. Silver and gold money found its way each year into the province when the train returned. But for the most part, transactions in New Mexico were completed in goods of the country, for almost no hard money circulated. A system of four kinds of pesos, dollars, came to custom among the people: silver dollars, which were very scarce, worth eight *reales,* "royals," or about an ounce of silver; "dollars of the future," worth six royals; "old" dollars, worth four royals; and "dollars of land," worth two royals. As all were called dollars, the Indians and simpler people accepted all as equal; but the traders always reckoned what they bought in "dollars of the land," or cheapest value, and what they sold in silver dollars, or highest value. It was a monetary system based on coinage but activated through barter. Blankets, hides, livestock changed hands instead of money.

iv. mischance

It was a picture of commerce somehow in harmony with the basic terms of production and survival in the valley estates. For in any day over the fields where the long thick low house sat in its boxes of light and shadow the thin distant cry of "Indios!" might be raised. The chapel bell would swing full circle and its clapper would now and then cleave to silence like a dry tongue in the mouth. All work was dropped. The men came running in a crouch from the fields. Children were angrily and dearly hauled up from their ditchside play. All streamed to the house, and once within the walls, they shut and barred the thick cotton-wood gates. The men took to the roofs where they lay down by the waterspout openings with their muskets. The plumed line of dust that had started to make a circle beyond the fields and close in toward them now was drawing nearer and the nodding gallop of Apache horses could be seen and the naked sprawl of their riders. "At the expense of our blood, with arms in hand," the household were ready to defend their common life. The attackers might have both arrows and firearms. If they wounded or killed a fellow on the roof, the household swallowed its grief, though confronting death the women usually sought comfort in screams. Muskets fired from the roof. The crazy thieves took casualties. One might come close with a brand hoping to fire the house. Another one or two might attack the rear gate or try to enter by the mill wheel. A man or a child from the house who had not gained sanctuary with all others might be found in the groves, dragged forth to view, and killed and killed, once in body, many times in idea, while the rooftops could only watch, and fire muskets, and rage. But the great house usually stood, though death and suffering had come in, and fields, if dry, might be burned, and ditches be broken and wanton flood result. The attack would be over as quickly as it had come. The swinging line of riders broke apart and their long dust plume died down. Each marauder streaked for the distant mountains by himself. Each made a column of dust that danced over the plain eastward like the little desert whirl-winds, the "sand devils," of hot afternoons. Long later, still watchful, the guards came off the roofs, and damage, wound and death were reckoned, as mischances were reckoned under the weather, or any other large, hard, and inescapable condition of living.

v. feast days

There were more joyful occasions, and these they made for them-selves in the river households. Religious feast days were celebrated with gaiety as well as devotion. In March there were prayers to San Isidro, patron of farmers, when the irrigation ditches were cleared of their golden winter stubble. If a ditch served several families, men from each came to do his share. The weeds were ignited. All day the ditches were

watched to see that fire did not spread to the fields. Food was taken out
to the watchers, and picnics for all the family sometimes followed. The
ditch fires showed after dusk and were guarded all night. At home, the
children before going to bed went to the heavy patio gates and looked
through the cracks at the magic glow across the fields. On June twenty-
fourth, the water in the river and the ditches was declared holy, for this
was the feast day of St. John, who had baptized Jesus in the river Jordan.
Early after sunup the women and girls went to the ditches or to the river
and bathed. Good health would follow. When they returned, little children went and then youths and men. This order was observed out of
decency, for they were people extremely modest and would not go to
bathe in mingled sexes.

The great feast of Christmas was celebrated with food, song,
prayer, theater and firelight. Special delicacies came out of the kitchen—
fried tarts of mincemeat and piñon nuts, white corn tamales, sweet cakes.
Little bands of young singers, called the Oremus Boys, went from house
to house in the villages, or in a hacienda toured the living quarters,
knocking at each door, before which they sang Christmas songs. When
their song was done, they received freshly baked sweetmeats. The house-
top was illuminated with dozens of lanterns burning candles. All day
before Christmas special fires were laid of piñon sticks, in squares of
four, and rising to eight or ten rows high. These were placed to outline
the plan of a rambling house, or the road of a village, and even the
profile of near-by hills. When darkness fell, they were lighted, and in
their orderly distribution, gallant columns of spark and smoke, and
spirited crackle, they made a spectacle that delighted all. But they had
more purpose than this. By the very signal of that firelight, the Holy
Child born that night was to find His way to the homes of those who
had made the fires. Boys ran among the bonfires, jumped over them, and
dared rebuke. It came, in the form of the Abuelo, or Bogeyman, who
appeared once a year, always at Christmas, to threaten boys with punishment for badness. He carried a great whip which he cracked after them
over the bonfires. He was a fright in tatters, with a false voice, and a
made-up face. They dreaded and dared him, laughingly. He chased
them home where he made them kneel down and say their prayers.
When he left they burst out again into the sharp clear night where the
aromatic piñon smoke smelled so sweet under a whole sky quivering
with stars of Bethlehem.

It was not a season of personal gifts. The greater gift of the infant
Jesus came to all in joyful renewal. In the great sala, by candlelight,

after much whispered preparation, at one end of the room a company
of family players appeared in costume to enact the tale of the Nativity,
in many scenes, before the rest of the household and guests and neighbors. The shepherds told in verse of the star in the sky. The three kings
appeared in finery with their gold, frankincense and myrrh. At the door
of an inn, someone knocked and sang, and all knew it was Saint Joseph:

> Where is there lodging
> For these wandering ones
> Who come so tired
> From long hard roads?

To this the landlord replied:

> Who knocks at the door
> In imprudent disturbance,
> Forgetting how late,
> And awakes all the house?

In the audience all knew what was coming but the littlest ones, and
they learned and would never forget, as Saint Joseph sang:

> Sir, I beg of you
> In all your charity
> To give shelter to this Lady.

It was anguish to know the sufferings of that small and Holy Family when
the landlord, reminding all of what mankind was capable, answered in
his hardness:

> My house awaits
> Him who has money.
> May God help him
> Who has none.

So the scene shifted to a stable, where through a window an ox and a
mule put their heads, and where attended by angels and visited by the
three kings the Child of the world was born again in the midst of homely
music and passionate belief.

At midnight the patio was alight with fires and all moved to the
chapel for services. Sometimes a priest from the town church was on
hand, and held midnight Mass. At the elevation of the Host, the bell

was rung, and with a hot coal a special salute was touched off from gun-powder poured on the blacksmith's anvil and covered by a big flagstone.

vi. wedding feast

Other than fixed feast days, marriages were the highest occasions. There was no courtship. One day the father of a promising youth, accompanied by the boy's godfather or best friend, called upon the father of a suitable girl and presented a letter, or made a formal speech, proposing marriage between the two young people. No answer was expected immediately. Pleasantries were exchanged over cups of chocolate, and the callers withdrew. After a few weeks, the call was returned, with a refusal or an acceptance. If accepted, the bridegroom may have heard something earlier that told him of his happiness, for the house of the bride's family would be redecorated throughout for the wedding, and news of unusual activity in her household perhaps travelled. Neighboring families might be joined by the marriage, or families living far apart. Cousins in the second and third degree frequently married, for the great families took pride in keeping intact their pure Castilian blood, and to do so, where there were fewer Spanish than mixed strains, would marry within the clan. Once the date had been agreed upon preparations went forward too in the groom's family, until at last they were ready to set out for the home of the bride. They went in their jarring carriage. In a wagon behind them came the groom's contributions to the wedding—all the food for the feast and cooks to prepare it; the leather trunks carrying the bride's wedding gown and her whole trousseau; and other gifts.

When they arrived, the groom's parents were given the freedom of the house, for they were to be in charge of the whole wedding festivity. The godparents of both bride and groom were there too, and would serve as best man and matron of honor, and counsel the young couple until they were married. Marriage was a sacrament. The godparents had solemn duties in connection with such a great stage in life. The betrothal took place as soon as the wedding party was complete. All relatives gathered in the sala, where the families came together. The bride's father brought her forward and presented her to the groom's father saying, "Here is she whom you sought." The groom's father introduced her to all his own people, and then introduced the groom to all her family. It was possible that this was the first meeting of the betrothed. All then turned toward the bride's godfather, before whom the young couple knelt down on white cushions, while he solemnized the engagement by putting a rosary of corals or pearls—the two precious sea growths from the faraway Pacific—first over the groom's head and then over the bride's.

Now the trunks were brought in from the groom's wagon and presented to the bride. They were taken unopened to her bedroom, where a few privileged girls could see their contents with her. Happiness and importance filled the air now as the preparations for the wedding went rapidly ahead. It would follow the next day. The bride stood for her godmother to see if the wedding dress needed alteration, and tried on all the other clothes. The visiting cooks went to work, helped by the resident cooks. The mud ovens outdoors were heated up. The groom's comestibles were noticed, to determine if he was generous or stingy. Musicians arrived. Lanterns were put everywhere in the open. If the time of year permitted, the patio was decorated and used. Pine boughs were tied to the posts of the *portal* all around the court. Guests kept coming to stay. Kegs of wine, flagons of brandy from El Paso were set about. If the chapel was large enough for all, the wedding would take place there, but if it wasn't, an altar was set up in the patio or the sala, where the priest could administer the sacrament of holy matrimony. He would do this only with the provision that at the first opportunity the married couple must come to town, bringing their godparents, to hear a nuptial Mass and receive the blessing in church.

At last all was ready, and the engaged youth and maiden, who though under the same roof since their betrothal had kept away from one another, now met again before the altar in the evening, accompanied by their godparents. They were married in candlelight, with the hand-shaped earthen walls of their family about them, and a burden upon them of solemn commitment. Tensions broke when the vows were done. All gathered in the sala for the wedding feast. Now a river house had put forth another reach of growth and promise of the future, all in proper observance of ways that were as old as memory. In her white silk wedding dress the bride went on the arm of her husband in his rich silver-braided suit and his lace-ruffled shirt. Everyone came past to embrace them, and then the feast began. Roast chickens basted in spiced wine and stuffed with meat, piñons and raisins; baked hams; ribs of beef; fresh bread of blue meal; cookies, cakes, sweets; beakers of chocolate and flasks of wine; bowls of hot chili; platters of tortillas, all stood upon extra tables draped to the floor with lace curtains. All feasted.

Then came music, and dark eyes fired up. The sala was cleared, while the musicians tuned up on two or three violins, a guitar and a guitarrón, or bass guitar. Servants came to spread clean wheat straw on the earth floor to keep dust from rising, or stood by with jars of water from which to sprinkle the floor between dances. In the candlelight the faces of the women, heavily powdered with Mexican white lead, looked an ashen violet, in which their eyes were dark caves deeply harboring the ardent emotion of the occasion. The orchestra struck up. They danced quadrilles and minuets, whose figures drew all dancers into fleeting touch with each other. There were paired dances, like la raspa, with its heel thunderings and its laughing fast walk. There were marching dances accompanied by spoken verses invented on the spot by someone who was famous as an improvisor. He would go to stand before a guest, bow, and without an instant's groping for what to say, recite an improvised ballad of eight-syllabled lines paying compliment to his subject whom he faced. He celebrated the beauty, charm and talent of the bride, weaving in episodes of her childhood, alluding to her gallant ancestry, and promising her a dazzling future. The groom he saluted in another decima as a superb horseman and buffalo hunter, or trail-driver, or heir of an illustrious house. Sometimes he sang a riddle poem, and all tried to guess the answer.

While the dancing went on, the bride had an obligation to fulfill. Retiring from the floor in her wedding dress, she reappeared presently in another gown from her trousseau, and later in another, and another. Everyone was eager to see what she had been given. Politely and proudly she gratified them. They fingered her silks and examined the set of jewels given her by the groom—matching earrings, necklace, bracelets, combs, brooches, of gold inlaid with enamel, or seed pearls, rose diamonds, amethysts or garnets.

Before midnight the bride retired not to reappear. Her maiden friends and her godmother went with her. The groom drank with the men in whose company he now belonged, while boys watched and nudged. The dancing continued, and humor went around. The groom's father calling above the noise in the hot, hard-plastered room, urged everyone to keep right on enjoying themselves. Presently the groom managed to slip away. In the bridal chamber the ladies admitted him and left him with his bride. Across the patio the merriment continued. Voices were singing. Someone shouted a refrain. The violins jigged along in a remote monotonous sing, and the gulping throb of the guitarrón was like a pulse of mindless life in the night.

So the river society renewed, celebrated and blessed itself.

On the following day the groom took his bride home to his father's house, where new rooms would be added as their home, in which they would have privacy, even as they shared the communal life of the hacienda.

When the children were born of the marriage, they were baptized as soon as possible. There was no greater token of love than to dedicate them to God. If they died in infancy, grief was put aside for a sort of exalted rejoicing that in their christened innocence they had been gathered straightway to God in Heaven. If they lived, they were cherished.

> Lullaby, little one,
> Lullaby, baby.
> For your cradle
> I give you my heart.

As they grew, like all children, they aped in their play what grownups did; but very early they were given tasks to do, and a little boy worked at a miniature share of his father's work, in field, corral or shed, and a little girl learned at sewing table, or in kitchen. They were an observant part of all the family's large or small occasions. The largest of these was death.

vii. mortality

There were sombre relish and conviviality in how death was received in the river kingdom. The Spaniard had a black mind and a morbid tradition. Philip II lived in him for centuries. Death was the gateway to an eternal life, whether, by his own choice, in heaven or hell. Its symbols were always before him. They clattered in gaiety on All Souls' Day—toy skeletons, candy skulls, tiny trick coffins like a jack-in-the-box—and they presided over him daily in all the painted and bloody agonies of his household saints. He did not fear death more than most men, but more than most, he was an informed critic of the emotions of mortality, and at proper times summoned them forth for their own sake, gave them style, and so became their master.

When death from natural causes was seen to be coming the family could only do its best to make the victim comfortable. There were no physicians anywhere on the river excepting the pueblo medicine doctors, and their concepts were too alien to Spanish life to be taken seriously. The parish priest was sent for if he was within reach. To die in sanctity was the most real of necessities. All prayers and observances were made. If the dying belonged to the sodality of Our Lady of Mount Carmel (who was the divine inspiration of Saint John of the Cross as theologian and poet) he knew that he might not die until once more he felt the earth. At his request a brick of clay was brought him to touch. Touching it, he believed his final struggles would be eased. His dear ones watched by his bed. When the last hour came they sent for the resador, who always led prayers aloud at devotional services. He now had a duty to perform, and he came to join the watchers. He was an expert at knowing the exact moment of death. Relying on his wide experience and his natural gifts, he kept his gaze upon the dying face; and when he recognized the first veil of final mystery as it came, he cried loudly three times, as was his duty, the name of Jesus. At the moment of death, the soul took flight to its Savior's name. The best friend of the deceased or the oldest man present closed the eyes. Men dressed the corpse if it was that of a man; women if that of a woman, or a child.

And now that death was among them, the bereaved women screamed in grief. They did it as a form of artistry. They threw themselves from side to side and wailed formless words. This was expected of them, a mortal politeness that was understood and even judged. In obscure wisdom they set out to exhaust, to cure, grief through its own excesses. Now and then in the midst of their working clamor, their interest might be seized by something beyond. They paused and gazed while their shrieks fell to whimpers. They were lost like staring children; and then, as always, life moved, their fixity was broken, and with a shake of the head they came back to their duty and redoubled their lamentations. Private loss became an experience to share in full measure with all who would partake of it. A woman shrieking and throwing herself required other women to hold her and give comfort. These in turn needed friends to relieve them at their enervating work. The whole society of women worked toward the seemliness of the event.

Men built the coffin of raw wood. The corpse was laid in it, and then with lighted candles at head and feet was placed on view in the sala for the wake, or velorio. All who could, attended to watch all night, while prayers were recited in unison, hymns of devotion to the patron saint were sung, and memories of the dead were exchanged. At midnight supper was served. The household was thronged and busy. Such an occasion was so much enjoyed that wakes were held even without death present. These were solemnized in honor of appropriate saints throughout the year. Men singing traditional laments in procession brought saintly statues from the church or the chapel, and communal meditations on death were observed as for a recent bereavement. A wake for a deceased person sometimes continued for two nights and was ended with burial. If the family lived near town, the coffin was borne to the parish church for a Requiem Mass, after which it was buried in the floor of the church while all present sang dolefully together. If the family lived far in the country, burial took place in the family chapel or in a cemetery upland from the river, out of reach of swampy soil. A fence of wooden pickets with ornamental tips stood around the family graveyard. A cairn of stones was put at the head of the grave to support a wooden cross. Late in the eighteenth century itinerant stone carvers sometimes appeared in the river settlements, and were hired to make a monument. One family, at Belén, had a carved stone mausoleum, built by sculptors brought from Italy. The funeral of a child was gay and impish, reflecting the happy fact that it died without sin. Dressed in white and decked with flowers and bright ribbons, the corpse was carried along in a procession that all but danced. The local musicians played furiously on their violins the tunes which everyone knew at their fandangos. The marchers chattered and laughed. Grief was out of place for one who had left the temptations of the world and already knew heavenly bliss.

For if life was a battle between good and evil, then the moment of decision came at the moment of death. Evil lived in the flesh, which would in the end lose the fight; but it also accompanied the spirit, and unless exorcised in piety before death promised eternal damnation. In the power of this conviction, Rio Grande Spaniards, like their most august forebears in Spain, strove to put down evil by punishing their own flesh. The flail of the Emperor Charles V, inherited and used by his son Philip II and willed in turn to his kingly heir, sounded in echo through the centuries amongst the villages and estates of the river kingdom. Their particular discipline in piety came alike to monarch and colonial from the thirteenth century, when self-flagellation in atonement was widespread amongst European religious orders and individuals, including the Third Order of Saint Francis. Searching for the river in the spring of 1598, Oñate's colony had paused in northern Mexico on Holy Thursday to seek redemption through pain, and "the night," wrote Captain Pérez de Villagrá later, "the night was one of prayer and penance for all. The soldiers, with cruel scourges, beat their backs unmercifully until the camp ran crimson with their blood. The humble Franciscan friars, barefoot and clothed in cruel thorny girdles, devoutly chanted their doleful hymns, praying forgiveness for their sins. . . . Don Juan, unknown to anyone except me, went to a secluded spot where he cruelly scourged himself, mingling bitter tears with the blood which flowed from his many wounds. . . ." By 1627, processions of flagellants in the Spanish river lands were mentioned as a matter of course in official reports of the Father President. When Vargas took the crown back to Santa Fe, "The Third Order of Penitence"—not to be confused with the Third Order of St. Francis—was established in the 1690s at Santa Fe and Santa Cruz, and legally recorded. In 1794 a cathedral document at Santa Fe named the same brotherhood, saying that it had "been in existence since the earliest years of the conquest." First administered under sacerdotal guidance, the brotherhood became more and more the responsibility of laymen, until in the latter half of the eighteenth century and throughout the nineteenth they alone conducted its ceremonies. For by then the Franciscans were rapidly losing their independent control of New Mexico's religious affairs, under pressure from the Bishops of Durango who worked, in the end successfully, to bring the river kingdom under their dominion. The Franciscan authorities were as a consequence withdrawing more and more of their friars from the vast province where few enough had ever been assigned.

Men of the Spanish villages and haciendas joined the fraternity to do bodily penance in atonement for their own sins and for the death of Jesus upon the cross. Calling themselves the Penitent Brothers, they were subdivided into two groups—the Brothers of Light, who administered the sodality, and the Brothers of Blood, who as the rank and file carried out its precepts. A village or a group of haciendas supported a morada, a chapter house of the Penitents. This was an earth chapel set away by itself. It had no windows, rarely a belfry, never more than one storey, often only one room. It was as secret and as plain as a kiva. It was closed to all but initiates. Within was the bare furniture of piety—an altar, a wooden cross great enough for a man, lengths of chain, blood-spattered whips bearing thongs of leather studded with cactus thorns, locally made images of saints painted flat or carved and colored, and various representations of Christ, and a life-sized figure of death in a cart. Here the chapter met for business, in secrecy, and, as the calendar demanded, in pain spiritual or pain physical. The members discussed good works that they might perform, together or individually. Apart from the great houses, there was deep poverty in the valley of the haciendas, and much suffering, and if charity could be done, it must be. The brotherhood met for prayer, and thinking of the poor souls in purgatory, prayed for their delivery into heaven—an act, under their faith, of supreme charity.

A young man taken into the chapter was initiated through memorized ritual and ordeals of pain. He came after dark on an appointed night to the morada, remembering and awed at what he was told to do, that would soon sweep his humdrum life into new wonder, prestige and expression of its deepest self. In the pathos of those who longed to conform, he lifted his hand and knocked upon the morada's door, and said,

"God's child knocks at this chapel door for His grace."

"Penance," replied a solemn voice from within, "penance is required by those who seek salvation."

"Saint Peter will open the gate," recited the novice, shivering at the analogy of heaven, "bathing me with the light in the name of Mary, with the seal of Jesus. I ask this brotherhood: Who gives this house light?"

"Jesus," answered the leader within.

"Who fills it with joy?"

"Mary."

"Who preserves it with faith?"

"Joseph."

The door was then opened to him. He was taken within and led to kneel and bend before a bench. His back was bared by the attendant Brothers of Light. He was exhorted in the duties of membership and secrecy. The sangrador, an officer empowered to draw the blood of the initiate, came to the kneeling youth and with a knife of obsidian cut three deep gashes the length of his back, and three more the width. Laying down his knife the sangrador took up salt which he rubbed into the wounds and stepped back expectantly. The novice remembered what he must now say.

"For the love of God bestow upon me a reminder of the three meditations of the passion of our Lord."

Nodding in propriety, the sangrador marked the three meditations with three lashes of a rawhide whip on each side of the kneeling man's bare body.

"For the love of God," begged the novice, "bestow on me the remainder of the five wounds of Christ."

And when these were given with the whip, he asked for the

bestowal of the Forty Days in the Wilderness, and the Seven Last Words of Christ, which were laid upon him. Then he was taken up and led aside, and his wounds were bathed for him, and he was by now lost in rapt endurance, and on his back were the welts of membership, as proofs of manhood, marks of prestige, and of faith.

When Lent approached, the Penitents made plans for its observance. In the whole Lenten canon of atonement they found the passionate theme of their own society, and led all others in public avowals of contrition and acts of penance. The tragedy of Christ's Passion was the central motive of their entire spiritual life, their art, and their acceptance of human estate. Through it they found the power to bear their own worldly sufferings and by it they were liberated from the burden of sin. Possessing so certainly a divine Champion they attained a strong dignity that was their consolation no matter what their material or social estate in life. If they were for the most part poor people without education save that which came from their daily experience and from the lessons of the pastor, they yet knew in a philosophical achievement of a high order that man's nature, capable of evil as well as of good, needed to be redeemed for his inner peace. Such a conviction was a universal commonplace in the Spanish society of the river kingdom.

Each year at the beginning of Holy Week the Penitents began their most intense demonstrations of faith. They retired to the morada, and were not seen to emerge for four days, while women prepared and brought food to the door for them. With the stripping of the altars on Holy Thursday came the tenebrous thoughts that prepared all for Good Friday. Litanies and prayers were heard in the morada. Plain song, far removed from the glories of old-world compositions, modified by strange accidental dissonances, and accompanied by the thin wailing of a homemade flageolet, rose above the praying brotherhood. In the darkness of Good Friday eve they emerged from the chapter house. Chanting in procession, while their countrymen watched in kneeling rows or walked beside them holding torches of pitch, they whipped themselves with chains and flails until their backs ran red. Girls, called Veronicas, ran to wipe their faces with cloths. In the valley, the tributary canyons, of the northern river, such nights were cold. Returning to the morada, the processional members watched all night, at intervals renewing their flagellations, and crying out the psalm of the Miserere.

> Deliver me from blood, O God!
> Thou God of my salvation,
> And my tongue shall extol Thy Justice!

And on the following day, Good Friday, within the walls of the morada an ordeal of spiritual pain was enacted. From infancy the Spanish people were poignantly aware of the whole drama of Calvary, and in various ways strove to share in humanity's guilt for the death of Jesus, and to claim the redemption promised to them by that very death. The Penitents of the river in passionate earnest sought to identify themselves with the sacrifice of Christ, and to renew in themselves the blessings to be drawn from it. They elected one of their number to the awful role of the Saviour. He was chosen for his goodness in life. Like any man, he knew fear when his life was in danger, and it was in danger now. Yet he was honored, and to face what was coming he was empowered by a sense of glory in his identity with Godhead. If the sweat stood out on his brow his soul rose within him. He was ready when within the blind walls of the morada his brothers seized him roughly, as soldiers had seized Jesus, and brought him to judgment. While the reader of the brotherhood intoned the Passion of Christ from the gospels, the events he narrated were acted out by men who knew and deeply believed in what they were to do. Christ was questioned before the High Priest and He answered, that He was the Son of God. The high priest cried, "He has blasphemed," and demanded of the populace what they desired, and they cried out for death, and struck at their brother in the morada. They took him a step or two elsewhere and faced him to Pilate, who washed his hands of him, and asked what was to be done with him? and they replied out of centuries and for all men, "Let Him be crucified!" The scene shifted in the narrow hall of the clay chapel, and was in the palace of the Procurator of Judea. There in mankind's reduction of all its victims to their animal being, the persecutors denuded the Christ and exposed him. They then put on him a royal scarlet robe, a crown of thorns made from wild rose branches, gave him a rude sceptre, and paid him mocking honor, while the hearts of the brothers were moved at what they did—to jeer as a false king the one who was King of all creation. Their ire rose with the gospel. They took his sceptre from their brother and beat him with it. They spat at him. He stood for them, entranced. They stripped him again and put his own clothes on him.

Outside the morada all knew what was transpiring within. History recorded in the gospels told them, and local memory, and sounds that came on the cold night. The weather was often bitter in Holy Week on the river, and snow fell on the little foothills that rose from the valley, and the sparse bushes looked black in daylight. One of the hills near the settlement stood a little higher than others. A path led to its top. This was Calvary.

Late in the morning on Good Friday the Passion within the morada came into daylight. A procession was formed. The Penitents went barefoot in their black hoods and white trunks. A group of flagellants led the way. The Christ followed, bent under the man-sized cross which he carried from the morada. A little group of honored brothers pulled the morada's rough wooden cart in which sat a wooden skeleton with gaping jaws—the carved image of Death. It held a drawn bow with a real arrow. Spectators from the settlement knelt to watch, and if the cart jolted against one of them this was counted a blessing. It was left to chance and the roughness of the cold ground whether Death's arrow would be jarred free from its stretched bowstring and fly away. The arrow, they said, once did so, and quivered into the flesh of a spectator, killing him. Death was everywhere. In fierce irony and challenge the people exposed themselves to its caprice, and ways of forgotten origin stirred in them out of the cultish death rituals of medieval Europe, as they now approached on the village Calvary the scene of the supreme death of their inheritance.

The mount was studded with rocks that pierced bare feet and with bushes that tore at bare bodies. Up a path worn by many generations that had walked the same hill for the same purpose the village Christ made his way, followed by all his neighbors. He fell three times and rose again to drag the cross to the appointed station at the top. The Veronicas wiped the faces of those who suffered in their imitations of Christ. The sound of whips on bleeding backs smote the air. To the cracked whistle of the flageolet, voices made their way in unison through the penitential psalms. With the marchers walked not only the history of Jesus Christ, but also the whole past of Israel, and Israel's whole past of Asiatic myth.

At the summit of the hill overlooking the lower river lands, the Christ was laid supine upon his cross, to which he was tied with bands of cotton cloth. His cross was raised against the white sky of the horizon. Those who watched saw a living bare body hanging upon the cruel tree and knew again what had been suffered for them in love at Golgotha. They fell to their knees at the instant of the crucifixion and beating their breasts cried out together, *"Peccado! Peccado!"*—"I have sinned! I have sinned!"—lost in the identity of the crucified. As the brother Christ hung on his cross wearing only black head-bag and white trunks, his body turned blue from the bindings that held him to it so tightly that his blood ceased to move in him. He was watched to detect the moment when he could endure no more and must die. When they saw it his brothers lowered the cross and took him from it, bearing him away to the morada to restore him if possible.

With that moment the village Christ had enacted the giving up of the Ghost, and out of the Gospel of Saint Matthew the words came back to all who watched—how "the earth did quake, and the rocks rent, and the graves were opened: and many bodies of the saints arose," and how for three hours there was darkness. And so on Good Friday night the brothers gathered in the morada to imitate the anguish and darkness of all nature, in the service of the Tinieblas. Twelve candles were lighted upon the altar. The Brother Reader recited twelve psalms. At the conclusion of each, one candle was extinguished until there was total darkness. With that, sounds imitative of the world in anguish and upheaval broke out in terrifying volume. All roared and groaned, while chains clanked, and wooden rattles whirred, and sticks thumped on drums, and hammers struck metal. After minutes, came sudden silence, and a single voice cried out asking for a sudario—the cloth that covered the face of a corpse. This was an elevated idiom, meant to signify a prayer for a soul in purgatory. The prayer was recited by a leader, to which all responded. The quaking uproar broke out again, and again a sudario was given, and for an hour in alternating clamor and prayer, the ceremony of darkness was observed, and at last the purifying terrors were over.

If the village Christ died he was buried by his brotherhood in secrecy, and his shoes were put the next day on the doorstep of his house to notify his family that he was dead. Grieved, they yet rejoiced, for they believed that in his ritual sacrifice he had gained for himself and them direct entry into heaven. His cross was left to stand all year on the summit of his hill, and sometimes two others were placed, one on each side of his, to recall the thieves who had died on Calvary with the Son of Man. From a distance they looked like twigs against the sky. Year-round they had the power to prick the thoughts of anyone who had sanctioned why they were there.

viii. the saints

For the crosses were in fact a form of monumental art at its most bare and artless. As such they stated starkly the whole purpose of visual art in the lives of the river people. That purpose was hortatory, not ornamental or esthetic. Rather than primarily to delight the eye, it was to compel goodness, which it did by means of images of the cross, the Deity and the saints, whose presence reminded the people of sufferings on earth that led to glories in eternity. And in their art—the art of the *santo*, or represented saint—the people revealed alike their longings and their own images, for the saints they fashioned were self-portraits.

In their first century on the river, Spaniards had brought their saints from Europe—large church paintings and carved images in the styles of the High Renaissance. In them along with piety echoed the civilized richness of court and cathedral, and through them shone conventions of drawing, modelling, and painting that adored the human body in its beauty, and strove to immortalize it with every elegance. The exuberance of patronal society was raised in works of art, even on religious themes, to a dazzling splendor, through superb techniques. Greek ideals of pagan beauty were revived to celebrate the persons and events of the Christian church. Through imported works of art, European sophistication presided over the worship of the river Spaniards and Indians in their rude adobe churches—until the terror of 1680. And then in one overwhelming gust of hatred, the Indians destroyed every vestige of the Spanish spirit that could be burned, ripped or uprooted, and the European likenesses of Christ, the Holy Family and the saints disappeared from their places of reverence in the homes and churches of the river. After their return to their impoverished kingdom, the colonists and the friars restored what they could of their property. But the Crown had lost interest in spending money on New Mexico. The Franciscan order on its own could afford only the most meagre of supplies to keep the missions alive. The barest necessities of life were all that came north in the wagon trains. The river kingdom began to recede more and more into its northern remoteness with every year as the home government in Spain found itself increasingly absorbed and on the defensive in European affairs. Imperial Spain was slowly bled of its life flow, and almost all the goods of life along the river were now created locally. Among these were the very saints themselves.

For, one way or another, there had to be saints in every house, chapel and mission, and if there were no saints from Europe, once again, the Franciscan friars, who when necessary could do anything, filled the need. They painted sacred pictures on buffalo skins. They remembered mannerisms of drawing and of coloring out of Europe, and their first efforts reflected these. On little tablets of wood they painted saints that could be hung up on a wall. Out of columns of cottonwood they carved statues which they colored. The friars fiercely preserved the seemliness of religious places by founding a local school of saint makers. They taught what they knew about drawing, painting and carving to those among their people who showed aptitude. As the eighteenth century passed, and the friars were gradually withdrawn, the work was left wholly with laymen. Born in the river world, they knew no direct European influence. A recognized profession of saint maker grew up, to create an original contribution of the Rio Grande to the art of the world.

It was an art that sought the universal divine, and expressed it through the humble daily likeness of the saint maker's own people. If this was the inevitable formula for the artist anywhere, then it was the qualifying locality, and the nature of the style, that made the Rio Grande saints unique. The faces and postures of those saints were those that prevailed in the bosky farms of the river—little cramped gestures without grace and yet tense with spirit; poor thin faces with great eyes that had always looked on poverty and in the mystery of hardship had found an identity with the divine. If the actors in the penitential events of Holy Week were fixed suddenly in their stark attitudes, with their dark eyes, their angled arms, their gaunt bodies, black hair, pale olive skins and brilliant lips, there, suddenly, would be seen the attitudes of the religious art of the Spanish Rio Grande. The santos at once gave and received a staring piety that exactly expressed the spirit of faith in all its vast, yet intimate, simplicity.

In time the saint maker became a familiar figure as he travelled up and down the river with his pack mule whose panniers contained a selection of saints to be sold at the rich houses or in the poor villages. He had tablets, or retablos, ranging in size from about four by six inches to about twelve by eighteen. He made these by first smoothing the wooden surface, then coating it with several washes of gypsum like that used on the walls of rooms. He ground his own pigments. Black came from charcoal, reds, browns and orange from iron ochre, yellows from ocherous clay, blue and green, which faded, from the copper ores used by the Indians for their kachina painting. For his medium he used water and egg yolk, and, much later, oil. He drew the outline of his saint in black or dark brown, and then filled in the color. His tablet often had an ornamental painted border, and at the top, a lunette carved in shell-like flutings. He tied a rawhide thong through a little hole by which to hang the tablet on the wall.

In his pack there were wooden figures fashioned in the round that stood from a few inches to several feet tall. These he called bultos. He made them like dolls. The torso was of one piece, the arms and legs of others that were attached, sometimes by sockets, sometimes by strips of muslin pasted as hinges. He covered the face and body with his gypsum wash, and then painted the features and the flesh. Every saint had his attribute by which he was recognized—Michael with his sword and the scales of justice, Raphael and his fish, Peter and his keys, Veronica and her veil, John with his long cruciform staff and his lamb. The saint maker carved such attributes separately, and affixed them to the figure. He worked to make his creations as lifelike as possible. If his bodily proportions were inaccurate, and the modelling of face and hands and feet faulty, it was only because his skill was not equal to his intention. But the passion that begot his works had more power to express than his technical ignorance had to constrain. His failures in realism did not deny life to his works—the life that he breathed into them out of the depth of his feeling, the power of his faith, and his desire to please his customers. He was an artist for whose productions there existed a lively demand throughout the society he was part of. This condition gave him dignity and fulfillment as man as well as artist. Fully integrated among his fellows, he gave in his work not only his own vision but theirs; and when he re-imagined their life in the presence of their reality, he became the means by which their society perpetuated its own image in art.

It was odd, but it was true, that though he had a set of severe conventions for painting faces, they never came out exactly alike, but had striking originality in characterization; and yet however individual they might be, all his faces were unmistakably Spanish. He gave them deep porched eyes, heavily rimmed with black, and thick, arching black eyebrows, and coal-black hair. The women's faces he finished with a paint that made them look like matrons made up for fandangos, with the ash-violet complexions that came from their lead powder. To his portraits of Christ and other masculine saints he gave beards, painted in shiny black. He often attached real hair to the heads of both male and female statues, and sometimes did not carve their clothing but made it out of cloth soaked in gypsum wash, arranged in folds when wet, and painted when stiffly dry.

Looking at the Mother of God bought from a saint maker, the owners could often see the living mother of their mud house in the valley. One statue showed her in sorrow, with a black rebozo, her brows lifted in pity above mica eyes, her full mouth trembling on the very taste of the grief that swelled in her round cheeks, with their touches of pink paint, and her full throat. Her dress was painted and so were its buttons, embroidery, and the rosary about her waist. Her hands were unduly large, and looked rough with work. Another divine-and-earthly mother had a calm, knowing gaze, above a great nose and a mouth shadowed with a wise smile, that seemed to rest upon daily concerns of husband, children, cooking pots and domestic animals. A Saint Raphael holding his fish was a heavy-browed youth with huge eyes full of the joy of the fisherman who has taken his catch out of the river beyond his family fields. In the right hand of a Saint Joseph was his flowered staff that bore a cluster of yucca blossoms. In his other arm he held the infant Jesus whose almond eyes and painted smile recalled the Mongol antiquity of the river Indians. The saint himself wore a look of grave, untutored wisdom in Indian fixity. In a crucifix were all the exhaustion, dryness, filthiness of caked wound and scab, the rivulets of painted blood, that countless people had seen on the village Christs of their own hill. His arms and legs were bound to the cross with miniature strips of cloth. In another carved Christ with real hair hanging lank the local face was focussed in staring rapture upon universal mystery unseen but believed. In another Christ, recumbent in a wooden cage symbolic of the tomb, the carved and painted mouth with a row of revealed tiny teeth was fixed open upon a silent unending scream. The power in his face was like that in the openmouthed masks of those clay figures buried with the dead in ancient Mexico. The Holy Trinity was represented by three bodies, joined, and three heads, as identical as the saint maker could make them, and the face of all was the square face of a handsome bearded farmer with roughly chiselled features who in obedience and patience drew the terms of his life out of the river earth. So in countless examples, stiff, angular, almost coerced into eloquence, the saints in tablet and statue spoke with passionate directness of the daily life whose daily need had called them forth in all their anguished divinity.

Though they had an awesome character, they had also an intimate personality. A favorite household saint was almost a member of the family, constantly included in the making of decisions, and consulted a dozen times a day in the comfort of half-thought and daydream. "What shall I do?" The santo would send the right answer. "May my harvest be good!" The santo would arrange it. "If the baby would only get well!" The santo must save it. "If I could only be loved!" The santo— if was a legitimate love—might bless it. Living as such a personality, the santo was subject not only to reverence but on occasion to displeasure, when prayerful requests were not answered. Then the santo was turned with its face to the wall, or put away in a trunk, until the request was answered, or its purpose dwindled through passing time. Addresses to the saints now and then took on an Indian character. When storms came, an Indian cook in a Spanish house went out the door and recalling the sacred use of corn meal in the pueblos threw a handful of salt to the sky, making the shape of a cross, and praying:

> Saint Barbara, holy maid,
> Save us, Lady.
> In thunder and lightning afraid.

ix. provincials

So in simplicity of spirit, and in direct productive life upon the land, with the most laborious of methods, the life of the hacienda valley took its way far from the great world. Out in the world, revolutions in psychology, and government, and science, were creating new concepts of living. But Spain, the mother country, consciously closed herself to these; and barely a ripple of late eighteenth-century European movement reached the river kingdom. The machine was being discovered as a power in civilization. Technology was born. Industry entered upon violent growth. But not in Spain, and not in the far valley of the Spanish river of North America. The Spanish had no gift for technology, generally speaking. Though the pure sciences were studied, their application was left to other nations. But even Spain's rich tradition of scholarly education did not reach to the river frontier. There were no schools for the haciendas, and no colleges. Even the Franciscan classes in the pueblo missions were disappearing in the last colonial century, as the teachers were withdrawn. Children of the river families learned what they could from their parents. This meant a sufficient skill at the jobs

ɔf working the land, and saving the soul. But it brought little for the
life of the mind. There were no printing presses in New Mexico. The
only books that came in the trade caravans went to the friars, and were
of a professional religious nature, with perhaps a copy or two of the
poems of Sister Juana Inés de la Cruz, Mexico's intellectual nun. An
occasional youth was taught to read, write and consider philosophy by
a priest who guided him toward a vocation in the religious life and
presently sent him to a seminary in Mexico. For the rest, only sons of
the richest river families could hope for a formal education. Such young
men were sent to Mexico City to college, or to Spain. They were promising scholars. Baron von Humboldt in Mexico found "that the young
men who have distinguished themselves by their rapid progress in the
exact sciences came for a great part from the northernmost provinces of
New Spain," where because of constant guard against wild Indians they
had led "a singularly active life, which has to be spent mostly on horseback." When they came home, they might become leaders in local politics, and enjoy the prestige of having seen the world. But the local
horizons and ways of the river prevailed over the sons as over the
fathers. Now and then a proud daughter of a hacienda was taken south
with the autumn wagons to be educated in a convent where she would
learn the crafts of ladyship. In due course she would return to her
family, ready to marry an eligible young man, and maintain with him
the combination of domestic grace and primitive husbandry that char-
acterized all life in the river estates.

For the rest, it was a life that had its arts. If these did not blaze
and tremble with the peculiar acrid glory of Spain at her greatest, they
yet glowed behind the sombre patience of the people like coals dying
under ashes. If their spirit longed for poetry, it had to be content with
the doggerel rhymes at dances, and in the nomenclature of the land,
like the name given to the mountains between Galisteo and the Rio
Grande, which were called the Sierra de Dolores. In such a place name
the Spaniards met the landscape of their souls. Their theatre was made
of the artless plays enacted by amateurs at Christmas and in Holy
Week with deep religious meaning. Their music sounded in the simple
scratches of violins at parties, funerals, the wail of the flageolet in the
Penitential passion, the singing of High Mass, the celebration of love
and adventure in ballads. Their painting and sculpture showed in the
saints made in the valley. Their architecture rose out of earth forms in
the universal style of the adobe house and church. All expression in art

was integrated in the occasions and forms of local living in the long valley. It was all unprofessional and traditional, and none of it was produced for its own sake, but always to serve primarily an intimate function of the society. As the ways of life were taken from the local earth, the texture of living more and more showed the face of local tradition with its Indian source. The river house, Indian dress, dyes, articles of trade, seasonal ceremonies like the opening of the ditches in spring, the drying of succulent foods, the kivalike form and secrecy of the morada, the bogeyman who benevolently scared children into goodness—such details stood for the gradual absorption of the Spaniards into the ancient environment where they came to conquer and remained to submit.

Did they see themselves in their long procession through the colonial centuries—thirsty for discovery, but often scornful of what they found; bearers of truth which all too often they bestowed with cruelty; lionhearted and greedy-minded; masters of great wildernesses that yet mastered them in the end?

Those who lived in the haciendas and villages of the river illustrated a last chapter of what it meant to be provincial in the Spanish empire. Through three centuries the colonials knew first how it was to move farther away from Spain; and then from Cuba, then from Mexico City, then from Culiacán; and from the big monasteries of New Biscay and Coahuila to the Rio Grande. Every stage brought reduced movement, less color, luxury, amenity, worldly importance in all things. In time, remote from their sources, the colonists lived on hearsay instead of communion. Folk artisanship replaced skilled professional craftsmanship. Barter substituted for money. Home-butchered animals instead of prepared commodities sustained life. Custom overshadowed law. It was a civilization falling asleep—remembering instead of creating, and then forgetting; and then learning the barest lessons of the new environment, until their meagre knowledge had to serve in place of the grandeurs of the source. As they were native lessons, so were they appropriate, but as their products in objects and ways were primitive, they were matters of marvel at what was produced not with so much skill, but with so little. A grand energy, a great civilization, having reached heights of expression in the arts of painting, poetry, architecture, faith and arms, had returned to the culture of the folk. Defeated by distance and time, the Rio Grande Spaniards finally lived as the Pueblo Indians lived—in a fixed, traditional present.

What they preserved were their distinction and grace of person and manner—all that was left of the Golden Age whose other attributes had once been so glorious, so powerful across the world.

And yet in their daily realities they found content. Escorials and armadas and missions over the seas were all very well, but now there was enough to do just to sustain life. All about them was a land whose forms of mountain, desert and valley seemed to pre-figure eternity. The brilliant sky called out life on the hacienda by day; and at night, with tasks done, and reviewed in prayer, and promised for the morrow, all seemed as it should be, with the sound of frogs and crickets, and the seep and suck of the river going forever by, and the cool breath of the fields, and the heavy sweet smell of the river mud, and the voluminous quiet of the cottonwood domes. The haciendas fell asleep under a blessing of nature.

39.

The World Intrudes

The Spanish community, scattered along the river for nearly two thousand miles from Taos to Reynosa, knew increasing trouble in meeting its own simple needs, whether of ceremony or material growth. In the 1750s there was only one man who knew how to beat a military drum, and at the end of the century there were no more than thirteen skilled carpenters, in all the New Mexico valley. Poverty ruled. It ruled in Spain, where monetary disasters followed upon wars long since bereft of adventure and triumph; and it ruled in the colonies, where the Crown could no longer afford to pay for far-flung garrisons, and missions, and new enterprises. Aside from the ancient pueblos, there were less than twenty villages and towns on the whole river. As royal support for the river frontier lessened, the haciendas and towns were more exposed to Indian dangers. Comanches swept over Taos in 1760, carrying off fifty Spanish women and children, who were never recovered. Even so, once a year, Plains Indians came to Taos to attend the fair, and the Spaniards from downriver met them there, and a Frenchman now and then appeared from the east. Loot from plains warfare changed hands in New Mexico. "They bring captives to sell," noted Bishop Tamarón of Durango after his visit to Taos in 1760, and "buckskins, many buffalo hides, and booty that they have taken in other parts—horses, guns, muskets, ammunition, knives, meat, and various other things. No money circulates in these fairs, but articles are traded for each other and in this way those people provide themselves."

Even such primitive energy in commerce was lacking on the Texas river, for in 1762 the government of New Spain relaxed its efforts to colonize Texas as a protection against the French. The French threat to Texas was removed when France ceded Louisiana to Spain. The lower river towns founded by Escandón were left with more local problems. At Laredo, in 1771, dispute raged as to which side of the Rio Grande was to be permanently settled. The original community had been established on the north bank, but safety from increasing Indian raids called for removal to the south bank. If the debate went beyond words, there were stocks in the old plaza into which the alcalde, José Martínez de Sotomayor, could clap offenders. Compromise resulted when some families moved across the river, while others remained on the north bank, and sought shelter on the south bank only when Indian alarms were given.

They came often. The big ranches on both sides of the Texas river were repeatedly raided, and the river towns knew one siege after another, with fire, pillage, and death. What could be done? The central government had neither money nor troops to add to the meagre garrisons of the Mexican river states. An effort was made to combine the forces of New Biscay, Coahuila, Tamaulipas and Nuevo León, so that a continuous patrol of the river frontier would be possible. New Mexico could add no troops to such a force, for the old river kingdom had all it could do to survive its own Indian troubles, falling back mainly upon attempts to pit one wild tribe against another so that warring they might leave the valley pueblos, farms and towns in peace. It was a forlorn policy.

But appeasement seemed all that was left to the lower river commanders and the governor of Texas at the end of the eighteenth century. To tribes agreeing to be friendly, annual tribute was paid. It seemed like a nightmare when each year the inert enemy came to be paid for a peace that was at best precarious. Who knew how long the bribes would satisfy, or when the recipients might become critical of the gifts they were offered? In one shipment to San Antonio meant for Indians there were one hundred English rifles, one hundred thirty dozen knives, some with horn handles, sixty hatchets, sixty dozen scissors, fifty dozen combs, thirty dozen little mirrors, fifty pounds of copper wire and fifty pounds of beads to string upon it, twenty pairs of braided and buckled short trousers, sixty-two copper kettles and sixty dozen jingle bells. In a typical year the Governor of Texas received one thousand nine hundred seventy-three Indians to whom he gave such nervous bribes.

New Mexico in the 1770s suffered under concentrated Comanche warfare which swept down the Rio Grande under the command of Cuerno Verde. An able governor, de Anza, transferred from Sonora, ended such hostilities for the time being by chasing the Comanche captain over the plains to Kansas and there destroying him and many of his warriors. Politics, in the same decade, persisted. From his hacienda near Albuquerque, Don Eusebio Durán y Chaves went to Spain in 1774 to see King Charles III, who as the empire's bonds wore thin had time for collections of birds, musical clocks, ingenious gardens and the re-decoration of palaces. It was Don Eusebio's purpose to acquire for life by royal grant the post of alcalde of the river pueblos of Sandía, San Felipe, Santo Domingo and Cochiti, with the right of succession for his son. He was received by the King, who listened to a recital of the Durán y Chaves family's achievements through many generations on the river; and in the end granted the petition. The personal exchange was one of the last between a Spanish monarch and any of his subjects from the Rio Grande. Don Eusebio made his long way homeward to New Mexico, where the reach of the Old World was losing its grasp.

But the river world was reaching out to tie itself to the life, east and west, of the North American continent. In 1776, Fray Silvestre Vélez de Escalante set out from Santa Fe and travelled up the Chama River from its Rio Grande confluence at Española, to find a path west to the missions at Monterey, California. His course was indirect. It took him to Mesa Verde, where he saw the silent cliff houses of the Indian ancestors of the Rio Grande pueblos, and in eight months of travel, he failed to reach the Pacific. But he returned with new knowledge which later pathfinders could use. In another direction, the Spanish capital of San Antonio sought to establish a regular route between that point, Santa Fe and St. Louis on the Mississippi. The roads were found, and if regular commerce was not yet possible, the future was waiting nearer than anyone knew, with its new energies. Across the lower Rio Grande at the end of the century an increasing trade in horses came and went. Foreigners—Frenchmen, Englishmen, Americans, even a few Irish—crossed Texas from Louisiana and entered the north Mexican provinces where they bought or traded for horses which they drove eastward for sale; and an old Indian trail was worn wider and deeper. Even Indians from the plains now and then went peaceably southward, pausing at the river to obtain permission to seek audience with the Viceroy in Mexico. And why? asked the Count of Sierra Gorda in Laredo and was told that the Indians wanted to establish colonies of their own over the Rio Grande in Mexico. Their request was humored. The Indians toured Mexico and went home again to the plains having seen what they had seen, which later could find use in their border warfare against the settlers who had let them pass by.

Lessons in human relations came hard—and late. In 1785 the Governor at Santa Fe received an official letter notifying him that the custom of branding Negroes on cheek and shoulder had been abolished. Under the guise of granting Indians their full privileges as subjects of the King, a government decree of 1794 took away from the Texas missions and placed under the care of civil justices all those who had been for ten years or longer the wards of the friars. Where the Indian had farmed his field and bred his cattle under the selfless teaching of the missionary, he was now to act alone. He could sell his crops, choose his occupation, and live where he pleased. Liberty was his. He was free to live like any Spaniard. The decree was a curious mixture of enlightenment and irresponsibility, and its motives were too bald to remain long hidden by rhetoric. In fact, there was no longer enough money to subsidize the missions, and their secularization was inevitable. No missions had ever been self-supporting. Part of their support had come from the Franciscan order, and the greater part from the Crown. Now the chapels were to become parish churches, to be supported by local population, or left empty to the weather. In many a mission friars would no longer teach Indians to read and write and work for the communal support of the settlement in modern fashion. There was no one else who holding duty and faith above worldly gain disinterestedly loved an Indian. In being granted with a flourish his equal status with the lay Spaniard, the Indian was in fact abandoned to a life of misery and exploitation. The civil justices assigned as his guardians were officially enjoined to guard the Indian against drunkenness, for drunk, he made a fool of himself and sold his meagre goods for a gulp of liquor. It was a fact used to advantage by Spanish traders. An Indian hiring out to labor was to be protected against unjust payment, but if he chose, he might accept commodities instead of cash, and their value was of course fixed by his employer. With no education for a gradual assumption of civil status, the Indian was abruptly required to be self-supporting and self-governing in the alien society of the Spaniard.

A bishop of northern New Spain saw the inevitable consequences and warned against them. He cited the corruption of the colonial and local governments, and he spoke of the nature of the Indian still so near to its savage inheritance. He pleaded that the friars lived and worked in close community with Indians, and gave to them guidance and love that no civil agent, however dedicated and honest, could ever match. The plea was useless. The missions were secularized, the Indians were cut adrift, many of the lower river chapels fell into disuse. The Texas-Coahuila parishes came under the jurisdiction of the Bishop of Linares, just as those of the New Mexico river became the responsibility, in due course, of the Bishop of Durango.

The act of secularization was the last blow for such a community as Fort St. John Baptist on the Rio Grande. Traffic crossing by its ford was long since diminished, as Laredo and other downstream towns grew to provide nearer gateways between interior Mexico and inhabited Texas. But a little cluster of mission Indians still lived at Saint Bernard's, and the fort still had a flying company in station to protect river ranches against wild raiders. Now asked to maintain the great stone temple with its convent, its granary, its baptistry, as a local parish church, the few families, the underpaid and often criminal soldiers of the garrison, could not do so. The friars were withdrawn. The other two missions of the triangle at St. John Baptist were abandoned also. These two of earthern structure weathered rapidly away. Saint Bernard's with its beautiful tapestried stone survived the elements, but in time lost much of its sound splendor to other uses, for as the decades passed, and a remote northern Mexico town was settled where the fort had stood, the townspeople tore at its walls to build their own houses, corrals and market shops out of the stones quarried by the Franciscans so long ago. The first and the finest stone mission of the Rio Grande gaped open to the weather when the roof of the nave fell in. Grass appeared in the high cracks of the walls where dust was packed by wind. Snakes came to cast off their micalike skins in the open rooms amid the warming stones of spring. The irrigation canals broke and the water ran idly. The fathers'

pool still mirrored its gray and yellow rock cliff. Saint Bernard's returned
to the wilderness from whose needs and materials it was built.

Up the river its first bridge was being erected at El Paso in 1797.
The wood for it had to be brought from far away in the north, and
was delayed in arriving, thanks to incompetence on the part of the engineer in charge. But in October three years later the bridge was completed, though it seemed to require constant repairs. More pine beams
were sent from Santa Fe in June, 1802, with a warning—wood was
precious—not to entrust it to the man in charge of the bridge, and a
strong suggestion that someone more suitable be found locally to direct
the work. A few weeks later the receipt of the timber was acknowledged
from El Paso, and a new engineer named. The governor himself, Fernando de Chacón, went to inspect the bridge, and finally took charge
of its repair. It gave him much trouble. He suffered injuries at the
bridge, there were no medical facilities in El Paso, or anywhere in New
Mexico, to cure him, and he ended by petitioning King Charles IV in
November, 1802, to relieve him of his post as governor and give him
an appointment in Spain. Fourteen months later the King granted his
petition. The bridge needed additional repairs in the following year,
and a party was sent to the Sierra de la Soledad from El Paso to cut
wood. Placed as it was, at the entrance of New Mexico, the bridge was
important to the whole kingdom. As late as 1819, Indians "and other
poor people" of Taos were pressed into service to haul mountain lumber
all the way down the river to the bridge at El Paso, often to their
personal hardship. In that year, the resident Franciscan of Taos wrote
to the governor at Santa Fe appealing to him to excuse the Taos farmers
from furnishing oxen for hauling timber to El Paso for the bridge until
late summer, so that they might work their crops. The governor scratched
his approval on the edge of the friar's letter, and ordered hauling
suspended.

But it was one thing to build a bridge for internal commerce,
quite another to allow foreigners to use it. At all her frontiers, New Spain
tried to exclude strangers. The Count of Revilla Gigedo, Viceroy, in
1792 issued an order received in New Mexico that required innkeepers
to report every day to the local magistrate who their transient lodgers
were. After the battle of Cape Saint Vincent in February, 1797, when
England's navy defeated Spain's, and followed this by raiding Spanish
possessions at home and in the Indies seas, a secret governmental dispatch
came to Governor de Chacón at Santa Fe in July with alarming news
and grave warnings. Spain believed that the English were readying an

expedition that was to sweep across North America from Halifax, Nova Scotia, aimed particularly at an invasion of New Mexico by way of the Mississippi and Missouri rivers. Observe every precaution, advised the dispatch, to protect Indian and Spanish subjects against English and American designs upon their loyalty. Intensify military reconnaissance at the borders. Arrest all foreigners. Go so far even as to employ Comanches and other erstwhile Indian enemies as allies in an unceasing vigilance. The home government was greatly exercised; but if its efforts could ever have stayed what it feared might come, they were already too late.

For the frontiers had been crossed not by a fantastic expedition from Nova Scotia, or a French army from Louisiana, but a handful of men here, another there, bearing passports in some cases, in others nothing but enterprise. Traders came to Texas, trappers entered northern New Mexico, and by 1804 sixty-eight foreigners had come to Texas to stay. They included Frenchmen, who arrived from Louisiana in 1778, Englishmen in 1783, Irishmen in 1786, and United States Americans in 1789. Spanish frontier officials had their orders against foreigners, but the spaces of the country were vast, the Spanish garrisons meagre, and occasional officers corrupt. Intrusions over the eastern border of Texas had the effect of shock-waves that travelled all the way to the Rio Grande and beyond into northern Mexico.

Louisiana, New Orleans, were Spanish in 1800, but the city was a turmoil of mixed foreigners, languages and intentions. Adventurers from the states were already to be seen there, and their intrigues overheard. In November, the principal towns of the lower Rio Grande were alerted by news that flew across Texas. An American of New Orleans, Philip Nolan, with thirty or forty followers, most of whom were from the United States, was making his way illegally toward Mexico on what he announced as an expedition to capture wild horses in New Santander, bring them back across Texas and sell or trade them in the southern States. But he had been in Texas before, and there was a standing order for his arrest. In the face of it, he persisted in his new adventure. It was known that his company was now heavily armed. He himself carried a double-barrelled shotgun, a carbine and a brace of pistols. In spite of Spanish protests to American officials against his violation of American neutrality agreements, Nolan was allowed—or was he encouraged?—to set out on his venture. The Supreme Court of the Territory of Mississippi, which heard the Spanish complaint against him, declared that "it is beyond our power and contrary to the constitution of the United

States to prevent one or more citizens from leaving their country when it cannot be proved with evidence that their intentions are hostile." Nolan gave assurances that his purpose was wholly commercial and peaceful. He was planning to be gone only three months. As for the heavy armament he and his men carried, the arsenal was solely to bring down game on which to subsist, and to repel Indians and bandits. He proceeded with his plans, many of which, in the rude unrest of New Orleans, became known to Spanish spies who sent rapid dispatches to San Antonio, the Rio Grande and Mexico City. Nolan was going to the Rio Grande by the Gulf Coast, dodging Spanish outposts. Then his plans were changed, he was entering Texas farther north, and would proceed to Revilla, on the Rio Grande, where, he said, he had things already well arranged so as to meet no resistance. What was behind it all? The Spaniards were distracted. Nolan evidently had the implicit support of the United States in his movements that were so formally unwelcome to the government of the Rio Grande. Did he seem to presage a future gathering of larger forces behind him to the East? If he were successful, would greater companies, with more on their minds than horse trading, move across Texas, and take the river, and perhaps northern Mexico? The Rio Grande was a strategic barrier, in any case. The garrisons stationed there received their orders when word came that Nolan, after a skirmish with royal troops on the Wichita River in north central Texas, was on his way.

The garrison commanders at Laredo, Revilla, Mier, Camargo, Reynosa and Refugio (a mission that stood on the site of later Matamoros) were ordered by the governor of New Santander to arrest any foreigner entering their posts without a passport. The towns were to mobilize their militia to two-thirds strength, and soldiers from each were sent to Reynosa as a large guard to hold Nolan when he should appear. For he was believed to be marching down the Gulf Coast in November to the mouth of the Rio Grande, and Reynosa was the most important river town near to the Gulf. He was expected to follow the river upstream and try to cross into Mexico at Reynosa. But the other river garrisons were not idle. All of them sent out daily scouting parties up to ten men each, while appeals went to the governor for trained officers, more men, better arms, and military supplies. The provincial governor, unable to send help, could only call for redoubled vigilance. At Laredo the horses of the cavalry were usually stabled on the north shore of the river. Fearing surprise attack and theft of the mounts, the commandant had them moved to the south bank.

Out of Texas came continued rumors—but no Nolan. For the last weeks of November, all of December and half of January, the river towns braced and waited for the thirty or forty invaders whose captain so insolently defied the official will of New Spain. What were the river Spaniards so afraid of, in their towns, and on their huge ranches? If their garrisons were poor, they yet outnumbered the invaders so far from home in so immense a land. The Spaniards in defending their sovereignty which already was losing its power from within seemed to know that the future was upon them already, from within and without. No effort was too great if Nolan could be halted, and with him, even for a moment, the energies that in so little time had swept from the Atlantic states to the Mississippi. The governors of northern Mexico in person moved with troops to the Rio Grande to take up the defense. Hererra of Nuevo León with a hundred men was at Revilla, where Nolan had airly said he would "not be detained two days." Cordero of Coahuila threw a line of a hundred and sixty men from Laredo inland to Monclova to intercept Nolan if he should penetrate south of the river. Blanco of New Santander marched with a force from San Carlos to the mouth of the river to find Nolan, but failed to encounter him. The Governor combed the coast for him, and then marched up the river all the way to Laredo. News had come that the Comanches, led by the invaders, were gathering for frightful descents upon Laredo and Fort St. John Baptist. For three months the whole lower river frontier was on a war basis to repel the first organized intrusion from the United States.

But it never came to the river. In March, 1801, the Rio Grande commands heard how on the twenty-first, Spanish troops from Nacogdoches in East Texas had surrounded Nolan in his camp near the Brazos river. The American expedition was now reduced to twenty-five members. Far from being a powerful invasion force, they were dug in at a permanent camp in the midst of hostile Indian country. Their defenses consisted of crudely made log bulwarks. They were hungry and hairy. They had been subsisting on horse meat. All their rumors and threats suddenly fell down like torn banners. The Spanish troops attacked and by midmorning it was all over. Nolan was killed. His ears were cut off to send to the Spanish governor at San Antonio. His survivors surrendered. On the Rio Grande, the militia were demobilized. Over four hundred soldiers had been waiting for nearly five months to repel the invasion. For the first time the river towns had known the posture of defense against another threat than that of horse Indians.

Their accustomed peace and poverty settled again over the towns and ranches of the Texas river.

But not for long, for in the following year a compact made by the home government of Spain gave Louisiana back to France. Once again, but now in vastly greater meanings, the dangers of an unprotected eastern border swept over the weakened governments of northern New Spain. The Rio Grande was again a political line on a map. LaSalle in 1682 had claimed the River of Palms as the western boundary of French Louisiana. In "Secret Instructions for the Captain-General of Louisiana," dated March 26, 1802, the French government set forth a claim to the Rio Grande "from its mouth to about the thirtieth parallel" as the western boundary of Louisiana. Alluding vaguely to former agreements with Spain, never substantiated, the document went on to note that "the line of demarcation stops after reaching this point, and there seems never to have been any agreement in regard to this part of the frontier. The farther we go northward, the more undecided is the boundary. This part of America contains little more than uninhabited forests or Indian tribes, and the necessity of fixing a boundary has never yet been felt there." The French claim took in almost half of the Rio Grande inland from the Gulf.

It was a claim that the French did not press; but its existence in 1802 created an horizon at the Rio Grande for all those who looked westward across Texas in the following decades, from the successive owners of Louisiana to the three republics of Texas, and ending with Texas as a state of the American federal union. The return of Louisiana to France was a shock to northern Mexico. Already impoverished by failing governmental support, and distracted by Indian troubles, where would the Rio Grande states find the means to guard the frontier, now moved so much closer by the treaty of 1802? The treaty did contain one crumb to allay anxiety for the future. It specified that if France ever gave up Louisiana, she must yield it only to Spain. From this clause the governors of New Spain took comfort while they could.

But secretly in the following year to raise monies to finance his war against England, Napoleon Bonaparte, dictator of France, sold Louisiana to the United States for $15,000,000. Once again, and with violence sure to come, the status of Texas, and the Rio Grande, was thrown in doubt. United States troops were mobilized along the Mississippi to support the American commissioners who entered New Orleans to take possession from the French. The question was soon raised as to how far, having bought Louisiana, might the Americans consider the territory to extend? The French had claimed all the way across Texas to the Rio Grande. Why should not the Americans? President Thomas Jefferson in fact did so. East Texas was agitated. Spanish garrisons were reinforced—but how pitifully. Border incidents occurred. New Spain made desperate plans to establish physical defenses, living possession, of the coastal wastes of Texas. The resources of Cuba and Mexico together were to be used for naval power and for the raising of colonial families. New sites inland in the Texas wilderness were to become towns and forts that would discourage the United States. But all such plans came to little or nothing, while the author of New Spain's latest trouble assumed in December, 1804, the crown of emperor in the metropolitan church of Notre Dame de Paris. His state was immense. It revived Roman splendors and improved them with designs by Isabey, involving miles of blue velvet, and millions of embroidered golden bees, and columns of upstart peers and peeresses in plumes and diamonds, and a captive Pope, and a clarion reminder that a field soldier could lead a revolution and make himself a throne that the world would acknowledge. It was a lesson that was to have its echo in Mexico one day, and as such exotically enough it had a waft of meaning for the Rio Grande. More immediately, off Trafalgar, in 1805, the navy of Spain, in bondage to Napoleon, was destroyed forever by England's Nelson. The lifeline of the Indies, thinning for so long, was ready to break.

Reduced to moral force, Spain agreed to arbitrate with the United States in conversations at Madrid the actual boundary between Louisiana and Texas. But these diplomacies had no outcome. The boundary was still the old western line of Louisiana on the Red River, or the Rio Grande, depending upon which party looked east or west. In February, 1806, the United States General Wilkinson moved with troops to Natchitoches, in disputed territory. An agreement was presently reached between New Spain and the United States to respect a neutral zone between the Arroyo Hondo and the Sabine River—despite the words of General Wilkinson that he would "soon plant our standards on the left bank of the Grand River." To believe Wilkinson, he had been working the whole broad West through his imagination "for sixteen years." The routes to Santa Fe from St. Louis; the strength of life along the Rio Grande; the interior empire of the prairies with its wealth and its possible independence through access to the sea by the Mississippi— what dreams did he have, and how far was he hoping to go to externalize them? There was no sure answer, but he was not far removed from the restless affairs of Aaron Burr, and at one time he received monies as an agent for Spain while wearing the uniform of an American general officer. In 1806 advancing from the Arroyo Hondo to the east bank of the Sabine with triumphant airs, he halted there and with him halted whatever ill-imagined glory he had been brooding alive. The royal governor of Texas, Salcedo, earnestly worked to keep the peace, while war sentiment was alight in the United States. When the issue of American sovereignty was talked of east of the Mississippi, it was focussed on Texas, and the lower Rio Grande. Nobody yet gave much thought to the rest of the river.

New Mexico was lost in the north, far removed from the fears and urgencies that kept all of Texas and the Rio Grande Mexican states in agitation. The death agonies that were beginning at the Gulf seemed hardly real or meaningful in the old river kingdom. Something of their tremors came up the river, as along a dying nerve, from time to time, in the form of official papers. These were examined at Santa Fe, noted, tied, and put into a box in the ancient governmental palace on the plaza. The general drift of policy was grasped; but there were more local matters that had to be given attention.

Periodically since the first coming of the Spaniards, epidemics of smallpox had swept through the river pueblos taking a fearful harvest. Now in 1805, with vaccination a proved preventative, the government sent Surgeon Larrañaga, of the Santa Fe garrison, among the settlements. He was the only doctor in hundreds of miles. His present task was difficult. Parents, both Indian and Spanish, were ignorant of science. The medium of vaccination seemed to them cruel and dangerous. They resisted him. On his travels, it was not easy for the doctor to preserve the vaccine under proper conditions. Moreover, he encountered epidemics of whooping cough, measles and dysentery in several pueblos, and was reluctant to vaccinate children already ill. But he did what he could, and reported mass vaccinations at El Paso, Cebolleta, Albuquerque, Santa Fe, Laguna and even Zuñi. In the same year, the governor of New Mexico proposed that an annual fair be held at El Paso in September. He invited skilled weavers to come from New Biscay, and he pointed out how unsatisfactory the present commercial organization of the province was.

Commerce had its oddities—and dangers. In June, 1805, there appeared in Santa Fe a man named James Pursley with two Plains Indians. They came from the Rocky Mountains to the north, as scouts for a great band of horse Indians who sent them to discover whether trade relations with New Mexico could be established. The main body of Indians—there were two thousand of them, and they had ten thousand animals—lurked in camp on the plains that were later called South Park, Colorado. The Governor of New Mexico, Joaquin Real Alencaster, agreed to "enter into a trade." The Indian messengers went back to their people, but Pursley remained in Santa Fe, among, as he thought, civilized people. A Kentuckian, he felt equal to the whole open West. But at Santa Fe he encountered persons and conditions that made him regret bitterly his decision to stay. He was not a prisoner, but he was told that he might not leave the province without a passport. He was free to ask for it at any time, but until he did so, he was under bond not to escape. He was forbidden to write letters. He knew that if he had but two hours' head start, "not all the province could take him." He was allowed to keep his gun. At home, in Kentucky, he had made his own gunpowder when needed; but when he did the same in Santa Fe, he was nearly hanged when discovered, for it was a capital crime to make explosives in the old kingdom. All he could do was resign himself to make a living at his trade, which was that of carpenter. When he worked for the Spanish officers, they paid him poorly and he was powerless to complain. But "he made a great deal of money" working for others, for his kind of skill was rare in New Mexico. He was the first citizen of the United States to penetrate the land of the upper Rio Grande, where no one might pass either way across the Spanish colonial frontier.

Everywhere on the river affairs all looked inward. Among the lower river towns a new colony was gathered together in 1806 from the people and resources of Mier, Camargo and Refugio, near the Gulf, to cross into Texas and found the town of San Marcos as an outpost against organized American intrusion. It was the old design that had been followed over Texas so often before; and it suffered a familiar fate. Harried by Indians, the settlers at San Marcos abandoned their town in 1812 and returned to the Rio Grande. Their purpose had never been tried in a dramatic resistance of American invasion. Not that invasion did not come—but it came through infiltration rather than frontal attack. Settlers arrived in modest little parties. If they entered Texas as travellers or traders or hunters, they yet contrived to stay. Wherever they put themselves on the earth, the American newcomers seemed able to take root against the wilderness. French settlements, Spanish outposts had come and gone. But the wilderness dweller from the United States clung to his advancing frontier at all its stages and never retreated.

Spanish intelligence travelled often and fast. Warnings were relayed from presidio to military district headquarters to provincial governor, and orders came back down the line.

Chihuahua learned, presumably from agents at St. Louis who sent their reports down the Mississippi and over Texas to the Rio Grande, of a venture approaching the river kingdom at the north, and warned Santa Fe in 1806. An American lieutenant with a small band of men travelling as traders, and perhaps even as settlers, had been dispatched by General Wilkinson to examine the plains and enter New Mexico from the north. His name was Pike, and with his men he should be intercepted and returned to the States, or captured and taken to Santa Fe. In a last marshalling of power, the old river kingdom gathered one hundred regular troops, and mobilized five hundred New Mexican militia, all mounted. In command was Lieutenant Don Facundo Melgares who with his two officers next-in-command rode black horses. All the troopers rode white horses, and the animal train totalled two thousand. With provisions for six months the party moved out eastward in June, 1806, to find Pike; to reconnoitre the wild land between New Mexico and the supposed plains boundary of Louisiana, which had not been fixed even by the United States; and to establish alliances with Plains Indians against the eastern Americans. In October Melgares was back in Santa Fe with his troops. He submitted his personal expense account immediately, and was obliged to report that he had not found his man.

Though his man was willing, even eager, to be found. On his own, he was trying to reach the New Mexico river and Santa Fe. As winter came Zebulon Montgomery Pike and his men were in the Rocky Mountains where they suffered greatly. On January twenty-eighth, probing southwestward through sand dunes and following a sandy creek, Pike made camp, and then "ascended one of the largest hills of sand" from which with his spyglass he "could discover a large river," which he "supposed to be Red River." But it was not the Red River, it was the Rio Grande, winding placidly through the vast open San Luis Valley of Colorado. In the mountains to the west, high on the towering slopes of the Continental Divide, the river had its source in three main branches. Gazing through his telescope, Pike could be sure of his mission now.

According to his orders from General Wilkinson he was like Melgares to make binding treaties with horse Indians (whom he addressed with some grandeur in French), and to make notes on the natural history, terrain and peoples of the areas he crossed. Mineral and botanical specimens were to be collected, and a careful log of mileages and astronomical observations recorded. Most important—and least covered by written orders—was the job of entering among the New Mexicans, discovering their temper, noticing their defenses, and considering means, including the military, of opening a way to Santa Fe. He was to avoid making trouble when he at last reached his goal: "Your conduct," wrote Wilkinson, "must be marked by such circumspection and direction as may prevent alarm or conflict, as you will be held responsible for consequences."

Travelling westward in September, 1806, Pike came to a Pawnee settlement on the twenty-fifth. The Indians said that a great troop of soldiers on white horses had been there a month before. They were the Spaniards from Santa Fe who had been looking for him. The Pawnee Chief showed Pike flags, medals, mules, and commissions written with a flourish which the Spaniards had given him. The Spanish commander was a young man—too young to make binding agreements, said the Chief; he had come only to open the way for further dealings later. But there had been certain courteous threats, and Pike wrote to Secretary of War Dearborn that the Spaniards had mounted "an expedition expressly for the purpose of striking a dread into these different nations of the Spanish power, and to bring about a combination in their favor," and he called the Spanish dealings with the Pawnees "an infringement of our territory."

Pike treated with the Pawnees for a fortnight. He tried to induce them to give over their Spanish trophies, but they would finally yield only the Spanish flag in trade for that of the United States. But it was possible that the Spanish troops might return, and finding that the Indians had disposed of their colors, give them trouble. Pike explained this, and returned the Spanish flag to the Indians, who were moved to "a general shout of applause."

Advancing westward with the autumn the Americans entered the mountains and encountered every hardship in wind, snow, cold and hunger. By the time Pike came to the river five men with frozen feet on which they could not walk had been left behind in the mountains. The remaining ten were exhausted but determined to establish a base from which they could go back to rescue their companions. Three days after viewing the river for the first time, they came to its bank. The first thing they looked for was timber with which to make boats for a descent of the river. Finding none, they marched downstream thirteen miles and came to the mouth of a confluent—the Conejos River—that flowed from the west. They turned up this stream for five miles and found a "small prairie" with cottonwoods within reach where Pike ordered a halt. On his map he marked the Rio Grande as the Red River. For the next several days he led his men in building a stockade against "the insolence, cupidity, and barbarity of the savages." It was a stout little fortress, thirty-six feet square, twelve feet high, built of cottonwood logs and protected at its open top by a crown of sharpened stakes that projected outward at a slant beyond the walls for two and a half feet. The lower ends of the stakes were lodged in a ditch that ran around the inside of the walls. There was no gate. The occupants moved in and out by a tunnel under the walls and a plank laid over the moat. Gunports were opened in the walls eight feet above the ground, and raised interior walks were built for riflemen and sentries.

For a week the party worked, rested, read, hunted—and schemed. With Pike travelled a young physician, Dr. John Hamilton Robinson, who had been assigned to the expedition by General Wilkinson. He was adventurous and personable, with "blooming cheeks, fine complexion, and a genius-speaking eye." He possessed "a liberality of mind too great ever to reject an hypothesis because it was not agreeable to the dogmas of the schools; or adopt it because it had all the éclat of novelty. His soul could conceive great actions, and his hand was ready to achieve them; in short, it may truly be said that nothing was above his genius." The problem now was how to make contact with the New Mexicans without arousing suspicion. Pike and the doctor developed an idea. Why not use Morrison's claim? This was a paper in Robinson's possession which had been given him by a friend in St. Louis to present for collection if he should ever come upon a trader named Baptiste LaLande, who now lived at Santa Fe. Under treaties between Spain and the United States, a mutual guarantee protected "the right of seeking the recovery of all just debts or demands before the legal and authorized tribunals of the country." The two schemers resolved to make "this claim a pretext for Robinson to visit Santa Fe." They gave the paper "the proper appearance." The doctor would take it to Santa Fe to collect Mr. Morrison's claim against Monsieur LaLande; would give over information about the party on the northern river; and after that it would not be long until Spanish officials came to the river fort. Pike's company would be taken to New Mexico, and their purpose—"to gain a knowledge of the country, the prospect of trade, force, etc."—would be near fulfillment. Dr. Robinson set out alone on February seventh to find

Santa Fe, and on the same day, a party went back into the mountains to rescue the soldiers who had been left behind a hundred and eighty miles away.

The doctor walked up the Conejos River on the first day, and on the second, bore south. Soon on the slope of a mountain he met two Yuta Indians with bows and arrows who were afraid of him, but he overcame them with some small gifts, and they agreed to take him to Santa Fe. On the following day he reached the village of Agua Caliente, where he spent the night on a mattress on the floor of the local commander's house, while word of his presence went to the capital by courier. He was escorted south on the trail early the next day, and before nightfall found himself in the presence of Governor Joaquin Real Alencaster, who saw in him a *"joven de presencia fina."* But even if he was "a young man of fine presence," the Governor was hard with him. He took possession of all his papers, interrogated him austerely, and learned readily that he came from a party of Americans, under a first lieutenant named "Mongo-Meri-Paike," whom he had left in their "excellent retrenchments" on a river to the north. For himself, the doctor said he had come to Santa Fe seeking a certain Baptiste LaLande, against whom he had a claim for monies due. He handed over the claim. The Governor said he would look into it. The interrogation proceeded.

When had he set out, with his friends, on the expedition that brought them here?

Last July.

And what had been their experience with Indians whom they must have met on the plains?

As to that, they had made friends with the Indians, and were authorized to make alliances with certain tribes on behalf of the United States.

Which tribes, in particular?

It seemed that the Comanches were included.

At this period of New Mexico's unstable Indian relations, the Comanches were formal allies of the Santa Fe government. The doctor's revelations were disturbing. He was ordered to a room in the Palace ordinarily used as a cell for officers in arrest and a noncommissioned officer was assigned to remain with him, though the doctor was not denied permission to walk about the town. Food was sent to him from the Governor's table.

On the next day he was taken again to the Governor, who had examined the LaLande affair, only to discover that LaLande had no property. The debt could not be paid, though at some future time the Governor would see what could be done.

The doctor now made "a spirited remonstrance." He invoked treaties and he spoke bitingly of any foreign government that gave asylum to a man evading his creditors.

The Governor scowled; but with more courtesy than before, he invited the doctor to dine with him, which was a welcome gesture. In the course of the meal, the Governor brought up a matter that troubled him. As his guest was a man of medicine, he could not forbear to mention that he suffered from dropsy, and though he was being treated by a certain reverend father who practiced medicine in the city, he would be glad now of professional advice. The doctor "prescribed a regimen and a mode of treatment." His prescriptions differed from those of the local physician, who as a result showed his enmity later.

With the next day, the doctor was told he would be taken south to Chihuahua, for further interrogation by the Commandant-General of the Interior Provinces. He resigned himself, and on the following day, glad of the opportunity to see more of the country, for which he was "willing to run the risk of future consequences," he marched south under escort.

It was not long until Pike, at his stockade, knew that Dr. Robinson's job was done. With one of his soldiers he was out hunting on February sixteenth when he met two armed horsemen, a Spanish dragoon and a civilized Indian. Both parties "acted with great precaution," but drew together to talk and all sat down on the ground. The strangers told Pike that they had left Santa Fe four days before; "that Robinson had arrived there, and been received with great kindness by the governor." Presently the spies—Pike knew they were spies—went to the stockade with him and spent the night. In the morning, after cordial exchanges, they left, and Pike with his little garrison fell to reinforcing the stockade, for they knew that they would presently have other visitors.

One morning ten days later a sentry at the cottonwood fort fired his musket in the air. Two strangers were approaching. Pike received them in the stockade. They were Frenchmen, from Santa Fe. Conversations began in which evasions were exchanged with every air of polite frankness.

The Governor, they said, had heard that Pike's little defense work in the wilderness was about to be attacked by Yuta Indians; and accordingly he had sent troops out to protect him—fifty regular dragoons, and fifty militia, all mounted. They would arrive in two days.

Pike answered nothing.

Two days? In a few minutes the main body of the Spanish detachment appeared, all armed with lances, carbines and pistols, with two officers: Lieutenant Ignacio Saltelo, in command, and Lieutenant Bartolomé Fernández. Pike sent word that the officers might enter the fort, leaving their troops halted in the cottonwood grove a little distance away. They agreed, entered by the miniature drawbridge which astonished them, and joined Pike for a breakfast of deer, meal, goose and some biscuit. After breakfast Lieutenant Saltelo got down to business.

"Sir," he said to Pike, "the Governor of New Mexico being informed you had missed your route, ordered me to offer you, in his name, mules, money, or whatever you might stand in need of to conduct you to the head of Red river; as from Santa Fe to where it is sometimes navigable is eight days' journey. . . ."

"What!" cried Pike, interrupting, "is not this the Red river?"

"No, Sir! The Rio del Norte."

As if in chagrin Pike ordered the United States flag to be hauled down. He knew also that in spite of manners, the Spanish officers had orders to take him to the capital regardless of his wishes. Lieutenant Saltelo said:

"The Governor has provided one hundred mules and horses to take in the party and their baggage. He is very anxious to see you at Santa Fe."

Pike explained that some of his men had not yet rejoined the party at the fort, and he could not leave without them. He said further, with every appearance of a free man, that his orders did not justify his entering Spanish territory. The Spanish officer insisted; Pike grew hot; and Lieutenant Saltelo mildly assured him that "not the least restraint" would be used. The Governor only had to have an explanation of Pike's business on the frontier. (This was the third new reason given for the Governor's solicitude.) Pike finally agreed to leave for Santa Fe, provided a large party were left behind to await the coming of the invalid soldiers and their rescuers to the stockade. Pike felt a certain professional regret as affairs calmed down. After all, he was confident of his military situation. The stockade was stout. "I could so easily have put them at defiance," he mused. He hated to see lost all the work he and his men had put into the defenses. The Spanish soldiers seemed overjoyed that the intruders did not intend to resist; but Pike's men felt otherwise, for they mistrusted the Spaniards, and besides, said Pike, they wanted to raise "a little dust."

But friendliness soon prevailed. The Santa Fe soldiers gave food and blankets to the eastern Americans. By eleven the next morning, February 27, 1807, the Santa Fe column set out. Fifty Spaniards stayed behind with Lieutenant Saltelo to await the men from the mountains; Pike and the rest were escorted by Lieutenant Bartolomé Fernández, of whom Pike made a good friend, referring to him always as Bartholomew. They marched up the Conejos, struck off southwestward, and four days later reached the Rio Grande from the west, coming down the Chama to San Juan. They had come from a country of deep snow to a land of plains where there was no snow and vegetation was sprouting. As they passed by villages, the inhabitants stared at the visitors, who were in wretched circumstance. Pike himself was "dressed in a pair of blue trousers, mockinsons, blanket coat, and a cap made of scarlet cloth lined with fox skin; my poor fellows were in leggings, breech cloths and leather coats." All were unshaven and thin, and none had a hat but the leader, and few had shoes.

Pike observed the Pueblo Indians of the region. He found that they were not slaves of individuals, but of the state, for they were "compelled to do military duty, drive mules, carry loads, or, in fact, perform any other act of duty or bondage that the will of the commandant of the district, or of any passing military tyrant, chooses to ordain." Nor was this all. "I was myself eye-witness," said Pike, "of a scene which made my heart bleed for those poor wretches, at the same time that it excited my indignation and contempt, that they would suffer themselves, with arms in their hands, to be beaten and knocked about by beings no ways their superiors, unless a small tint of complexion could be supposed to give that superiority." It seemed that one night on the way to Santa Fe, two of the Indian riders with the Santa Fe troops ran off to a near-by pueblo which was their home. In the morning, all Indian riders were turned out in mounted formation to tell who had gone absent without leave in the night. All refused to speak. At once, for their silence, several were "knocked down from their horses by the Spanish dragoons with the butt of their lances." The Indians got up and stood like stone. Their faces streamed with blood. They held weapons in their hands. But they gave no sign of what they must have felt—"the boiling indignation of their souls at the indignities offered by the wretch clothed with a little brief authority! The day," said Pike, who knew nothing of 1680 and 1696, "the day of retribution will come in thunder and vengeance!"

On March second the company came to San Juan on the Rio

Grande and were received by the Father President, who had lived there for forty years. He gave them coffee and chocolate to drink, and asked Pike back to dinner, and saw to it that his men had a place to stay. Pike on his way to visit the soldiers' quarters was accosted at the door by a man who said to him in broken English,

"My friend, I am very sorry to see you here; we are all prisoners in this country and can never return; I have been a prisoner for nearly three years, and cannot get out."

Something about the creature, plucking and fawning, repelled Pike.

"As for your being a prisoner," said Pike, "it must be for some crime. As for myself, I feel no apprehension. And when you speak to me, talk French. I can hardly understand your English."

Pike turned to join his men in their room, and at his heels a stream of questions followed. How had Pike come into northern New Mexico? Why? Where was he going? The importunate wretch followed him into the billet, and Pike ordered his men to shut and lock the door and faced him. He was sure now that the man was sent to worry some damaging admission out of him.

"You are a spy, sent by the Governor, or someone, to trick me, aren't you? All men of that description are scoundrels, and should never fail to be punished, while I have the power to do it . . . " and he ordered his soldiers to grasp the man. "If you make a sound, or resist, I'll be obliged to make use of this . . . " and he drew his sabre.

The man broke down. Yes—only let him for God's sake not be harmed—yes, he was an agent of the Governor. He had been told to meet Pike and by raising complaints against the Spaniards, inspire him to pour forth all the information the government hoped for. He was a miserable man who harmed nobody, but whose goods had all been taken by the New Mexicans, who would not even turn him loose to go back to St. Louis. He was Baptiste LaLande.

Pike ordered him released, and said to him,

"I consider you as too contemptible for further notice. But you may tell the Governor, the next time he employs emissaries, to choose those of more ability and sense. Moreover, I question whether His Excellency will find the sifting of us an easy task."

Pike saw to his men, and returned to the priest's house. LaLande accompanied him; but not to make any complaints about his rough handling. Instead, he announced that Pike was a former governor of

Illinois. The effect of this absurdity was a marked increase in the respect shown by the old priest, who now gave dinner to Pike—"the first good meal, wine, etc."—that he had had in eight months. He overindulged, while the father talked for two hours about his hobby, which was botany. Later, in exchange, Pike demonstrated his sextant to the pastor out of doors, to the astonishment of the hundreds of San Juan Indians who surrounded them, and, indeed, of the pastor himself, who shook his head. He knew no mathematics and would never be able to use a sextant. How was this? wondered Pike. The Father President explained that it was Spanish governmental policy to prohibit the study of science in the Indies so that the colonial inhabitants would have no basis of comparing their conditions with those of other lands.

The march was resumed the next day. As the party drew nearer to Santa Fe, Pike thought of his papers. It would be awkward if certain of these came into the hands of the New Mexicans. Since he was likely to be the one who would be most thoroughly examined, he found it wise to distribute some of his documents among his five men to conceal inside their clothing. The rest of his papers he placed in "a little chest" where in innocence they could be revealed if asked for. The party with horse and pack mule jogged on, now on the east bank of the river. Passing on through Pojoaque and Tesuque, they came in late afternoon within sight of Santa Fe. (In his field notes he spelled it "St.Afee.") "Its appearance from a distance," said Pike, "struck my mind with the same effect as a fleet of flat-bottomed boats which are seen in the spring and fall seasons, descending the Ohio river." As he entered the city he saw that it straggled along the Santa Fe creek for about a mile, and that it was only three streets in width. The streets were narrow—twenty-five feet across. A great crowd accompanied the cavalcade to the Palace where Pike and his people were taken through a long vista of several rooms that had rugs of buffalo, bear or other skins, into a far room where they sat down. After a wait, Governor Joaquin Real Alencaster entered, and everyone stood. Pike's new friend Bartholomew was present. The Governor spoke to Pike in French.

"Do you speak French?" he asked brusquely.

"Yes sir," replied Pike.

"You come to reconnoitre our country, do you?"

"I marched to reconnoitre our own."

"In what character are you?"

"In my proper character, an officer of the United States army."

"And this Robinson," said the Governor, "is he attached to your party?"

Pike thought for a moment. Robinson was already a prisoner. What if, unknown to either of them, their country and Spain might now be at war over boundary issues? Under the rules of war, Robinson might be subject to execution as a spy. To protect the doctor, Pike replied, "No."

And now it was the Governor who grew thoughtful. Why should the eastern American lie so brazenly if there were not something equivocal about his whole presence within these borders?

"Do you know him?" asked the Governor.

"Yes; he is from St. Louis."

"How many men have you?"

"Fifteen."

"And this Robinson makes sixteen?"

"I have already told Your Excellency that he does not belong to my party, and shall answer no more interrogatories on that subject."

"When did you leave St. Louis?"

"July fifteenth."

"I think you marched in June."

"No, sir!"

There was bad temper in the air. The Governor dismissed Pike, ordering him to go to Bartholomew's house, and return in the evening at seven with all his papers. As they went out, Pike saw that his friend Bartholomew "seemed much hurt at the interview."

In the evening at seven they returned to the Palace.

"Where are your papers?" demanded the Governor.

"I understand my trunk has been taken possession of by your guard."

The Governor received this with surprise, sent for the trunk, and a new interpreter, who when he arrived turned out to be Sergeant Solomon Colley, one of the prisoners taken from Philip Nolan's abortive invasion of Texas six years before. The Governor permitted all to sit down, and through the interpreter began to question Pike, starting all over again, with his name and birthplace. Pike answered Sergeant Colley in English, and then spoke directly to the governor in French, and with energy. All this narrow questioning, he said, was useless. Only let the governor read Pike's commission from the United States, and his orders from his general, and he would see that he came with no hostile intentions toward the Spanish government. On the contrary, urged Pike, he had express instructions to guard against giving offense or alarm. Do this, and His Excellency would be convinced that far from deserving treatment as undesirables, Pike and his men would be "objects on which the so much celebrated generosity of the Spanish nation might be exercised. . . ."

The governor seemed mollified. The trunk had arrived, and he glanced through its contents, noting a diary, and "an exact map, in ink, of all the rivers and lands that they had reconnoitred," and some official papers. Which were the commission and the orders? Pike read them to him in French. The governor sprang to his feet and for the first time gave his hand to Pike.

"I am happy," he said, "to know you as a man of honor and a gentleman," and added kindly that Pike could go now, and take his chest of papers with him. They would make other arrangements tomorrow. Pike retired with his trunk. He found now that his soldiers were drinking with some hospitable citizens of St. Afee. He was alarmed. His men still carried papers that least of all he wanted the local authorities to see. Taking his men aside, he retrieved all his documents, went to his room at Bartholomew's house, and with relief put them into his chest, where they would now be safe, for he was convinced that "the examination of papers was over."

But he was deceived; for early the next day an officer brought orders from the governor for Pike to appear before him, and to bring the trunkful of papers, as he wished to make some observations on Pike's route, and other matters. There was no chance to remove any of the papers. The governor's messenger waited for him. Pike was helpless. Bringing the trunk he came before the governor.

In silence the governor went through the enlarged collection of documents. There was much to consider. The box held letters to and from Wilkinson and Pike; maps; diaries giving carefully observed data of the journey to this province, and of New Mexico itself; a pasteboard folio quarto, "containing copies of official communications to the Secretary of War and to General Wilkinson, and various observations relative to the mission of the said lieutenant, with 67 used folios"; and other significant materials. Surely it was in itself significant that the lieutenant had tried to hide some of the now revealed documents? With the evidence of such mysterious behavior, and of the documents themselves, Real Alencaster resolved to send Pike and his men to Chihuahua in their turn. He told Pike of his decision, and added, "You have the key of your trunk in your own possession; the trunk will be put under charge of the officer who commands your escort."

"If we go to Chihuahua," asked Pike, "must we be considered as prisoners of war?"

"By no means," answered the governor.

"You have already disarmed my men without my knowledge; are their arms to be returned or not?"

"They can receive them at any moment."

Now something else troubled Pike. It was a professional matter of some delicacy. His reputation as an officer was involved. He said,

"But, sir, I cannot consent to be led three or four hundred leagues out of my route, without its being by force of arms."

The Governor understood.

"I know you do not go voluntarily; but I will give you a certificate from under my hand of my having obliged you to march."

He then asked Pike to dine, and said that arrangements were already made for him to set out immediately afterward on his journey down the Rio Grande. On the river, below Albuquerque, a relief escort was waiting for him, said the Governor, with "the officer who commanded the expedition to the Pawnees."

Pike did not want to be impertinent; but he had to ask:

"Pray, sir! do you not think it was a greater infringement of our territory to send 600 miles in the Pawnees', than for me with our small party to come on the frontiers of yours with an intent to descend Red river?"

"I do not understand you," said the governor coldly. Pike rejoined with sarcasm:

"No, sir! any further explanation is unnecessary," and took his leave for the moment, returning to Bartholomew's house. Presently he received by messenger from the Governor twenty-one dollars in cash for his current expenses, which would be charged against the United States, and a gift of a shirt and a new neckcloth that had been made in Spain by the Governor's sister. At midday he returned to dine at the clay Palace. The meal was "rather splendid, having a variety of dishes and wines of the southern provinces." The Governor, enjoying his own wine, "became very sociable." It was soon time to go. Pike left a note for his men who were yet to come from the northern stockade, bidding them to "keep up a good discipline and not be alarmed or discouraged." In the plaza Sergeant Colley, "the American prisoner, came up with tears in his eyes," and begged Pike not to forget him when he arrived home in the United States. Pike had also seen and talked with James Pursley, who was still a prisoner at large in New Mexico, and not fated to leave until 1824. The Governor's coach was waiting. They climbed in—the Governor, Bartholomew, Pike and Captain D'Almansa, who commanded the escort—and drove out in a snowstorm for three miles, drawn by six mules and attended by a guard of cavalry. When it came time to say good-bye, the Governor struck an attitude, and declaimed:

"Remember Alencaster, in peace or war!"

He then returned to the city, and the travellers, mounted on horses, rode on through the heavy snow as darkness fell. At ten o'clock that night they found their way with great difficulty down the escarpment of La Bajada and came to a village where they were taken in for the night by the resident priest, and given supper. After supper Pike and the two officers talked for a while. D'Almansa—he was an elderly native of New Mexico—complained sadly that he had been a soldier of the King for forty years. In all that time he had risen only to the rank of first lieutenant of the line, and captain by brevet; while many a youngster from Spain, serving in the colonies, had been promoted over his head. After the old man went to sleep, Bartholomew in his turn bared his heart to Pike. He was one of those New Mexicans who "longed for a change of affairs, and an open trade with the United States." He believed that the United States would invade New Mexico by the next spring. In vain Pike denied this. Bartholomew insisted, and wondered how he would fare when the time came. Pike ended by solemnly writing out for him "a certificate addressed to the citizens of the United States, stating his friendly disposition and his being a man of influence." The paper was a comfort to Bartholomew.

As it was still snowing hard the next morning, the march was delayed. Bartholomew took Pike to call on an old, infirm Spaniard who received them hospitably, gave them chocolate, and asked many questions about the United States, drawing comparisons with Spain. "What appeared to the old veteran most extraordinary," noted Pike, "was that we ever changed our president." The old Spaniard was astonished to hear Pike say that "there was a perfect freedom of conscience permitted in our country. He, however, expressed his warm approbation of the measure." But once again it was time to march, and now Bartholomew had to return to Santa Fe. He embraced Pike and the other eastern Americans, and Pike "could not avoid shedding tears" as they parted;

his friend had been good to him. The southbound column set out once more.

Pike examined everything and kept a journal, for his information would be of vital importance to the men and women of the United States who fulfilling individually some pressing instinct to enter new lands to the west fulfilled together what all felt to be the historic destiny of their country. At Santo Domingo pueblo, now situated on the east bank of the Rio Grande, Pike saw rich paintings in the church, and a life-sized statue of the patron saint, ornamented with gold and silver. The view from the church roof was "one of the handsomest" in New Mexico. The next day at San Felipe he made notes on a bridge over the river. It had eight spans, with "pillars made of neat woodwork, something similar to a crate, and in the form of a keel-boat, the sharp end or bow to the current; this crate or butment was filled with stone, in which the river lodged sand, clay, etc., until it had become of a tolerably firm consistency. On the top of the pillars were laid pine logs, lengthways, squared on two sides; being joined pretty close, these made a tolerable bridge for horses, but would not have been very safe for carriages, as there were no hand-rails." With the bridge at El Paso, this was one of the only two on the whole river. At Albuquerque on March seventh Pike received animated entertainment at the priest's house, where beautiful orphan girls waited on the company, and embraced the guests "as a mark of their friendship." It was the season of opening the ditches after winter, and he saw men, women and children at work in the fields by the haciendas, giving "life and gayety to the surrounding scenery." The scene put him in mind of what he had read of the irrigation works of Egypt. Downstream at the next village, in the house of the local commander, Pike saw someone sitting by the fire reading a book, who arose and spoke. Pike searched him with his eyes for a moment, and then exclaimed,

"Robinson!"

"Yes."

"But I do not know you!"

"But I know you. . . . Yet, my friend," said the doctor, "I grieve to see you here and thus, for I presume you are a prisoner."

"No! I wear my sword, as you see; all my men have their arms, and the moment they dare to ill-treat us we will surprise their guards in the night, carry off some horses, make our way to the Apaches, and then set them at defiance."

But he could not get over Robinson's improved appearance. When

he had last seen him, Robinson was "pale, emaciated, with uncombed
locks and beard of eight months' growth." And now he was well-fed,
smooth-faced, and ruddy, with sparkling eye. Captain D'Almansa entered, and Pike introduced the doctor, saying that he had been a member
of the party from the start. The Captain smiled. It was plain that he
had known as much all along. Pike was sheepish, and resolved to write
to the Governor, when he could, to explain why he had denied the doctor
as one of his group. Robinson told Pike of his adventures, and ended
with a word about Lieutenant Don Facundo Melgares, who was to
command the escort from that point on. In him, said the doctor, Pike
would find "a gentleman, a soldier, and one of the most gallant men
you ever knew."

    But when Pike and Melgares met, there was constraint. Pike was
chagrined to be delivered after all, and by his own actions, into the
hands of a Spanish officer who had been away from home looking for
him for ten months, and had spent for his government over ten thousand
dollars on the mission. But Melgares received him "with the most manly
frankness and the politeness of a man of the world," and seeing Pike
out of sorts, "took every means in his power to banish my reserve, which
made it impossible on my part not to endeavor to appear cheerful." The
young Spanish officer did not affect the haughty manners of the Castilian, but behaved more like an urbane Frenchman. He confessed himself to be one of the few Spanish officers in the New World who still
remained loyal to the King, and deprecated the idea of revolution.
Melgares and Pike soon became warm friends—as befitted the past and
the future.

    In the afternoon, the escort commander sent a note to the
alcaldes of nearby villages:

> Send this evening six or eight of your handsomest
> young girls to the village of St. Fernández, where I
> propose giving a fandango, for the entertainment
> of the American officers arrived this day.
>   (Signed)   Don Facundo.

    The command was obeyed. Pike observed that such obedience
"portrays more clearly than a chapter of observations the degraded state
of the common people." The girls arrived, they were indeed beautiful,
and the ball was given. But as to women in New Spain, Pike noted
primly: "Finding that the men only regard them as objects of gratifica-
tion to the sensual passions, they have lost every idea of that feast of

reason and flow of soul which arises from the intercourse of two refined and virtuous minds." They were, in fact, like creatures in a Turkish harem. He believed that their men actually thought more of their horses than of them. Yet he was eager to record the "heaven-like qualities of hospitality and kindness" with which he was received in his march down the Rio Grande, when at overnight halts in villages, there were banquets, fandangos and cockfights. But soon there were no more villages on the route, for the column had come to the Dead Man's March. They crossed to the west bank and stayed with the river, and Pike noted the great difficulty of the trail. Fording again where the river turned east at the end of the desert passage, they continued on the east bank until they came to the bridge two miles above El Paso. There they crossed, and entering El Paso were surrounded with hospitality, and pleased with the river lands. Gambling was rampant. Pike watched Melgares play cards during three days in a row, and win so heavily that to keep his luck he gave away five hundred dollars to the ladies in whose house they were billeted. After several days at El Paso, the march was taken up across New Biscay to the south, and in nine days the prisoners were pleasantly received at Chihuahua, where they were detained for many weeks while Pike's documents were translated and studied.

Finally he and his men were expelled from New Spain, granted a loan of a thousand dollars by the commandant-general at Chihuahua, and escorted across northern Mexico to Coahuila and the lower Rio Grande. Pike's records were rich, despite the trouble he had in making and keeping them in Spanish territory—toward the end he concealed his daily pages in the rifle barrels of his soldiers. His whole journey and its observations brought the Spanish west for the first time into the knowledge of the United States. With him the source country of the Rio Grande entered history. The Spanish instinct to exclude him—and his kind—was from its own point of view correct, even if it was fated never to succeed. A veiling mist had been blown away from the map, and there before the gaze of the United States lay shining the mountains of New Mexico, and the Rio Grande, and farther away, and just visible, but real, the Pacific. . . .

The departing guests came to the Rio Grande on June 1, 1807, at Fort St. John Baptist. They stayed only one night there. Pike thought there were twenty-five hundred residents, and he saw "three or four handsome missions," and a powder magazine, and barracks for the garrison, and as the defenses of the fort, "a few iron field-pieces on miserable truck carriages." The place made a poor impression. There was trouble finding supper. Pike's compass was stolen from him there. He heard of an American who stayed at Fort St. John Baptist practicing medicine, and sent for him. The man told a long, adventurous tale, of hardship and misfortune, playing on the sympathies of his hearers; but when one of Pike's men recognized him he turned out to be a murderer and an imposter, and Pike delivered him over to the local authorities. A troupe of entertainers were in town for the moment, and in the evening gave a show. They were slack-wire artists. Everyone went to see them. But they were "in no wise extraordinary in their performances, except in language which would bring a blush on the cheek of the most abandoned of the female sex in the United States." Late in the following day the Americans with their escort crossed the river and camped at a ranch on the other side. The next morning they set out across Spanish Texas, and in three weeks reached Louisiana, where on July first, at four in the afternoon, at Natchitoches, Pike felt his heart leap when he saw the United States flag.

At Santa Fe, Governor Real Alencaster did his duty by calling attention once again to "the necessity of putting this Province on a respectable basis and of maintaining advanced forts and establishments on the principal rivers in order to contain the ambitious ideas expressed by the Anglo-American government." He could do no more. His superiors did nothing. In the following year, his successor ordered the military commander at Taos to conduct scouting expeditions, in order to keep out foreigners; and not long later the pastor of Taos sent a report marked "Private" to Santa Fe to tell that Indians of the pueblo were holding secret meetings in their kivas with white men, who were thought to be French or American.

While such local matters blew hot and cold the dying Empire knew a major change at its heart. In 1808 the legitimate King of Spain, Ferdinand VII, brutalized by Napoleon, gave up his crown. Napoleon at once bestowed it upon his brother Joseph Bonaparte. Ferdinand, whose name with a "Viva" was carved in the ceiling beams of a high stately room in the town of St. John Baptist on the river, was jailed in Talleyrand's French château while Spain became a theatre of war. For contrary to Napoleon's contemptuous guess a great body of Spaniards resisted the conquest which he had taken for granted, and established beyond his reach a legitimist capital at Cádiz on the short Atlantic coast of southern Spain. Soon the Spanish patriots had the powerful wits of Wellington leading their defense. And for the first time in history, and even in the midst of war against the master of Europe, who whether as enemy or ally was Spain's sorrow, the motherland gave to the Indies what they had never owned: a right to representation in the national govern- ing body. In January, 1809, the Cádiz parliament decreed that delegates were to be elected in the colonial states, which now received full mem- bership as partners in the government. In 1810, the Rio Grande provinces of New Mexico and Coahuila-Texas named their deputies and sent them to take their seats in the parliament of Cádiz. From Coahuila-Texas went Don Miguel Ramos Arizpe, who held the degree of doctor of laws from the university in Mexico City. From New Mexico went Don Pedro Bautista Pino. Both provinces of the Rio Grande grasped eagerly at their first chance to present their needs directly to the home government.

Dr. Ramos Arizpe carried with him a great list of instructions. He was to ask the parliament to unify the many local jurisdictions of the lower Rio Grande states; to improve the wretched roads that precariously connected the wilderness communities; to stimulate agriculture, cattle raising and industry; to provide for a cigar factory at Saltillo after all the centuries when it had been forbidden to Spanish colonials to utilize their own tobacco crops in local manufacture; to abolish the odious tariffs on wool and cotton and with funds thus available to set up various textile mills; to grant the status of incorporated city to Saltillo; and to found a college where the youth of the provinces could be taught grammar and philosophy.

Don Pedro Bautista Pino, who owned great estates east of the Rio Grande along the Galisteo Creek in New Mexico, sailed from Veracruz with a party of several persons, including his private secretary. During his three years in Spain he presented an urgent program of recommenda- tions on behalf of the upper Rio Grande province. He addressed his papers to King Ferdinand VII, and quoted the instructions under which he came to the córtes from New Mexico: "The function of our represent- ative is not limited to looking after the welfare of this province; he must at the same time guard the general welfare of the monarchy." Within this frame of political orthodoxy he proposed, then, "1. The establish- ment of a bishopric at Santa Fe; 2. The establishment of a seminary college of higher learning, and of public schools for the instruction of the youth; 3. Uniformity in military service, the addition of . . . five presidios . . . and payment of salaries to all settlers who may be enlisted . . . as is done in Durango, Sonora, Texas, and other adjoining provinces; 4. The establishment of a civil and criminal court in Chihuahua." By what was asked it could be seen what was missing. The nearest bishop was at Durango; the nearest civil and criminal court was at Mexico City. Don Pedro spoke proudly in his sense of injury and justice. "These four petitions, Sire, should not be called petitions, for, could any other province in the monarchy claim to have existed fifty years without having seen a bishop? Is there any other province six hundred leagues from the seat of the administration of justice? There is no such province, no matter how miserably poor it may be. Consequently, the requests made by my province as petitions should be called claims and not petitions."

Don Pedro went to Paris before his return home, and to London, where he bought a beautiful and very costly landau in which for years he was to be seen riding over the frightful roads of New Mexico. No one ever asked in vain for a ride if Don Pedro had a seat empty.

As for what he and Doctor Ramos Arizpe had presented to the parliament—nothing came of any of it. With acid wit, the people of Santa Fe in after years sang a popular couplet that expressed what the river province felt about the politics of the homeland and the gullibility of the colonies:

> Don Pedro Pino went;
> Don Pedro Pino came back.

Deputies from all the Indies answered the call; but if she had counted on them to hold the Empire together, Spain had called them too late. Three centuries of taking without giving in proportion had done their work. The Spanish Americas found their opportunity for freedom in the distracted exhaustion of their motherland. Out of the wedding of the old world and the new had come a new people on their own lands, where in the end they must be their own masters. Freedom's work was already making. Don Pedro Bautista Pino closed his state papers to the King by saying in alarm, ". . . America and Spain must work in closer and closer co-operation, without permitting any difference to arise whereby the colonies might become victims of the great and horrible misfortunes now suffered by some of the provinces of New Spain, which in regard to the glory and prosperity of the nation are deceived by a few malicious enemies."

It was a loyalist's gallant effort to dismiss the power that was abroad in the new world; but no such effort could any longer succeed. No misfortune seemed so great to people hungry for freedom as the weight of the dying yet grasping hand of Spain upon them; and those were more than malicious reports that told how Spanish glory and prosperity were things of the past. In the very year when the Rio Grande deputies took their seats at Cádiz the first revolution of Mexico broke out, and spread fast to the dusty towns and brush-grown ranches of the lower river.

40.

The Shout

On September 16, 1810, at Dolores in the province of Guanajuato, a proclamation of liberty was made by the parish priest, Father Miguel Hidalgo. The "grito de Dolores"—the shout from Dolores—rang out over Mexico, and overnight won a tremendous response, especially in the internal and northern states. Priests, soldiers, ranchers, merchants, Christian Indians, laborers, adventurers and fortune hunters—men of every class threw in their fortunes with the revolution. They marched under the banner of the patroness of Mexico, the Virgin of Guadalupe. For the first time there was a powerful, organized movement, under an inspiring leader, to express the hopes of the Mexicans for their freedom, though there had been little uprisings earlier, local in nature and quickly suppressed. A month after Hidalgo's shout the royal council in Spain issued an offer of amnesty to rebels in New Spain who bowed again to Spanish authority. As it still took from two to three months for official business to pass either way over the ocean, the government in this order referred to earlier rebellions, that lacked the scale and fury of Hidalgo's movement with its hundred thousand volunteers, many of whom came from the lower Rio Grande.

These were recruited by the lively efforts of two brothers. One was a blacksmith and merchant named José Bernardo Gutierrez de Lara who came from New Santander. Aroused by Hidalgo's cry, he threw himself passionately into the fight. In the 1750s his ancestors had founded the river town of Revilla under the Count of Sierra Gorda;

and his brother José Antonio Gutierrez de Lara was a priest well known in the river settlements. With Hidalgo sweeping through the interior towns and cities, Father José Antonio Gutierrez de Lara went back and forth along the Rio Grande in the autumn of 1810, visiting Laredo, Revilla, Mier, Camargo and Reynosa with such effect that in the following February the governor of New Santander, who had fled his capital before the revolutionists, reported to Mexico City that "revolution and terror rage in the settlements along the Rio Grande."

While Hidalgo's forces, styled the Army of America, after a feint at the capital of Mexico, turned north again and spread toward the Rio Grande, the river towns heard of how the revolution had sprung into flame in Texas. At San Antonio the royal governor, Manuel Salcedo, and his officers were captured by army rebels and forced to proceed in heavy chains to the Rio Grande where at Fort St. John Baptist they were jailed. With a Bonaparte on the throne of Spain, the Latin Texans feared that future diplomacy would see them thrown to the French by the royal Spanish government. A strong belief in Mexican independence ruled the Texans. They took the United States for their model, and called themselves Americans, and spoke of setting up for their own a government of Americans by Americans. Spanish by inheritance, they hated both Spain and France. In the great urge of the hour they forgot their frontier troubles with the United States and turned to Washington hoping to find an ally in the struggle.

In February, 1811, the rebels were feeling the rallied strength of the royalists; and when two emissaries of the revolution, General Ignacio Aldama and Father Juan Salazar, came to Laredo on their way to the United States to raise men and munitions for their cause, they found the local garrison loyal to Spain. Captain José Días de Bustamante, in command of all government troops on the river, declared that he would sooner turn his forces over to the French, the English, the murderous Indians, than to the rebels. But he let Hidalgo's messengers pass. On their mission rested Hidalgo's hopes, for his Army of the Americas was already on the run. Not long since, with nearly a hundred thousand men, Hidalgo had been ready to take Mexico City; and now, turned back from the capital by his own doubts and beset by swiftly gathering royalist troops, he was coming north with only five thousand ragged men and a straggling supply train. His one great resource was a treasury of two millions in gold and silver bullion that he carried along. His sympathizers were in power in Texas, and he would join them, restore his forces, and return to the liberation of Mexico.

But after only three months, the revolutionary regime was over-thrown in San Antonio. In March royalist deputies arrived at St. John Baptist. This old river fort was now ardently royalist. The deputies were on their way to find and deliver the imprisoned Governor Salcedo, who was held on a ranch near Monclova, and who soon would resume his duties in San Antonio. The river line knew every move made by loyalist and insurgent, as the fortunes of each surged back and forth between interior Mexico and Texas. At Saltillo on March sixteenth Father Hidalgo and his commanders held council. With two millions in gold and silver they would be able to do good business buying arms and influence in the States. Texas, over the river, was to be the floodgate for the great tide of help that would win the revolution. While in the midst of their starving army they made plans, they were joined by an unexpected guest. It was José Bernardo Gutierrez de Lara, who came to offer to the failing revolt all that he owned—his fortune, his services, his life. The rebel staff took heart from his fiery spirit. He was accepted as one of them, he was given a commission as lieutenant colonel, he was charged with raising an army in the river states and bringing them to Fort St. John Baptist. Perhaps by now, the messengers Aldama and Salazar already had arms, men and money promised in the United States. The Shout would sound again with new power.

But now came word that Aldama and Salazar had been taken when the royalists overthrew San Antonio. Gutierrez de Lara offered to carry out their mission. He would go to Washington himself. The rebel chiefs thanked him, and authorized him to do so, but first, let him go to the Rio Grande and recruit men. The Army of America was dying away by desertion. Gutierrez de Lara saw the need and obeyed. When Hidalgo and the staff moved out for Texas, only a thousand men were left to escort them. On March twenty-first, near Baján, in the desert, by ambush and treachery, the Army of America was cut to pieces by royalist forces. Hidalgo and almost all the rebel leaders were taken, and their supplies, and their gold and silver, and their hopes. In four months Hidalgo and all his commanders would be executed. The liberation would seem to be a lost cause. There was a flurry at Laredo, there was a spark of hope at Fort St. John Baptist with most of its garrison absent, but only from Revilla came action that kept the revolution alive.

For Bernardo Gutierrez de Lara managed to get away unseen by the royalists, cross the river, and vanish into Texas. With him he had twelve men and Captain Miguel Menchaca, who seemed to be an ardent revolutionist. If the revolution lay shattered, it had the sympathy of most of the civilized world. Gutierrez de Lara refused to see it abandoned. He now set out to accomplish the mission for which he had applied before the disaster in the Mexican desert. Menchaca, who knew the trails, guided him across Texas to Louisiana where, after passing through great dangers from royalist troops who searched for his party, he arrived in August. He immediately found sympathizers for his cause. A plot was hatched. While he went to Washington to enlist aid from the United States, Menchaca was to return secretly to Texas, recruit an army, and overthrow Governor Salcedo. Once done, this deed would permit Menchaca to establish a new revolutionary government, and to send Gutierrez de Lara its credentials, and money, and proof that it was a reality worth supporting. They were great dimensions of belief and daring which Gutierrez de Lara took with him when he left for Washington—"Guazinton," as he wrote it—in October.

He arrived on December eleventh and encountered policy on two levels, as its spokesmen might have said. One was official, whereby the Government of the United States observed strict neutrality in the affairs of Spain and her rebellious colonies. The other was private and unofficial, whereby aid and encouragement were to be given to the Latin American rebels. In spite of his odd status, for he had no credentials to submit, and he could speak of himself though with pride only as a "Lieutenant-Colonel, an American of the Kingdom of Mexico," Gutierrez de Lara was warmly received at the State Department. His position deserved respect, for who knew what was at stake if war should break out between the United States and England? Who knew what would be the key that would unlock Spanish America to the trade of the United States? He was not an experienced statesman; but his blacksmith shop, his small mercantile ventures on the Rio Grande did not benumb him in high circles now.

He told of Menchaca's activities, which he felt sure would succeed. So soon as they did, there would be a new government in Texas to deal with. When that day came, let the United States permit the shipment of arms and supplies to the Rio Grande and the north Mexican states.

He proposed that in return for such waiving of neutrality, a newly free Mexico would ship silver, wool and other exports to the United States. The trade impasse would be broken. Perhaps in time the Western Hemisphere would be wholly independent of European trade.

Finally, with a touch upon the most raw nerve of all, he pointed out the disadvantages to the Americas if upon local political disagreements there should suddenly intrude "any malignant effort that might come from Europe"; and to prevent any such possibility, he asked for military aid from the United States to join forces with the revolutionary movement.

The chief clerk of the State Department heard him on December twelfth, and much impressed, brought him to the Secretary, James Monroe, with whom he had three interviews. The Secretary was interested to hear of Captain Menchaca's great enterprise that was even then launched in Texas. He urged Lieutenant Colonel Gutierrez de Lara to remain in Washington until such time as would see the stabilization of the Menchaca government at San Antonio, when proper credentials could be issued to him. Speaking for his government, the Secretary could agree that freer trade relations between the United States and Mexico were most desirable. As for outright aid in men and arms—this was a matter with many aspects. One of these had to do with the *pretext* under which the United States could move troops into Texas. Luckily, there was an old issue available. The Secretary, wrote Gutierrez de Lara in his diary, ". . . told me that it would be easy to send an army to the Rio Grande under the pretext that they were going to take possession of the lands which France had sold to them." As the Mexican patriot listened his heart sank within him, for he saw then the price of help. The Secretary continued his argument, and pointed out as though to a questioning world that once on the Rio Grande, the American army could then, more or less incidentally, "help the Creoles."

Gutierrez de Lara thought quickly, and made a despairing counter-proposal that might just gain him American troops and leave his land free. He would accept the plan, he said, provided the United States forces would come under his command.

At this, the Secretary lost interest in his own proposition, and Gutierrez de Lara was obliged to reject it himself. He could not trade all of Texas for the support he so greatly wanted. He saw vanish the aid he had come to enlist; but the price was too great, and in any case he had no authority to agree to such a bargain. Indeed, he must go further than rejection of it, if what lay in the thoughts of the State Department people really constituted a threat. He proposed new agreement upon the old idea of a neutral zone "to separate the two nations, or Americas, for thereby would be obviated many discords which commonly result from the close contact of two powers." This idea aroused no interest, though Monroe was cordial, and ordered arrangements to be made for Lieutenant Colonel Gutierrez de Lara's expenses while in Washington, and for his return passage when he should depart.

Between his second and third conferences with Monroe there were evidently further discussions in the State Department. A crisis was approaching in British-American relations. When he returned for his final talk with Monroe, Gutierrez de Lara was amazed to hear the Secretary say that if war were declared between the United States and Great Britain, the United States would send an army of fifty thousand men to Mexico on the side of the revolutionists. Gutierrez de Lara could scarcely believe his ears. It was a prize of undreamed-of proportions to take home to the struggling liberators of Mexico. They would never believe him. He would have to carry proof. He asked the Secretary for a copy in writing of what he had just promised.

The Secretary regretted that he would be unable to provide this.

Gutierrez de Lara lost his elation. What he felt was plain in his diary when later he made notes on the interview. "Mary Most Holy!" he ejaculated, "help me and rescue me from these men!"

The Secretary dismissed him kindly, urging him to return home, to pursue his plans, to assure his associates that the United States regarded favorably their intentions; and indicated that there was no reason now to wait for credentials from Captain Menchaca and the new government of Texas. For Menchaca, with three hundred American volunteers, entering into Texas to win a new nation, had met a large Royalist patrol, whom he had joined immediately, abandoning his adventurous followers. The Americans had fled without casualties. Gutierrez de Lara so was left alone in his determination. But the State Department gave him every assistance in making his way homeward, and presently he had the powerful help of new friends—one of them the American agent William Shaler, another a Cuban patriot called José Alvarez Toledo, who was ready to die for the freedom of the Indies. In January Gutierrez de Lara sailed from Philadelphia for New Orleans with new plans for the independence of Mexico, while Spain, if she had lost the power to nourish, seemed also to have lost the wits to understand the Indies. In January, 1812, with revolt in the whole air over the Western Hemisphere, she issued a state edict calling upon the colonies for their aid in her war against Napoleon, that *"moderno Atila,"* with his *"ferocidad,"* his *"crueldad calculada,"* his *"arte infernal."* Come, cried Spain to the embittered colonials, restore *"las dulces ideas de fraternidad y de unión"* which had marked *"nuestra común felicidad"* throughout three centuries. . . .

Aid? What aid? Mexico, riven by battles over many a dusty city, was poor and hungry. Food, all commodities, became scarce. Local merchants at Laredo agreed with others in other towns: if supply ran short, prices had to rise. The alcalde of Laredo, Manuel Dovaline, took measures in March, 1812, against the inflation and profiteering that resulted from the revolution and caused hardship to so many of his citizens. Prices were fixed on such items as meat, beans, candles and hay—green or dried. Those who came to market at Laredo to sell were required by law to offer consumers a fair chance to buy. All produce had to be displayed for sale at fixed prices in the public plaza for three days before it could be offered for sale wholesale or in bulk to jobbers. Not long later the same officer established, for Laredo, a bureau of standards. Sellers were required to bring their measuring sticks and bulk measures to be checked and approved. Europe and its strivings seemed very far away.

Throughout the spring and summer of 1812 rumors of Gutierrez de Lara came to his own part of the river. He was in New Orleans. He was in Nachitoches. He was coming down the Gulf Coast with fifteen thousand soldiers and eight thousand Indians. He was marching for San Antonio. He was in a rage because his property at Revilla had been confiscated by the royalist government, his family had been imprisoned. Surely he would come to their rescue? Not all such rumors could be true at the same time, but actually he was moving into Texas, and ahead of him went a cloud of printed manifestoes and proclamations. A printing press, and a wandering American printer who fed his own rickety radicalism into the clanking platens, seemed to be indispensable articles of equipment to the filibustering armies that reached across Texas toward the Rio Grande in the last royal decade. Gutierrez de Lara, said a broadside, was on his way to free "the hemisphere of Columbus." Another entitled "The Friend of Man" exhorted the "sons of Montezuma" to unshackle themselves from Spain. These papers of sedition reached their goal. Captain Bustamante, the royalist commander on the lower Rio Grande, was obliged to write to the governor at San Antonio that in spite of every precaution to intercept the agents of Gutierrez de Lara and confiscate their revolutionary pamphlets, the flood of dangerous ideas had rolled through. River Indians were openly discussing, for all the world like Rousseau's savages, the philosophy of government. What right, asked the Indians, had a King to rule over other people? All people must have, they asserted, the right of self-government. Liberty and freedom were the natural states of man. It was uncanny to hear murdering horse Indians at large with such opinions. Near Revilla an Indian shepherd was often seen driving his sheep up and down the river.

As he went he left behind him the pamphlets of Gutierrez de Lara, who was coming, said the shepherd, back to Revilla.

And in fact a large force sprang to arms under Gutierrez de Lara, though nothing so large as it was rumored to be. But all those who by neutrality laws had been stayed for years in Louisiana, gazing with hunger toward the spare and beautiful land of Texas, now saw their chance to make their fortunes. What did the pretext matter? Let the printer grind out the passionate ideals of the revolution. Texas was waiting for the settler. Gutierrez de Lara took for his second in command the American officer Augustus Magee. The men of the "Republican Army of the North" were on their way by August, 1812, to Nacogdoches. The town received them as liberators. Texas had been breached. On the seventeenth, Governor Salcedo wrote in desperation to the Viceroy. He mentioned the two battalions of soldiers who had recently been sent to Mexico from Spain to help defeat the revolution, and he asked for a thousand of those men at once. The Viceroy's reply was not drafted until seven months later, when no matter what it said it would be of no use. On the same day, Salcedo sent couriers to the Rio Grande states asking for immediate reinforcements. Only one out of four commanders of royal troops sent aid. The royal governor of Texas waited with his doom at San Antonio.

In October a familiar figure reappeared at Fort St. John Baptist, travelling toward Chihuahua. He was Dr. Robinson, Pike's old comrade. His purpose now was secret, though he carried credentials from both the United States government and the new regime of Gutierrez de Lara. He disappeared into Mexico, and four months later was again at the river outpost, having spoken for Secretary Monroe to the Mexican authorities on behalf of better relations between the United States and the loyalist Mexican government. It was a strange message, for Washington was openly supporting Gutierrez de Lara's agitations. Dr. Robinson, with his usual animation, spoke to proponents of all points of view; and returned without bringing any official satisfaction. At St. John Baptist on his return trip, he proposed himself as mediator between the revolution and the royal government. His spirited offer was declined, and he returned to the United States across Texas in March.

On his way he paused briefly at San Antonio. He found the Governor bitter against the royal officials in Mexico who had sent him no help. Gutierrez de Lara and Magee were advancing fast, now. By late March San Antonio was under siege, and news of the end came to Laredo on April eighth when an escaped royalist officer rode into the

river city to tell of what he had seen. The Republican Army of the
North took San Antonio on April second. On the following day a trial
was held at which Governor Salcedo and sixteen of his officers were
sentenced to be shot. Gutierrez de Lara, some said, pardoned them; but
before they could be taken safely away, they were led on horses out on
the southern road of San Antonio by one hundred rebels in the darkening evening. They were ordered to dismount. They were tied hand and
foot. Their throats were cut. They were stripped naked. They were
left to lie waiting dead for beasts of prey and carrion birds. Gutierrez
de Lara at once set about drafting the declaration of independence and
the constitution of the first Republic of Texas, which he proclaimed
with grandiloquence on April seventeenth, 1813.

Four months later the Republic was in ruins. Spanish royal forces
converging on interior Texas from Laredo and Fort St. John Baptist
brought down the republic in the battle of Medina on the eighteenth
of August. Gutierrez de Lara was already in the discard. His American
allies had shelved him in favor of the Cuban Toledo. Royal government
was officially restored in Texas, and everywhere on the Rio Grande, in
September.

At Santa Fe the French were still a menace to upper Rio Grande
officials, and in April a certain José Antonio Casados of New Mexico
was interrogated as to whether or not he had given "topographical
information" to a Frenchman resident at Santa Fe. In 1813 King Joseph
Bonaparte fled Spain before the allied armies led by Wellington, and
Ferdinand VII was brought back from his French prison to Madrid to
occupy his throne once more. In his absence the Cádiz parliament had
preserved the frame of a legitimate Spanish government, and had sought
to conciliate the Indies with liberal decrees, including declarations of
equality for Indians and colonials, and the abolition of the Inquisition.
Now the returned King repudiated as many as he could of the parliament's reforms, and in 1815, with the tireless concern for trifles that was
his inheritance on the Spanish throne, he approved a circular—a copy
reached Santa Fe—regulating the mustaches of army officers.

The energies of the nineteenth century colonies, straining for
freedom, were not conciliated by Spain. Authority was if anything
drawn tighter by the hands of the home government. If new towns
struggled to come alive on the Rio Grande, the colonial administrators
were referred to the Laws of the Indies, which provided clearly that no
one, neither viceroy, nor council, nor governor, nor "any other officers
of the Indies, however high they may be," might grant city or town

titles in the New World, "because this favor must be asked of our Council of the Indies" in Spain. Any such title granted from within the New World was declared void in advance. For the rest, all the old precise conditions still had to be met if a colonial desired to found a town. He agreed by contract to gather "at least thirty persons," each of whom was to have "a house, ten breeding cows, four oxen, or two oxen and two yearlings, one brood mare, one breeding sow, twenty Castilian breeding ewes, and six hens and one cock." The founder was also to choose a priest, and provide a church, and equip it. All this was to be established and ready by a certain fixed time. If he failed to finish his enterprise by the date agreed upon, the contract with the royal power said "he shall lose all that he may have built, cultivated or earned, which we shall apply to our Royal Patrimony, and he shall also incur the penalty of one thousand dollars in gold for our Chamber. . . ." If he completed his contract in order, he was to receive four square leagues of land; and he retained the powers that had been granted to him; for he received "the civil and criminal jurisdiction . . . for the days of his life and for those of a son and heir; he also received authority to appoint alcaldes of ordinary jurisdiction, aldermen, and other officers of the council of the town. . . ."

Such exhaustive paternalism played its part in the early periods of conquest, when the first responsibility was to transplant intact in the new land the image of home; but home long since had taken a new definition; and oversea names were scrawled in blood on the whole map of that New World which Alexander VI had given forever to the Spanish kings and queens.

Along the Rio Grande after 1813 the revolutionary spirit was not extinguished. Occasionally its flicker and glare showed like watch fires on the horizon of royal north Mexico. Mischief harassed the government from many quarters. A seditious courier was taken on the river and made to reveal that in New Orleans Gutierrez de Lara, Toledo, a party of pirates and a band of ambitious traders were concocting plans for a co-ordinated attack by land and sea against northern Mexico. In a larger affair there seemed to be relief, for by royal order the Te Deum was sung in the river chapels in September, 1813, to celebrate the disaster that had overwhelmed Napoleon in the snows of Russia in the previous autumn, news of which had just come to Santa Fe. But the relief was short, and after Napoleon's escape from Elba, Ferdinand VII circularized the New World with warnings against possible surprises by Napoleon's agents in the Americas.

In fact, Joseph Bonaparte was now living at Point Breeze, on the Delaware River in New Jersey, and was said to be interested in various movements against Spanish Texas and Mexico. At Philadelphia, in 1816, he met with conspirators headed by a young Spanish revolutionary named Francisco Xavier Mina. He listened to Mina's plan. With the volunteer forces he was raising—his support drew upon adventurous men from England, Spain, Cuba, Haiti and the United States—Mina intended to go by sea to the mouth of the New Santander River in the Gulf of Mexico, disembark, march overland and capture Mexico City. Joseph, the ex-king, gave Mina a letter of credit on a London bank for one hundred thousand dollars. Was it not possible that the crown of an independent Mexico might descend upon this Bonaparte if, aided by his letter of credit, the conspirators should succeed? In April, 1817, Mina's fleet, headed southwestward, dropped anchor off the mouth of the Rio Grande. There were two frigates, two brigs, and two schooners carrying about four hundred motley troops. On shore was the royalist outpost, consisting altogether of a corporal and four privates, to defend the entrance to the river. Mina flew the Spanish flag. When he sent an officer and some men ashore they were unsuspectingly received by the corporal. Where were they from? The officer replied that they were "a Spanish squadron from the Havannah for Vera Cruz." And what did the landing party require?—and the corporal helped the filibusters to round up some cattle and slaughter them. Other boats came inshore. One was upset, an officer was drowned. The water casks were filled from the fresh if muddy river, while the corporal in command of the river's mouth cheerfully chatted about the positions of other government troops on the Mexico Bay. Along with his nine cannon, Mina had a printing press. On it while at the mouth of the Rio Grande he had a bulletin printed, under the date of April 12, 1817, which was afterward believed to be the first Texas imprint. In a few hours the little squadron set sail; and in a few weeks its mission was a failure, its forces divided and scattered, its leaders dead.

But Joseph Bonaparte backed another venture in the following year when he put money at the disposal of a Bonapartist general, Charles Lallemand, who had plans for a colony in Spanish Texas. The Viceroy of Mexico countered with secret orders to his outposts, including those of the Rio Grande, to exclude the French general. There was a rumor —it was enough to appall the Spanish colonial government—a rumor that said if Napoleon were rescued from St. Helena, he might very well take up his residence in General Lallemand's Texas settlement. And was Joseph Bonaparte still looking for another crown in Spanish America? In spite of orders from Mexico City, Lallemand, with his followers, came to the Texas coast in 1818, to establish the colony known as Champ d'Asile. But under Indian pressure and before rumors of Spanish power gathering to expel the intruders, it was abandoned in six months.

So for the better part of two decades Texas, with its part of the Rio Grande, was regarded as fair game by any person or faction able to muster enough strength to invade her territory. By far the greatest interest was shown by Americans of the United States; and with each repeated attempt against the soil of Spanish Texas the Americans, as though sanctioned by habit, seemed to feel that their claim to Texas increased in power and virtue. There was a shred of precedent for American claims to all of Texas as far as the Rio Grande—the famous, and ambiguous, French view of the territory involved in the various sovereignties of Louisiana, beginning with that of Louis XIV. So long as the issue remained in doubt, frontier struggles to settle it by seizure were inevitable. But now in 1819, the instrument known as the Florida Treaty settled all disputes between Spain and the United States over boundaries and territories. Among its other provisions, the Treaty gave Florida to the United States, fixed the Sabine River as the western boundary line of Louisiana and—most significant of all—established that the United States ceded to Spain and renounced forever all its "rights, claims and pretensions" to Texas, with the long Rio Grande boundary.

If the agreement seemed acceptable to the northern and eastern regions of the United States, on the frontier west it produced roars of fury. The land-hungry adventurers lingering in Louisiana, the frontier fighters of many races and nations who answered every cry, wherever raised, for the freedom of Texas, saw themselves betrayed. Once again a small volunteer army came together, now under the leadership of James Long, in the summer of 1819. Against active discouragement by the United States their plans proceeded, and by June they were across the Sabine, conventionally accompanied by a printer named Eli Harris, who struck off on the twenty-third a declaration of independence for the second Republic of Texas. Long was named as president, and gathered about him a supreme council whose membership included José Bernardo Gutierrez de Lara, as a sort of elder statesman of border revolt. The royalist powers opposed Long's venture; but the opponents never came to serious battle. Texas was a waste, after a decade of march and counter-march by invaders and defenders. The whole immense province had scarcely four thousand inhabitants of the white race. For those who tried to live there outside the struggle, there was a third foe who took advantage of it on his own ground: the Indian.

For to him the manifestoes of liberators and the retaliations of royal militia meant only a chance to sweep down upon isolated ranches and border towns and wilderness trails, to kill, steal and burn. The Rio Grande garrisons were frequently off on expeditions against filibusters, and their home stations were left open to Indian attack. At Laredo the north-bank settlers abandoned their side of the river and gathered on the opposite, where they built watchtowers and kept vigil. Indians entered into the illicit commerce in stolen horses between the Rio Grande states and East Texas, dealing with American traders who paid them well for the wild herds they drove north over the river and all the way to Louisiana. Such trade relations did not make the Indians into allies of white Americans at large. Party to neither side in the struggle for Texas, the Indians preyed upon both. In 1818 the Comanches staged their greatest raids upon the lower river. They drove off thousands of head of livestock, and murdered settlers, and burned down towns—among them, the Villa de Palafox, which had been founded thirty miles above Laredo on the north bank of the river in 1810. They left it depopulated and destroyed. It was never resettled. Several coal mining settlements in the same region were also wiped out. If the Florida Treaty gave Texas to Spain, the Spanish authority had little left with which to keep it in peace and safety.

On January 1, 1820, the home government suffered a blow that paralyzed it further. A Spanish army mutiny, led by Colonel Rafael Riego, gathered popular support. Spain's last military power had been exhausted in attempts to put down the revolutionary outbreaks in the colonies. The home army declared against any such further service. It was believed that out of forty thousand troops recently sent to the Americas, north and south, not a man had returned. Spain was shaking apart, and the effect of this was felt in the New World. It was with some hope of success that Henry Clay attacked the Florida Treaty in Congress on April 3, 1820, for the treaty had not yet been ratified by Spain, and sentiment in the American West was wild against it. Clay demanded that the treaty be repudiated, and that by the division of Spanish lands the United States must take in all of Texas, all the way to the Rio Grande. John Quincy Adams disagreed with him. "The appetite for Texas," he declared, "was from the first a Western passion," and he added that it was "stimulated by no one more greedily than Henry Clay," who, he said, "preached the doctrine that we should have insisted upon our shadow of a claim to the Rio del Norte. . . ."

While such passions affecting the destiny of the Rio Grande were felt in Madrid, and Washington, and over Texas, the acting governor at Santa Fe, Facundo Melgares, Pike's old royalist friend, summoned the alcaldes of New Mexico to convene on November first in the Palace of the Governors. Their purpose was to consider ways and means for the journey of Don Pedro Bautista Pino who was once again readying himself to return to Spain and take his seat in the parliament. Ferdinand VII on his release from France had abolished colonial representation; and now, as a consequence of Riego's revolt, it was restored. As in the old days, when service to the Crown was undertaken so often by great figures of the Indies conquest "at no expense to His Majesty," the colonial delegate was obliged to pay his own way, or have it paid for him by his province.

The meeting was symbolic of what had been. Presided over by a royalist governor, it soberly went to work on a routine matter that tied the Spanish Rio Grande to Spain—for almost the last time.

In the same autumn, and symbolic of what was to come, a mild but tenacious man from Missouri named Moses Austin appeared in San Antonio to request official permission of the royal authorities to settle a group of Anglo-American families in Texas. After some hesitation, he was granted approval of his petition on January 17, 1821, and he returned to Missouri to make preparations with his people for their exodus. They would surrender their United States citizenship, and enter Texas as subjects of the King of Spain. But the nature of that sovereignty was soon altered in a series of events that when it began moved swiftly.

41.

The Broken Grasp of Spain

At Washington on February 22, 1821, Spain ratified the Florida Treaty. But two days later, at Iguala, a town halfway between Mexico City and Acapulco, the rallying call of a new Mexican revolution was sounded by Colonel Agustín de Iturbide, an officer of the viceregal army, and the days of Spain in Mexico were numbered. Riego's mutiny in the home country had provided a precedent, and Napoleon's airs had provided a manner, for Iturbide's sudden rise to eminence.

His revolutionary call was the Plan of Iguala. It consisted of three points to which all the dissident parties of Mexico could rally— clergy, people of property, the American-born colonials. It proposed, first, the continuation of the Catholic Church as the established church of Mexico; second, the establishment of an independent limited monarchy; and third, equal rights for Spaniards and creoles.

With only twenty-five hundred troops to support him at Iguala, Iturbide soon had overwhelming approval from the mass of Mexicans. He won his revolution with an idea. Not a shot was fired. He marched across the country taking on volunteers in great numbers. The popularity of his Plan spread like wildfire. In vain, orders were dispatched on March third by the viceregal office to all its branches warning against Iturbide's propaganda, and calling for loyalty to the government. All circumstances—turmoil in Spain, long-frustrated desire for freedom in Mexico—created an atmosphere of success for Colonel de Iturbide. There were signs that he saw in his destiny a repetition of that of another field soldier who had suddenly become more than a commander—had embodied a glorious ideal—had swept a nation into ardent dedication to himself—and had finally consented to wear a crown. For Bonaparte he was willing to read Iturbide.

By summer one province after another was taking the oath supporting the independence of Mexico. On July third orders went to the river provinces from one of the last royal strongholds sanctioning the oath to the new regime and giving instructions for its form. All people were to assemble before a crucifix and a book of the Gospels, and swear—the military on the hilts of their swords, the civil on the cross— to uphold the holy, Roman, Apostolic faith; to defend the freedom of the empire of Mexico; and to keep the peace between Mexicans of European and Mexicans of American blood. Later in the month New Biscay was urged to capitulate, and, up the river, New Mexico on September eleventh took the oath by order of Melgares, the last northern royalist.

He had every legal right, now, to give his order; for in August the tremendous act of separation had been done. A new viceroy, General O'Donojú, had arrived from Spain to mollify the rebellion and to urge Mexico to await the action of parliament which assuredly would recognize her claims to independence. But he found that Mexican freedom had gone beyond claim and was fact. Iturbide met with him at Cordova, in the province of Vera Cruz. It was soon clear to the last Viceroy that unless he accepted at once the fact of Mexican independence, a massacre of Spaniards living in Mexico, a civil war of fearful dimensions, must come. On July twenty-fourth he signed away Spain's dominion over Mexico and all the outlands she embraced—the Central Americas, California, New Mexico, Texas. The Florida treaty would hold—but now between the United States and Mexico. The grasp of Spain was broken at last, and forever.

Mexico's first Consul now proceeded to the capital, where he was ecstatically received. He named a provisional governing body, and appointed a regency of five members, including General O'Donojú, with himself as president. On September twenty-second the "Act of Independence of the Mexican Empire" was solemnly proclaimed. Its creator was styled "Most Serene Highness." In Texas James Long was captured with what remained of his filibustering group, and claimed that he had heard nothing of all Iturbide's works in Mexico. Far from admitting that he was an aggressor against Mexican soil, Long declared that all he had ever worked for was the liberation of Texas from Spain, and the further freedom of Mexico. He was taken to Mexico City for examination of such doubtful statements, and there not long later was shot to death in a scrape with a Mexican sentry.

Meanwhile the Empire was coming into its new state. The Most Serene Highness in November sent out to his far-flung provincial gover-

nors the news that he had founded an order of merit—the Order of
Guadalupe. He asked Santa Fe for confidential nominations of those who
deserved to receive the cross and ribbon of the new honor. News still
came slowly to the New Mexico river. At Santa Fe they heard on
December twenty-sixth how the liberator had entered his capital city,
and on January sixth, led by Governor Melgares, who was now a passionate servant of the new Empire, New Mexico celebrated the triumph.
Santa Fe at dawn heard artillery salutes. A parade was held. The post-
master, Juan Bautista Vigil, painted new decorations for a ball held in
the Palace, at which the alcalde, Pedro Armendaris, led a cotillion. Later
in the evening a brilliant tableau was staged, in which the Plan of
Iguala was dramatically represented in all three of its exhilarating
clauses, with Father Juan Tomás Terrazas as The Church, Alférez Santiago Abréu as Independence, and Chaplain Francisco Hocio as The
Union of Spaniards and Creoles. The whole affair recalled the eloquence
of Governor Melgares spoken a few days earlier: "New Mexicans . . . let
us show tyrants that although we live at the very extremity of North
America we love the holy religion of our fathers; that we cherish and
protect the desired union between Spaniards of both hemispheres; and
that, with our last drop of blood, we will sustain the sacred independence
of the Mexican empire!"

It was not long before the empire had its crown. The Most
Serene Highness was proclaimed as Emperor Agustín I, with his wife
as Empress, by the Mexican congress on May nineteenth, 1822. Like any
proper Bonaparte he promptly created his father and mother, his sons
and daughters, all princes and princesses. It was a satisfying gesture for
one who had once resigned from the Army in the face of official charges
of squalid misconduct in military and private affairs. All turned now
to him, even those who had hopes in his far provinces. A worried provincial was in Mexico City, and on May 21, 1822, wrote to the Emperor
Agustín I:

Sir:

Having become a citizen of this Empire, by the formation
of a settlement of three hundred families from the United States
of America in the Province of Texas, under authority from the
Deputation in the Internal Provinces; and participating in the
Sentiments of Joy manifested by the nation at the recent political
change, I respectfully approach His Imperial Majesty, and offer
my congratulations on the happy consummation of the inde-

pendence of Mexico, by the election of the hero of Iguala, the Liberator of his Country to the Imperial Throne—

I make a tender of my services, my loyalty, and my fidelity to the Constitutional Emperor of Mexico; a tender which I am ready to verify by an oath of allegiance to the Empire.

This solemn act cuts me off from all protection or dependence on my former government—my property, my prospects, my future hopes of happiness, for myself and family, and for the families I have brought with me, are centered here— This is our adopted Nation:—We look to the Sovereign Congress as the pure fountain whence those blessings are to flow which will diffuse peace, improvement, intelligence, and happiness over this new born Nation:

We raise our eyes and hearts to him, whose virtues have elevated him to the station he merited, as the Father, who is to distribute those blessings to his people with a firm, impartial, and benevolent hand—

I therefore supplicate that his Imperial Majesty will have the goodness to take the Settlement I have formed under his protection, and that we may be received as Children of the great Mexican family.

The prostrate appeal was signed by Stephen F. Austin, who had succeeded upon his father's death to the leadership of the Missouri exodus. The future of Texas and the river hung upon his letter; though in terms which none foresaw.

For two months preparations went furiously ahead toward the coronation of the emperor. The Napoleonic analogy there reached its climax; for in great engraved folios by Percier, the designs of Isabey for Napoleon's fabulous coronation had been preserved, and Mexican designers, artisans, couturiers and masters of ceremony must have had access to them. Improvising desperately, they did what they could about blue velvet, and golden bees, and precedence, and state coaches. But the results, with an emperor and empress in borrowed diamonds, served mainly to reveal ambition and poverty together; and foreign observers smiled with terrible tact, as the President of Congress placed a crown upon the head of Agustín I, who in turn crowned the Empress Ana María with a diadem, while a memory of Joséphine moved in the shadows. The American consul wrote home that the affair, lasting five hours, was "a most tiresome Pantomime," and General Wilkinson, who also attended, fell asleep twice, and later said it had all been "clumsy and tinselled."

And everywhere along the Rio Grande—from the mountain towns and pueblos of the north, and the high bosky valleys of the farming haciendas, and the gravelly garrison villages of the turn of the river, and the dusty little cities of the thorned brush country, to the lone sentry outposts in the sweet heavy air of the Gulf beaches—the Spanish colors were down; and for a little while in their place hovered the first imperial eagles of modern Mexico.

Sources for
Volume One, By Chapters

Sources for
Volume One, by Chapters

RATHER THAN INTERRUPT THE FLOW OF THE NARRATIVE by the use of footnotes on each page, or of superior numbers referring to a later listing of notes, I have adopted a simplified form of reference in order to identify my sources. I hope my system will provide relief for the general reader who is not concerned with authorities, and yet will reassure the scholarly reader with respectable evidence, given here, of my efforts to make my long story a true one. Each source is here noted in brief form which corresponds to its alphabetical position in the General Bibliography (Appendix C), where the reader will find full bibliographical particulars.

prologue

1. Creation: Croneis; Milham; Talman.
2. Gazetteer: Bartlett; Emory, *Report;* Federal Writers Program, WPA, *Colorado,* and *New Mexico,* and *Texas;* Lane, F. C.; Peyton.

book one: the indian rio grande

1. The Ancients: Coolidge; Huntington; Martin, P. S.; Watson; Wissler.
2. The Cliffs: Bandelier, *Delight Makers,* and *Final Report;* Benedict; Bryan; Fergusson, E.; Fewkes, *Two Types;* Hewett, *Ancient Life;* Kroeber; Lummis, *Mesa;* MacClary; Martin, P. S.; Renaud; Twitchell, *Leading Facts.*
3. To the River: Bandelier. *Final Report;* Benedict; Bryan; Fergusson, E.; Gilpin, *Pueblos;* Hewett, *Ancient Life,* and *Pueblo Indian World;* Hoffman; Martin, P. S.; Reagan; Renaud; Twitchell, *Leading Facts;* USDA, *Survey Report (Rio Puerco)*, and *Tewa Basin Study;* Watson.
4. The Stuff of Life: Alexander; Bandelier, *Delight Makers,* and *Diaries* and *Documentary History,* and *Indians of the Rio Grande Valley;* Benedict; Brand; Bryan; Castetter; Coolidge; Crane; Davenport; Denver Art Museum, *Leaflet Series, 1936,* and *1939;* Dobie, *Vaquero;* Douglas; Fergusson, E.; Frazer; Harrington; Hewett, *Ancient Life,* and *Pueblo Indian World;* Hrdlička; Jeançon, *Pueblo Indian Clothing,* and *Pueblo Indian Foods;* Kelley; Kidder; Lummis, *Mesa;* MacClary; Martin, G. C.; Martin, P. S.; Palmer, R. A.; Parsons; Renaud; Smith, V. J.; Thoburn; Twitchell, *Leading Facts;* USDA, Field flood control co-ordinating committee, *Survey Report . . . Rio Puerco;* USDA, SCS, *Report on Rio Grande Watershed,* and *Tewa Basin Study;* USDI, *Reclamation Handbook;* Watson; White; Wissler.

book two: the spanish rio grande

1. The River of Palms: Bandelier, *Hemenway Southwestern Expedition;* Benavides; Castañeda, C. E.; Hoffman, Fritz L., in Céliz; Watson.
2. Rivals: Castañeda, C. E.; Cortés; Diaz del Castillo.
3. Upland River: Bishop; Bolton, *Coronado,* and *Spanish Borderlands,* and *Spanish Exploration;* Hallenbeck, Álvar Nuñez; Hodge; Nuñez Cabeza de Vaca.
4. The Travellers' Tales: Bandelier, *Hemenway Southwestern Expedition,* and *Historical Introduction;* Bishop; Díaz del Castillo; Foscue; Hallenbeck, *Álvar Nuñez;* Hammond, G. P., *Narratives of the Coronado Expedition;* Hammond, G. P., and Rey, in Montoya; Hodge; Nuñez Cabeza de Vaca; Wright.
5. Destiny and the Future: Bolton, *Coronado;* Castañeda de Náxera.
6. Faith and Bad Faith: Bolton, *Coronado;* Castañeda de Náxera.
7. Facing Battle: Bolton, *Coronado;* Castañeda de Náxera; Díaz del Castillo.
8. Battle Piece: Bolton, *Coronado;* Castañeda de Náxera.
9. The Garrison: Bandelier, *Historical Introduction,* and *Indians of the Rio*

Grande Valley; Bolton, *Coronado;* Castañeda de Náxera; Díaz del Castillo; Gilpin, *Pueblos;* Hammond, G. P., *Narratives of the Coronado Expedition;* Towne; Watson.

10. Siege: Bolton, *Coronado;* Castañeda de Náxera; Hammond, G. P., *Narratives of the Coronado Expedition.*

11. The Eastern Plains: Bandelier, *Historical Introduction;* Bolton, *Coronado,* and *Southwestern Exploration;* Castañeda de Náxera.

12. Prophecy and Retreat: Bolton, *Coronado;* Castañeda, C. E.; Castañeda de Náxera; Cervantes Saavedra; Hammond, G. P., *Narratives of the Coronado Expedition;* Vásquez de Coronado.

13. Lords and Victims: Bolton, *Coronado;* Castañeda, C. E.; Castañeda de Náxera; Hammond, G. P., *Narratives of the Coronado Expedition;* Hammond, G. P., and Rey, in Montoya; Sanford.

14. The River of May: DeGolyer.

15. Four Enterprises: Bandelier, *Historical Documents;* Bolton, *Spanish Exploration;* Castañeda, C. E.; Gonzales de Mendoza; Hackett, in Bandelier, *Historical Documents;* Hallenbeck, *Land of the Conquistadores;* Hammond, G. P., Hodge, Rey, in Benavides; Hammond, G. P., in Montoya; Hewett, *Pueblo Indian World;* Hodge, in Nuñez Cabeza de Vaca.

16. Possession: Bolton, *Spanish Borderlands,* and *Spanish Exploration;* Hackett, in Bandelier, *Historical Documents;* Hammond, G. P., and Rey, in Montoya; Pérez de Villagrá; Trend.

17. The River Capital: Artiñano; Bandelier, *Documentary History,* and *Historical Documents;* Benavides; Bolton, *Spanish Borderlands,* and *Spanish Exploration;* Fergusson, E.; Hallenbeck, *Land of the Conquistadores;* Hammond, G. P., and Rey, in Montoya; Montoya; Oñate, in Bandelier, *Historical Documents;* Oñate, in Montoya; Pérez de Villagrá; Towne; Vega.

18. Collective Memory: Armstrong; Artiñano; Bell; Buckle; Cervantes Saavedra; Columbus; Crane; Díaz del Castillo; Fitzmaurice-Kelly; Gautier; Gibson, C. E.; Goldscheider; Hanke, *First Social Experiments,* and *Spanish Struggle;* Hewett, *Ancient Life;* Hume; Huntington; Leonard; Madariaga, *Fall,* and *Rise of the Spanish American Empire,* and *Spain;* Martialis; Maugham; Meier-Graefe; Prescott; Priestley; Trend.

19. Duties: Bandelier, *Indians of the Rio Grande Valley;* Benavides; Bolton, *Spanish Exploration;* Crane; Hallenbeck, *Land of the Conquistadores;* Oñate, in Montoya; Pérez de Villagrá.

20. A Dark Day in Winter: Hallenbeck, *Land of the Conquistadores;* Horgan, *Habit of Empire;* Montoya; Pérez de Villagrá.

21. The Battle of Ácoma: Hallenbeck, *Land of the Conquistadores;* Horgan, *Habit of Empire;* Pérez de Villagrá.

22. Afterthoughts: Pérez de Villagrá.

23. Exchange: Bandelier, *Final Report;* Benavides; Bolton, *Spanish Exploration;* Bourke; Burkholder; Denver Art Museum, *Leaflet Series,* 1940; Hewett, *Ancient Life,* and *Pueblo Indian World;* Montoya; Oñate, in Montoya; USDA, SCS, *Rio Grande Watershed in Colorado and New Mexico.*

24. The Promises: Bandelier, *Historical Documents,* and Hackett, in same; Hallenbeck, *Land of the Conquistadores;* Hammond, G. P., and Rey, in Montoya.

25. The Desert Fathers: Bandelier, *Historical Documents;* Bell; Benavides; Bourke; Crane; Dickey; Fergusson, E.; Francis of Assisi; Gilpin, *Pueblos;* Hammond, G. P., Hodge, Rey, in Benavides; Kubler; Leonard; Leonard in Siqüenza y Góngora; Madariaga, *Fall,* and *Rise of the Spanish American Empire;* Maugham; Siqüenza y Góngora; Towne; USDI, Reclamation Handbook.
26. The Two Majesties: Armstrong; Bandelier, *Historical Documents;* Benavides; Díaz del Castillo; Ellis; Hanke, *First Social Experiments,* and *Spanish Struggle;* Hewett, *Pueblo Indian World;* Madariaga, *Fall,* and *Rise of the Spanish American Empire;* Trend; Underhill.
27. The Hungry: Alessio Robles; Bandelier, *Historical Documents;* Benavides; Castañeda, C. E.; Crane; Hewett, *Ancient Life;* Morfi; USDI, NPS. *San Buenaventura Mission.*
28. This Miserable Kingdom: Bandelier, *Historical Documents;* Crane; Hackett; Hallenbeck, *Land of the Conquistadores.*
29. The Terror: Bandelier, *Historical Documents;* Burkholder; Chavez; Crane; Gilpin, *Pueblos;* Hackett; Hammond, G. P., Hodge, Rey, in Benavides; Kubler; Madariaga, *Fall of the Spanish American Empire;* Peyton; Underhill; USDA, *Rio Grande Watershed in Colorado and New Mexico.*
30. Limit of Vision: Hackett; Hallenbeck, *Land of the Conquistadores.*
31. A Way to the Texas: Bandelier, *Historical Documents;* Benavides; Bolton, *Spanish Exploration;* Castañeda, C. E.; Hammond, G. P., Hodge, Rey, in Benavides.
32. The Great Captain: Bandelier, *Final Report,* and *Hemenway Southwestern Expedition,* and *Historical Documents;* Chavez; Crane; Espinosa, in Vargas; Hallenbeck, *Land of the Conquistadores;* Hammond, G. P., Hodge, Rey, in Benavides; Twitchell, *Spanish Archives;* Vargas; Wallace, S.
33. Fort St. John Baptist: Bandelier, *Historical Documents;* Céliz; Hammond, G. P., Hodge, Rey, in Benavides; Hoffman, Fritz L., in Céliz; McKellar; Morfi; Priestley.
34. Early Towns: Alessio Robles; Bandelier, *Historical Documents;* Burkholder; Hallenbeck, *Land of the Conquistadores;* Pino; Twitchell, *Spanish Archives.*
35. Colonial Texas: Castañeda, C. E.; Céliz; Hoffman, Fritz L., in Céliz; Morfi.
36. Mexico Bay: Alessio Robles; Castañeda, C. E.; Wilcox, *Conversations.*
37. Forgotten Lessons: Bandelier, *Historical Documents;* Bolton, *Spanish Borderlands;* Bryan; Castañeda, C. E.; Chavez; Conkling; Díaz del Castillo; Dougherty; Fergusson, E.; Kubler; Madariaga, *Rise of the Spanish American Empire;* Priestley.
38. Hacienda and Village: Bandelier, *Final Report,* and *Historical Documents;* Benedict; Benavides; Beshoar; Bevan; Bolton, *Coronado,* and *Spanish Borderlands;* Boyd, E.; Castañeda, C. E.; Chavez; Dickey; Dougherty; Fergusson, E.; Fisher; Forrest; Hackett, in Bandelier, *Historical Documents;* Horgan, *Colonial Life;* James, G. W.; Jaramillo; Kincaid; Kubler; Madariaga, *Fall,* and *Rise of the Spanish American Empire;* May; Pérez de Villagrá; Priestley; Salpointe; Twitchell, *Spanish Archives;* Underhill; USDA, Field flood control co-ordinating committee, *Survey Report . . . Rio Puerco;* USDA, SCS, *Rio Grande Watershed in Colorado and New Mexico;* Wilder.

39. The World Intrudes: Alessio Robles; Altamira y Crevea; Castañeda, C. E.; Dickey, Dougherty; Grant, B.; Hollon; Pike; Pino; Rives; Sibley; Sitwell; Twitchell, *Spanish Archives;* Watson; Wilcox, *Conversations.*
40. The Shout: Barker, *Austin Papers;* Castañeda, C. E.; Cox; Gutierrez de Lara; Rives; Twitchell, *Spanish Archives;* Wilcox, *Conversations;* Wortham.
41. The Broken Grasp of Spain: Barker, *Austin Papers;* Castañeda, C. E.; Percier; Rives; Robertson; Twitchell, *Spanish Archives;* Wilcox, *Conversations.*